Contemporary British Conservatism

Contemporary British Conservatism

Edited by

Steve Ludlam

and

Martin J. Smith

First published 1996 by
MACMILLAN PRESS LTD
Houndmills, Basingstoke, Hampshire RG21 6XS
and London
Companies and representatives
throughout the world

ISBN 0-333-62948-5 hardcover
ISBN 0-333-62949-3 paperback

A catalogue record for this book is available
from the British Library.

10 9 8 7 6 5 4 3 2 1
05 04 03 02 01 00 99 98 97 96

Copy-edited and typeset by Povey–Edmondson
Okehampton and Rochdale, England

Printed in Malaysia

Published in the United States of America 1995 by
ST. MARTIN'S PRESS, INC.,
Scholarly and Reference Division
175 Fifth Avenue, New York, N.Y. 10010

ISBN 0-312-12935-1

Contents

List of Tables and Figures

Tables

viii   *List of Tables and Figures*

Figures

Preface

All the chapters in this book have been written by specialists in British politics who are actively engaged in academic research in the areas that they describe and analyse here. Some, where appropriate, have been encouraged to incorporate the results of their recent empirical research. We hope that such findings will enrich readers' grasp of the issues under discussion. All the authors have concentrated on developments under the leadership of Margaret Thatcher and John Major, and where pertinent have assessed their relative impacts on ideas, policies and the party itself. They have also put the events since 1975 in the context of the experience of post-war Conservatism.

In any collection of this kind, there are inevitably gaps. Fortunately (as the list of references at the end of the book makes clear) British Conservatism, long an underresearched topic, has become much examined in recent years, so that serious studies now abound in monographs, journals and conference proceedings. Our aim has been to collect in one volume a set of studies to satisfy the curiosity of both institutionalised students, like us, and private students looking for more detail and analysis than is generally available in scholarly journalism or in general textbooks on British politics. To the extent that the book succeeds, it is thanks to the contributors whom we applaud for their efforts and their patience with us, and to our publisher, Steven Kennedy, and his colleagues. We are not the first, and neither will we be the last wayward scribblers to benefit from Steven's ever-cheerful combination of mild insistence and enthusiastic tolerance. Finally, we offer our thanks and apologies to Fiona, Julia, Joe and Thomas, who have had to put up with even more of our inexplicable preoccupations than usual.

STEVE LUDLAM
MARTIN J. SMITH

ix

Notes on the Contributors

David Baker is Senior Lecturer in British Politics, Nottingham Trent University. His main publications are on British Conservatism and fascism. He is co-director of the Conservatives in Parliament Project.

Jim Buller is completing a PhD at the University of Sheffield. His research interest is in the European Community (EC) and Thatcherite statecraft, and he has published on Britain and the EC.

Imogen Fountain was Research Officer of the Conservatives in Parliament Project at the University of Sheffield. Her research and publications are on the social composition of Conservative parliamentarians, and their attitudes to European integration.

Andrew Gamble is Professor of Politics, University of Sheffield. He has published widely on political economy and British Conservatism. His published books include *The Conservative Nation*, *The Free Economy and the Strong State: The Politics of Thatcherism* and *Britain in Decline*. He is co-director of the Conservatives in Parliament Project.

Stephen George is Jean Monnet Professor in Politics at the University of Sheffield. He has published extensively on the European Union (EU). His recent books include *Politics and Policy in the European Union*, *Britain and European Integration since 1945*, *An Awkward Partner: Britain in the European Community*, *Britain and the European Community: The Politics of Semi-Detachment* (editor) and *The United Kingdom and EC Membership Evaluated* (co-editor).

Ron Johnston is Vice-Chancellor of the University of Essex. Between 1974 and 1992 he was Professor of Geography at the University of Sheffield. He is the author of many books and papers on political and electoral geography, including *A Nation Dividing* (co-author) and *The Geography of English Politics*.

Steve Ludlam is Lecturer in Politics, University of Sheffield. His recent publications are on Conservatism, European integration, and the last Labour government. He is co-director of the Conservatives in Parliament Project.

Adam Lent is completing a PhD at the University of Sheffield, and is Convenor of the Political Studies Association's Post-Structuralism and Radical Politics Specialist Group. His research interests and publications are in opposition politics and new social movements.

Charles Pattie is Senior Lecturer in Geography at the University of Sheffield, and has taught at the University of Nottingham. His main research interests are in political geography, and in collaboration with Ron Johnston he has published *A Nation Dividing* and numerous papers on the spatial aspects of voting in British elections.

Chris Pierson is Reader in Politics at the University of Stirling and Visiting Research Fellow at the Australian National University, Canberra. He has written extensively on the welfare state, social democracy and the theory of the state. His recent publications include *Beyond the Welfare State?*, *Socialism after Communism* and *The Modern State*.

Ben Rosamond is Lecturer in European Integration, Department of Politics and International Studies, University of Warwick. His recent publications are on European integration, British party politics and trade unions.

Patrick Seyd is Senior Lecturer in Politics, University of Sheffield. He has researched widely and published widely on British party politics. His recent books include *The Rise and Fall of the Labour Left*, *Labour's Grassroots: The Politics of Party Membership* (co-author) and *True Blues: The Politics of Conservative Party Membership* (co-author). He is co-director of the Party Membership Survey.

Martin J. Smith is Senior Lecturer in Politics, University of Sheffield. He has published widely on British pressure groups and public policy. His recent books include *The Politics of Agricultural Support*, *The Changing Labour Party* (co-editor) and *Pressure, Power and Policy*. He is currently conducting research under the Economic and Social Research Council (ESRC) Whitehall Programme.

Matthew Sowemimo is completing a PhD at the University of Sheffield. He was formerly an economic policy researcher for the Liberal Democrat parliamentary party. His current research interest is the Conservative Party and European integration. He has published on British party politics.

Helen Thompson is Fellow in Clare College and Assistant Lecturer in Social and Political Sciences, Cambridge University. She has published articles and chapters on Britain and the European Exchange Rate Mechanism (ERM), and the British core executive.

Paul Whiteley is Professor of Politics, University of Sheffield. He has published extensively on political representation and political economy. His recent publications include *The Labour Party in Crisis, Pressure for the Poor: The Poverty Lobby and Policy Making* (co-author), *Political Control of the Macroeconomy, Labour's Grassroots: The Politics of Party Membership* (co-author) and *True Blues: The Politics of Conservative Party Membership* (co-author). He is co-director of the Party Membership Survey.

List of Abbreviations

ACE	Action Centre For Europe
ACAS	Advisory, Conciliation and Arbitration Service
AIA	Anglo-Irish Agreement
BES	British Election Survey
CAP	Common Agricultural Policy
CFSP	Common Foreign and Security Policy
CSA	Child Support Agency
DFE	Department for Education
DSS	Department of Social Security
DTI	Department of Trade and Industry
EC	European Community
ECSC	European Coal and Steel Community
ECU	European Currency Unit
EDM	Early Day Motion
EMF	European Monetary Fund
EMS	European Monetary System
EMU	Economic and Monetary Union
EP	European Parliament
EPC	European Political Cooperation
ERM	Exchange Rate Mechanism
ESRC	Economic and Social Research Council
EU	European Union
FMI	Financial Management Initiative
GATT	General Agreement on Tariffs and Trade
GDP	gross domestic product
GLYC	Greater London Young Conservatives
GM	grant-maintained
GP	General Practitioner
IGC	Inter-Governmental Conference
INF	intermediate nuclear forces
IRA	Irish Republican Army
LEAs	Local Education Authorities
LET	Local Exchange and Trading
LMS	Local Management of Schools
MP	Member of Parliament

List of Abbreviations

MoD	Ministry of Defence
NATO	North Atlantic Treaty Organisation
NEC	National Executive Committee
NEDC	National Economic Development Council
NHS	National Health Service
NUM	National Union of Mineworkers
NUT	National Union of Teachers
OMOV	one member one vote
PCP	Parliamentary Conservetive Party
PSBR	Publice Sector Borrowing Requirement
QMV	qualified majority voting
SALT	Strategic Arms Limitation Talks
SDP	Social Democratic Party
SEA	Single European Act
SERPS	state earnings-related pension scheme
TURERA	Trade Union Reform and Employment Rights Act
VAT	Value Added Tax
WEU	Western European Union

1

Introduction

MARTIN J. SMITH and STEVE LUDLAM

In 1895, the Conservative Party was led by Lord Salisbury, who was widely portrayed as colourless and fatalistic. He led a minority government under pressure from a resurgent Liberal Party and a rising labour movement. The party was approaching a debilitating split over a grand issue of political economy – tariff reform – that posed the question of what was the proper place of the British state in a changing world economy? A hundred years later, John Major, widely portrayed as a colourless and fatalistic leader, was rapidly losing ground and seats to a resurgent Labour Party and to the Liberal Democrats. He voluntarily turned his into a minority government in 1994 by expelling Euro-rebels from the parliamentary party, only to readmit them unconditionally. In 1995 he resigned the leadership, challenging his critics to 'put up or shut up'. The party seemed to have stumbled to the very edge of a split over a grand issue of political economy – European integration – that posed the question: what was the proper place of the British state in a changing world economy?

The party seemed to be in the grip of multiple crises. Its election performances since the 1992 General Election victory were breaking all the records for loss of support. The opinion polls were similarly breaking records in terms of unpopularity between general elections, and of public respect for the leader. The parliamentary party had been engaged in fratricide over Europe almost since the general election. Media-hyped personal 'scandals' had taken a heavy toll of ministers who had undermined the moral content of their leader's injunction to get 'back to basics'. The party's finances were breaking new records for debt, and attracting public disquiet over the sources of private donations. The party's mass membership was revealed as shrinking in number, and getting older. The Cabinet was characterised as being divided between consolidators tired of the 'Thatcher revolution' and Jacobins determined to put fresh 'clear blue water' between their party and the opposition parties. This book considers whether the 'Thatcher revolution' has survived its leader's sacking, and covers such questions as what was the ideology of Thatcherism? Which elements of the Thatcherite programme have become permanently embedded in British public policy? Has Major developed a programme of his own, or a distinct ideological stance? What state is the party in, after such a long and stressful period in office?

Party

Harris has argued that, 'The continuity of the Conservative Party consists above all in the existence of the party itself, with common symbols and terminology, rather than a coherent ideational system' (Harris, 1968, 115). The longevity and success of the party is certainly unparalleled in modern history, anywhere. The historic achievement of the Conservative Party as an electoral winner is extraordinary. It has survived radical constitutional reform, the rise of industry and of labour, depression and mass unemployment, and association with appeasement and military disaster. The obverse of the heroic Dunkirk evacuation was the public evidence it appeared to present of the consequences of the Conservatives' controversial inter-war foreign policy (Ponting, 1990). The party's serious divisions over relations with fascist governments (Blake, 1970) took on new meaning as a result of the war. The Conservative 'guilty men' of Munich made way for a coalition that was obliged to promise post-war social reform to secure popular commitment to the war effort. In spite of Churchill's personal reputation as a victorious war leader, Labour swept into office in 1945. The coalition government's initial response to the Beveridge report on social reform was perceived as half-hearted, and the Conservative charge that Labour's 1945 manifesto would need the Gestapo to enforce it backfired. The party shifted quickly towards support for the post-war settlement, and regained electoral dominance, holding office from 1951 to 1964. After Harold Macmillan's and then Labour's interventionist economic modernisation programmes foundered, Edward Heath launched a new Conservative electoral platform emphasising economic liberalisation, and won in 1970. His U-turn towards industrial intervention and incomes policy in 1972 ended in humiliation and failure in the 1974 election. But others in his party had taken the neo-liberal turn more seriously and captured the party leadership under Margaret Thatcher, proclaiming a new commitment to free market economics (Conservative Party, 1977). Like Heath in 1970, Thatcher offered to liberate Labour's supporters from high taxes and oppressive incomes policies, and triumphed over a labour movement divided and demoralised by the sacrifices demanded by the 'Social Contract' with the Labour government. Chapter 3 surveys the post-war electoral record and considers explanations of Thatcher's repeated electoral triumphs and Major's victory in 1992.

One feature of the Conservative Party, the privileged social and educational background of most of its MPs, was supposed to have slowly changed in the era of the post-war settlement of the 'social question', in the wake of the party's attempts in the 1940s to give its parliamentary ranks a more egalitarian profile to match its shift in policy (D. Butler and Pinto-Duschinsky, 1980). Reform in the 1960s of the party leadership selection process produced in succession three grammar-school leaders from humble families, resulting in fresh claims that the party's elite was becoming more socially representative. Research a decade ago detected a more substantial shift towards a socially representative leadership taking place in the wake of the 'Thatcher revolution' that was suppose to value individual merit above class origin. How far such a shift was under way is measured in Chapter 5.

In the parliamentary party loyalty and respect for the authority of its leaders have been important when rapid shifts of policy have been required to sustain electoral support. Such loyalty, so often contrasted with the conflict within Labour's leadership, also came under pressure as the post-war consensus weakened and conflict over alternative platforms increased. Backbench dissidence turned into repeated parliamentary rebellion under Heath, was largely isolated under Thatcher until her defence of the Poll Tax combined with Cabinet divisions over Europe to undermine her leadership, but then erupted under Major. The focus of rebellions under Major was European integration. Chapter 6 traces the origins and forms of this debilitating feature of contemporary Conservatism.

Neither political popularity, nor discredited or divided oppositions, nor the obedience given to its leaders, and certainly not their class origin, can explain the full extent of post-war Conservative electoral success. A crucial component has been the legendary efficiency of the party's organisation, the envy of its opponents (K. Baker, 1993, 288). Two elements stand out: the party's ability to outspend its rivals, and the strength of its constituency organisations. By the mid-1990s both elements appeared to be at risk. The party's ability to attract colossal donations from foreign supporters, one a prominent fugitive from British justice, was threatened by public unease with 'sleaze' in British politics (Fisher, 1994). The party yet again had to streamline its central organisation and its fulltime constituency agent network to cope with a financial crisis after the 1992 election. In 1993/4, after a sustained economy drive, the party centre recorded the largest annual surplus in the party's history (Conservative Party, 1994c). It still had a record overdraft, however, and a major *Financial Times* investigation discovered that business leaders were increasingly reluctant contributors (*Financial Times*, 19 December 1994). How far this was the usual parsimony between election campaigns was unclear, though one large multinational company with a long-standing links with the party seemed to have taken a longer-term decision, saying it had become inappropriate for an international company to support national parties. Arguably even more serious was the revelation that the source of a significant proportion of the party's funds and of its election campaigning strength – its mass membership – was falling away (Whiteley, Seyd and Richardson, 1994). Chapter 4 interprets the evidence of this crucial development.

An important external measure of the impact of Thatcherism is its impact on the main opposition parties and on political opposition in general. Charges of accommodation with Thatcherism have come to symbolise discontent with the 'modernisation' of policy platforms of Labour and Liberal Democrats. Chapter 7 surveys the political and organisational responses of the two main parties competing with the Tories, and considers the significance of the 'new opposition politics' that turned away from a parliamentary state dominated by one party.

Conservative Ideology and Policy

In the popular (and to some extent the academic) mind, the election of Major provided the Conservatives with a leader who was the opposite of Thatcher. As one biographer put it, 'He arrived in No. 10 with no ideological baggage, beholden to no faction' (Anderson, 1992).

Thatcher was radical, ideological, dogmatic and colourful. Major was a consolidator, pragmatic, consensual and grey. In more academic accounts John Major represented continuity, but at the same time without the conviction and radicalism of Thatcher: 'Thatcher's resignation is more than just the end of one political leader. It signals the end of a regime. Thatcher was not only a dominating personality like Churchill, but also the focus of a distinctive political project. It is the future of this project that is now in doubt' (Gamble, 1991, 15).

According to this view Major was circumscribed by the Thatcher inheritance, but was unlikely to maintain the ideological conviction of Thatcher, and was prepared to make non-Thatcherite commitments to the public sector in order to win a broad base of support. Several of the most important of his early speeches as Prime Minister proclaimed his promise to make state services second to none, a marked change of Downing Street tone (Anderson, 1992, 365–70). Yet, despite the fact that Major has become the third longest serving Conservative Prime Minister since the war, relatively little has been written on the long-term impact of Thatcherism on Conservative ideology and policy. Has the Thatcherite political project been institutionalised, or has Major managed a return to an earlier 'progressive' Conservatism?

Like most ideologies Conservatism is open to various interpretations and indeed is very flexible and changeable. Many people calling themselves Conservatives have held very different views of the world. However, there are some elements of Conservatism that appear fixed:

> basic Conservative doctrine has been said to rest on: a sense of religion and divine order coupled with veneration of Christian virtues; a rather pessimistic view of human nature combined with a scepticism about rationalist possibilities; an organic and hierarchical conception of society founded on the family as the basic social unit and of the importance of private property; a sense of empire; an acceptance of political and spiritual authority; a stress on tradition and prescriptive experience and thus on solely mediated change; and the understanding that the reality of politics is essentially limited. (Greenleaf, 1983b, 191)

Nearly all Conservatives accept the importance of order, tradition and nation. Central to the conception of Conservatism is the idea of the nation-state with fixed boundaries, a clear identity and a particular tradition. Tradition is important as a means of maintaining stability within a nation. It defines the relationships between actors in society and governs the nature of change; change is acceptable as long as it is within the context of a society's traditions. For Conservatives such as Oakeshott, rational plans and ideology should be rejected in politics. In his view Conservatism is 'not a creed or a doctrine, but a disposition' (Oakeshott, 1973, 23). Underlying this conception of politics is the notion that human beings are fallible and prone to wrong-doing. This leads to the ultimately contradictory notion that the state needs to be strong in order to constrain the evil doers and thus maintain order, but its power must be limited because of the fallibility and essential badness of those who might control it. However, the ultimate goal of most, if not all, Conservatives is order. They wish to retain peace within society, to preserve the social order and to protect private property.

Throughout its long historical defence of property rights, the party has responded flexibly to new challenges whether they came from radical democrats, Chartists, Socialists, the labour movement, riots by the unemployed, or simply from the weight of public opinion expressed in elections. Edmund Burke, commonly held to be the founding thinker of modern Conservatism, was haunted by the political potential of that 'hideous phantom', the people; one of his most celebrated warnings was that, in consequence, 'A state without the means of some change is without the means of its conservation' (Burke, 1968, 9, 106). The party has indeed often preferred reform, and has pioneered both political and social reforms in its history. When necessary, however, and whatever the ideological preference of its leadership at the time, the party has been willing to crush threats to the social order by any means necessary, including force. It has also adapted successfully to secular changes in society. Having been widely reviled as the party of 'unproductive' land-owning property by both liberal industrialists and by radical labour leaders, the Conservatives succeeded in time in attracting both the institutional support of industry and the votes of a significant proportion of the labouring poor. Such historical flexibility and opportunism underlies the judgement that:

> Conservative ideology is British public ideology, its precise nature depending on which groups are dominant in British society at any time and what is the nature of the radical attack upon the British *status quo*. If there is no radical attack, or if it is so marginal as not seriously to impinge on public politics, then Conservative ideology becomes 'common sense', embodying relatively few general propositions of any kind. (Harris, 1968, 99)

From within this breadth of policy responses to the rise of democracy and of modern industry, and out of such a broad ideological tradition, Greenleaf has identified a dualism within Conservatism: a twin inheritance of collectivism and libertarianism (Greenleaf, 1973, 1983a, 1983b). Collectivist Conservatism sees the state power being used for social welfare, economic intervention and even wealth redistribution. It can be traced back to the social concerns of Disraeli's Young England, through Joseph Chamberlain's municipal conservatism and social imperialism, the social policy of Neville Chamberlain and Macmillan's 'middle way' (O'Gorman, 1986; Macmillan, 1938). Joseph Chamberlain's collectivism did not seem far from social democracy:

> Chamberlain continually urged the positive role of the state to achieve social reform. It was a kind of new unauthorized programme and ranged from proposals for labour exchanges and municipal control of the drink trade to supporting a state mortgage system and the idea of industrial arbitration courts; from cheap train fares for workers and the extension of smallholdings to improved insurance schemes and stronger housing legislation. (Greenleaf, 1983b, 229)

The Chamberlainite tradition has dominated the thinking and policy agendas of most of the party's twentieth-century leaders (Chapter 2). The alternative libertarian strand was based on a mistrust of the state, and the liberal belief that people should be free to do as they wish so long as they do not harm others. The main inspiration behind libertarian Conservatism was Herbert Spencer, and it developed in the face of growing pressure from newly enfranchised voters for greater social protection and welfare. Although on the defensive throughout most of the twentieth century, libertarian Conservatism was supported by a substantial minority within the party.

However, in the period immediately following the Second World War, it was the 'progressive right' that gained ascendancy within the party (Gamble, 1974). The progressive right was clearly influenced by the collectivist tradition of Conservative thought. It was also affected by the 'corporate bias' of public policy that, even in the inter-war period, had witnessed growing attempts to draw interest groups into an 'extended state' (Middlemas, 1979). The Second World War and the shock of the 1945 election defeat forced the Conservatives into a more interventionist and collectivist position. The policy documents produced after the 1945 defeat rejected a reversion to *laissez-faire* and accepted watered-down Keynesianism, full employment, social security and the maintenance of 'strong central guidance over the economy' (R.

Butler, 1971, 146). In this 'corporate society', the Conservatives had become the party of state intervention and state-sponsored competitiveness (Harris, 1972).

Progressive Conservatism retained some of the principles of traditional Conservatism whilst recognising the social demands of the working class and the legitimacy of the trade union movement. For progressive Conservatives, order, evolutionary change and the inherent evil of man were still important. They remained totally committed to the maintenance of capitalism and private property. They accepted the inevitability of inequality, but believed in the necessity of state welfare provision to maintain a just and stable society. The central economic goal of progressive Conservatives was growth and prosperity, and this was not necessarily achieved through the market but through state intervention and corporatist policy-making. They were also aware that Britain was no longer a world power and that if it was to retain influence in the world, to 'punch above its weight', it was important to be integrated into Europe (Chapter 13). More generally, they did not believe that the Conservatives had a monopoly of truth and therefore Conservative domination of society and the state was not desirable (Hogg, 1947, 13). It was thus vital to sustain free associations, including trade unions, and to have strong opposition parties.

Thus the progressive right retained elements of traditional Conservatism: the fallibility of humans, the desire for gradual change; the importance of order; and the maintenance of capitalism. In its suspicion of ideological approaches to politics it contained important elements of Oakeshott's Conservatism. However, it also defined an important role for the state in both economic and welfare policy. In retrospect, progressive Conservatism was very historically specific. It was result of the combination of the collectivism of the war, the success of Labour, the strength of the trade union movement, the post-war boom, the international acceptance of Keynesianism, and the failure of inter-war Conservatism. The war had changed the balance of power and the political agenda. The Conservatives were pragmatic and concerned with regaining power, and therefore they were willing to adapt to circumstances.

This ideology influenced the policies of Conservative governments from Churchill to Heath. The Conservative government in 1951 accepted the spending commitments of Labour, the welfare state, public ownership and the need to work with the trade unions. Throughout the post-war period economic policy was conducted with maintaining welfare and full employment in mind. Such was the alleged profligacy of Macmillan that his Chancellor and Treasury ministers all resigned in 1958 because the Prime Minister refused to support cuts in public expenditure. Faced with growing economic problems and the signs of Britain's relative economic decline, there was no attempt at doctrinal *laissez-faire* solutions. Instead Macmillan pioneered indicative planning, and through the National Economic Development Council (NEDC) consulted the trade unions and business over how to solve Britain's economic problems. After the industrial relations policy of the Thatcher government (Chapter 10), it is worth recalling that in 13 years of Conservative rule between 1951 and 1964, with large parliamentary majorities, the Conservatives made no attempt to legislate against trade union activity. When signs of conflict appeared between government and trade unions, the unions were incorporated into economic decision-making (Middlemas, 1979).

Heath came to power in 1970 with a new Conservative economic policy committed to disengaging the government from the economy, strengthening the free market, reducing taxation and reforming industrial relations. His new direction should not be seen as simple proto-Thatcherism. First, Heath only changed tack after the obvious failure of indicative planning by Conservative and Labour governments. Second, the aims of the policy were the 'progressive' goals of full employment and maintaining welfare. Third, when that policy failed to prevent rising unemployment and was unpopular he was prepared to abandon it and to attempt a Keynesian 'dash for growth', increased industrial intervention, and renewed consultation with union leaders. Heath's 'Selsdon Man' project was a pragmatic attempt to modernise the British economy, not a dogmatic attachment to free market economics. According to Campbell, Heath had never intended to break the post-war social settlement, rather, 'His purpose was to persuade the country to perform better by means of relatively minor tinkering with incentives and restraints; it was not fundamentally to change the government's role in relation to the economy' (Campbell, 1993, 267).

However, Heath, like Wilson's Labour government before him, failed to solve the underlying problems of the British economy. Simultaneously rising inflation and unemployment (stagflation) poor industrial relations, weakening of sterling and balance of payments deficits started in the 1960s and worsened dramatically in the 1970s. The resulting disillusion with the post-war consensus gave fresh impetus to the party's small libertarian wing, such that 'By the late

1960s . . . a substantial, or at least very vocal body of opinion in the Conservative Party was moving in a libertarian direction' (Greenleaf, 1983b, 335). A 'neo-liberal' faction in parliament repeatedly rebelled against Heath's economic policy U-turn (Norton, 1978). Through a range of think tanks such as the Centre for Policy Studies, pressure groups such as the Aims of Industry, and sympathetic journalists like Peter Jay and Samuel Brittan, the libertarian wing mounted an effective critique of the post-war consensus that reached a wide audience (Greenleaf, 1983b; Gamble, 1994).

It was against this background of that Thatcher became leader of the Conservative Party in 1975, and then Prime Minister. Her election as party leader was more a result of accident and luck than the growing support for New Right ideas (Chapter 2). However, she took over a demoralised party that was divided and lacking direction, and was able to fill the vacuum with a clear agenda and a set of policies that provided a distinct alternative to the Labour government. In opposition, she was helped by the difficulties Labour faced in managing its inheritance from Heath, as the 'oil shock' plunged the industrial world into recession. Labour was divided between a resurgent left which wanted a return to reformist Socialism committed to international neutrality, increased public ownership, greater planning and workers democracy, and an entrenched right, dominating the government and committed to a mixed economy, European integration, fiscal conservatism and wage controls. The Labour government was failing to deliver. Unemployment rose to record post-war levels, unprecedented public expenditure cuts were announced, and real incomes fell faster than anyone could remember under the pressure of wage controls, inflation and tax increases. There was increasing disillusion amongst Labour's traditional supporters (Whiteley, 1983). The failure of the Labour government in the winter of 1978/9, and the Conservatives' presentation of a clear set of alternatives, notably lower taxes and freedom from wage controls, resulted in electoral victory for Thatcher. She became Prime Minister with policies that were distinctive in many respects from both Labour and from post-war Conservatism. Thatcher offered a libertarian form of Conservatism and serious pursuit of many of Labour's economic policy innovations. Labour had, usually reluctantly, adopted monetarist rhetoric and policy instruments, abandoned full employment, cut public spending, and imposed arbitrary 'cash limits' on spending programmes (Ludlam, 1992). Thatcher promised to follow this path with conviction.

For Thatcher, the role of the state in the economy should be limited to providing the conditions for a free market; the state should not plan or intervene in industry; there was no room for subsidies; regional policies were to be cut, and nationalised industries sold off (Chapter 9). The role of the state in welfare was also to be limited and public expenditure cut (Chapter 11). No longer was the welfare state to be a means of social justice: it was a mechanism for neutralising the failures of the market economy. Where possible welfare was to be provided by the private sector, or the family, and not the state. Thatcher also abandoned the pluralism of traditional Conservatism. First, she seemed to proclaim a monopoly of truth, admitting to an 'inner conviction' that she could save the country (Thatcher, 1993, 11). Her way was the only way to run the economy and to organise the state. Second, she had little time for the intermediate organisations that provide a framework for civil society. They were seen as special interests that would hinder the implementation of Thatcherism and consequently many were undermined or abolished. It was this perspective that led to the assault on the trade unions and local authorities.

The nation-state was also important to Thatcherism. Promises of devolution disappeared. There was a commitment to making Britain great again in the world and increasing suspicion of the EC as a threat to Britain's sovereignty (Chapter 13). Thatcher also committed Britain strongly to Reagan's prosecution of the second Cold War (Chapter 12). The concern with the nation-state demonstrates that Thatcherism was not pure liberalism (see Table 1.1). It retained many elements of traditional conservatism: a strong belief in the family, opposition to liberal morality, a commitment to law and order, discipline and authority. The essential feature of Thatcherism was the need for a strong state as a mechanism for achieving a free economy (Gamble, 1994).

Table 1.1 highlights contrasting progressive and Thatcherite positions on a range of political issues that are discussed in the chapters of this book. It suggests that Thatcherism is very different from the progressive Conservatism that dominated the party for 30 years. As she later put it, 'Ted Heath's Government . . . proposed and almost implemented the most radical form of socialism ever contemplated by an elected British Government' (Thatcher, 1993, 7). In spite of the certainty with which Thatcher herself described her beliefs, however, her record as party leader has produced a considerable range of interpretations.

TABLE 1.1   *Broad characteristics of progressive and Thatcherite Conservatism*

	Progressive	Thatcherite
Change	Gradual	Rapid
Economy	Mixed	Free market
State	Extended/interventionist	Limited/directive
European integration	'Pool' sovereignty	Assert independence
Policy-making	Consultative	Executive
Civil society	Pluralist	Individualist
Trade unions	Legitimate/constructive	Undemocratic/destructive
Welfare state	Universal right	Safety net
Morality	Social obligation	Private self-help

Interpretations of Thatcherism

The literature on Thatcherism and its impact is immense. Marsh distinguishes between unidimensional explanations based on political, ideological, or economic characterisations of Thatcherism, and inclusive explanations that attempt to draw on all three factors (Marsh, 1994). However most interpretations tend to concentrate on one factor. These are discussed in Chapter 2, and can be characterised as follows.

Thatcherism as Personality

Kavanagh and King tend to emphasise the personality of Thatcher. They focus on her domination of her Cabinets, and her ability to set her own agenda and force it through (King, 1985; Kavanagh, 1990). Riddell takes this approach in a slightly different form, arguing that 'Thatcherism is essentially an instinct, a series of moral values and an approach to leadership rather than an ideology' (Riddell, 1983, 7; 1991).

Thatcherism as Party Political Statecraft

Bulpitt sees Thatcherism as a continuation of traditional Conservative statecraft. The concern of Conservative governments is to govern competently and win general elections. Consequently, the goals of the Thatcher government were not particularly ideological but were concerned with ensuring that the Conservatives won the next election (Bulpitt, 1986). Gamble has developed an alternative political explanation. He sees Thatcherism as a political project aimed at restoring the 'conditions – electoral, ideological, economic and political – for the Conservative Party to resume its leading role in British Politics'; central to this project was the restoration of the domestic and international authority of the British state and the reversal of Britain's economic decline (Gamble, 1994, 4).

Thatcherism as Pursuit of Ideological Hegemony

An early study, that popularised the very notion of Thatcherism, defined it as a hegemonic project (Hall and Jacques, 1983). According to Marsh, this involved:

> a conscious strategy adopted by calculating subjects. The hegemonic project is characterised as authoritarian populism involving: increasing centralisation with the state; the rejection of consultation with interests; and the greater use of coercion but also a greater awareness of the importance of manufacturing consent among the population and, indeed, a recognition of the need to really incorporate some strategic elements of popular opinion into its hegemonic project. (Marsh, 1994, 9)

Thatcherism was an attempt at moral and ideological leadership which could create a new historic bloc of finance capital, the skilled working class and the middle class.

Thatcherism as a Post-Fordist Modernisation Strategy

For Jessop, Thatcherism was an attempt to restructure the Keynesian welfare state and the British economy towards a post-Fordist economy which was based on finance capital, and which was also highly flexible, non-unionised, and divided into a skilled highly paid core and low skilled, low paid, peripheral workforce. This required breaking the power of the unions and shaking out Britain's traditional manufacturing industries. However, this strategy was essential flawed because of the conflicts within British society and the fundamental weaknesses of the British economy (Jessop, Bonnett, Bromley and Ling, 1988; Jessop, 1989).

Thatcherism as Inconsistent Policy Implementation

Marsh and Rhodes emphasise the need to assess not what Thatcher said it would do, but what it actually achieved. They note that the success of Thatcherism varied greatly from one policy area to another (Marsh and Rhodes, 1992). Undoubtedly there were radical changes in areas like relations with local government and privatisation (Chapter 8), but in policy areas such as trade union reform, economics and health, there was either a high level of policy continuation or policy had unintended consequences which meant that the government did not always achieve its initial goals (Chapters 9, 10 and 11). Rose similarly demonstrates how most of the policies undertaken by the Thatcher government – at least up to 1985 – were policies introduced before 1946, concluding that, 'Of the 118 different programmes that constituted the inheritance of the 1945 Labour government, more than five-sixths are still in effect more that four decades later; only nineteen have been terminated' (R. Rose, 1990, 273).

It is important to see Thatcherism as a complex political phenomenon, and as both a cause and an effect of wider change. In a sense Thatcherism was a response by the libertarian wing of the Conservative Party to the failure of collectivism, the post-war consensus and social democracy. It was also a response to the left-wing shift of Labour, the disillusion of the working-class voters, and middle-class fears of inflation and high taxation. At the same time it was a strategy for dealing with much wider changes in the economy and society. Thatcherism was a response to the increasing internationalisation of the economy, which made the modernising Keynesian strategy appear impossible, and to the changes in the class structure which weakened the link between class and voting. Thatcherism was a British Conservative response to trends that are affecting polities throughout the world. It was not unique, as Riddell has observed:

> Thatcherism has been working with the grain not only of domestic developments but also of international trends. The shift in economic policy towards tighter financial and public spending restraint began in the mid-1970s not only in Britain but also in the US and on the continent of Europe. There have been similar problems and solutions in social provision and industrial policy based on the spread of privatisation. These trends have been common under both left- and right-wing governments. (Riddell, 1991, 13)

It is nevertheless important to remember the domestic political context. The Thatcher government was made up of politicians who had to operate not only within the context of Britain's position in the world economy but also within existing political structures. Such contexts were continually changing, providing new opportunities for a radical political programme. Hence the state of the world economy, relationships with government departments and interest groups, and relationships within the Cabinet and party, all constrained the Thatcher government but also created opportunities to pursue a radical agenda (M. J. Smith, 1994a).

Initially Thatcher was faced by the politics of power of a previous era. The policy networks established in the post-war era still dominated most policy areas. It took the Thatcher government a long time to introduce radical policies in welfare: she was limited by incomplete support in her own Cabinet and by opposition from interest groups and professionals who dominated policy-making. Her inability, or unwillingness, to make progress in this area was regarded as her one significant failure by her most loyal lieutenant in Cabinet (Ridley, 1992, 85). By 1988, however, she had removed most of her Cabinet 'wets' and challenged the established policy networks in health and education, and was starting to introduce radical policies. Only after nine years of Thatcher government did the structures of the state and the politics of power start to shift in a Thatcherite direction. It was this politics of power that then confronted Major, making it difficult for him to shift away from Thatcherism, even when he wished to without another period of activist government.

Conservatism after Thatcher

Despite Thatcher's domination, 'The Conservative Party never became a Thatcherite party. It remained the Conservative Party led by Mrs Thatcher' (Gamble, 1994, 213). In these circumstances, it is to be expected that a leader could build support for a return to a more pragmatic progressive Conservatism. However, such a conclusion would underestimate the impact of social and economic change. Thatcherism was a response not just a cause. It was a way of coping with social and economic change: Britain's weakening position in the world economy, the failures of the welfare state and weak corporatism, and the changes in the class and occupational structure. Such changes made a return to progressive conservatism difficult. Very few Conservatives now call explicitly for a return to Keynesian demand management.

Given the changes in state structures (Chapter 8), it has become more difficult for Major – or any other Prime Minister – radically to change policy direction. As John Gray has pointed out: 'The current centralist structure of the state is an artefact of the New Right, constructed to make the shift of power to market institutions irreversible' (Gray, 1994). To reverse privatisation, the position of trade unions, the changes in the tax structure or the reforms of health and education would involve considerable will and high political costs. Thatcher, and economic change, have affected the context within which decisions are made. Few Conservatives would want to re-enact the battles of the 1980s. Progressive Conservatism was historically specific, and the factors which created that ideological formation are either gone or greatly altered. There is, in any case, little sign that Major wants to challenge the new state structures or policies established by the Thatcher government. In a keynote speech on 'The Role and Limits of the State', he insisted, 'In the 1980s, Margaret Thatcher began to roll back the frontiers of the state, with privatisation, deregulation and the restoration of personal incentives . . . But more is needed . . . At all levels my ambition is smaller government, efficient government, effective government, *responsive* government' (Major, 1994b).

This is not to suggest that Major and his successors have no room for manoeuvre. There is an argument both within and outside the Conservative Party over whether Major is continuing the Thatcher inheritance. According to Edward Leigh, a minister sacked after Major's extensive 1993 reshuffle, 'The left of the Tory party has now achieved its ambitions to control economic, foreign and industrial policy. The right sits beleaguered in isolated fortresses in the Home Office, Social Security and Wales' (*Spectator*, 5 June 1993). Others on the right have complained that Major has abandoned the Thatcher legacy, and Thatcher has dissociated herself from some of Major's policies, notably on Europe (Chapter 6). Major's reshuffles since 1990 have seen a decline in the number of Thatcherites in the Conservative government from 20 in 1987 to 12 in 1993. In the Cabinet Thatcherites had been reduced to a rump of three by 1993 (Ludlam, 1993).

There have been significant policy differences between Thatcher and Major. Major did abandon the Poll Tax, supported membership of the ERM (Chapter 13), made Michael Heseltine President of the Board of Trade with a commitment to a more active industrial policy, and professed a stronger commitment to public service. However, there is also an argument that the changes are more in style than in substance. Major is perceived as more consensual and pragmatic leader than Thatcher, but still acting in line with Thatcherite principles and overall policy (Riddell, 1991; Marsh, 1994). For Ian Lang, Major is 'more Thatcherite than the lady herself', and he is 'taking the Conservative agenda further than his predecessor did' (Lang, 1994, 3–4). Indeed, in terms of health policy, education policy, the reform of government and public services, privatisation and fiscal policy there appears to be very little shift from the Thatcherite agenda, as one of his most outspoken Cabinet rightwingers has acknowledged (Redwood, 1995). Facing colossal government debt, the 'damp' Chancellor, Kenneth Clarke, has presided over a far more radical public spending review than the one that Thatcher disavowed when its existence was leaked before the 1983 election. Michael Heseltine seems to have placed his energies into deregulation rather than industrial intervention, and the long delayed privatisations of railways, coal mines and postal services have been tackled under Major.

Despite the change in personnel, the Thatcherite agenda in welfare and economic policy seems to be the new centre ground in Conservative Party policy. Nowhere within the party is there sustained criticism of the welfare policy, fiscal conservatism, or taxation policy inherited from the Thatcher era. Indeed, the key ideological division within the Conservative Party is no longer over the level of state intervention, although it is still important. The recent ideological disputes within the party concern the limits of national sovereignty and how far legislative sovereignty should be ceded to supranational institutions, particularly in relation to Europe (Chapter 6; D. Baker, Gamble and Ludlam, 1993b). On this view Thatcherism is 'a return to a limited government tradition but also to a mainstream national sovereignty tradition' (D. Baker, Gamble and Ludlam, 1993b, 287). What now divides Conservatives is less the role of government, and more Britain's position in relation to Europe. So those who ostensibly accept a Thatcherite economic agenda, such as Edwina Currie or Major, are in conflict with those, like Teresa Gorman and Thatcher, who are economic liberals who remain unwilling to pool national sovereignty.

Is the only difference between Major and Thatcher the issue of Europe? Major has attempted to distinguish himself through policies such as 'back to basics' and the Citizen's Charter but it is clear that, in key areas of policy, the Major government has been concerned with implementing policies that were already been initiated. For any party, turning around the ship of state is exceedingly difficult. As Riddell highlights: 'For all but the most passionate adherents to Mrs Thatcher's cause, the shifts that occurred were more a response to changed circumstances and changed times rather than any dramatic reversal of policy' (Riddell, 1991). At the same time Major's view of the welfare state and the public service appears less hostile than that of Thatcher. He affirmed that government 'must provide high quality education and health – and security for the old, the sick, and others who depend on our welfare system' (Major, 1994b). His emphasis was to be on the management of such services, not on their legitimacy.

Therefore, the impact of Thatcherism on her successor's agenda appears mixed. Major has continued the curious mix of collectivism, authority, free economy and order that has characterised the Conservative Party. How far is his a new mix? Despite the fact he has been Prime Minister for so long, there are curiously few assessments of party under his leadership (Kavanagh and Seldon, 1994). There seem to be three general hypotheses about 'Majorism':

- Thatcher has changed the balance of power within the party and the state, and hence Major is constrained to continue with a Thatcherite agenda;
- Major has again remixed the historic elements of Conservatism, offering a combination of neo-liberal economic policy with a progressive commitment to public services tailored to the political circumstances of the 1990s;
- Thatcher was not as radical as has generally been supposed. She pursued Conservative statecraft, and any adaptions by Major are a modified Conservative statecraft.

The concluding chapter will assess the validity of these hypotheses, and of the interpretations of Thatcherism outlined above, and consider the state of the party, in the light of the evidence presented in the chapters that follow.

2

An Ideological Party

ANDREW GAMBLE

Margaret Thatcher was elected leader of the Conservative Party in 1975 and resigned in 1990, having served 11 years continuously as Prime Minister. She became leader at a time of crisis for the party. It had lost four of the previous five general elections, its policies were in disarray after an unsuccessful term in government, and its vote in October 1974 was the lowest it had achieved at any election this century. The crisis within the Conservative Party reflected a more general sickness of the political regime which had existed in Britain since the 1940s and within whose parameters governments of both parties had worked. In the two elections of 1974 both main parties had below 40 per cent support. This was the first time either had gone below 40 per cent since 1945. This loss of legitimacy had external and internal causes. The disintegration of the Bretton Woods system in 1971 had caused inflation to accelerate. The quadrupling of oil prices in 1973 had been a trigger for the first generalised world recession in 1974, which sharply raised unemployment, and ushered in an era of restructuring and adaptation to the requirements of a more open and interdependent world economy. All the institutions and organisations which had grown up in the national protectionist era of the previous 50 years now came under scrutiny and challenge. Britain had an economy which had performed well by its own previous standards but poorly in relation to its main competitors. The adjustment required was therefore deeper and more immediate in Britain than in many other countries. Internally the government was seen to be failing because it had become overloaded in respect of the tasks it was seeking to undertake, and weak in relation to the claims of special interests upon it.

The Thatcher myth in the Conservative Party developed against this background. Her supporters portrayed her from the outset as a heroic leader with a mission to restore the Conservative Party to its rightful place as the leading party of the state, and to renew British national purpose and confidence. The idea that Thatcherism was a radical, even revolutionary force, which sought to overturn much that had become established and legitimate in twentieth-century Britain, originated with her own supporters, and in particular with some of the intellectual auxiliaries who were drawn to her flag (Cosgrave, 1978; Ranelagh, 1992).

The assessment of Thatcher and Thatcherism was a source of considerable controversy during her period as leader. Since her enforced departure in 1990 the controversy has not subsided. It has been given a new perspective with the election of John Major as Conservative leader. Major's personal style has been a marked contrast to Thatcher's and some of his policies have also been different. Although he was Thatcher's preferred successor out of the three candidates who contested the election a rift soon developed between them, and Major became a target of derision and contempt for many of the Thatcherites. If he had lost the 1992 election he would have been merely a footnote to the Thatcher era, and the party would have regrouped under a new leader in opposition. But because he won the election he ensured that his premiership would not be a short-lived affair, and that increasingly it would be compared with Thatcher's (Kavanagh and Seldon, 1994).

One key comparison concerns ideology. Under Thatcher the Conservative Party became noted for its attachment to ideology. Thatcher is supposed to have declared on one occasion in the 1970s at a Salisbury Club meeting that 'the other side have an ideology; we must have one as well.' Were the Conservatives still an ideological party under Major, or did they revert to their traditional pragmatic, non-ideological approach to government? Did they repudiate the policies of the previous 15 years or continue them? Was Thatcherism an aberration, a bad dream from which the Conservative Party and the country awoke in 1990? Or was the outlook of the party and the direction of policy permanently transformed? Was the Major government merely a continuation of the Thatcher government, or did it introduce new themes, and a new direction?

The Chamberlain Tradition

Before seeking to answer these questions the strangeness of the phenomenon of Thatcherism for the Conservative Party is worth stressing. The previous great political enthusiasm to grip the Conservative Party in the twentieth century had been tariff reform, spearheaded by Joseph Chamberlain, at one time a leading radical in the Liberal Party and a prominent Birmingham manufacturer. Chamberlain was a Unionist and an Imperialist rather than a Conservative who allied with the Conservatives over the issue of Home Rule for Ireland. The thrust of Chamberlainite politics was imperialist, protectionist and collectivist, and it left its legacy on the twentieth-century Conservative Party (Semmel, 1962).

Apart from Churchill, who left the Conservative Party and joined the Liberals over the issue of tariff reform, all the other twentieth-century leaders of the Conservative Party after Arthur Balfour – Bonar Law, Austen Chamberlain, Baldwin, Neville Chamberlain, Eden, Macmillan, Home and Heath – belonged to the Chamberlainite tradition in the party. In the Chamberlainite vision British security and prosperity depended on Britain being at the centre of an economic, geographical and political association which was much wider than the British Isles. At the beginning of the century this was the Empire; as the dream of Empire faded and its foundations crumbled after 1945, the EC gradually became the new focus. The formula however was similar. External involvement was to be matched by a commitment to national efficiency, institutional modernisation and social reform.

The novelty of Thatcherism within the Conservative Party was that it signalled a decisive rupture with the Chamberlainite tradition of social imperialism. Thatcherism was a post-imperial, post-welfare, post-labourist vision of Britain and its place in the world. The break was most apparent over collectivism in economic and social policy, and least clear-cut over the Empire and foreign policy. There were occasionally regressions, most notably the Falklands War in 1982, a final imperial gesture. But overall the Thatcher years did little to halt the retreat from Empire. The granting of independence to Zimbabwe and the agreement returning Hong Kong to Chinese jurisdiction were more significant than the Falklands, which in any case the Thatcher government had been trying to dispose of before the Argentine army invaded (Chapter 12; Young, 1990, 259).

The most distinctive aspect of foreign policy in the Thatcher era was the division that emerged over the relative merits of the Atlanticist alliance and the EC, which in time came to divide the Thatcherites themselves (D. Baker, Gamble and Ludlam, 1993a). The Thatcherites who stayed loyal to Thatcher gave priority to Atlanticist over European relationships, particularly in the security field, and became fierce critics of the momentum within the EC to some form of federal union (Chapter 6). Many Conservatives in the Chamberlainite tradition had always been suspicious of the USA because of the imbalance in the relationship between the two countries. With the demise of the Empire the EC appealed to many former imperialists because it possessed some of the same features. Although Britain could not dominate the EC as it dominated the Empire, the EC offered another extended sphere for British influence which could safeguard British security and prosperity (Chapter 13).

From this perspective the last major success of the Chamberlainite tradition in the Conservative Party was the successful negotiation of entry into the EC by Edward Heath in 1971. Thatcher did not openly repudiate this commitment and the Conservative Party campaigned for a yes vote in the referendum in 1975. But in the course of her premiership her hostility to the EC increased, and by the end of it the threat which the EC posed to national sovereignty had become a key dividing line in the party (Chapter 6). Defence of national independence had become a core element of Thatcherism.

The other key part of the Chamberlainite tradition which Thatcherism repudiated was the emphasis on welfare and social reform as the means of incorporating the labour movement within the British state. Thatcherism reasserted the central role of private property and individual liberty as the touchstones of public policy, and rejected the established policy consensus of welfare Keynesianism (Chapter 11), as well as the need to make concessions any longer to the organised labour movement (Chapter 10). Chamberlain had spoken of the ransom that property had to pay if it wished to ensure its security. The ransom took shape in the first four decades of the twentieth century. It involved higher levels of taxation to pay for collective welfare programmes in social security, health and education; the maintenance of legal privileges to trade unions which gave them immunities from actions for damages in respect of strikes and other industrial action; and the extension of government controls over the private sector. Thatcher rejected the need for all three parts of the ransom. Her call to roll back the state was a repudiation not just of the consensus of post-war politics but of the main line of direction of Conservative politics in the twentieth century. In defining the Conservatives as the party of national independence, economic liberty and moral order the Thatcherites were attempting to return to basics and abandon many of the causes and commitments which had come to define the Conservative Party.

The Concept of Thatcherism

The political project of Thatcherism took time to develop, and many people had a hand in shaping it. In some areas it remained incomplete and undeveloped; in others it was strongly influenced by events and the problems which were encountered in government. The term Thatcherism remains a controversial one because it attributes a coherence and consistency to the ideas held by Thatcher and her associates which is hard to reconcile with the improvisation, muddle, opportunism and changes of direction which characterised the Thatcher government in so many areas of policy (Marsh and Rhodes, 1992; Jordan and Ashford, 1993). It also suggests that the most important causal factors in the explanation of what happens in public policy and government are ideas. Thatcherism was first formulated as a new *Weltanschauung*, which won hearts and minds in the Conservative Party, in the opinion-forming elites and in the electorate, and was then translated into practice through the actions of the Thatcher governments. In this conception Thatcherism is an external and self-contained force which entered British politics like a fireball, transforming all institutions and policies with which it came into contact. Some were burned away quickly, while others resisted stubbornly.

Crediting ideas with autonomous power to effect social change is an old theme in social science. Despite their disagreements about other matters Keynes and Hayek were strongly in agreement about the importance of ideas. In Keynes's famous words,

> the ideas of economists and political philosophers, both when they are right and when they are wrong, are more powerful than is commonly understood. Indeed the world is ruled by little else. Practical men who believe themselves to be quite exempt from any intellectual influences, are usually the slaves of some defunct economist. Madmen in authority, who hear voices in the air,

are distilling their frenzy from some academic scribbler of a few years back. I am sure that the power of vested interests is vastly exaggerated compared with the gradual encroachment of ideas. (Keynes, 1973, 383)

Applying this notion to Thatcherism, what happened to the Conservative Party in the 1970s and 1980s was that one grand vision – welfare Keynesianism had become exhausted and was successfully challenged by another, market liberalism. The Conservatives under Thatcher's leadership became the vanguard in Britain for the new ideas which gradually undermined the old institutions and the old policies.

One rationale for this account of political and social change is provided by Milton Friedman, who speaks of three great intellectual tides in modern history: the Adam Smith tide which led to the *laissez-faire* individualism of the nineteenth century, the Fabian tide which produced the twentieth-century welfare state, and the Hayek tide which has seen the revival of free markets in the last decades of the twentieth century (Friedman and Friedman, 1980). Long waves of ideas like long waves of economic development, provide a framework within which political parties and other political groups act and which set the parameters within which policies are introduced. As with economic long waves there may be cycles within each long wave, but as with a tide the overall direction remains constant.

The existence of such long waves is hard to prove or disprove (certainly in any precise form), but the idea has always been an influential one. Dicey's famous argument that the tenets of individualism were losing their hold on public opinion and being replaced by the tenets of collectivism is one example; and the idea is central to Greenleaf's recent characterisation of the British political tradition (Greenleaf, 1983a). He argues that there is a single tradition of ideas which cuts across political parties. The tradition has two main strands, libertarian and collectivist, and for long periods one of these strands can be dominant. On this view Margaret Thatcher in the Conservative Party, and more recently Tony Blair in the Labour Party, are political leaders who are expressing the libertarian strand of the political tradition, after a long period in which the collectivist strand was dominant as articulated by Chamberlainite Tories, Fabian Socialists and New Liberals.

There are many difficulties with these accounts. For political scientists concerned with the analysis of policy, ideas never have such a self-contained role in prompting decisions. They might accept a notion like the 'climate of ideas', but dispute that a particular climate directly affects what is or is not done. There are many factors that intervene and mediate the outcomes. In looking at a specific period such as the Thatcher period, and estimating how much was actually changed by decisions taken by government ministers and how much change originated from other sources, the concept of Thatcherism can be an obstacle to understanding. A better procedure is to disaggregate the programme of the government into different policy areas, and examine each in turn. Underlying this approach is the assumption that a government is not a unified actor with a single will, but is composed of many different agencies and individuals, often with conflicting and incompatible agendas and interests.

If government is seen primarily as an arena rather than as an actor, a concept such as Thatcherism takes on a different meaning. Since there is no actor, either political party or government, on which Thatcherism can seize, but rather a complex network of interests and agencies, the main role of general doctrines like Thatcherism is to offer retrospective accounts which seek to knit together the often chaotic, unplanned, and accidental character of policy-making. Such a view of politics and policy-making is decidedly unheroic, in marked contrast to the heroic view of Thatcherism described earlier. It can go too far in denying any role for ideas and political will in shaping events, but it is a useful corrective to the notion that there was some seismic political revolution in the 1980s which transformed British politics permanently. There was a significant change, but many things did not alter, or changed much less than was sometimes claimed.

Thatcherism as Ideology: Authoritarian Populism

Against the scepticism of the policy analysts the significance of Thatcherism as a political project has been asserted by a number of analysts. Stuart Hall's account of Thatcherism which gives special emphasis to its ideological features as authoritarian populism has been the most influential (Hall, 1988). Hall argued that Thatcherism was something new in the politics of the right. Thatcher had grasped that the disorientation of British and world politics in the mid-1970s provided a set of opportunities and spaces for a new politics. Established institutions and practices could be questioned and new discourses developed to change the boundaries of political possibility.

As an ideological project Thatcherism operated on several different levels: seeking to promote a new public philosophy against which particular government programmes could be assessed; challenging the intellectual merits of particular doctrines, such as the Keynesian doctrine of demand management; and attempting to establish a new common sense, which contradicted many long-established assumptions about policy, for example, that governments had a responsibility to maintain full employment (see Chapter 9).

One characteristic response to Thatcherism was to brand it as an attempt to go back to the nineteenth century and to resurrect nineteenth-century values of self-help, limited government and *laissez-faire*. Hall argued instead that the novel feature of Thatcherism was that it was a modernising project. It offered a way of adjusting to new realities and removing outworn and failed institutions. It was populist in its appeals to the people to rally against the dead hand of bureaucratic collectivism. This populist aspect gave it a dynamism and an appeal which enabled it to take the offensive. During the Thatcher era the normal roles were reversed between the parties. Instead of it being the Conservatives anxious to protect and conserve, they became the radical party, eager to tear down and rearrange institutions throughout the state and civil society. The Labour Party became the party seeking to protect the status quo including trade union privileges, the nationalised industries, the NHS, public housing, local government control over services, and even the rates.

What made Thatcher populist was her habitual stance, which she did not abandon even when she was head of the government, of opposition to the state. She stood with the people against the bureaucratic leviathan of the extended social democratic state. Hall described her populism as authoritarian because it was not aimed at increasing popular participation and democratic control, but at reducing it. The flaws in the institutions of the collectivist order were to be used to reduce the public sector and public provision, weaken organisations like trade unions, and limit the scope of government responsibilities and capacities in economic and social policy, while increasing them in the fields of social and public order (see Chapters 10 and 11).

Hall saw Thatcherism as a response to the crisis of legitimacy in the British state in the mid-1970s. By taking the offensive against many of the institutions and practices of the existing state it broke new ground and began to reconfigure British politics (Chapter 8). Many things thought impossible or beyond limits suddenly became possible again.

The importance of ideology and intellectuals for this project was not that they provided blueprints or detailed policies and proposals, but that they questioned the key assumptions on which the economic and political structures of the extended state had been based. In this way they helped to undermine the legitimacy and the inevitability of existing arrangements, and made it possible to imagine quite different ones. They helped create the space within which politicians could act, often in an opportunistic and unplanned way, but informed by the strategic possibilities which the prior debate about policy and objectives had opened up. An example of this process was privatisation. Denationalising state industries was one of the key strategic objectives which was identified by New Right intellectuals in the 1970s for rolling back the state, but no commitments were made in the 1979 manifesto, and no detailed plans existed. The government began with a few small sales of government shares in manufacturing companies; but the privatisation programme only really got under way when the opportunity to privatise British Telecom (BT) arose because of the problems of funding its investment requirements through the public sector (Veljanovski, 1987). The success of the British Telecom (BT) privatisation encouraged other experiments and a rolling programme of privatisations developed, which served a number of objectives and built a wide-ranging coalition of interests including the managers of the existing companies, parts of the workforce, members of the public who bought shares, and the Treasury which profited from the contribution to general revenue. The thesis of authoritarian populism does not depend on the claim that Thatcherism achieved a great popular endorsement for its new policies. Thatcherism was successful because, on most of the crucial battles in which the Thatcher government became engaged, it was able to assemble a winning coalition and to disorganise and demoralise the opposition. Confident in its aims and sure of where the political and moral high ground actually was, the Thatcher government was able to ride out conflicts and win. It triumphed in all its major confrontations with the trade unions, including the all-important defeat of the National Union of Mineworkers (NUM) in 1984–5; it fought long battles with several key professional groups; and it engaged in protracted struggles with local councils. It developed a confrontational style to force through reorganisation and change throughout the public sector, while relying on the disciplines of market forces, bankruptcy and competition to achieve it in the private sector.

The success of Thatcherism as an ideological project in Stuart Hall's sense is more evident at the elite than at the popular level. The Conservatives achieved electoral success under Thatcher but no popular endorsement of Thatcherite values. By the end of the Thatcher period there were higher percentages expressing support for collectivist values than at the outset (Crewe, 1988). The real success which Thatcherism achieved was that it reunited the party in opposition and restored its morale; rebuilt its electoral support (Chapter 3) and its support within the business community; won the 1979 election following the débâcle over the public sector strikes in the winter of 1978–9 and the loss of the devolution bill; and then in government was able to keep the confidence and support when it mattered of both its electorate and its key allies in business, finance and the media, while the opposition remained fragmented, defensive and unimaginative (Chapter 7).

Does this make Thatcherism hegemonic? There is no doubt that in its aspirations Thatcherism sought to be hegemonic. Thatcher wanted to bury Socialism. In some moods she wanted to see the trade unions, the Labour Party and local authorities all disappear. She wanted to create a new consensus informed by her values of economic individualism, national independence and conservative morality, so that even if the Conservatives lost office at some point in the future (a possibility she could not bear to contemplate) any successor government would be obliged to govern within the new constraints which she had established. It would no longer be possible to go back to large nationalised sectors, high marginal rates of taxation, strong trade unions, exchange controls, council housing and corporatist structures in economic management, such as industrial strategies and incomes policies.

Hegemony has a number of different meanings. Social or class hegemony, in the sense of the fundamental social and economic relationships of the society, was not under serious threat in Britain in the 1970s. What was under threat was the survival of the two main governing parties. The crisis of hegemony was a crisis of political authority, which afflicted both main parties, and arose because of widespread doubts about their competence first to govern successfully, second to be nationally representative, and third to deal with new external and internal challenges.

This crisis of hegemony affected both Labour and the Conservatives, but after their demoralisation in 1974 the Conservatives adapted much more quickly under Thatcher's leadership to the new national and international realities than did Labour. They found a winning political and electoral strategy, while Labour disintegrated, touching lower depths in popular support in 1983 than the Conservatives had ever done. By 1987 the Conservatives were well on the way to establishing a dominant party system. They had a commanding electoral lead over Labour, they dominated the policy agenda and they had established a reputation for economic competence. They were not loved, but their statecraft had been highly effective in strengthening their position through council house sales, the increase in share-owners, the encouragement of private health insurance and opt-out schools, and the weakening of the main institutional strongholds of their political opponents (in the public sector, trade unions and local government).

Thatcher's primary purpose when she became leader was to restore the political hegemony of the Conservative Party within British politics. Given the rules of the electoral system and the highly centralised organisation of the British state it was possible to achieve comfortable parliamentary majorities with electoral support of only 42–3 per cent in four successive general elections (Chapter 3). What marked out Thatcherism was that it was a political project which aimed not just to win electoral victory but to reshape the British state in ways which would benefit the Conservative Party. For most of the twentieth century Thatcherites argued that at least as far as economic and social policy were concerned the Conservatives had been on the defensive, operating on ground which had been marked out by their opponents. They sought to redefine the key issues in British politics so that in future their opponents would have to operate within a Conservative agenda.

How successful they were in these aims has been much discussed. Reference has already been made to the lack of success the New Right had in shifting the British electorate from its support for collectivist welfare provision in certain fields, particularly health and education. The later privatisation measures were extremely unpopular and, although the early trade union legislation had majority support, opinion soon flowed back to the unions. Majorities also declared that they would prefer more public services even if it meant higher taxes (Chapter 3). The Conservatives could comfort themselves that pocket-book voting resulted in many voters still voting for the Conservatives and tax cuts, even if morally they still preferred the old centre-left consensus. Economic individualism had been given free rein, but its values were still widely resisted, even among Conservative Party members (Chapter 4).

One view on the New Right was that there was a time-lag between the introduction of new patterns of behaviour and acceptance of the values underlying them. Others following Hayek concluded that the circumstances of modern economies meant that most citizens were employees rather than self-employed, and that this created a democratic politics in which the majority would vote for programmes which provided security and protection rather than ensuring enterprise and risk. A New Right programme would always have interests against it, and skilful statecraft would be necessary to create coalitions to support New Right policies (Pirie, 1988).

Many analysts have stressed the unevenness of the Thatcher achievement (Jessop, 1989). The ability to unify the business community and most of the print media behind the programme was impressive, and the support did not diminish but in some cases increased as time went on. But support from other areas of civil society was small, and little was done to rectify it. The churches, the universities, the schools and the health service all became embroiled in long struggles with the government. The initiative remained with the government on most issues, until the unprecedented revolts over the Poll Tax, education and health. One consequence was that much less was achieved in transforming the welfare state or reducing the overall burden of taxation than the Thatcherites had hoped. The direction was laid out, but the implementation was inconsistent.

The economy was the greatest disappointment of all. The economic miracle of the 1980s was based on unsustainable foundations and reality returned in the recession of 1990–2, as unemployment climbed again and inflation accelerated. Transforming the economy was to have been the bedrock on which the new order was founded. The high hopes of 1987 proved at best premature (Michie, 1992).

Thatcherism as Limited Politics

Stuart Hall's emphasis on Thatcherism as an ideological project inspired a great deal of research and writing on Thatcherism. By emphasising that Thatcherism did have a coherence, however flawed and incomplete it might have been in practice, he established the concept as an important framework for thinking about the political changes of the 1980s.

A different approach, but one which agreed in part with Hall, was Shirley Letwin's analysis of Thatcherism (Letwin, 1992). Like Hall she saw Thatcherism as displaying a coherence, but located the source of the coherence in a particular attitude to the task of government rather than in the objectives of a political project. Thatcherites believed, according to Letwin, that government must be organised so as to encourage individuals to embrace and practice the 'vigorous virtues'. This involved choosing those policies which would enable individuals to be self-reliant and to make their own choices. A Thatcherite policy is therefore one of limited politics in which the state deliberately withdraws from making decisions which could be made by individuals for themselves.

Letwin argues that this conception of human nature and the role of politics and government in a state that is understood as a civil association which has no directing will or purpose is what informs Thatcherism and its policy choices. In some areas, particularly education, the government at times did not follow these precepts and began intervening and attempting to impose its own pattern. In Letwin's terms this was not true Thatcherism, but an aberration from it. However, across the broad range of policy, there was an attempt to disengage and to transfer responsibilities from public bodies to individuals.

The process was always an uneven one. Nicholas Ridley confessed that the government often had to centralise in order to decentralise. To create a new pattern of less dependency on the state the Thatcher government sometimes took measures which increased that dependency, sweeping away intermediate institutions and established mechanisms of accountability and representation. To its critics on right and left the neo-liberal project of the 1980s involved an extension of state powers and state interference. The preference for market solutions in all areas of policy became a dogma which involved the suppression of many valuable institutions and non-market relationships. The hollowing-out of the state and civil society then led to fears about the erosion of community, the increase in selfishness and the rising tide of crime.

Conservatism after Thatcher

Thatcher left a difficult ideological legacy to her party. She broke decisively with the Chamberlainite tradition in economic and social policy, rejecting the accommodation with the organised labour movement and attempting to release the government from responsibility for economic outcomes and commitments to universal welfare benefits. She failed, however, to reconcile the conflict which emerged between the agendas of the liberal and the conservative New Right. Thatcherites proclaimed their belief in the traditional family, but never developed a coherent family policy. Many of the consequences of their policies undermined the kind of family they were committed to preserving (Chapter 11). Although Thatcher herself combined a rhetoric of individualism with a rhetoric of responsibility, in practice the two were not easily reconciled. The policies of the governments over which she presided promoted individualist rather than communitarian values.

Under Major this tension has increased. The social consequences of a decade of individualism have become ever more apparent, and the Conservatives have begun rediscovering the virtues of communities and non-market relationships for a successful and stable market order. After a decade of promoting solutions involving exit, the Major government through its Citizen's Charter began to experiment with solutions involving voice as well (Chapter 8). However, the main direction of policy was not changed. The reform of the Sunday Trading Laws went ahead, as did more privatisation measures, and market reforms in health and education continued (Chapter 11). The principle of limiting government responsibility wherever possible was not abandoned. The impact of the 1980s boom and the subsequent recession forced the raising of taxes in 1993 and 1994, but the Conservatives remained committed to lowering (direct) taxes whenever they could.

Despite early indications that there might be some changes, Major did nothing to revive industrial strategy. The logic of competition in a global economy was permitted to govern patterns of ownership and production in the UK. The passing of the Rover Group into German hands and the ending of shipbuilding on Tyneside, and above all the virtual extinction of the coal industry, were all allowed to occur. No attempts were made to reform or control the financial markets (Chapter 9), while in the labour markets the government continued to advocate greater flexibility and the reduction of financial burdens on employers (Chapter 10), and fiercely resisted the imposition of controls from the European Commission. The ideal of Britain as an off-shore Hong Kong, with a policy regime which emphasised privatisation, deregulation, low taxes and flexibility, still burned brightly under Major. Underlying it was the neo-liberal analysis that all the problems of the economy were due to market rigidities. If these were removed and markets allowed to clear then the economy would operate at full employment and its potential for growth would be increased. This policy doctrine was inherited from the Thatcher years and continued to govern policy.

Major managed to sound more concerned about the community than Thatcher ever had, but the thrust of policy did not change. If anything it was applied more inflexibly and with less political skill than under Thatcher. It is hard to see Thatcher making the political mistake of selling out the Nottinghamshire miners, crucial allies of the government during the miners' strike of 1984–5, quite as ruthlessly and comprehensively as the Major government did in 1992–3. Certain policies were changed or abandoned by the Major government, most notably the Poll Tax, but this was largely for practical and electoral reasons rather than because of any fundamental change of heart about the ideological principle lying behind it.

In education and health the policy also remained the same. No frontal assault was made on the principle of collective provision, but the continuing squeeze on budgets and the impact of the reforms in the organisation of the health service and education meant that the scope of private provision continued to expand. The internal markets in the National Health Service (NHS) and the incentives provided for schools to opt out of local authority control created pressures for more radical changes in funding and organisation, as they were intended to do (Chapter 11).

The recent direction of economic and social policy has become deeply ingrained in the thinking of the contemporary Conservative Party. One indication of this is the party's response to one of the consequences of its economic and social policies, namely the record crime wave. Its attempted reforms of the police and the prison service have introduced the principles of privatisation, competitive tender and commercial accounting into public services which had in the past been organised on hierarchical military lines. For all the ruminations on the importance of community by traditional Conservatives such as Douglas Hurd and Ian Lang, in policy terms the party continues to draw most of its ideas and its organisational models from the commercial sphere.

Thatcher's other ideological legacy to her party has been more divisive. In economic and social policy the party does seem to have shifted permanently away from the extended towards the limited state, but in relation to Britain's role in the world the party remains deeply divided. Major has sought to balance the two wings of his party, and has been perceived as a weak leader as a result. In ideological terms he has tried to position the Conservatives as the party of national sovereignty, but this has been hard to square with his enthusiasm for Britain being at the centre of Europe, his commitment to the ERM and his negotiation of the Maastricht Treaty (Chapters 6 and 13). Until the forced suspension of sterling from the ERM in September 1992, Major appeared to prepared to commit the Conservative Party once again to a much more positive role in Europe than Thatcher had been willing to entertain. But his policy was shipwrecked on Black Wednesday (Chapter 9) and although ultimately successful, he was severely bruised by the long parliamentary struggle over ratification of the Maastricht Treaty.

With the waning of the Atlantic relationship the consistent ideological position for the party is that put forward by Enoch Powell over many years, and by Thatcher at the end of her premiership: an uncompromising defence of national sovereignty and security, combined with free market principles in the conduct of economic and social policy. The first is incompatible with the EU as it currently operates and as the majority of its members wish to see it develop. Recognition of the increasing interdependence of the European economy is an argument for the pooling of sovereignty and the transfer of national powers to supranational bodies.

The European project belongs to the Chamberlainite tradition in the party, the search for a wider sphere in which Britain can exercise influence and protect its interests. Rejection of the European project would involve the distancing, and possibly the withdrawal, of Britain from the EU, and the revival of a specifically English nationalism, which might have consequences for the Union with Scotland, Wales and Northern Ireland. Major's position here is ambiguous. For tactical reasons at the 1992 election he gave strong backing to the Union with Scotland and ruled out any measure of devolution. His policy in Northern Ireland, however, has been to establish the basis for a political settlement which would involve devolution of power, and accepts the possibility of an eventual withdrawal of Northern Ireland from the UK (Chapter 12). Major's Unionism does not run deep, and this vestige of the old Conservatism looks in deep trouble.

One of Major's problems has been that, compared to the years of high drama and political confrontation under Thatcher, he has presided over a country in which many of the issues which once used to be dominant have lost much of their former significance, and some have disappeared altogether. Many of the fiercest dragons which Thatcher set out to slay have been slain. The most notorious, the USSR, simply collapsed. The trade unions have been considerably weakened and are no longer a serious constraint on the conduct of economic policy. Most of the nationalised industries have been sold, and local authorities have been stripped of many of the powers and functions which they once possessed. The lack of visible enemies and Major's leadership style has given the impression of weakness and lack of direction. The split in the party over the ERM and Maastricht has compounded the problem.

Conclusion

The argument of this chapter is that during Thatcher's leadership of the Conservatives there was a substantial ideological shift within the Conservative Party, and that this shift has proved to be permanent under her successor. The party has abandoned the interventionist and collectivist social and economic programme it adopted in stages during the twentieth century, and shows no signs of returning to it. Economic liberalism now shapes the party's thinking about policy.

The other shift which took place during the Thatcher years was towards a narrower English nationalism and a rejection of any compromise of British national sovereignty. Support within the party has been shifting in this direction but the issue is still divisive in the parliamentary party and in the leadership, in a way in which economic issues have ceased to be (D. Baker, Gamble and Ludlam, 1993).

Thatcherism succeeded in regaining the political hegemony for the Conservative Party which they have enjoyed for most of this century. The movement of the opposition parties on to their ground (particularly in economic and social policy) was one of the surest signs of their success (Chapter 7). This trend has continued and been amplified during Major's leadership. The modernisers in the Labour Party are not merely responding to Thatcherism; they are also responding as Thatcher did to changed opportunities and realities as well as building on earlier debates and initiatives within the party (Chapter 7, M.J. Smith, 1992). But it is clear that the ideological polarisation which took place between the parties in the 1970s and early 1980s is over, and that the new parameters of policy debate and the new estimate of what is politically possible substantially reflect the priorities which Thatcherism established.

Political hegemonies are fragile; they have to be constantly guarded and maintained, and the Thatcherite hegemony has developed a fault line through its centre in the shape of Europe. Major has sought to contain the disagreements within his party and avoid a split, but although he has been forced on the defensive he is not prepared to go all the way in proclaiming the party a Thatcherite party, dedicated to national independence, economic liberty, moral order and the old constitutional state. But there is little else on offer.

3

The Conservative Party and the Electorate

CHARLES PATTIE and RON JOHNSTON

Throughout its long history, the Conservative Party has been a formidable electoral force. Between 1832 and 1992, and not counting inter-election changes in government, the Conservatives emerged on the winning side in 18 out of 41 elections, a record unsurpassed by any other modern party (Blake, 1985). The party was the most successful in twentieth-century British politics: while it won only two of the 13 elections between 1832 and 1885 outright, it won eight of the 14 elections between 1886 and 1935, and eight of the 14 between 1945 and 1992. Conservative-led governments have presided over almost two-thirds of the years between 1900 and 1995.

This has been a considerable achievement during a century and a half of rapid social change. Paradoxically the 'conservative' party built its success upon an ability to adapt to new and threatening challenges. The emergence of a mass electorate implied permanent opposition for an establishment party, but under Disraeli the party built a working-class base (McKenzie and Silver, 1968). In the twentieth century, the welfare state was embraced quickly and the party kept Labour out of office between 1951 and 1964. In the 1970s, the Conservatives pursued another new political agenda, based on monetarist economics and deregulation, winning four elections in a row between 1979 and 1995, and thus staying in power for 16 unbroken years, a unique achievement.

How has the party managed to survive so successfully as an electoral machine, and what are its longer-term prospects? This chapter focuses

37

on the period from February 1974 to April 1992, a period of considerable change in British politics, much of it led by the Conservatives. After 1974, the so-called 'post-war consensus', based on broad support for Keynesian economics and for welfare state services, fragmented (Kavanagh and Morris, 1989). The two-party system which had dominated politics from 1945 was replaced by a multi-party system. After their double defeat in 1974, a new leader, Margaret Thatcher, took the party on a rightward trajectory. She became an iconic figure, claiming to speak for the 'common sense' of the British people, and exhibiting a strong radicalism. But did the Conservatives win voters' 'hearts and minds' in the 1980s and 1990s? How did they make the transition from a party widely seen as a spent electoral force in 1974, to one which seemed 'unassailable' in elections during the 1980s?

Post-war Trends in Conservative Support

In this section, we consider post-war trends in Conservative electoral support (Table 3.1), a period during which the party 'revisioned' itself twice, first to support the welfare state and later as an opponent of state involvement, these shifts paralleled wider economic developments.

After the war, recollections of the inter-war Depression were still clear. In most western countries the need for a welfare state and for Keynesian economic management was accepted. The Conservatives were no exception, adapting quickly to the post-war 'settlement' (Chapter 11). The Keynesian welfare state delivered economic stability and prosperity until the post-war boom faltered in the 1970s. Spending on state benefits and services threatened to outstrip tax yields (Newton, 1980). Theorists on the left and right began to argue that welfare states were becoming ungovernable (Brittan, 1975; Habermas, 1976). Monetarist economic ideas were embraced enthusiastically under Thatcher's leadership as a way out of the apparent 'crisis of Keynesianism'. Throughout her leadership the market served as an ideological goal for the party, freeing people from the 'dead hand' of the state and allowing personal freedom full rein (Chapter 2). The changing economic and political climate had consequences for Conservative electoral support too, but in more complex, indirect ways. To understand the consequences of the changing times for electoral support, however, we must take account of the wider electoral context.

TABLE 3.1 *Election results, 1945–92*

Year	Conservative* Vote %	Seats	Labour Vote %	Seats	Liberal† Vote %	Seats	Nationalist Vote %	Seats	Other‡ Vote %	Seats
1945	39.8	213	48.3	393	9.1	12	0.2	0	2.5	22
1950	43.5	299	46.1	315	9.1	9	0.1	0	1.2	2
1951	48.0	321	48.8	295	2.5	6	0.1	0	0.6	3
1955	49.7	345	46.4	277	2.7	6	0.2	0	0.9	2
1959	49.4	365	43.8	258	5.9	6	0.4	0	0.6	1
1964	43.4	304	44.1	317	11.2	9	0.5	0	0.8	0
1966	41.9	253	47.9	363	8.5	12	0.7	0	0.9	2
1970	46.4	330	43.0	288	7.5	6	1.3	1	1.8	5
1974F	37.8	297	37.1	301	19.3	14	2.6	9	3.2	14
1974O	35.8	277	39.2	319	18.3	13	3.5	14	3.2	12
1979	43.9	339	37.0	269	13.8	11	2.0	4	3.3	12
1983	42.4	397	27.6	209	25.4	23	1.5	4	3.1	17
1987	42.3	376	30.8	229	22.6	22	1.7	6	2.6	17
1992	41.9	336	34.4	271	17.8	20	2.3	7	3.5	17

* Includes Ulster Unionists, 1945–70.
† Liberal–SDP Alliance, 1983–7; Liberal Democrats, 1992.
‡ Mainly Northern Ireland MPs.
Note: Figures in this table have been rounded and therefore may not total 100.
Source: D. Butler and Kavanagh (1992).

Two-Party Politics, 1945–70

Electorally, the post-war years can be divided in two periods. From 1945 to 1970, elections were two-party contests. the Conservatives and Labour between them routinely won around 90 per cent of the votes cast (Kavanagh, 1987; Kavanagh and Morris, 1989). Despite leading the wartime government, the Conservatives lost the 1945 election having secured only 40 per cent of the vote. They did not do so badly again until February 1974. But post-war austerity damaged Labour, and the Conservatives embraced the new welfare state. The Conservative vote recovered in 1950, and sufficed in 1951 to beat Labour, even though Labour won marginally more votes. Three successive victories between 1951 and 1959 enabled them to govern for 13 unbroken years, attracting almost 50 per cent of those who voted, a level of popular support unmatched since (though somewhat exaggerated as the Liberals did not contest every seat). Rising living standards, low unemployment, low inflation, and a developing welfare state all seemed to guarantee the party continued victory (Abrams, Rose and Hinden, 1960).

Economic problems and political scandals eroded the Conservatives' position. Labour recovered from the Bevanite 'rebellion' of the 1950s, won narrowly in 1964 under a popular new leader, Harold Wilson, and consolidated its position in 1966. Of the five elections fought between 1964 and 1979, the Conservatives won only one, in 1970. Edward Heath's recovery proved short-lived, weakened by economic failures and industrial strife, culminating in confrontation with the miners. Heath went to the country in February 1974, campaigning on the issue of 'who governs, government or unions?', and lost despite winning a small majority of votes cast. For some, Labour had emerged as the new 'natural party of government'.

Multi-Party Politics, 1974–92

The second period also opened inauspiciously for the Conservatives, but the 1974 elections signalled a major change in the nature of British electoral politics, from which the party evenually benefited. Neither major party had been able to halt Britain's long-term economic decline, and voters deserted both major parties at the February 1974 election. Labour and Conservatives recorded new post-war lows, both struggling to get above 37 per cent of the vote. A quarter of the electorate voted for other parties. The main beneficiaries were the Liberals, who began to fight most constituencies, and the Scottish and Welsh Nationalist parties. At all subsequent elections, substantial minorities have voted for third (and in Scotland and Wales fourth) parties. The two-party system became a multi-party system.

After falling to only 36 per cent in October 1974 under Heath, the Conservatives recovered better than Labour. At the 1979 election, Thatcher capitalised on disaffection with the economy and strikes in the winter of 1978–9, winning 44 per cent of the vote, and a parliamentary majority of 43 seats. The 1979 election marked another sort of watershed: prior to 1979, the expectation was that parties would alternate in office. Thereafter, the Conservatives re-established themselves as the natural party of government, winning the next three elections with around 42 per cent of the vote. Depending on how the non-Conservative vote has split, parliamentary dominance has varied from a peak of 144 seats in 1983 to just 22 in 1992 (Johnston, Pattie and Fieldhouse, 1994). But whatever the majority, British electoral politics seemed no longer an 'alternating two-party system' but a 'dominant one party system' (Crewe, 1988).

From 1979 governments introduced a range of far-reaching policies, many of which weakened sources of political opposition and strengthened Conservative-supporting groups. Trade unions were taken on and neutralised through a series of Acts of Parliament and the failure of the 1984/5 NUM strike. Policies such as financial deregulation and right-to-buy legislation for council tenants also helped bolster Conservative support and create the conditions for continued electoral success. Local government came under early and sustained attack, as Thatcher sought to control public spending. Inner-city Labour-controlled councils in particular were targets of legislation that limited their autonomy and abolished the Labour-controlled metropolitan counties, seriously undermining one important bastion of opposition (Duncan and Goodwin, 1988). Ironically, the culmination of attempts to control local authorities, the extremely unpopular Poll Tax, almost proved the Conservatives electoral undoing (D. Butler, Adonis and Travers, 1994).

A number of reasons can be advanced for the Conservatives' dominance in the 1980s and 1990s. Labour responded to defeat in 1979 with an acrimonious internal debate, culminating in 1981 with the breakaway by the Social Democratic Party (SDP). In alliance with the resurgent Liberals, the SDP was an instant success. For a time it seemed that the SDP–Liberal Alliance could beat both the Conservatives and Labour, and it came within 2 percentage points of displacing Labour as the largest party of opposition in terms of vote share at the 1983 election, Labour's worst defeat since 1918. Although Labour's vote share increased in 1987 and 1992, the Alliance's (Liberal Democrats by 1992) decreased. The opposition vote remained split, allowing the Conservatives to win on vote shares that would have meant defeat before 1970. The absence of a unified opposition was a major fillip in the 1980s and 1990s, but it is important not to push this argument too far. Third-party supporters may not have voted against the government, but against Labour. Adding Alliance and Labour votes to produce an anti-Conservative majority is a spurious exercise (Crewe, 1988).

A second important event in consolidating Conservative electoral hegemony was the Falklands War in 1982. The government had been languishing in the polls, blamed for rising unemployment and inflation. After the war, they were buoyed up by national sentiment. The other parties could not compete, and the Conservatives won by a landslide in 1983. More than any other event, the Falklands War helped build Thatcher's image as a 'resolute' leader.

The third important factor underlying Conservative electoral success in the 1980s and 1990s was the changing geography of the vote. Under a first past the post electoral system like Britain's, the geography of a support is crucial to winning seats (Gudgin and Taylor, 1978). In 1951 and February 1974 the party with the largest share of the vote did not gain most seats because of the geography of its support. In 1983 the concentrated Labour vote in old industrial and metropolitan areas won 209 seats on only 27.6 per cent of the vote. On 25.4 per cent of the vote the Alliance won only 23 seats because their support was much less spatially concentrated.

The importance of the changing electoral geography was not limited to the link between votes and seats. One of the most striking features since the early 1970s has been the rapid development of regional divides in voting (Johnston, Pattie and Allsopp, 1988; Johnston and Pattie, 1992a). The geography of party support is a long-established feature of British voting. Traditionally, the Conservatives have done best in southern and rural areas, and Labour in northern, industrial seats. Between 1974 and 1987, this pattern became even more pronounced (Figure 3.1). Disraeli's 'one nation' party had become a 'two nations' party, drawing support disproportionately from only a few populous regions with most parliamentary seats. The Conservatives could pursue policies which widened inequalities between citizens and between regions, so long as conditions improved in their heartland regions (Jessop *et al.*, 1988). Up to the 1992 election, they enjoyed virtually unassailable majorities in a great many of their key seats, while the number of marginal constituencies declined. A post-war record swing against them would have been required before they lost control of Parliament (Johnston, Pattie and Fieldhouse, 1994). Regional polarisation of the vote reversed somewhat in 1992 (Johnston and Pattie, 1992b; Pattie, Johnston and Fieldhouse, 1994). The Conservatives staged a very small recovery in Scotland, but Labour's vote share recovered in the south and in strategic Midlands constituencies, leaving the Conservatives more vulnerable than at any time since 1979.

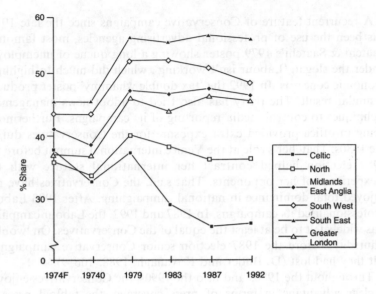

FIGURE 3.1 *Conservative vote as a percentage of three-party vote, February 1974–92*

Accounting for Electoral Success

The task of explaining the Conservatives' contemporary electoral success remains. In this section, we consider four potential factors: electoral campaigning, social change, ideological change, and government competence and economic management.

Electoral Campaigning

Compared to its rivals, the Conservative Party is a well-resourced organisation, though recent research has cast doubts on the health of its mass base (Chapter 4). The party normally commands a larger income than either of the main opposition parties, and is generally able to outspend its rivals by wide margins (Pinto-Duschinsky, 1981, 1985, 1989; Johnston and Pattie, 1993a). In 1992 the Conservatives spent £10.1 million on their national election campaign, compared to £7.1 million for Labour and £2.1 million for the Liberal Democrats (D. Butler and Kavanagh, 1992, 260).

A recurrent feature of Conservative campaigns since the late 1970s has been the use of professional advertising agencies, most famously Saatchi & Saatchi's 1979 poster showing a long queue of unemployed under the slogan 'Labour isn't working', which did much to highlight economic concerns. In 1992 the 'tax double whammy' poster produced a similar result. The party has also tried to adopt news management techniques to control media reporting of its campaigns. Furthermore, being in office provided extra exposure for the Conservatives during the 1980s: Thatcher's role at the Venice international summit before the 1987 election helped contrast her international stature with the inexperience of her opponents. That said, the Conservatives have not enjoyed total dominance in national campaigning. After 1983 Labour professionalised its campaigns. In 1987 and 1992, the Labour campaign was widely felt to be at least the equal of the Conservatives. On 'wobbly Thursday' before the 1987 election senior Conservative campaigners felt they had lost (D. Butler and Kavanagh, 1988, 106–9).

Throughout the 1980s and into the 1990s, the Conservatives enjoyed a clear advantage in terms of press coverage, the tabloid press in particular being heavily weighted in their favour. Only the *Daily Mirror* gave unequivocal support to Labour. Recent estimates suggest that favourable and free press coverage was worth an extra £16 million campaign spending for the Conservatives, compared to an extra £5 million for Labour (Linton, 1994, 31). But some caution is needed when discussing the impact of press support. Voters may be influenced by the views of their newspaper, but equally, voters choose their papers to match their views (Newton, 1992; Sanders, Ward and Marsh, 1993). Even so, research suggested that the largest swing towards the Conservatives during the 1987 campaign came from regular readers of the pro-Conservative tabloids (Miller, Clarke, Harrop, Leduc and Whiteley, 1990, 89).

The advantage in campaign resources is not just national. The party also enjoys a large financial advantage in the constituencies, where campaign spending is limited by law, but the Conservatives still outspend their rivals (Johnston and Pattie, 1993a). In 1992, their average constituency campaign spending was £5787, compared to £5055 for Labour and only £3218 for the Liberal Democrats. That local advantage is not trivial. The amount spent is linked to the amount of effort put into that campaign, and the more a party spends locally the better it does (Johnston, Pattie and Johnston, 1989; Pattie, Whiteley,

Seyd and Johnston, 1994). In 1992, *ceteris paribus*, the Conservatives' share of the electorate rose by 0.12 percentage points for every percentage point increase in their spending (Johnston and Pattie, 1993a). Constituency campaigning by other parties reduced the Conservative share and boosted their own standing; but overall, local spending did more to raise the Conservative vote than spending by their opponents did to lower it.

It is hard to quantify overall the electoral advantage the Conservatives derive from their resources and press support, but the balance of evidence suggests that they do boost the party's standing. After the 1992 election, however, Tory party finance became more of a publicity liability, as 'sleaze' allegations followed the revelation that an important private donor was on the run from the police, and fluctuations of corporate donations left the fabled 'war chest' shallower than in the 1980s (Fisher, 1994).

Social Change

Over the post-war period, and particularly since 1970, there have been fundamental changes in British society. The class structure has altered markedly as the economy has shifted from manufacturing to services, a trend accelerated by government policy during the 1980s when, for the first time, the majority of the British workforce was in white-collar jobs (Table 3.2). The electorate has changed in other ways, too.

A key area of change has been housing tenure. Since the 1960s, there has been steady growth in the number of home-owners, and rapid decline in the private renting sector. During the 1980s, government right-to-buy legislation made it easier for council tenants to purchase their homes (R. Dunn, Forrest and Murie, 1987). After 1979, the proportion of the electorate owning their own home rose rapidly to 72 per cent in 1992, while the proportion renting from their council declined to 19 per cent (Table 3.3).

Privatising nationalised industries, and selling the shares to small investors, saw the proportion of the population owning stocks and shares rise from around 7 per cent in 1979 to 22 per cent in 1992 (*Social Trends 1993*). By looking in more detail at class and housing tenure, we will see how the Conservatives have benefited, but we will also see that something other than social change has been occurring.

TABLE 3.2   *Shifting class structures, 1971–91 (%)*

Class	1971	1981	1991
I Professional, etc.	3.6	3.9	4.8
II Managerial and technical	17.8	22.0	27.8
III(N) Skilled non-manual	21.1	23.0	23.3
III(M) Skilled manual	28.4	25.5	21.7
IV Semi-skilled manual	20.9	18.9	16.2
V Unskilled manual	8.2	6.7	6.3

Note: Figures in this table have been rounded and therefore may not total 100.
Source: Census.

TABLE 3.3   *Changing patterns of housing tenure, 1964–92 (%)*

Year	Home-owners	Council	Other
1964	48.5	28.9	22.7
1970	54.5	29.7	15.8
1974F	53.8	30.9	15.3
1974O	53.4	29.5	16.4
1979	57.2	31.4	11.5
1983	65.7	27.7	6.7
1987	71.0	22.9	6.1
1992	71.8	19.3	8.1

Note: Figures in this table have been rounded and therefore may not total 100.
Source: British Election Survey (BES).

Class Cleavages

Social class is one of the most fundamental factors influencing voting. Traditionally, the majority of working-class voters supported Labour, and the majority of middle-class voters supported the Conservatives. In the 1960s the majority of voters were members of the manual working class, and an increasing proportion of voters had been brought up in Labour-voting households, producing predictions that Labour was becoming the natural party of government (D. Butler and Stokes, 1969).

The Conservatives have lived with this problem since the extension of the franchise in the late nineteenth century, but a sizeable minority of the working class has always voted Conservative, and has allowed the party to survive and prosper in the twentieth century (McKenzie and Silver, 1968). Furthermore, despite Butler and Stokes' projections, social change since 1970 has increased the proportion of voters in traditionally pro-Conservative classes. But changes in the sizes of the classes were not the only factor to affect the impact of the class cleavage: consumer affluence changed the relationship between class and political partisanship. As the working classes began to enjoy increasingly middle class life styles, an 'embourgeoisement' process was meant to weaken their support for Labour (Abrams, Rose and Hinden, 1960). In the late 1960s the 'affluent worker' study suggested that a generational divide was developing. Older manual workers remembered the Depression and the war and voted for Labour no matter what. Younger manual workers who had only known post-war prosperity were much more 'instrumental' in their professed attachment to Labour, supporting it on condition that it continued to deliver affluence (Goldthorpe, Lockwood, Bechhofer and Platt, 1968; Heath, 1990; Devine, 1992). Here were the seeds for a decline in the class cleavage.

During the 1970s, class declined in importance as voters became disillusioned with the failures of the two major parties. The electorate became more volatile, more influenced by issues and short-term factors (Särlvik and Crewe, 1983; Franklin, 1985; but see Heath, Jowell and Curtice, 1985; Weakliem, 1989). This is illustrated in Figure 3.2, which adopts a fourfold class division: professional and managerial workers (AB); skilled non-manual workers (C1): skilled manual workers (C2); and semi- and unskilled workers (DE). All survey data are taken from the BES. In a strongly class-aligned electorate, the Conservative/Labour (C/L) ratio should be well above 1.0 for white collar workers, and well below 1.0 for blue-collar workers. Blue-collar workers have generally been more likely to vote Labour than Conservative, and white-collar workers more likely to vote Conservative than Labour. But from the 1970s, class alignment became weaker: the Conservative lead declined among the middle classes, while in the 1980s the skilled working class were almost as likely to support the Tories as Labour. Something had happened to the link between class and voting.

To understand what, we need to go back to the regional polarisation of voting in the 1970s and 1980s. The regional geography of class dealignment was not even over that period. While class was a declining influence on individuals, it was an increasing influence on constituency voting: working-class areas were becoming more likely to support Labour (W. Miller, 1977; Johnston, Pattie and Allsopp, 1988). This

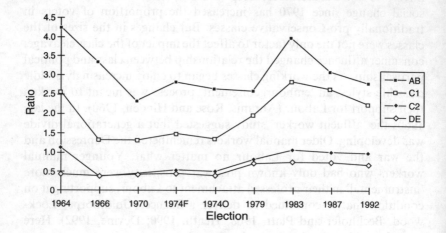

FIGURE 3.2   *Conservative/Labour ratio by class 1964–92*

paradoxical combination of individual de-alignment and constituency realignment was linked to the regional polarisation in voting behaviour outlined above.

We have calculated the C/L ratio since 1974 in each class in five regions (the South West was excluded because of small samples). Figure 3.3 reveals marked and widening regional differences. AB voters in the South East have been much more likely than ABs in Scotland and Wales to support the Conservatives than Labour, and the gap between the regions widened between 1979 and 1987, narrowing slightly in 1992. The same story is repeated for the other social classes. Skilled non-manual workers in the South swung heavily behind the Conservatives, particularly from 1979, but in Scotland and Wales they were just as likely to vote Labour. The most dramatic shifts are among working-class voters. In 1974 skilled manual workers living in the South East were already more likely than skilled workers in the North to vote Conservative rather than Labour. But all skilled manual workers then were more likely to vote Labour than Conservative: the difference was one of degree, not of substance. Since 1979, skilled

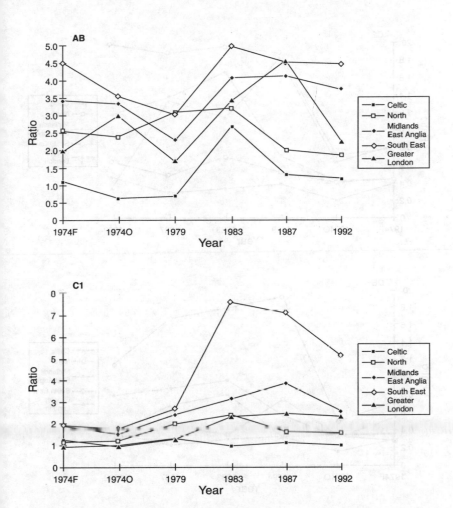

FIGURE 3.3   *Conservative/Labour ratio, voters, by region, February 1974–92*

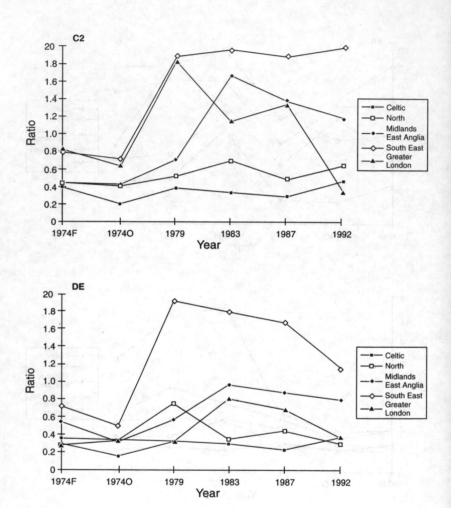

FIGURE 3.3   *Conservative/Labour ratio, voters, by region, February 1974–92*

manual workers in the South East, the Midlands and London have become more likely to vote Conservative than Labour. In 1983 and 1987, skilled manual workers in the South East were roughly 2.5 times more likely to vote Conservative than Labour. Skilled workers in the North and in Scotland and Wales, however, remained twice as likely to vote for Labour. A similar story holds for semi- and unskilled workers.

This turnaround is a consequence of changing economic geography. Until the recession of the late 1980s and early 1990s, the South East enjoyed a prolonged boom, but the North remained mired in recession. In the South, workers' earning power was high in relative terms and grew: in the North it declined for the large numbers affected by growing unemployment. Goldthorpe's 'affluent worker' study, for all its problems, proved prescient in the 1980s (Johnston and Pattie, 1989). After 1989 the geography of recession reversed, and the southern economy was hard-hit. Government support fell back in the blighted areas, narrowing the North–South electoral cleavage, but not removing it. The working-class 'Essex men and women' who backed the Conservatives in the 1980s began to turn away in 1992, though they were still more likely to vote Conservative than Labour.

Analysis of the geography of the class cleavage therefore gives an important clue to understanding Conservative electoral success in the 1980s and early 1990s. The party built an electoral coalition in the South based not only on its traditional supporters, but also heavily on working-class voters. Driven back into its northern redoubts, Labour was effectively neutralised.

Consumption Cleavages

The 'affluent worker' thesis implied that changing consumption patterns would have electoral consequences favouring the Conservatives. In the early 1980s, new research explained class de-alignment in terms of consumption-based cleavages (Dunleavy, 1979; Dunleavy and Husbands, 1985; but see Franklin and Page, 1984). The welfare state introduced new political conflicts between those dependent on the state for services and jobs, and those dependent on the market. Voters relying on state provision would support parties committed to an expanding welfare state (mainly Labour), while those reliant upon the private sector would support a party which aimed to reduce the state sector (the Conservatives). One of the major sources of consumption cleavage was housing tenure. Between 1974 and 1992, over half of owner-occupiers voted Conservative but only a quarter voted Labour.

Over the same period, between 55 per cent and 65 per cent of council tenants voted Labour (Table 3.4).

This new cleavage 'cross-cut' social class. Working-class home-owners were pulled in conflicting directions. Their class location suggested support for Labour, while their consumption location suggested support for the Conservatives. The key element seems to be home-ownership as a source of investment: working-class owners in areas where house prices were high were more likely to vote Conservative than were working-class home-owners where prices were low (Johnston, 1987). We can get some impression of the importance of this by dividing the classes up according to their housing tenure, and calculating the C/L ratio for each sub-category (Table 3.4). Not surprisingly, owner-occupiers in social classes A, B and C1 were much more likely to vote Conservative than Labour, and council tenants in social classes C2, D and E were much more likely to vote Labour than Conservative: class and consumption location reinforced each other. Voters in cross-cutting locations are more interesting. The large group of blue-collar workers who own their homes was consistently more pro-Conservative than other blue collar workers in council properties, and from 1979 were more likely to vote Conservative than Labour.

During the 1980s, the Conservative government made clear its goal of achieving a 'property-owning democracy': the electoral consequences of achieving that policy are plain to see. The social demographics of consumption locations imply a growing advantage for the Conservatives. On the face of it, by changing the consumption locations of large

TABLE 3.4   *Housing tenure and voting*

| Year | % share of vote | | | | C/L ratio | | | |
| | Owner-Occupier | | Council | | ABC1 | | C2DE | |
	Con.	Lab.	Con.	Lab.	Owner	Council	Owner	Council
1974F	50.0	27.7	17.4	63.6	2.75	0.44	0.79	0.22
1974O	46.7	29.6	17.8	65.3	2.49	0.46	0.66	0.21
1979	56.3	26.7	27.8	59.5	3.17	0.64	1.04	0.44
1983	53.0	19.4	23.3	54.7	4.65	0.72	1.49	0.33
1987	50.9	22.8	21.4	58.1	3.64	0.61	1.18	0.32
1992	52.7	26.5	18.2	64.8	3.07	0.43	1.07	0.24

Source: BES.

numbers of working-class voters, the right to buy should have helped convert Labour voters into Conservative supporters, further adding to the Conservatives' advantage. However, in practice the policy's electoral consequences have been more complex. It was relatively pro-Conservative council tenants who bought their homes, not home buying council tenants who became Conservatives (Heath, Jowell, Curtice, Evans, Field and Witherspoon, 1991). However, the same study showed that, having made the purchase, they were less likely to vote Labour than in the past. Council house sales seem to have had little direct impact upon the Conservatives' fortunes, but indirectly they helped erode an important source of potential support for Labour.

Ideological Change

Analysing the changing social bases of the vote does not, however, tell us why the Conservatives were so successful after 1979. To answer that, we need to look at other factors. One of Conservatism's distinctive features in the 1980s was its very strong ideological element. The party offered a radical programme, very different from the post-war consensus. Thatcher presented herself as a 'conviction politician', promoting market economics allied to a reassertion of 'moral values' and of the police powers of the state (Gamble, 1988). She often presented herself as speaking for a silent majority. If this claim is true, it might help account for the Conservatives' victories.

However, the evidence for an ideological sea-change or for pre-existing public support for Thatcher's agenda looks slight (Table 3.5). Studies of public political attitudes in the 1970s and 1980s suggested increasing rejection of it (Crewe, 1988; Edgell and Duke, 1991: Studlar and McAllister, 1992). There was widespread support for the notion that government should spend more to alleviate poverty, and widespread concern over the powers of 'big business'. On nationalisation and privatisation, and on trade union power, opinion moved towards the Conservatives during the opposition years of the 1970s, only to move away in the 1980s and 1990s. In part, this reflects changing contexts: declining concern over union power after 1983 is influenced by government success in controlling the unions. Even so, there was no rightward drift in public opinion after 1979. Even more strikingly, an overwhelming majority of voters rejected the control of inflation, the government's own priority, in favour of putting people back to work (Table 3.6).

TABLE 3.5   *Public opinion and the Conservative agenda, 1974–92 (%)*

	1974O	1979	1983	1987	1992
Nationalisation					
More	32	17	18	17	24
Enough	46	43	40	50	52
Less	22	40	42	32	24
'Government should redistribute wealth'					
Should	56	55	48	44	59
Neutral	16	16	15	20	12
Should Not	28	28	37	36	29
'Government should spend to reduce poverty'					
Should	87	84	86	88	93
Neutral	6	8	3	5	2
Should Not	7	8	11	7	5
'Trade unions have too much power'					
Too much	81	82	74	46	34
About right	–	–	–	43	–
Not too much	19	18	26	12	66
'Big business has too much power'					
Too much	62	60	68	32	73
About right	–	–	–	55	–
Not too much	38	40	32	13	27
'Measures to improve race equality have gone'					
Too far	27	30	20	29	26
About right	44	41	53	42	41
Not far enough	29	29	27	29	34
'Measures to improve sex equality have gone'					
Too far	19	23	9	9	5
About right	46	48	58	48	39
Not far enough	35	30	32	43	57

Source: BES.
Note: Figures in this table have been rounded and therefore may not total 100.

TABLE 3.6 *Choosing Thatcherism or social democracy (%)*

	1983	1987	1992
Government priority should be to cut unemployment/reduce inflation			
Cut unemployment	65.0	73.9	72.3
Both equally	18.4	12 5	14.1
Reduce inflation	16.6	13.6	13.6
Prefer: spend more on services and high taxes/low taxes and service cuts			
More services	45.1	60.8	66.9
Both equally	37.2	26.5	20.6
Low taxes	17.8	12.8	12.5

Source: BES.
Note: Figures in this table have been rounded and therefore may not total 100.

Similarly, when asked to choose between better public services and higher taxes, or lower taxes and cutting public services, the largest proportion of the electorate increasingly rejected the Thatcherite position. There may well be a difference between what people report as an ideal and what they do in practice. For instance, survey evidence suggests that in 1992 public support for low taxes at whatever cost was at its weakest since before 1983, but it is unlikely that the 1992 'Labour's Tax Bombshell' campaign had no impact. Nevertheless, the electorate did not wholeheartedly agree with some of the main tenets of Conservative policy.

Yet there is a paradox here: if voters did not agree with Conservative policies and ideology in the 1980s and 1990s, why did they keep that government in power? Part of the answer can be found by dividing the electorate into different groups. For instance, there is evidence to suggest that those who joined the electorate for the first time in 1979 and 1987 were more right-wing than were those who joined the electorate before then (Russell, Johnston and Pattie, 1992). However, those who joined the electorate in 1983, having just experienced the deepest post-war recession, were more left-wing than the 1979 and 1987 cohorts. More telling are the class structure and geography of public opinion. At both the 1983 and 1987 elections, middle-class and southern voters were significantly more right-wing in their views than were working-class and northern voters (Pattie and Johnston, 1990b). Whether Thatcherism created or tapped into this southern streak of

Conservatism is hard to say, but it was clearly on more fertile ground in the South than in the North. Overall, the electorate was not won over by Conservative ideology in the 1980s and 1990s, but strategic sections of voters were amenable.

Government Competence and Economic Management

If the Conservatives had not won hearts and minds in the 1980s and 1990s, why were they winning elections? A large and growing literature has linked support for political parties to public perceptions of their fitness to govern and their records on economic management. During the 1980s, a large gap opened up between public perceptions of the Conservative and opposition parties. Table 3.7 gives the ratio of the number of respondents with one view of a party to the number with the opposite view. At first glance, the Conservatives did relatively poorly despite Major's attempts to give his party a softer edge. The opposition parties were seen as more caring.

Furthermore, more voters thought the party worked in the interests of one class rather than of the whole nation. That said, voters thought Labour was a 'one class' party too. Only the Alliance (and the Liberal Democrats in 1992) were seen overwhelmingly as acting in the national interest. A majority of voters at the 1983 and 1987 elections thought each main party extreme. Polls showed that Labour's leaders were not trusted with high office. The emollient effect of Major, and Labour's swing back to the centre under Neil Kinnock changed this perception. At the 1992 election twice as many voters thought the Conservatives and Labour were moderate parties as thought they were extreme. But the Conservatives were able to play effectively on public fears of Labour's 'extremist' reputation in 1983, 1987 and 1992: 'loony left' local authorities and 'tax double whammies' proved powerful slogans.

The Conservatives were helped after 1979 by public perceptions of party unity. Very large numbers saw Labour as deeply divided, particularly after the SDP split, and voted accordingly. The Conservatives' greatest asset in terms of public perceptions was undoubtedly their reputation for strong government: in 1987 almost 20 times as many voters thought the Conservatives provided strong government as thought they were weak. Labour and the Alliance/Liberal Democrats were never able to compete. However, the Conservative reputations for unity and strong government were badly undermined after the 1992 election by policy reversals, notably sterling's exit from the ERM,

TABLE 3.7 *Public perceptions of parties' fitness to govern*

Party	1974F	1974O	1979	1983	1987	1992
Party caring or uncaring? (Caring/uncaring ratio)						
Con.	–	–	–	–	0.93	1.12
Lab.	–	–	–	–	3.69	4.13
Lib.	–	–	–	–	7.67	9.49
Party good for one class/goods for all classes? (One class/all classes ratio)						
Con.	1.88	1.88	–	1.66	1.66	1.42
Lab.	0.83	1.02	–	1.56	1.78	1.55
Lib.	–	0.30	–	0.13	0.18	0.15
Party extreme or moderate? (Extreme/moderate ratio)						
Con.	0.82	0.90	–	1.21	1.17	0.48
Lab.	0.79	1.20	–	1.33	1.32	0.48
Lib.	–	0.27	–	0.08	0.06	0.08
Party united or divided? (United/divided ratio)						
Con.	–	–	–	2.86	3.10	2.61
Lab.	–	–	–	0.09	0.32	0.48
Lib.	–	–	–	0.87	0.14	5.13
Party strong or weak government? (Strong/weak ratio)						
Con.	–	–	–	–	19.28	6.78
Lab.	–	–	–	–	0.57	0.69
Lib.	–	–	–	–	0.26	0.44

Source: BES.

backbench rebellions over Europe and perceived policy drift between 1992 and 1994 (Chapters 9 and 6).

The focus of public perceptions of Conservative competence since 1979 has been on the economy. The economic voting model is straightforward: voters reward governments which deliver prosperity and punish those which produce lower living standards. This fills the explanatory gap between public disapproval of Conservative policies, and public support for the government. One much-discussed model of this kind was proposed by David Sanders and his co-workers who linked Conservative popularity in monthly opinion polls between 1979 and 1983 to four factors (Sanders, Ward and Marsh, 1987). Higher exchange rates, unemployment rates and Public Sector Borrowing Requirement (PSBR) figures all meant less support for the government; lower figures meant increased support. But crucially, voters who were optimistic about the future were more likely to support the government than pessimistic voters. Such personal expectations were improved by rising consumer spending, lower taxes, less short-time working, and lower interest rates. This model was able to account for 87 per cent of the variance in Conservative support during the first Thatcher government. Later studies have applied the Sanders model to the 1979–87 (Marsh *et al.*, 1992) and 1979–92 periods (Sanders, 1993b), one offering a successful prediction of the 1992 election 18 months before polling day (Sanders, 1991)!

Each Conservative victory since 1979, then, can be attributed in part to public concerns about the economy. In 1979, the party benefited from public dissatisfaction with the Labour government's record. In 1983 and 1987 over two-thirds of the electorate thought that the governing party had handled inflation and taxes well (Table 3.8). Few thought the government had handled unemployment well but, although concerned about the minority of unemployed, voters supported a government that made them better off as individuals, particularly in areas where unemployment was low (Johnston, Pattie and Allsopp, 1988; Johnston and Pattie, 1993b). This logic held even at the 1992 election, when the government had to defend a recession. There was a clear correlation between people's perceptions of how their personal standard of living had changed since 1987, and how they voted in 1992 (Table 3.9).

TABLE 3.8   *Public perceptions of Conservative handling of the economy, 1979–87 (%)*

	1979	1983	1987
*Conservatives handled prices:**			
Well	46.5	79.7	65.7
Not well	53.5	20.3	34.3
Conservatives handled taxes: †			
Well	–	66.1	68.7
Not well	–	33.9	31.3
*Conservatives handled unemployment:**			
Well	55.5	26.8	19.8
Not well	44.5	73.2	80.2

* In 1979, question was 'If in government, Conservatives would have handled . . .'.
† Question not asked in 1979.
Source: BES.

TABLE 3.9   *Changes in personal living standards since 1987 general election,
and vote 1992 (%)*

'Since the last general election, would you say your own standard of living has
increased or fallen?'

	Increased a lot	Increased a little	About same	Fallen a little	Fallen a lot
Conservative	66.3	56.7	48.7	30.8	18.7
Labour	18.5	22.8	32.4	47.6	57.6
Lib. Dem.	13.6	18.3	15.2	18.2	20.9
Other	1.7	2.2	3.7	3.5	2.8
Total	8.7	26.0	37.5	15.2	12.6

'Compared with other parts of Britain over the last 10 years would you say this
part of Britain has been getting more prosperous than average?'

	Much more prosperous	Little more prosperous	About same	Little less prosperous	Much less prosperous
Conservative	63.0	57.6	53.6	39.9	21.1
Labour	17.9	20.1	30.0	37.8	56.4
Lib. Dem.	18.4	19.2	13.5	18.8	18.2
Other	0.7	3.1	2.8	3.5	4.3
Total	7.1	17.3	33.0	26.1	16.5

Source: BES 1992.
Note: Figures in this table have been rounded and therefore may not total 100.

Among the 8.7 per cent who thought their personal standard of
living had increased a great deal since 1987, 66 per cent voted
Conservative in 1992, and only 18 per cent voted Labour. Among
the 12.6 per cent who felt that their standard of living had declined a
great deal, only 19 per cent voted Conservative, compared to 58 per
cent who voted Labour. What saved the government was their ability
to retain the votes of those who had at least held their own since the
last election.

Economic voting also helps account for regional voting trends. While
in all regions optimistic voters were more likely than pessimists to

support the government, optimists in depressed regions were less likely to do so than optimists in boom areas (Johnston Pattie and Allsopp, 1988). A question in the 1992 BES demonstrates the importance of voters' regional contexts (Table 3.9). Those who felt that their region had become much more prosperous than the national average were much more likely to vote Conservative (63 per cent), and much less likely to vote Labour (18 per cent) than were those who thought their region had become much less prosperous over the same period (21 per cent of this group voted Conservative; 56 per cent Labour). During the 1980s, recession badly affected the traditional northern manufacturing centres, while the service sector in the South East prospered, resulting in discussion of an emerging 'North-South economic divide' (Hudson and Williams, 1989; Lewis and Townsend, 1989; Pattie and Johnston, 1990a). Not surprisingly, as the economic divide between the regions widened, so did the electoral divide (Johnston, Pattie and Russell, 1993). After 1989, overheating of the south-eastern economy and renewed recession put the process into reverse: the recession hit hardest at the southern service sector. At the 1992 election, the regional electoral divide narrowed as the Conservatives lost support in the recession-bound South and Midlands (Johnston and Pattie, 1992b). If the analysis advanced above is correct, the party faces a gradual erosion of its support in its heartland region if it fails to deliver prosperity again. Southern skilled manual workers who voted Conservative in the 1980s may desert in the 1990s if their living standards remain under threat.

The economic downturn and recession which followed the Lawson boom of the late 1980s undoubtedly did much to damage public support for the Conservatives, but in 1992 a new leadership could blame the recession on its predecessors. After the 1992 election the Conservatives could not repeat this trick. 'Vote Conservative on Thursday, and the recovery starts on Friday', Mr Major promised electors in 1992. It did not happen, and within six months of winning the election, the government was forced out of the ERM. This was perhaps the most serious blow to Major's government and his credibility, as the Chancellor who had persuaded Thatcher finally to take Britain into the ERM and made it the cornerstone of economic policy. On average, only about 14 per cent of respondents to Gallup polls in 1993 felt that the government 'was handling the economic situation properly', a figure worse than in previous post-war lows for sitting governments (Crewe, 1994). The Conservatives' main electoral asset, their reputation for economic competence, had been shattered. The related 'Euro-rebellion' by Major's backbenchers (Chapter 6) added unprecedented disunity to the image of incompetence.

To add to the government's woes, the opposition parties were quick to recover from their defeat in 1992. John Smith's leadership revived Labour confidence, and the party put the factional fighting of the 1980s behind it. Tony Blair's succession to the Labour leadership, following Smith's sudden death in 1994, only helped consolidate Labour's new-found moderate and electable image. The Liberal Democrats re-estab-lished themselves after the traumas of the collapse of the Alliance.

After the collapse of sterling on 'Black Wednesday', Conservative popularity fell alarmingly. Opinion polls consistently gave the party around 25 per cent of the vote. The party also performed disastrously in actual elections. The Liberal Democrats scored dramatic by-election victories in previously rock-solid Conservative seats such as Christch-urch, Newbury and Eastleigh, and Labour's victory at Dudley in 1994 produced the biggest Conservative to Labour by-election swing for 60 years. In the 1993 county council elections, the Conservatives won the equivalent of only 31 per cent of the national vote (Crewe, 1994, 110), and lost control of previously safe shire counties like Surrey, Kent and Norfolk which had been Conservative-held for around 100 years. They only returned to power in one county, Buckinghamshire. The 1994 district council elections were even worse, giving the party only an estimated 27 per cent of the national vote, 'certainly the worst local election performance by a major party since 1945. It was probably the worst ever' (Crewe, 1994, 113).

Worse was to come a month later. In the only nation-wide ballot since the 1992 General Election, the June 1994 European elections, the Conservatives' share of the vote was, at 27. 8 per cent, 'the lowest . . . obtained by either major party in any nationwide election this century' (Crewe, 1994, 115) Major survived only after a concerted effort to 'talk down' Conservative chances, such that the party's eventual tally of 18 Euro-seats seemed a triumph compared to the five or six seats being predicted in some quarters. The Liberal Democrats had taken two seats for the first time, but failed to break out of their south-western strongholds to challenge the Conservatives' southern heartland as the Labour Party swept south, taking 62 seats. In April 1995 the party's vote slumped to an all-time low at 11 per cent in Scottish local elections. In May 1995 another record fell, as the party tumbled to 25 per cent of the national vote, in local elections in England and Wales that saw 2042 Tory councillors lose their seats.

And the Future . . . ?

At the beginning of the chapter, we argued that the Conservatives were a formidably successful electoral force. However, as we have seen in this chapter, electoral success in the 1980s and 1990s is built on potentially shaky foundations. Support for the party since 1979 has been lower than at any previous election since 1922: yet it has managed to win convincing parliamentary majorities. The party has been helped by a deeply divided opposition vote. However, as Labour gradually recovers from 1983, that advantage declines. After 1992, the Conservative majority was down to just 21 seats. In 50 of the seats won by the party in 1992, less than 5 percentage points separates its electoral share from that of its nearest rival: in 36 of those highly marginal seats, Labour is the challenger. The Conservatives are now more vulnerable to defeat than at any time since before 1979, especially as unemployment rose faster in those 50 Tory marginals between 1992 and 1994 than elsewhere in the country.

Conservative Party officials argued that the poor election results in 1993 and 1994 represented little more than normal mid-term blues, pointing to slumps in support for the party in each Parliament since 1979 (all of which were followed, about two years later, by election victories). However, there are good grounds to suspect that the reverses since 1992 represent something more fundamental. After 1992 the Conservatives plumbed historical depths in both opinion polls and actual ballots. The Conservative Party replaced Labour as the disunited party, this time over Europe. Even more crucially, the party lost public confidence in its economic competence. If the factors which helped them win between 1979 and 1992 are still in place, the Conservatives face the prospect of electoral defeat. By 1995, the party's legendary electoral machine faced its biggest challenge for over two decades.

Note

BES data were supplied by the ESRC Data Archive at the University of Essex.

4

Conservative Grassroots: An Overview

PATRICK SEYD and PAUL WHITELEY

No party has had a better claim to be a mass party than the Conservatives. The Conservative Party claimed that it had over two million members in the late 1940s, making it the largest membership party of any in post-war Western Europe (Von Beyme, 1985; Katz and Mair, 1992). The recruitment of a mass membership of this size was a remarkable achievement, especially when considering the party's aristocratic and parliamentary origins. However, this also poses a puzzle since it is not clear why the party leadership should want to recruit such a large membership or, for that matter, why individuals should want to join a party whose values and procedures so limit the scope for personal political influence.

The answer, as far as the party leadership is concerned, is that the members have been regarded as both an electoral resource and a source of funds. Robert McKenzie's description of local Conservative associations in the 1950s, with their 'block system' and 'canvasser corps', conveys the essence of the party as an impressive local electoral machine. He describes the activities of local party members in the following way:

> Ideally the block should be looked after by the same party workers both between and during elections. Their functions are to distribute party literature: to spread verbal propaganda; to deliver invitations to meetings and social functions; to collect information for the associations 'Marked Register', to enrol members in the Association; to recruit active workers and

helpers of all kinds; to act as 'intelligence officers'; to undertake election work during campaigns for both parliamentary and local government elections. (McKenzie, 1964, 255)

This elaborate network of party members ensured that the Conservative Party had both a strong presence and numerous advocates in almost every constituency. In this period, before television and advertising developed their mass markets, the Conservative Party leadership had its local ambassadors to help articulate the case for Conservatism, and legitimise its standing in every part of the nation. Furthermore, these were loyal, reliable voters. Before the polling stations even opened on general election days the party could rely on a guaranteed minimum vote from which to build the additional support necessary to form a government.

McKenzie's description was rooted in the 1950s; since then, however, the development of modern communications techniques – in particular television, advertising and public opinion polling – might have persuaded the party leadership that it no longer required party members in order to maintain local electoral machines. However, despite the 'nationalisation' of recent elections, the Conservative Party leadership continues to stress the importance of its constituency membership as electoral campaigners. Evidence taken from the 1987 General Election and subsequent analysis suggest that it can ill-afford to ignore the electoral impact of its grassroots' activists (Whiteley, Seyd and Richardson, 1994, 213–18). After the party's poor performance in the local elections of May 1993, an internal post-mortem stressed the unwillingness of party members to go out and campaign as a significant factor. In his address to the 1993 Conservative Party conference, the Party Chairman emphasised the importance of party members as electioneers.

These loyal campaigners become of even greater electoral importance when, as increasingly occurred during 1993 and 1994, traditionally loyal parts of the print media became party critics. In addition to their electoral role, members also provide the Conservative Party with money. For a start, the member usually pays a subscription to the party. The party at national level has never fixed a specific sum of money as the party subscription, and it is left to each constituency association to gather what money it deems appropriate from each member. The average subscription paid in 1991–2 was £12; only 2 per cent of members failed to pay anything (Whiteley, Seyd and Richardson, 1994). This subscription income goes, however, into local associa-

tion funds and not to the national party. The decentralised nature of
the Conservative Party means that considerable income is often held at
the local level.

Since 1948 every Conservative constituency association has been set
an annual financial 'quota' by the national party, calculated since the
early 1950s on the basis of the Conservative vote in each constituency,
which it has been expected to send to Central Office. Each year since
1968 the quota targets and the actual quota payments made by each
constituency association have been published in the Conference handbook, and rewards are distributed to the successful, and the defaulters
are publicly identified. Initially the quota scheme was successful, and
almost all local associations had made some contribution to central
party funds. Ball calculates that in 1967 only 149 associations in
England and Wales had submitted less than 30 per cent of their quota
payment; but by 1992–3 this figure had risen to 343 (Ball, 1994). In the
latest returns available (1993–4) only 22 per cent of associations met or
surpassed their quota obligations; on the other hand, 17 per cent failed
to send any money whatsoever to Central Office (Conservative Party,
1994c, 152–66).

The pressures on local associations to meet their quota obligations
requires members to engage in regular money-raising activities.
Whether it is soliciting donations from local dignitaries, business
leaders or other financially well-endowed local people, or whether it
is organising bring-and-buy and jumble sales, the activity is constant.
Among the one-third minority who attend local association meetings,
more of their time is taken up with fund raising and administrative
matters than with either local or national political issues (Whiteley,
Seyd and Richardson, 1994).

It has always been difficult to assess the proportion of central party
funds raised locally by members because the Conservative Party has
always maintained considerable secrecy about its financial affairs. The
extent to which the Conservative Party is reliant upon the donations of
individual members rather than corporate organisations is open to
dispute. Recent public revelations regarding donations from prominent
foreign businessmen have prompted considerable debate over the
Conservative Party's finances (Fisher, 1994). Some authorities suggest
that the money raised and donated by Conservative Party members is a
relatively small proportion of the total compared with company
donations; on the other hand, the Conservative Party chairman, in
evidence to a Home Affairs Select Committee enquiry into party

funding, suggested that in 1992 around 70 per cent of the party's total national income was raised by individual members' fund-raising activities (Home Affairs Committee, 1993, 51).

If the party leadership recruits members primarily for electoral and financial reasons why would individuals want to pay a subscription and identify with the Conservative Party's objectives? They are not required to do either, and if they do so in order to influence political outcomes, they are likely to be disappointed since the party structures, procedures and values provide little encouragement for membership participation and influence.

The fact that it was the Conservative Party in Parliament which initiated an extra-parliamentary organisation, the National Union of Conservative and Constitutional Associations, later renamed the National Union of Conservative and Unionist Associations, to mobilise electoral support among the newly-enfranchised voters after the 1867 and 1883 electoral reforms has since determined the internal distribution of power within the party. Power has been located within the parliamentary party and, for most of the time, with one single parliamentarian, the party leader.

The Conservative Party is made up of three separate organisations. First, there is the parliamentary party, managed and run by the party Whips' office; second, there is Conservative Central Office, which employs the full-time professional staff at national and regional headquarters; and, third, there is the National Union to which constituency associations in England, Wales, Scotland and parts of Northern Ireland are affiliated.

The fragmented nature of the party has been confirmed in the courts of law. In 1982 the Court of Appeal stated that the party leader provided the only common link in the organisation and, apart from him or her, 'the separate bodies which make up the party, cooperate with each other for political purposes but maintain separate existences for organisational purposes' (All England Law Reports, 1982, 60).

This fragmentation reinforces the party leader's powers. He or she is free to choose senior colleagues in a Conservative Cabinet and shadow Cabinet, is responsible for the party's election manifesto, and appoints the party chairman. These arrangements prompted Sir Charles Marston, a member of the National Union Executive Committee, to describe the Conservative Party in the inter-war years as 'an autocracy masquerading as a democracy' (McKenzie, 1964, 181). Similar such unflattering comments have been made in more recent years by small groups of Conservative activists campaigning for internal party reforms. For example, a group of Greater London Young Conservatives (GLYC) described the party as 'one of the least democratic organisations in Britain outside the Freemasons' (GLYC, 1969, 20). And the Charter Movement, a current group of party reformers, describes party management as akin to 'an old style East European way of running politics' (Charter Movement, 1991, 2). These reformers are arguing for the election of those party officers responsible for organisational and financial affairs, and then their answerability to directly elected executive bodies, the publication of the party's financial accounts, and the control of annual conference agendas and debates by an elected committee.

The rather unflattering view of intra-party democracy held by the Charter Movement is one shared by most academics and political journalists. The most comprehensive study of the post-war Conservative Party concluded that the party leadership paid only scant attention to the views of the party members (McKenzie, 1964). In addition, most political commentators regard the party's annual conference as more of a rally and public relations exercise than a deliberative assembly. These views are not shared, however, by Kelly, who argues that an elaborate 'Conservative conference system' exists, made up of functional and area meetings, at which activists articulate opinions and leaders take note of them (R. Kelly, 1989, 184). There may not be the formal resolutions or leadership accountability of Labour or trade union conferences, but the 'mood' and 'atmosphere' of these gatherings are fed back into the policy-making process. Kelly argues that intra-party democracy exists in an 'oblique and informal way' (R. Kelly, 1989, 188).

Kelly's reminder that an extensive activist network of conferences exists is valuable. However, his estimate that 20 000 participated in this conference system in 1986 is almost certainly a gross exaggeration of the numbers involved today (R. Kelly, 1989, 179). The serious haemorrhaging of membership in recent years will have cut this figure considerably.

What is difficult to test is Kelly's argument that the party leadership is sensitive to the moods and opinions of these active party members. If one examines recent instances where party members have appeared to hold strong opinions – for example, on the privatisation of the post office, the additional Value Added Tax (VAT) charge on domestic fuel, or Britain's membership of the EU – it is extremely difficult (and in fact impossible) to disentangle the relative influence of voters and active party members on these issues. And there are other issues, such as capital and corporal punishment, and coloured immigration, where party members' opinions have been very clearly expressed at the annual party conferences, yet the leadership has ignored these moods and atmospheres.

The present party structure lacks any sense of formal accountability of the party leadership to the individual members. The party leader is not elected by a ballot in which the party members play a direct part; there is no formal accountability of platform speakers to the representatives at party conferences; there is no elected executive body accountable to conference representatives; and there is no election or confirmation of party officers. Finally, there is no constitution which stipulates the rights of individual members; thus, there is no formal way in which members' equality or participation in party affairs is legitimised. Rather, it is the historic norms and values of hierarchy and deference upon which the party is organised.

Notwithstanding Conservative Party members' lack of formal powers, they either may not be activated to join in order to obtain political influence, or they may be well aware of the structural limitations on their power, yet wish to 'stand up and be counted'. Alternatively, they may join to secure personal benefits; for example, membership may provide rewards, either in the sense of career opportunities or in terms of social networks.

What are the motivations which lead people to join the Conservative Party? This, together with an analysis of who the Conservative Party members are, what they do within the party organisation, and the views they hold on political issues are the themes of this chapter. Answers to these questions have not generally been available because very few studies of the members have ever been conducted; the studies available have tended to be either examinations of local Conservative associations as part of a broader study of a particular locality (Bealey, Blondel and McCann, 1965; Newton, 1976), or more qualitative participant-observation studies (Morris, 1991). The evidence used in this chapter is derived from a survey of approximately 2500 members carried out in 1992 in 34 constituencies in Great Britain (see the note at the end of this chapter).

A Mass Membership Party

In 1953 the Conservative Party reported a membership of 2 800 000. This figure, and other such figures issued periodically by the party, is obtained from local records, since the Conservative Party does not have a national membership list. An individual joins one of the 634 constituency associations in England, Wales and Scotland in which he or she resides, or has business premises. Since 1991 nine Conservative constituency associations have also been established in Northern Ireland. Membership recruitment has always been the responsibility of local constituency associations, and there is no formal requirement that they return membership figures to party headquarters at Conservative Central Office. A proposal to require all constituency associations to submit an annual return detailing their membership activities failed to secure the necessary two-thirds majority at a meeting of the Central Council in 1993 because local representatives were suspicious that the proposed change would lead to centralised control of constituency activities. The total membership figures have, therefore, been dependent upon both the efficiency and the goodwill of over 600 constituency association officers; anyone who has researched the grassroots Conservative Party will know that neither can always be guaranteed! So the claims made regarding the number of party members need to be regarded with a significant degree of caution.

Periodic attempts by academic researchers to estimate the membership figure have produced varied results. The most comprehensive and detailed study of the Conservative Party suggested a figure of 2 250 000 members in the 1960s (McKenzie, 1964). Blondel estimated a figure of 2 800 000 at this time, while Rose suggested a figure of 1 500 000 by 1970 (Blondel, 1973, 89; R. Rose, 1976b, 153). In his study of party finance, Pinto-Duschinsky reckoned on a figure of 1 400 000 and, finally, Tether, on the basis of a survey of 30 constituency associations, suggests a figure of 1 000 000 (Pinto-Duschinsky, 1981, 154; Tether, 1991).

The constituency associations in our survey had an average membership of 1193; projecting these figures nationally would suggest a total national membership of 756 000. However, as we point out later in the chapter, we calculate that the Conservative Party is losing members at a rate of 64 000 per year, implying a figure for 1995 of around half a million.

Why Join the Conservative Party?

We have suggested in our earlier study of Labour Party members a 'general-incentives' theory of participation, based upon the proposition that individuals participate in politics in response to incentives of various kinds (Seyd and Whiteley, 1992). Thus individuals participate in order to achieve collective goals, including policy objectives of various kinds. Other individuals participate to achieve private, or selective, returns. Others are motivated by a sense of loyalty and affection for the party, or by a sense of civic duty. Finally, we suggest that individuals are often motivated by social norms of various kinds; for example, by the desire to conform to the wishes of other people who are significant in their lives, or whose opinions are listened to with respect. The theory suggests that individuals similarly join the Conservative Party as a response to incentives of various kinds (Whiteley, Seyd and Richardson, 1994, 80–99). In response to the first of the questions we posed in our survey, which was why certain people decide to become party members, we asked respondents to describe in their own words their 'most important reason' for joining the party. Their answers are reproduced in Table 4.1, under five broad categories of incentives theory. We can see from Table 4.1 that the most common reason members gave for joining was that they had either an expressive or affective attachment to the party. In other words, they had a general sense of commitment and loyalty to the party.

The second most common reason was to achieve or support particular policy goals, which we describe as collective positive incentives. Almost as many members, however, are motivated to join by their aversion to other parties, which we describe as collective negative incentives. Thus the Labour and Liberal Democratic parties, and also the trade unions, are significant recruiting agents for the Conservative Party! The spiral of membership decline which we have already referred to might be slowed down or even reversed, therefore, if a Labour government is elected at the next general election. Sixteen years of Conservative governments will have had some impact upon membership levels.

Others join for quite distinct personal reasons. They either join in order to meet people who are also involved in the political process, or to satisfy their own personal political ambitions; the latter may involve becoming a school governor, a local councillor, or even running for Parliament. Conservatives in government, whether at national or local level, will provide an added incentive to such people. We describe these as selective process and selective outcome incentives.

Many also join because of social norms, or the influence of family and friends in the community and the workplace. Finally, a few join for

TABLE 4.1   *The most important reason for joining the Conservative Party (N = 2467)*

(Question: What was your MOST important reason for joining the Conservative Party?)	Percentage
Altruistic motives	
To promote freedom	2.5
To promote the interests of the nation	3.3
To help the party financially	1.9
	7.7
Collective positive incentives	
To support free enterprise or capitalism	3.4
To support Thatcherism	3.3
To achieve economic prosperity	2.2
Because of general Conservative policies	8.4
Because of specific national policy concerns	1.4
Because of specific local policy concerns	1.5
	20.2
Collective negative incentives	
To oppose the Labour Party or trade unions	11.5
To oppose other parties	3.7
To oppose the local council	0.2
	15.4
Expressive attachments	
An attachment to Conservative principles	10.5
Belief in the Conservative Party leadership	1.0
Generalised loyalty to the party	10.5
	22.0
Selective outcome incentives	
For career reasons	1.0
In order to become a councillor	0.4
	1.4
Selective process incentives	
For social reasons	11.4
To work in elections	1.5
To support the local MP	1.5
	14.4
Social norms	
Through the influence of parents	8.3
Through the influence of a spouse or children	2.2
Through the influence of friends or colleagues	1.1
Persuaded by a canvasser	2.0
	13.6
Unclassified	5.3

altruistic reasons; they believe in making a contribution to society, to democracy, to freedom, and to other broadly defined social goals.

Who Belongs to the Conservative Party?

The grassroots of the Conservative Party is made up of aged inactivists. The typical Conservative Party member is 62 years old, and has either never worked, or is now retired from work. In Table 4.2 we see that the age profile of the membership is skewed very markedly; almost one-half of the membership is aged 66 or over, while only 5 per cent are under the age of 35. Unless the Conservative Party renews itself by recruiting many more younger members in the future, it could face a very drastic decline in its membership. On the assumption that the average life expectancy of a party member is 75 years, the party stands to lose more than 40 per cent of its membership over the next decade.

The experiences of party members are far removed from today's world of schools, colleges and universities. Over one-half left school at the age of 16 or under, and almost one-third have no educational qualifications at all. Although private education has played a major part in Conservative politics by training future Conservative elites, the great majority of party members have been educated in state schools, with only about one-quarter having a private education.

It is often assumed that local Conservative associations are dominated by businessmen who own their own companies and employ a small labour force. Recently, however, there have been some suggestions that these traditional pillars of the local party have been replaced by new 'upstarts', such as estate agents. In fact, the party's membership is much more varied in terms of occupational backgrounds than these ideas would suggest.

Using the occupational classifications adopted in the BES (Heath *et al.*, 1991), we find that 55 per cent were or are in salaried positions. These include teachers, marketing and public-relations executives, and financial-service workers, most of whom are accountants, underwriters, brokers and tax specialists. However, some of the traditional professions, like law and medicine, are less well represented.

The Conservative Party is overwhelmingly a middle-class party; fewer than 10 per cent are traditional manual workers. Working-class Conservatism may be of considerable significance in explaining the

TABLE 4.2 *Socio-economic characteristics of the Party membership (%)*

	%
Age (N = 2424)	
25 and under	1
26–35	4
36–45	11
46–55	17
56–65	24
66 and over	43
Type of school last attended (N = 2429)	
Primary/elementary	13
Secondary modern/technical/Scottish secondary	26
Grammar/Scottish senior secondary	28
Comprehensive/Scottish comprehensive	3
Direct grant/grant aided	1
Private fee-paying/Scottish independent	23
Other	5
Type of work organisation or sector (N = 2082)	
Private company/firm	59
Nationalised industry	5
Local authority	14
Health authority/hospital	7
Central government/civil service	6
Other	10
Socio-economic occupational classification (N − 2109)	
Salariat	55
Routine non-manual	17
Petty bourgeoisie	14
Foreman and technician	6
Working-class	8
Type of housing tenure (N = 2419)	
Own property	91
Rented from council	3
Rented privately	3
Rented from housing association	1
Living with family/friends	1
Household income (£p.a.) (N = 2295)	
Under 5 000	8
5 000–10 000	18
10 000–15 000	19
15 000–20 000	15
20 000–30 000	19
30 000–40 000	10
40 000–50 000	5
50 000 and over	8

Note: Figures in this table have been rounded and therefore may not total 100.

party's electoral dominance, but it is of only limited importance at the party's grassroots.

Almost one in five members are routine, non-manual workers, most of whom are clerks, cashiers, typists, secretaries and receptionists. The self-employed have been a loyal pillar of the Conservatives' electoral support, and just over one in ten of the party membership fall into this category (Heath *et al.*, 1991).

Given the age profile of the membership, it is not surprising that less than a third are in full-time work. Among those still working or previously employed, a clear majority earned their living in the private sector of the economy. Just as members' work experiences have been in the private sector, so also their living experiences are in the private sector of the property market. Nine of every ten own their own property, and only 3 per cent rent accommodation from a local council.

With such a large number of elderly and retired members, it is not surprising that more than a quarter of them had household incomes in 1992 below £10 000 per year. However, at the other end of the scale, just under a quarter had a household income above £30 000 per year, with almost one in ten receiving more than £50 000 a year. The median income of members is in the £15 000–£20 000 range.

Conservative Party membership is rather ill-defined; as we pointed out earlier, there is no fixed subscription (not even a minimum figure) and the party requires only generalised support for its political objectives. We now turn, therefore, to what membership actually means in terms of political activities.

What Do Members Do?

A battery of questions in the survey was designed to elicit information about the political activities of the members. The activities listed were chosen to be representative of a full range, arranged in increasing order of costliness, from a comparatively low-cost activity (like putting up an election poster) to a very high-cost activity (like running for elected office). It is interesting to note in Table 4.3 that only in one case, that of donating money to the party, is it true that a majority of respondents 'occasionally' or 'frequently' undertake this activity. The second most popular activity, displaying election posters, frequently engages fewer than a fifth of the respondents. Relatively few Conservatives deliver

TABLE 4.3   *Political activities undertaken by Members (%)*

Question: We would like to ask you about political activities you may have taken part in during the last FIVE years:

Activity	How often have you done this?			
	Not at all	Rarely	Occasionally	Frequently
Displayed an election poster in a window	51	8	23	18
Signed a petition supported by the party	53	14	26	8
Donated money to Conservative Party funds	16	12	45	28
Delivered party leaflets during an election	63	4	13	20
Attended a party meeting	53	13	19	15
Helped at a Conservative Party function (e.g., jumble sale)	58	9	17	16
Canvassed voters on behalf of the party	77	6	9	9
Stood for office within the party organisation	89	2	4	5
Stood for elective office in a local government or national parliamentary election	94	1	2	3

Note: Figures in this table have been rounded and therefore may not total 100.

leaflets during election campaigns, and even fewer canvass voters on behalf of the party.

At the highest end of the activism scale, some 9 per cent of members stood for office inside the party organisation, and 5 per cent stood for office in a local or national election. These are the really active members who keep the party organisation running at the local level on a day-to-day basis.

Overall, the results indicate that for most party members their membership means donating money to the party on a regular basis, and little else. For the most part, they do not get involved in campaigning, canvassing or attending meetings. Assuming a total membership of 750 000 at the time of the survey, this implies that around 135 000 members (that is, 18 per cent) frequently or occasionally canvass during elections. However, if we ask respondents the question 'How active do you consider yourself to be in the Conservative Party?', some 20 per cent considered themselves to be 'very' or 'fairly' active, which would imply an active membership of approximately 185 000. These figures would suggest that when active party membership is considered the differences between the Conservative and Labour parties are minimal. A survey of Labour Party members carried out in the same year (1992) reveals more Labour than Conservative election canvassers and similar numbers of 'very' or 'fairly' active members (Whiteley and Seyd, forthcoming).

These political activities set out in Table 4.3 do not constitute an exhaustive list, but they do encompass most of the important aspects of party work. We can see if in fact there is a single underlying activism scale by means of a factor analysis of the responses to the questions in Table 4.3. The factor loadings listed in Table 4.4 suggest that there are two independent factors underlying the responses in Table 4.3. The first factor, which is easily the more important of the two, explains nearly 50 per cent of the variance in the data, and loads strongly on relatively high-cost measures of participation. Thus individual members who canvass quite a lot also attend meetings, deliver leaflets and help at party functions. This factor is labelled the 'Activist' scale.

The second factor, which is independent of the first, relates principally to low-cost political activities such as donating money to the party, signing petitions, and displaying election posters. Individuals who do these things tend not to canvass during elections or to get involved in the party organisation, although some of them attend meetings or help out at party functions on occasions.

These results reveal that two distinct grassroots Conservative parties exist. One is a party of activists who are involved in campaigning, attending meetings, and running elections; the second is a party of supporters who do not get involved in these activities at all, but who do get involved in fairly low-cost things like signing petitions and giving money to the party.

What are Members' Opinions?

Conservatives often claim to adopt a non-ideological, common-sense approach to politics (Gilmour, 1977). Even if academic commentators detect more of an ideological consistency than these pragmatic claims

TABLE 4.4   *Factor analysis of political activity items*

Activities	Factors	
	Activist scale	Supporter scale
Canvassed voters on behalf of the party	81	
Stood for office within the party organisation	78	
Attended a party meeting	74	41
Delivered party leaflets during an election	72	
Helped at a Conservative Party function (e.g., jumble sale)	70	40
Stood for elective office in a local government or national parliamentary election	70	
Signed a petition supported by the part		79
Displayed an election poster in a window		68
Donated money to Conservative Party funds		64
Eigen value	4.36	1.17
Percentage of variance Explained	48.5	13.0

Note: The table contains the varimax rotated factor loadings which exceed 0.40 in value, multiplied by 100 for ease of interpretation. The initial factor scores were obtained by means of a principal components analysis of the items in Table 4.3, using pairwise deletion of missing data and Kaiser's criterion for factor extraction. The latter extracts all principal components with eigen values ≥; 1.

might suggest, it is often felt that Conservatism is a 'non-operational' ideology (Harris, 1972). By examining party members' attitudes on a range of specific contemporary issues, we can see whether there are any underlying principles to their opinions. We asked members' opinions of 32 statements and asked them to place themselves on two left–right scales, one relating to the Conservative Party, and the other to British politics in general. The confirmatory factor analysis derived from the members' responses produces four significant independent factors. The analysis suggests that while regular combinations of attitudes do appear among party members, the degree of such structuring is not very high (for technical details, see Whiteley, Seyd and Richardson, 1994, 132–7).

The first factor revealed is a progressive factor. Thus Conservatives who support public spending on poverty are also likely to be in favour of the regulation of markets, the redistribution of income and wealth, incomes policy and the provision of adequate unemployment benefits. They are also likely to favour giving workers more say in the workplace. The second factor is an individualism factor. Thus those respondents favouring privatisation of the coal industry will also favour private education, private medicine and the introduction of market mechanisms into the NHS. The two left–right scales load highly on this factor also, both with negative signs. This indicates that left-wing Conservatives, as measured by these scales, are likely to disagree with privatisation and tax cuts.

The third factor is a traditionalism factor, loading significantly on attitudes to immigration, the death penalty and opposition to further European integration. The left–right scale for the Conservative Party was also significant here, suggesting that left-wing Conservatives oppose the death penalty and further restrictions on immigration, and tend to favour European integration. A further feature of the traditionalism indicators is a distinction between general traditionalism and moral traditionalism: attitudes to abortion, divorce and Sunday trading. This suggests that traditionalism is less cohesive a tendency than either progressivism or individualism. Members who favour the death penalty or the repatriation of immigrants do not necessarily favour restrictions on abortion or divorce.

In Table 4.5 we show the distribution of opinions on the 24 questions from which the four factors emerged. It seems clear that grassroots Conservatives are more progressive than conventional wisdom would suggest. Thus majorities of members favour pursuing policies designed to 'capture the middle ground of politics'; they favour making unemployment benefit adequate to support a reasonable standard of living. In addition, they favour protecting consumers from the free market and regulating industries which have been privatised. Equally, majorities favour spending more money on the health service, on reducing poverty and giving workers greater say in the workplace. Only two of the progressive indicators are opposed by majorities; these are the indicators of redistribution of income and wealth, and electoral reform.

There is also clear evidence in Table 4.5 that many grassroots Conservatives support individualism in the form of privatisation and tax cuts. Majorities favour privatisation of the coal industry, introducing market mechanisms into the NHS, and encouraging private education and private medicine. However, roughly one-quarter of respondents oppose these privatisation programmes, and so market

TABLE 4.5   *The distribution of opinions on the indicators in the factor structure (%)*

Progressivism	Strongly agree	Agree	Neither	Disagree	Strongly disagree
Protect consumers from free markets	13	44	18	22	3
Introduce prices and incomes policy	12	31	12	32	14
Make unemployment benefit reasonable	14	60	13	11	2
Redistribute income and wealth	5	22	21	41	11
Capture the middle ground of politics	16	54	14	14	2
Regulate privatised industries	25	48	13	13	1
Introduce proportional representation	5	18	12	42	22

	Definitely should	Probably should	Doesn't matter	Probably should not	Definitely should not
Spend more on poverty	29	52	8	9	2
Spend more on the NHS	31	49	7	11	2
Give workers more say in the workplace	16	48	13	18	4

Individualism	Strongly agree	Agree	Neither	Disagree	Strongly disagree
Markets in the NHS will improve the service	15	53	15	14	3
Privatise British Coal	11	43	17	22	6

	Definitely should	Probably should	Doesn't matter	Probably should not	Definitely should not
Encourage private education	28	36	20	12	3
Encourage private medicine	17	35	16	26	7
Introduce stricter trade union laws	27	38	12	20	3
Cut income tax	20	40	13	22	4

(Table 4.5 continues)

(Table 4.5 continued)

Traditionalism: general	Strongly agree	Agree	Neither	Disagree	Strongly disagree
Reintroduce the death penalty	36	33	7	17	7
Encourage repatriation of immigrants	32	38	12	15	4
Resist further European integration	19	34	16	28	3
Give more foreign aid to poor countries	2	21	25	41	11
Abolish Child Benefit	7	13	12	53	15

Traditionalism: moral	Strongly agree	Agree	Neither	Disagree	Strongly disagree
Make abortion more difficult	12	21	19	35	13
Divorce is too easy	18	42	13	23	4
All shops should open on Sundays	16	31	10	23	20

Note: Figures in this table have been rounded and therefore may not total 100.

solutions to economic problems are not without their critics within the grassroots party.

The distribution of opinions on the two traditionalist factors are more divided. There is strong support for the repatriation of immigrants and the reintroduction of the death penalty and significant support for resisting further European integration, but much less support for restricting abortion, and little support for abolishing child benefit. Equally, most favour no restrictions on Sunday trading.

Overall, these results suggest that Conservative Party members tend to be progressive, individualistic and to some extent traditionalist. On the one hand, they tend to be rather chauvinist, anti-immigrant and anti-trade union, and in favour of market solutions to economic problems; but on the other, they are also concerned about protecting consumers from the free market, regulating privatised industries and ensuring that children and the unemployed get adequate financial support.

Some of these responses run counter to the image and policies of the Conservative Party during Margaret Thatcher's leadership. We conclude, therefore, by considering to what extent the Conservative Party members shared her ideological enthusiasms.

Thatcherism and the Grassroots Party

In terms of the four factors of progressivism, individualism, general and moral traditionalism, Thatcherism represented a clear shift away from progressive ideas towards individualism and traditionalism. With regard to individualism, it favoured privatisation, deregulation, tax cuts and free-market solutions to economic problems. But it also represented a shift towards traditionalism, as exemplified by Margaret Thatcher's support for capital punishment, her vocal opposition to European integration, and her unease over immigration.

Given this, if Thatcher succeeded in radicalising the Conservative Party, we would expect to/ see significant majorities of grassroots members opposing most of the progressive indicators and favouring the individualism and traditionalism indicators. It is apparent from Table 4.5, however, that the grassroots Conservative Party is rather anti-Thatcherite. On the one hand, there is significant support for distinctive Thatcherite policies such as privatisation, capital punishment and opposition to further European integration; but, on the other hand, grassroots Conservatives favour 'capturing the middle ground of politics', support welfare for the poor and unemployed, and approve of the regulation of markets. Furthermore, although they support the privatisation programmes, they also want the newly privatised industries to be closely regulated, in order to safeguard the interests of consumers. Finally, they support stricter laws to regulate trade unions but support the idea of giving workers more say in the workplace.

It is difficult to answer the question as to whether Margaret Thatcher shifted grassroots ideology to the right since we have no data on grassroots beliefs prior to her premiership. However, there is no reason to believe that pro-Thatcherite beliefs, such as opposition to immigration and to further European integration, and support for capital punishment, are the result of her 're-educating' the party. Evidence from voting surveys which pre-date the Thatcher era and from a survey of representatives attending the 1979 Conservative Party conference both show strong support for capital punishment and restrictions on immigration into Britain.

The voting evidence shows that both Conservative and non-Conservative voters were pro-capital punishment and anti-immigrant long before Thatcher became party leader. Butler and Stokes report that 71 per cent of the electorate wanted to retain the death penalty, and 83 per cent thought that too many immigrants had been let into Britain in their first survey of the British electorate in 1963 (D. Butler and Stokes, 1974, 461, 465).

The 1979 survey of Conservative conference participants is not representative of the membership as a whole, but nevertheless it is representative of the elite of activists who attend the party conference (Reif, Cayrol, and Niedermayer, 1980). Some 59 per cent of them agreed that 'The voluntary repatriation of immigrants should be supported by the allocation of government grants'; and 82 per cent agreed that 'Capital punishment should be reintroduced in Britain for certain types of murder.'

Thus the limited evidence we have from pre-Thatcherite surveys suggests that Thatcherism merely aligned itself with pre-existing attitudes within the Conservative Party, rather than shifted opinions in a new direction. Thatcherism as a doctrine appears to have done little to 're-educate' the Conservative Party by transforming it into a more strongly traditionalist and individualistic organisation. In this respect, this finding is similar to the evidence relating to the electorate as a whole, who appear largely untouched by Thatcherite ideas. Of course, there are many traditionalists and individualists within the grassroots party, but that appears to have been the case for many years, long before Margaret Thatcher became leader.

The Future of the Grassroots Party

We began this chapter by referring to the Conservative Party's success in creating a mass membership; it has succeeded more than any other British party in attracting large numbers of voters and members. It can claim with some justification to be one of the most successful political organisations in any democratic political system. Today, however, the Conservative Party appears to be going through a precipitous decline in membership. This decline has serious implications for the future of the party, since members are important in raising funds for the national organisation, for winning elections and acting as ambassadors in the community (Whiteley, Seyd and Richardson, 1994). It needs to revive the grassroots party as a matter of urgency.

An accurate assessment of trends in Conservative Party membership is only possible by tracking the membership over time. We have already pointed out the fragmentary nature of national membership figures. In a recently-published handbook of party organisations, Paul Webb provides five separate observations for the national membership between 1960 and 1989 (Katz and Mair, 1992, 847). If we add to these the estimates for membership for 1992 obtained from the present survey, and then regress the membership data against time, the resulting model is:

Membership = 6486.8−63.89 (Year)
              (12.3) (9.9)

Adjusted R^2 = 0.95 (membership is measured in thousands)

This model should be interpreted with care, since it is estimated from only six observations, but the adjusted R^2 shows that it fits the data very closely, and the *t* statistics (in parenthesis) show that time is a very statistically significant negative predictor of membership. The model suggests that on average the Conservative Party has been losing some 64 000 members each year since 1960. On the assumption that the model is a good predictor of future trends it implies that, if nothing is done to change this, the party membership will fall below 100 000 by the end of the century.

We suggested earlier that the Conservative Party has an active membership of around 185 000. We asked members about their perceptions of their rates of activism over time. Compared with five years previously (1987), some 25 per cent of the members thought that they were less active and only 8 per cent thought they were more active. If we subtract the percentage more active from the less active, some 17 per cent have become 'de-energised' over a 5-year period. The results of a further ESRC panel study will shed further light here (Whiteley and Seyd, forthcoming). There are various reasons why this has occurred. A number of cultural and social factors, such as class de-alignment, social and geographical mobility, increased leisure opportunities and a higher female participation in the labour market are at work to produce a long-term decline in membership and levels of activism. However, our evidence suggests that this decline seems to have accelerated during Thatcher's leadership.

Margaret Thatcher shifted the centre of political gravity within the Conservative Party to the right. Yet, in terms of the nine point left–right scale (with 1 to 4 categorised as left), 15 per cent classified themselves as on the left of the party. Furthermore, members who coded themselves on the left were rather more active than members who placed themselves on the right. Thatcher's particular brand of Conservatism will most likely have resulted in a decline in activism over time, as many active members found themselves out of sympathy with ideological trends within the party. In addition, it appears that Conservatives who joined the party during the Thatcher years were much less attached to the party in comparison with those who joined earlier (Whiteley, Seyd and Richardson, 1994, 225–6). This weakening of attachment is clearly related to the politics of the Thatcher era.

Thatcher appeared to be very popular among grassroots members. Asked to rank her on a scale from 0 to 100 (the higher the score the greater her popularity) her mean thermometer score was 78. But the range of scores on this scale was high, too, the standard deviation being 18.9. This means that even though many Conservatives thought highly of her, a significant group did not like her at all.

We have already noted that many members are progressive, 'one nation' Conservatives. Supporters of poverty programmes, advocates of the NHS and sympathisers with the idea of generous unemployment benefits will have found themselves increasingly at odds with the party during the Thatcher era. To be fair, many grassroots members are clearly strong supporters of Thatcherite policies, but the fact that many progressives exist in the grassroots party is likely to have caused problems during her period as leader. Moreover, if they followed the Conservative tradition of avoiding public criticism of the party leadership and quietly withdrawing from the party, their departure would have been relatively unnoticed.

Conclusions

In response to this decline in both membership and activism, the Conservative Party clearly needs to develop a strategy for reviving its grassroots. Policy successes, particularly in relation to the management of the economy, are a key factor in a revival strategy. However, the party leadership also needs to provide political incentives to encourage participation at the local level. In order to satisfy those who wish to play an active part in their local community, the importance and prestige of local government needs restoring. Party members, however, need also to be given greater influence in the party's policy-making procedures. Part of the strategy for reviving the grassroots means giving members a meaningful influence in all aspects of party life.

The evidence is that Thatcher, though apparently successful at the time, damaged the grassroots Conservative Party. The Conservative Party has always been a broad church with distinct ideological groupings among the members. We made the point earlier that three broad ideological tendencies exist within the mass membership: progressivism, traditionalism and individualism. Thus the relentless drive away from progressive Conservatism produced disillusion and detachment on the part of many local supporters. Moreover, the policy failures, particularly in relation to the management of the economy, added to this trend. The leadership has to return to a strategy of balancing these diverse ideological tendencies. The Conservative Party's long and successful history can be explained largely by its leaders' ability to adapt to changing circumstances and times. Thatcher strove to abandon this long tradition of pragmatic Conservative leadership, and the party is now paying the price for this abandonment.

Note

This national sample of members used a two-stage design. First, a 5 per cent sample of constituencies was drawn at random from the party's regions. The use of a sampling frame stratified by Conservative Party regions ensured that a representative regional distribution of constituency associations was obtained. A one in ten systematic random sample of party members in 34 constituency associations was selected. In January 1992, we sent out 3919 questionnaires, and by the cut-off date in April 1992 a total of 2466 usable replies had been returned: a response rate of 63 per cent. The research was funded by the ESRC (Grant No: Y304253008). Fuller details of the research methodology can be found in Whiteley, Seyd and Richardson (1994), Appendix 1.

5

Eton Gent or Essex Man? The Conservative Parliamentary Elite

DAVID BAKER and IMOGEN FOUNTAIN

Are measures more important than men? Do we judge our parties more by what they do than by who the people are who do them? The answers to these questions are complex and unclear. (D. Butler and Pinto-Duschinsky, 1980)

As policies and ideology have shifted in response to social and economic change, one aspect of Conservatism apparently remained constant: the social background of the Conservative Party's Members of Parliament (MPs). Throughout most of the twentieth century the Parliamentary Conservative Party (PCP) has been dominated by men drawn from backgrounds of social privilege, typically old boys of the most exclusive private schools in occupations associated with four main elements: the land, the military, business, and the professions. As one recent commentator has said, 'Wealth, whether landed, industrial or commercial, or professional (almost exclusively the Bar), was the essence of the pre-1939 House' (Criddle, 1994). Between the wars the balance shifted towards a wider elite of private school/Oxbridge educated businessmen, although 172 of the 415 Conservative MPs elected in 1935 were aristocrats by birth or marriage (Haxey, 1939). The wider accusation that this élitism undermined British social and economic progress has recently been revived (Ellis, 1994).

The face of privilege was somewhat eroded by wider socio-economic changes, and by the need to adapt to a changing electoral context in which social deference was in decline and the Labour Party appealed to the party's crucial working-class electoral base (Chapter 3). Fears of appearing socially unrepresentative after the crushing Conservative defeat of 1945 led to the 1948 Maxwell Fife Report which recommended an end to the practice of requiring Parliamentary candidates to have private wealth to fund their own election campaigns (D. Butler and Pinto-Duschinsky, 1980). But the informal nature of the selection process remained unchanged until 1980, when tough management-style selection boards were introduced to filter out the less able from the candidate lists (Criddle, 1994). As a result the socio-economic profile of the PCP changed very little. Mellors analysed standard socio-economic data on all MPs who contested general elections between 1945 and 1974 and demonstrated that candidate selection continued to reproduce social exclusivity (Mellors, 1978).

Following the discontent with the leadership selection process in 1963 from which the aristocrat Sir Alec Douglas-Home emerged, and his subsequent election defeat at the hands of a modernising grammar-school Labour leader, the party introduced leadership elections. The next three leaders, Edward Heath, Margaret Thatcher and John Major, all came from humble families and were all educated at state secondary schools. In the 1980s the media, supported by the rhetoric of the Thatcher Conservative Party – and, more significantly, academic analysis – detected real social changes in the Conservative Parliamentary elite (Burch and Moran, 1985). The Parliamentary party, measured by its education and occupational background, was seen as finally showing signs of becoming more 'meritocratic' and 'classless'. This was underlined by Thatcher's education and provincial 'corner shop' childhood.

The rise of the professional politician in the party was also seen as important, with a growing number of candidates having risen through the party organisation and relying on political consultancy work for extra income (Hollingsworth, 1991; Kavanagh, 1992; Riddell, 1993). In addition, under Thatcher and later Major, the party has aggressively marketed itself, in the words of Norman Tebbit, as the party of the 'upwardly mobile', the restless achievers personified by the East End barrow boy turned City dealer. This mood was perhaps best summed up by Julian Critchley, who saw the modern Conservative activist as personified by the suburban car-dealer rather than the landed aristocrat (Tebbit, 1988; Critchley, 1992).

During Major's post-election 'honeymoon' period in office in 1992 much was made by the media of his relatively modest roots, his lack of university education and his proclaimed commitment to a 'classless society' given symbolic form by the open access granted to public suggestions for the award of public honours. The *Sunday Times* claimed that the 1992 election saw for the for the first time a majority of state-educated Conservtive MPs in the new Parliament. David Willetts, the MP for Havant (King Edward's School, Birmingham, and Christ Church, Oxford), said, 'This development adds credibility to our claims to be the party of opportunity and of classlessness.' Judith Chaplin, the new MP for Newbury (Wycombe Abbey, and Girton College, Cambridge) commented, 'This is very good news. What the Prime Minister means by classlessness is everyone having opportunity. This news underlines this message' (*Sunday Times* 12 April 1992). More recently Criddle has claimed that the Conservative political class is decisively changing: 'A more meritocratic, socially mobile Conservative elite had arisen, its leaders in the 1980s assaulting the very institutions and values with which the party was once synonymous' (Criddle, 1994). But the case for social convergence remains weak. Even the *Sunday Times* article quoted above pointed out that a Conservative MP was more likely to have been to Eton than any other school (a total of 34), and only 3 per cent gained their degrees from a polytechnic rather than a university. True, the absolute social privilege of Conservative Parliamentarians has declined in recent years, but by how much and in what manner? Has state school educated Essex University Man really replaced Eton and Oxford Man at the core of the British Conservative Party elite?

Problems of Methodology

The study of social background of elites is notoriously fraught (Edlinger and Searing, 1967). The fundamental problem is that although social background data is easy to collect, it is not easy to demonstrate causal links between social background and political behaviour. Middle-class radicals and working-class conservatives abound in British society. In a famous critique Crewe queried whether British elite studies, while amassing a great deal of information, were contributing to a better understanding of elites (Crewe, 1974). Those who used the social background approach typically assumed, without further need for demonstration, that if the social background of an elite could be established it was evidence of shared values, goals and purpose.

The crisis of methodological self-confidence in elite studies that Crewe's analysis brought into sharp focus did not, however, mark a complete collapse of such academic work. One of Crewe's most important suggestions was for analysis to focus on generations, namely the time and entry of individuals into cohorts of the elite. The hypothesis that political consciousness might be linked to generational cohorts influenced, for example, by inter-war mass unemployment, wartime experiences or even the 1979 'Winter of Discontent' offered valuable lines of research. This is particularly important if we ask whether recent ideological changes in the Conservative Party, notably under Thatcher's leadership, might be linked to a cohort effect. Most obviously the divisions in the Conservative Party over the European integration (Chapter 6) could be related to the socio-economic composition of the party's younger cohorts, with the older cohorts fearing the rekindling of conflict in a disunited Europe, and many of 'Thatcher's children' more concerned with federalist European encroachments upon British sovereignty.

The main academic studies of the British Parliamentary elite since Crewe's strictures against the 'harmless voyeurism' of counting 'tired old variables' indicating socio-economic background, have followed his advice to use cohort analysis. Mellors justified such longtitudinal studies because they provided measures of party cohesion, revealed factors that might at least influence opinions and attitudes, and enabled estimates to be made of opportunities for elite recruitment (Mellors, 1978). His work was extended by others to cover the 1979 and 1983 general elections (Burch and Moran, 1985), and was further deployed to analyse the professionalism of political careers (King, 1981). Burch and Moran's contribution has similarly been further discussed and extended (Borthwick, Ellingworth, Bell and Mackenzie, 1991; D. Baker, Gamble and Ludlam 1992a, 1992b). Such studies acknowledged the force of Crewe's critique of the unproven assumption of a direct link between an elite's social origin and political attitudes and behaviour, but argued that the collection and analysis of data on elite recruitment remained important tasks of political science. Norris and Lovenduski have further argued, on the basis of the 1992 British Candidates Study, that while the social background of legislative elites does not generally matter, gender does: women legislators appear to give stronger support to feminist, social policy and local constituency issues (Norris and Lovenduski, 1995).

The Parliamentary Elite under Grammar-School Leaders, 1965–95

The problems of measuring social class through educational background are well known, especially given the wide range of status which separates the top private schools from the bottom ones. Nevertheless, given the fact that, even after over a decade of pro-private school government policy, less than 5 per cent of UK children attend such schools, socio-educational exclusiveness remains very significant (Westergaard and Resler, 1975; Mellors, 1978; Burch and Moran, 1985). Against the background of a large influx of new Conservative MPs in 1979 and 1983, Burch and Moran studied the socio-economic backgrounds of these intakes of MPs, from both the major parties. Setting their findings in historical perspective by using Mellors' 1945–74 data, they concluded that this period was characterised by only marginal movement towards a socially representative PCP (Burch and Moran, 1985). In short, the High Tory 'grandees' were still in control of the Parliamentary party. However, the 1974–83 period had, they suggested, witnessed the Conservative elite becoming somewhat less exclusive, thus challenging the conventional wisdom of the period that, in spite of its *petit bourgeois* leader, the Thatcher Conservative Party was still dominated at the top by a self-perpetuating private school/ Oxbridge elite.

Burch and Moran identified several key elements of change in the educational background of new Conservative MPs in this period: MPs drawn from Oxbridge, those with a private school background, Old Etonians; those with state secondary educations who attended non-Oxbridge universities, and those with an elementary/secondary educaion only. They also identified those with combined private school/Oxbridge educations. Of these categories they considered the first three to be the most significant indicators of elite status, and suggested 'that in terms of educational background the Conservative Party has become more open and less exclusive in its source of recruitment' (Burch and Moran, 1985, 5–6). The Conservatives in Parliament Project updated these studies to include the 1987 and 1992 election cohorts of new MPs (Table 5.1; D. Baker, Gamble and Ludlam, 1992b; D. Baker, Fountain, Gamble and Ludlam, 1994c). Up to 1974 Oxbridge attendance was consistently high, peaking at 60 per cent of all new Conservative MPs, but falling off dramatically thereafter.

One significant long-term trend is the declining number of Conservative MPs with no higher education, down to 9 per cent in 1992

TABLE 5.1   *New cohorts of Conservative MPs by educational background*

MP election cohort	1964/6	1970	1974 I/II	1979	1983	1987	1992
Conservative majority (absolute)	−22/ −124	30	−41/ −81	43	144	102	21
Number in cohort	75	91	70	82	104	57	57
	%	%	%	%	%	%	%
All private secondary	85	68	81	70	63	63	65
Eton	21	12	14	13	6	5	7
Private secondary + Oxbridge	52	36	50	32	30	35	39
State secondary + Oxbridge	4	7	10	5	9	7	4
All Oxbridge	56	43	60	37	39	42	43
Private secondary + all old university	61	44	60	54	50	47	53
Private secondary + other higher ed.	4	4	3	6	6	11	5
Private secondary + all higher ed.	65	48	63	60	56	58	58
State secondary + all old university	11	16	13	16	20	19	21
State secondary + other higher ed.	0	7	1	9	9	14	12
State secondary + all higher ed.	11	23	14	25	29	33	33
State secondary + all higher ed.	11	23	14	25	29	33	33
Private secondary + all higher ed.	65	48	63	60	56	58	58
All higher education	75	71	77	85	85	91	91
No higher education	24	29	23	16	15	9	9
Private secondary only	20	20	19	10	7	5	7
State secondary only	4	9	4	6	9	4	2

Source: D. Baker, Fountain, Gamble and Ludlam (1994a).

Notes:
1. These election cohorts differ from previous analysts such as Burch and Moran for four reasons: (a) they include by-election victors retaining their seats; (b) MPs re-entering Parliament after broken service may not be counted as new MPs, depending on their previous history; and (c) because of the small numbers in the two short Parliament cohorts in 1966 and October 1974 (1964/6 and 1974I/II) are combined cohorts; and (d) MPs entering for a fraction of a Parliament and losing at the subsequent general election, never winning again, are excluded.
2. The educational categories are not exclusive, so that percentages may not total 100.
3. University refers to 'old' universities (i.e., only those so named before 1992). Former polytechnics appear here amongst 'other higher education' institutions like agricultural and military colleges.

from 24 per cent in 1964/6, paralleled by a rise in the significance of other higher education institutions (including agricultural and military colleges and the old polytechnics). If these institutions are included, the figure for state secondary educated MPs with higher education rises to 33 per cent in 1987 and 1992, though the figures for those with private educations and some form of higher education also rises to 58 per cent for those elections. The number of university-educated MPs who went to state secondary schools almost doubled from 11 per cent in 1964/6 to 21 per cent in the 1992 intake, having levelled off after 1983.

The data also reveals that the proportions of the 1987 and 1992 cohorts who attended Oxbridge rose above 1979 and 1983 levels to 43 per cent in 1992, though these were markedly below the figures for the 1964–74 cohorts. Private school attendance was consistently high throughout the post-war period until 1979, but fell from 1983 and then levelled off at between 63 and 65 per cent. Burch and Moran's indicator of combined private school/Oxbridge educations, down to 30 per cent in 1983 from over one-half in 1964/6 and 1974, was a major finding informing their portrayal of a reversal of post-war trends. Again the more recent figures show that this indicator 'recovered' in 1987 and rose again to 39 per cent of the new Conservative intake in 1992.

The decline in old Etonians, the core of the traditional Tory Parliamentary elite, is clear. Between 1945 and 1974 a slow fall occurred in Old Etonians joining the ranks of Conservative MPs, down from 26 per cent of new MPs in 1945 (Mellors, 1978) to 14 per cent of the combined 1974 cohorts. Again, this decline accelerated between 1974 and 1983, with a dramatic decline from 13 per cent 1979 to 6 per cent in 1983, levelling off thereafter. Nevertheless, Eton remains the single most represented school in the PCP and is significantly overrepresented in the ranks of government (see Table 5.2).

One explanation Burch and Moran considered for the less exclusive social profile they identified by 1983 was the conventional perception that MPs from more educationally exclusive backgrounds are often awarded the safest seats, so that unusually large cohorts, such as that in 1983, let in unusually large numbers of non-elite candidates fighting marginal constituencies, who might be expected to lose their seats at subsequent elections. They plotted the 1983 figures for education background against the marginality of the seat contested, and discovered that many of the less socially exclusive candidates won 'safe' seats in 1983. They therefore argued that these changes reflect deeper and more enduring developments within the PCP.

TABLE 5.2 *Educational background of ministerial appointments by Heath, Thatcher, and Major, (as percentages of all appointments)*

Ministerial Ranks	Appointment Cohort		
	Heath	Thatcher	Major
All private secondary			
Under Secretary	81	76	74
Minister of State	94	81	79
Cabinet	86	79	73
Eton			
Under Secretary	19	14	10
Minister of State	39	19	22
Cabinet	27	15	9
Private secondary + Oxbridge			
Under Secretary	54	50	50
Minister of State	61	62	58
Cabinet	73	63	55

Source: D. Baker, Fountain, Gamble and Ludlam 1994c

Notes:

1. 'Appointment' is defined as any promotion of an individual into one of the three ranks of government post defined in D. Butler and G. Butler (1994), so that an individual may appear as an 'appointment' on more than one occasion. Re-appointment at the same rank to another department is not counted, even if the new department is conventionally considered to be more prestigious.

2. These figures do not include changes resulting from the reshuffle in July 1994.

Applying a similar technique on seats with majorities of 10 per cent or above to the 1987 and 1992 intakes produces some interesting results (Table 5.3). Our data suggests that 1983 was not a watershed election as far as the onward march of 'classlessness' was concerned. In fact those with the most privileged educational backgrounds have made something of a comeback, especially in 1992. They remain throughout the period even more disproportionately represented in the safest seats than they are in each cohort as a whole (Table 5.1). Seen from this perspective 1983 was the point at which the post-war trend away from social exclusivity amongst Conservative Parliamentarians was halted and, so far, reversed.

Overall, earlier suggestions that the broadening social base of recruitment in the 1983 cohort of new MPs could reflect deeper and more enduring developments do not appear vindicated by trends in 1987 and

TABLE 5.3   *Privately educated Conservative MPs taking safe seats (percentages of cohorts in seats with majorities of 10 per cent or higher)*

Election cohort	1964/6	1970	1974 I/II	1979	1983	1987	1992
All private secondary	88	74	84	71	67	63	72
Private Sec. + all old university	65	57	73	58	53	48	54
Private Sec. + Oxbridge	65	52	57	48	35	37	44

Source: D. Baker, Fountain, Gamble and Ludlam (1994c).
Note: See Table 5.1 for definitions.

1992. Indeed, the general picture is of a somewhat less 'open' party in the post-Thatcher era, although the rise of those with 'new university' or other higher educational backgrounds could indicate a gradual erosion of some of the traditional university/Oxbridge grip on the party so disliked by the new, more 'upwardly mobile' MPs in the party.

The Ministerial Elite under Grammar-School Leaders, 1965–95

The rise of Cabinet ministers from less privileged backgrounds, personified by Heath, Thatcher and Major, also concerned Burch and Moran, who concluded that no significant advance was made by state-school educated MPs (Burch and Moran, 1985). They acknowledged Guttsman's observation of a reduction in Cabinet access by social privilege in the post-war period, exemplified by a reduction in Eton and Harrow old boys who had accounted for half the Cabinet in 1955 (Guttsman, 1967). Burch and Moran suggested that this slow flattening of the social profile of Conservative Cabinets had accelerated since 1979, a factor revealed most clearly in the decline of private schools/Oxbridge dominance in 1983. They argued that the long-term changes in the social composition of Conservative Cabinets had been modest, with Heath and Thatcher being atypical. There was, however, a decline in aristocratic and upper-middle-class representation. Overall, they suggested that real 'convergence' was occurring, with the professional elite numerically dominating Conservative Cabinets. They also speculated that the more meritocratic patterns of recruitment revealed amongst ordinary MPs in 1983 could, in time, dilute the privileged social background of future Conservative Cabinets (Burch and Moran, 1985). Table 5.2 shows that there is still disproportionate access to

Conservative governments from amongst this elite, particularly those from Eton. The flattening of social profile at ministerial level noted by Burch and Moran appears slow, even under Major. Overall there is a downward trend of disproportionate promotion of members of the British socio-educational elite across the past 30 years of government appointment cohorts. However, socio-educational elite access to government posts in Conservative governments remains even more disproportionate than its access to Conservative Parliamentary seats.

Table 5.4 appears to suggest that ministers with the most privileged socio-education backgrounds are nevertheless forced to wait longer than their less privileged colleagues for promotion. This, however, is due to their disproportionate access to promotion. Only around one-third of private secondary-educated Conservative MPs could actually hold office simultaneously since there are usually only around 80 ministerial posts available; in theory all their state secondary colleagues could hold office at the same time. This creates a 'crowding out' effect with members of the elite obstructing each other's progress up the 'greasy pole'.

TABLE 5.4 *Average number of years as an MP before appointment to ministerial rank, by education*

Ministerial rank	Appointment cohort		
	Heath	Thatcher	Major
All ministers			
Under Secretary	7.01	6.45	8.47
Minister of State	11.37	10.27	11.7
Cabinet	16.4	15.01	13.18
Private secondary			
Under Secretary	7.38	6.76	8.9
Minister of State	11.48	10.47	11.81
Cabinet	16.38	15.86	14.21
Eton			
Under Secretary	8.14	7.28	8.85
Minister of State	13.94	11.48	14.59
Cabinet	20.57	21.45	14.15
Private secondary + Oxbridge			
Under Secretary	7.69	7.11	9.31
Minister of State	11.35	9.97	11.7
Cabinet	16.88	15.91	13.53

Source and notes as Table 5.3.

Another possible approach to confirming elite status is to look at occupational data. The problems associated with measuring class by occupation are complex, notably because Conservative MPs have frequently held several jobs simultaneously or in succession, and continue to accumulate jobs after entering office. Deciding which job is significant is often impossible. Thomas's pioneering study counted all multi-occupations, while Mellors selected just one occupation where MPs listed several (Thomas, 1958; Mellors, 1978). Some preliminary work done by the Parliament Project team on declared occupations between 1964 and 1994 supports Mellors' view of a long-term decline in the land-owning/farming group (D. Baker, Fountain, Gamble and Ludlam, 1994c). By 1990, indeed, there was no declared land-owner/farmer at all in the Conservative Cabinet; a situation which, if accurate, is unprecedented in modern times. Less seriously, the supposed invasion of the Parliamentary party by estate agents, so often announced by commentators and satirists, has seemingly not materialised. While the predominance of businessmen and lawyers appears to continue, there is a decline in the numbers of MPs describing themselves as directors or business consultants, although the numbers of bankers/financiers and executives/managers appear to have risen since 1979. An increase in the number of Conservative academics entering Parliament since 1979 is also noticeable, though there has been a parallel decline in the arrival of print and broadcast journalists and other authors and publishers. The increase in the 1980s in new Conservative MPs previously active in urban, as opposed to rural, local politics, has also continued (Mellors, 1978; D. Baker, Gamble and Ludlam, 1992b; D. Baker, Fountain, Gamble and Ludlam, 1994c).

Conclusion

Burch and Moran's picture of a slowly flattening social profile of Conservative Parliamentarians is not sustained by the 1987 and 1992 intakes and governments. If anything, the measurable decline in social exclusivity in the early 1980s had been reversed by the early 1990s. The Conservative Party is led in Parliament largely by men and women whose education, particularly in the more exclusive institutions such as private schools, Oxford and Cambridge, indicates a continuation of social exclusivity. Major and Tebbit remain unrepresentative examples of the 'upwardly mobile' in the top ranks of the Parliamentary party.

The 1992 media image of Major as the leader and creator of a more 'classless' Conservative Party and the architect of a future 'classless' society appears largely groundless on these figures. The media tends to concentrate on grammar-school educated individuals such as Major and Kenneth Clarke, when dealing with the rise of the less privileged individuals to the top of the party, while ignoring the continuing social exclusivity of those around them. Such speculation is also fuelled by the undoubted decline of the Etonians in the Cabinet and the increase in numbers who have pursued higher education outside the 'old' pre-1992 university sector. If 'meritocracy' or 'classlessness' is growing in the Conservative Party, there are few clear signs of change yet visible in its Parliamentary elite.

In their 1980 essay on the continuing unrepresentativeness of the Conservative Party elite, Butler and Pinto-Duschinsky concluded that,

> Etonians though untypical in their background, are not necessarily so unrepresentative in their opinions. Some of the party's leading moderates have been drawn from the upper-classes . . . whereas some of the most vocal right-wingers in the party have recently been those with relatively modest social origins . . . In reality, there is no clear connection between class and the policy views of MPs. (D. Butler and Pinto-Duschinsky, 1980)

The above evidence supports this view. Social composition effects cannot be used to explain the apparently radical shifts in Conservative policy since 1964, most notably since 1979 under Thatcher. The evidence available on educational background confirms that the Thatcherite project of the 1980s for governing Britain did not emerge from any strong shift in the socio-economic composition of the Conservative Parliamentary elite, and neither did it construct such a shift (Crewe and Searing, 1988; Norton, 1990). If 'Thatcherite' policies cannot be explained as the result of changes in the social composition of the PCP, greater attention needs to be given to the formation and persistence of ideological groupings in the party and their interaction with the party leadership in specific historical conditions.

Note

The authors thank Andrew Gamble and Steve Ludlam for their contributions to the research on which this chapter is based, and the University of Sheffield Research Stimulation Fund for financial support.

6

The Spectre Haunting Conservatism: Europe and Backbench Rebellion

STEVE LUDLAM

> The stress placed upon loyalty and unity within the Conservative political tradition is an instinct as old as politics itself, all the more potent because Conservatism defends the privileges of a minority. Divisions within ruling strata are potentially more subversive and destructive than manifest divisions between those strata and the majority of the less privileged ... The Conservative stress on pragmatism, compromise and the tempering of policy disagreements has its roots in the fear that confrontation between factions within the privileged groups could of itself undermine the whole structure of the political organisation of society. (Norton and Aughey, 1981, 50–1)

Long before John Major could celebrate five years as Conservative Party leader, the party had fallen prey to the worst bout of in-fighting since the war, and arguably in this century. Such intra-party rebellion by backbench MPs can take many forms, from mild and private to wild and public; it can be intra- or extra-parliamentary, and can take place when the party is in opposition or in office. One occasional but serious form is backbench pressure to remove ministers, generally channelled through the 'men in grey suits', the leaders of the backbench 1922 Committee (Norton, 1994). Organised dissent in single-issue ginger groups, or in factions that pursue a range of linked policy objectives, is more serious, especially when it affects parliamentary behaviour. The once-conventional view of a PCP free of internal tendencies, factions and ginger groups has long been challenged, and from the perspective

98

of 1995 it is hard to imagine how such a view was ever credible (Seyd, 1980; Brand, 1989; Barnes, 1994). Signing Early Day Motions (EDMs) is an important indication of dissent, but not rebellion against the Whips, as such motions are never 'whipped' (Finer, Berrington and Bartholomew, 1961; Berrington, 1973). Rebellion against the Whips in parliamentary divisions is far more serious (Jackson, 1968; Norton, 1975, 1978, 1980). Major suffered most of the serious forms of rebellion to a degree unprecedented since the war. A succession of his ministers left office on the insistence of the backbenches, some after receiving his public support. The activities of party ginger groups and factions, in terms of publications, running slates in party elections, and open dissent in the mass media, all reached new heights. Political journalists increasingly sought and broadcast the views of Lollards, Positive Europeans, No Turning Backers, Bruges Groupists, Conservative Way Forwarders, 92 Groupers, Fresh Starters and European Foundationists. In June 1995 Major invited the most serious form of revolt of all, the one that brought him into office: the removal of a sitting Prime Minister in a leadership election. Angered by repeated Euro-rebel threats to challenge his party leadership, he forced a vote. John Redwood resigned from the cabinet to run, and Major won on a platform of no change of policy, by 218 to 89 votes, with 20 abstentions or spoilt ballot papers.

The sanctions available to leaders to restrain such dissent are at best only partly effective. Conservative whips have traditionally been reluctant to impose harsh sanctions on rebels, and the marked increase in rebellion in the 1970–4 Parliament, including the first post-war rebel defeats of a government, did not produce a single withdrawal of the whip, even when rebels repeatedly defied three-line whips or cross-voted on a confidence motion (Norton, 1978, 163–75). Throughout this chapter the distinction is maintained between a cross-voter who votes against the party line, and an abstainer who deliberately declines to vote when instructed (as opposed to absence by agreement); collectively those who defy the Whips are referred to as rebels. Appeals to constituency parties to discipline or deselect rebels have rarely achieved the Whips' aims and have more often backfired. By the time of the Maastricht rebellion the Conservative Whips had adopted a much tougher approach, producing howls of protest that included allegations of physical and sexist abuse (D. Baker, Gamble and Ludlam, 1993b; Gorman, 1993). Nevertheless, after repeated rebellion and procedural obstruction during the passage of the Maastricht Bill, only one MP finally lost the whip for abstaining on Major's Social Chapter confidence vote in July 1993. The risks of such sanctions rebounding were spectacularly illustrated when Major withdrew the whip from eight Euro-rebels who abstained in a vote of confidence in November 1994. Mass expulsion from the PCP was almost unprecedented; that the expulsions voluntarily turned Major's into a minority government was totally without precedent. The immediate consequence was a further rebellion that defeated Major on a budget measure. This, and several cases under Edward Heath's leadership, illustrate the fact that a small government majority does not always guarantee that rebels will avoid inflicting outright defeats on their leaders. Harold Wilson's law of Labour rebellions, that they always fell one short of his majority, has not applied to the contemporary Conservative Party.

This chapter concentrates on parliamentary rebellion, focusing on the most serious and sustained disputes, namely those over European integration. Europe is central for several reasons. It is a grand issue that raises the place of Britain in the world economy, like the historic disputes over Corn Law repeal and tariff reform that actually split the party (D. Baker, Gamble and Ludlam, 1993a). It tests the soul of British Conservatism because, unlike these earlier disputes, it also threatens the sovereign status of the nation and state whose defence has been crucial to the Tories' extraordinary electoral appeal since the mid-nineteenth century as the party of the Union, the Constitution and the Empire. Insofar as it is also in part a dispute over economic intervention and monetary policy, it also follows the other main fault-line of historic Tory divisions over economic policy (Barnes, 1994). It is one of the most explosive features of the European issue that it combines such ingredients in ways that cut across the familiar left–right, 'wet'/'dry', ideological wings of the party (Finer, Berrington and Bartholomew, 1961, 87ff; Seyd, 1972, 478; Berrington, 1973, 167; Aughey, 1978, 14; Dunleavy, 1993, 130; D. Baker, Gamble and Ludlam, 1994a). Since the formation of the Anti-Common Market League in 1961 Conservative MPs have been involved in at least 80 ginger groups on Europe which have often recruited from opposite wings of the party. Europe promoted the formation of single-issue groups in a party consequently viewed as a plurality of groupings, rather than a coherent hierarchy (Ashford, 1980, 124).

In practice European integration has stimulated by far the most serious rebellions in the party's post-war history. It made Heath's backbenches more rebellious than those of his predecessors. The havoc wreaked over Europe since the mid-1980s is unprecedented in scale, scope and impact. When, as Labour's new leader, Tony Blair first faced John Major across the despatch boxes, he chose to confront him on European integration. It was a remarkable reversal of party games. In the early 1980s, the Conservatives still enjoyed watching Labour divide, and then split over Europe when the short-lived SDP broke away. Yet within a few years Tory divisions over Europe had contributed crucially to the damaging removals from the Cabinet of Defence Secretary Michael Heseltine in 1986, Industry Secretaries Leon Brittan in 1986 and Nicholas Ridley in 1990, Chancellors of the Exchequer Nigel Lawson in 1989 and Norman Lamont in 1993, Deputy Prime Minister Geoffery Howe in 1990 (already sacked as Foreign Secretary in 1989), and of course Prime Minister Margaret Thatcher in 1990. The Maastricht rebellion resulted on 22 July 1993 in the most serious defeat sustained in Parliament by any Conservative government in the twentieth century, which Major was only able to survive by resorting to a vote of confidence, threatening his back-benchers with electoral annihilation. In November 1994 Major took the unprecedented step of expelling eight Euro-rebel MPs, suffered a serious parliamentary defeat in consequence, but then readmitted them unconditionally. By June 1995 the constant sniping of Euro-rebels stung him to force the leadership election that he won, resisting the rebel campaign demand that he denounce the single currency.

Rebellions from Churchill to Heath

Early rebellions against British membership of the EEC were manifestations of a wider opposition to policies perceived as weakening British imperialism that provoked most of the serious rebellions before Thatcher became leader. The first opposed the 1945 Washington Loans and Bretton Woods Agreements that signalled the subordination of British to US foreign economic policy. Seventy-four and 52 rebels respectively defied Churchill, including a frontbencher who resigned his post (Norton, 1975, 3–5). 'Imperialist' rebellions were generally reactive and hence sporadic, although organisational continuity was provided by the membership of the Monday Club, founded and named after Macmillan's so-called Black Monday speech heralding the 'winds of change' decolonisation of Africa (Gamble, 1974, 177). A 'Suez Group' attracted 40 Tory MPs to oppose closure of the British canal base, but they only rebelled in Parliament once, when 28 rejected Churchill's reassurances in 1954 (Norton, 1975, 107–9). After the Suez crisis in 1956 only half as many abstained in votes in protest against Eden's retreat, while outright Tory opponents of the invasion came under much more serious party pressure (Berrington, 1961; Gamble, 1974, 175).

Although the Monday Club coordinated opposition to the dissolution of the Central African Federation, there was no parliamentary rebellion until 1965, when 50 Tory 'imperialists' opposed Labour's imposition of sanctions on the illegal white regime in Southern Rhodesia (Norton, 1975, 255–6). Twenty-one voted with Labour. This was the biggest voting rebellion since the 1945 votes. It has been noted that Tory MPs rarely did more than speak against their governments or abstain on votes during the 1950s, but cross-voted regularly against the 1970–4 government (Norton, 1978, 215 *et passim*). This was true of votes on Rhodesia sanctions, where around 20 backbenchers regularly opposed sanctions orders. One hundred and sixteen rebels opposed a Labour sanctions order in 1978, the record post-war Conservative rebellion in a 'whipped' vote.

Another 'imperial' policy issue that generated repeated rebellion was immigration control. It would, however, be wrong to assume that such revolts invariably involved racist 'imperialists'. Tory cross-voting against the 1962 Commonwealth Immigrants Bill did involve 'imperialists', but these sought to retain free entry into the imperial homeland from the Commonwealth and colonies (Norton, 1975, 195–6). Tory rebellions against the party line on Labour's 1968 Commonwealth Immigrants Bill, which rose to 25 MPs in one vote, mostly represented the unease of the 'progressive' left wing of the party, involving future 'wets' like Ian Gilmour, Norman St. John-Stevas and Michael Heseltine (Norton, 1975, 280ff). It was when immigration rules became entangled with the requirements of EEC membership in 1972 that the issue produced what was at the time the worst post-war government defeat (Norton, 1978, 240). A roll call of at least 56 anti-marketeers and old 'imperialists' rebelled, seven of them cross-voting (Norton, 1975, 523–5).

Europe 1945–75

Controversy over EEC entry in the 1950s and early 1960s concentrated on several key areas of policy dispute. Five backbench groupings on

Europe were identified from EDM signing in the 1955–9 Parliament: European Stalwarts, Europe and Empire, Empire Moderates, Empire Stalwarts, and Uncommitted. Pro-European backbenchers were just outnumbered by Empire/Commonwealth protagonists (Finer, Berrington and Bartholomew, 1961, 89, 187–94). Sovereignty fears focused on the threat to the legislative process and the English legal tradition. Economic policy disputes focused on whether trade would best be served by developing Commonwealth links or by entering the EC. The impact of entry on farmers, a core Tory interest group, the cost-of-living implications of the Common Agricultural Policy (CAP), together with a more general fear of becoming identified with a foreign bureaucracy, raised fears of losing votes, especially in the party's crucial working-class electorate. By the time of Heath's 1971 entry application, the National Farmers' Union was for entry, and opposition had shifted from imperial sentiment towards a general concern with sovereignty and 'open seas' economic liberalism (Gamble, 1974, 199). More pragmatic opponents claimed that unemployment would rise and cost votes (Aughey, 1978, 19).

Labour's more serious crises over European integration from the 1960s to the 1980s have tended to conceal the fact that there were Conservative rebellions from the 1950s (Table 6.1), but the rebels were successfully marginalised by the strenuous efforts of party leaders. Harold Macmillan's first entry application was potentially even more divisive than the Maastricht Treaty. The symbols of Britain's sovereign power, visibly weakened by subordination to US economic policy and by North Atlantic Treaty Organisation (NATO) membership, nevertheless remained for all to see in the Commonwealth and remaining colonies (Norton and Aughey, 1981, 137–9). No senior minister rebelled, though Rab Butler hesitated and warned Macmillan, as Macmillan warned the Queen, that the party might well split over Europe (Macmillan, 1973, 128, 27). Macmillan issued a personal Euro-manifesto designed to win over party conference delegates in 1962 (Macmillan, 1962), and easily defeated an anti-Market amendment (Macmillan, 1973, 140). In Parliament just one MP cross-voted, though 24 abstained. De Gaulle's veto terminated Macmillan's entry application and the party's disputes, though the rebellion maintained its numerical strength in the 1967 vote on Labour's proposed entry application (Table 6.1).

Unlike Macmillan, Heath faced a rebellion involving a senior colleague; the sacked Cabinet minister, Enoch Powell, would eventually

TABLE 6.1.   *Key Conservative parliamentary rebellions against European integration, 1961–95*

Year	Vote	Cross-voters	Abstainers	Total rebels	Rebels as % of backbench MPs	Notes
1961	Con. government motion supporting EC entry application	1	24	25	9	Lab. support
1967	Lab. government motion supporting EC entry application	26	0	26	10	Con. support
1971	Con. government motion supporting EC entry application	39	2	41	16	Lab. oppose (Con. free vote)
1972i	Con. government European Communities Bill 2nd Reading. Heath's vote of confidence	15	5	20	8	Lab. oppose Govt majority 8
1972ii	Con. rebel pro-referendum amendment	22	9	31	12	Lab. support (Con. oppose)
1972iii	Con. government European Communities Bill 3rd Reading	16	4	20	8	Lab. oppose
1975	Lab. government Motion accepting 'renegotiated' entry terms	8	18	26	9	Con. support (Lab. free vote)
1978	European Assemblies Elections Bill Third Reading	9	0	9	3	Con. support Lab. Government
1986	European Communities Amendment (Single European Act) Bill 3rd Reading	7	0	7	2	
1992i	European Communities Amendment ('Maastricht') Bill 2nd Reading	22	4	26	10	
1992ii	European Communities Amendment ('Maastricht') Bill Paving Motion	26	6	32	13	Government maj. 3, with Lib.–Dem. votes

1993i	European Communities Amendment ('Maastricht') Bill, Council of the Regions amendment	26	18	44	17	Government defeat by 22 votes
1993ii	European Communities amendment ('Maastricht') Bill referendum amendment	38	13	51	20	Government win by 239 votes
1993iii	European Communities Amendment ('Maastricht') Bill Third Reading	41	5	46	18	Goverment majority 180
1993iv	Postponed Social Chapter vote, 22 July	23	1	24	9	Government defeat by 8 votes
1993v	Major's confidence vote, 23 July, on Social Chapter	0	1	1	0	Government maj. 40. Whip removed from abstainer
1994i	Major's confidence vote, 28 November, European Communities (Finance) Bill 2nd Reading	0	8	8	3	Lab. abstain. Govt majority 241. Whip removed from 8 rebels, 9th resigns
1994ii	Vote on Labour amendment to Finance Bill to abandon stage 2 of imposition of VAT on fuel	7	10	17	6	Government defeat by 8 votes. All but one of 'unwhipped' Euro-rebels rebel

Note: 'Abstainers' here refers to MPs known to have abstained on principle, rather than through non-political absence. Approximate percentage figures assume 80 MPs on the 'payroll' vote, (ie frontbenchers in government). A total of 86 Labour MPs defied their government in the 1967 vote, 89 in the 1971 vote, and 178 in the 1975 vote. 71 Labour MPs defied the official line to abstain on the Maastricht Bill Third Reading vote in 1993; 66 voted against the Treaty, 5 voted with the government.

Sources: Norton (1975, 1980); D. Baker, Gamble and Ludlam, (1994b); Gorman, (1993); McKie, (1993); House of Commons, Hansard.

leave the party and call for a Labour vote in 1974 to secure a referendum on continued Community membership. At the 1970 General Election a Voters Veto Campaign extracted pledges from many Conservative candidates to oppose entry (Spicer, 1992, 35). Opinion polls showed heavy majorities in 1970 against even applying again (George, 1994, 49). Heath launched an unprecedented campaign inside the party culminating in a meeting of 3000 activists who overwhelmingly supported application. At the 1971 party conference he forced a card vote that produced an eight to one majority for entry (Ashford, 1980, 104–6). Nevertheless in the Commons he was forced to rely on Labour rebels to win the vote ,on opening negotiations. This manouevre needs to be kept in perspective. No post-war government before Heath's had lost a Commons vote as a result of backbench dissent. Heath, starting with a majority of 15 that fell to 10, lost five such votes, but none was on Europe (Norton, 1975, 610ff). Aggregating Norton's figures shows that in 79 votes during the passage of the 1972 European Communities Bill, the average rebellion involved less than ten MPs (Norton, 1975). Only once did more than 20 rebel, demanding a referendum (Table 6.1). No rebels were disowned by their constituencies (Norton, 1980, 466).

Rebellions under Thatcher and Major

Although outright parliamentary disorder grew dramatically in the 1980s, it was confined to opposition MPs frustrated by Thatcher's radicalism and impregnable parliamentary majorities (Judge, 1992). There was frustration among Tory MPs but very little organised 'wet' dissent to Thatcher's programme in the early 1980s. Gilmour has subsequently blamed this failure on the absence of clear leadership from himself and other Cabinet 'wets' who were 'guilty of grave dereliction of duty' (Gilmour, 1993, 38). Following his sacking from the Cabinet, Francis Pym did launch a Conservative Centre Forward group to rally the 'wets' but it was 'virtually still-born', with an average attendance of just six MPs until it disbanded in 1987 (Pym, 1985; Brand, 1989). The important rebellions were on single issues. Thatcher's assault on trade unionism attracted dissent over the closed shop in 1980, and over ballot rules in 1984 when 90 MPs cross-voted, but the government was not defeated. It was defeated in 1982 when 50 cross-voted against the tightening of immigration rules, and at the Sunday Trading Bill's second reading in 1986, and also over social security benefits for the elderly in 1990 (D. Butler and G. Butler, 1994, 185). The old imperial sentiments resurfaced in the same year when Tebbit organised 80 MPs against the government's Bill on the status of Hong Kong citizenship. General discontent mounted in 1990 towards the end of Thatcher's premiership, by which time 70 backbenchers had stopped supporting the government on a range of issues, according to the Chief Whip (K. Baker, 1993, 330).

Arguably the most important rebellion under Thatcher was one of the least successful in terms of parliamentary voting. In the critical votes on the readings of the Poll Tax Bill in 1987–8 only 17 cross-voted; 29 cross-voted on a related local government Bill in 1990. Thirty-eight backed Michael Mates's amendment in 1988 to make the tax income-related, but Mates himself never expected to win (D. Butler, Adonis and Travers, 1994, 234ff). The overwhelming majority of the Poll Tax cross-voters were ex-ministers or longstanding backbenchers with no ambition to enter government. One, however, Heseltine, would use the Poll Tax to launch his leadership bid in November 1990, producing what was by any criterion the most spectacular act of rebellion by MPs in the party's history. A sitting prime minister had been removed by backbench rebellion comparatively recently, when Chamberlain won the vote on the conduct of the war but lost the support of 98 of his MPs in 1940 and resigned. In November 1990 Thatcher was preparing for war in the Gulf, a fact considered likely to protect her from removal by patriotic Tory MPs. Having won three elections in a row, and wars against military enemies without and class enemies within, how could they sack her? In November 1989 no fewer than 57 MPs had declined to support Thatcher when challenged by a 'stalking horse' protesting against the Poll Tax. After the shattering by-election loss at Eastbourne in 1990 where the Poll Tax had been virtually the only issue, 152 backed Heseltine in the first leadership ballot, with Thatcher four votes short of the 15 per cent majority needed to secure re-election. After vowing to fight on, she lost the support of the majority of her Cabinet and resigned (Alderman and Carter, 1991; Smith, 1994a). The Poll Tax and Europe, over which Howe's resignation had triggered Heseltine's challenge, had combined to produce the greatest rebellion of the party's long history.

Europe 1975–95

> Mrs Thatcher seems content with a broad church on Europe, a freer
> discussion, whereas Mr Heath desired the Community of Saints to follow the
> European vision. Differences of opinion remain, but this tolerance has
> dissipated much of the bitterness. Mrs Thatcher does not want a divided
> party. (Aughey, 1978, 24)

> It was always clear to me that the Conservative Party could be successfully
> led only by someone who took their stand in the centre of the spectrum on
> this issue [Europe], where the silent majority dwelt. Margaret's evident
> determination to lead the Party from one of the two extremes of that
> spectrum spelled nothing but trouble. (Lawson, 1992, 923)

By 1975, the parliamentary advantages of maintaining unity, against a
fractured Labour Party that had won four of the previous five
elections, overwhelmed the hesitations of all but the most irreconcilable
opponents of European integration. Powell's defection in 1974, calling
for a Labour vote to secure a referendum, and Heath's removal from
the leadership that he was widely felt to have abused in pursuit of entry,
lessened Conservative divisions in the referendum campaign. Thatcher
did not adopt a prominent stance. Her commitment to membership at
the time was unquestioned (Thatcher, 1977). She initially thought that
Heath might lead the party's referendum campaign that she left to her
Europeanist deputy leader, William Whitelaw. There remained a
persistent group of backbench rebels who had campaigned for a
referendum (Goodhart, 1976), but Labour's open divisions and
Thatcher's less fervent pro-European image lowered the temperature
of Tory dissent. The 67.2 per cent 'yes' vote reduced rebel morale and
suggested calmer times ahead. The biggest rebellion on Europe while
Thatcher was Leader of the Opposition was by 14 pro-European Tories
opposing an amendment, moved by Powell and supported by the
Conservative frontbench, to prevent proportional representation being
used in European elections (Norton, 1980, 318). She gave unprecedented opposition party support to Labour's guillotine motion to
secure direct elections to the European Assembly (Ashford, 1980,
116), and in 1978 she harassed Labour for not joining the new
European Monetary System and its ERM (J. W. Young, 1993, 134).
At the same time she offered a more cautious vision of Europe as 'a
partnership of nation states each retaining the right to protect its vital
interests' (cited in Aughey, 1978, 24). Ashford characterised this

attitude as 'confederalist', and argued that this view dominated the party by 1979. Confederalists supported inter-governmental cooperation on economic, foreign, and defence policies. The federalists, believers in a United States of Europe, were a small grouping, but influential because of their long-term association with the Europeanist cause. The majority of the party were less enthusiastic, generally positive about membership but irritated by the CAP and other interventionist policies. Outright 'anti-marketeers', in Ashford's view, had become 'virtually irrelevant' (Ashford, 1980, 110–12).

Europe hardly seemed a divisive issue in Thatcher's early Downing Street years, when she conducted a prolonged and nationalistic campaign to reduce the UK contribution to the EC budget (Chapter 13; J. W. Young, 1993, 140–51; George, 1994, 137–66). Cabinet disagreements over how far to press the 'British Budgetary Question' did exist (Pym, 1984, 90ff). Thatcher and her Foreign Secretary traded resignation threats over the deal Lord Carrington had brokered (Gilmour, 1992, 293), but such divisions did not produce significant parliamentary dissent, and Thatcher's successful campaign to reform the CAP received widespread support (Peterson, 1992, 162). The striking development from the mid-1980s was not rebellion by Ashford's federalists against Thatcher's confederalism, but the bitterness within the ranks of the party's triumphant 'Thatcherite' confederalists. Thatcher's struggle from 1985 against her Chancellor and Foreign Secretary over membership of the ERM, including the vital confrontation before the 1989 Madrid Summit followed by Howe's removal from the Foreign Office and Lawson's later resignation, are described in Chapter 13, and the main protagonists have now published their accounts (Lawson, 1992; Thatcher, 1993; G. Howe, 1994; cf. K. Baker, 1993). The divisions still did not lead to organised backbench dissent. The passage of the Single European Act (SEA) in 1985/6 produced only minor dissent (Table 6.1). Rebels highlighted the commitment in the Act's preamble to the eventual aim of Economic and Monetary Union (EMU), conceded to achieve the single market (Ridley, 1992, 142–3; Thatcher, 1993, 555). Veteran anti-marketeers also opposed the introduction of the qualified majority voting (QMV) procedure that removed the national veto. Thatcher had pushed for the use of QMV for the limited purpose of overcoming protectionist resistance to the single market (Thatcher, 1993, 550–3). It would be the extension of QMV to new policy areas in the Maastricht Treaty that most alarmed many of the party's increasingly hostile confederalists. To the Bruges

Group QMV was 'extinguishing the last vestiges of sovereignty necessary for self protection' (Bruges Group, 1991, iv).

Thatcher's Bruges speech in September 1988, after which the group was named, was widely seen as re-opening the party's Euro-divisions. The speech's content was more ambivalent than its reputation (Parsons, 1989, 163), and did little more than repeat her well-known view that 'willing and active cooperation between independent sovereign states is the best way to build a successful European Community' (Thatcher, 1988). The widely-quoted remark that, 'We have not successfully rolled back the frontiers of the state only to see them reimposed at the European level' gives the clue as to why the speech caused such a stir: its intended audience was not only in Brussels, but within her party and Cabinet. Lawson argues that it was Thatcher's subsequent 'crude populist anti-Europeanism' in the disastrous 1989 European election campaign that lit a fuse under a 'hitherto largely quiescent' party (Lawson, 1992, 922). Within eighteen months of Thatcher's sacking, her wing of the party was divided and openly mobilising against her chosen successor. The divisions widened in part because of Major's commitment to membership of the ERM. The fact that Thatcher had taken Britain in just before her sacking reduced the factional impact of the issue, but this constraint weakened as the deflationary impact on the economy worsened. The humiliation and the financial cost of resistance to expulsion from the ERM in September 1992 (Chapter 9) unleashed rebel fury, which seemed vindicated when the then-Chancellor published his own bitter account of Black Wednesday (Lamont, 1993).

The Maastricht Rebellion

What mainly detonated the rebellion, however, was the Maastricht Treaty, whose acceleration of the pace of political integration was precisely what Thatcher had sought to thwart by promoting the Single Market. When the Danes' first referendum in June 1992 rejected the Treaty, a Commons EDM urging Major to 'make a fresh start' was signed by 84 Conservative MPs, far more than had voted the month before against the Second Reading of the Maastricht Bill (Table 6.1). When exit from the ERM reduced Major's economic and European policy to ruins, a second 'fresh start' EDM quickly attracted 65 'Euro-sceptics' (Spicer, 1993, 201ff). Major's opt-outs from the Maastricht

Treaty (Chapter 13) had been intended in part to preserve party unity in two contentious areas, economic and monetary union, and social policy. But for the Euro-rebels they merely highlighted the federalist trend, and they also alienated Labour and Liberal-Democrat leaders who backed the Treaty in its entirety. The rebels regarded the notion of irrevocability in the Treaty as setting it apart from previous developments. Assurances, of the kind offered since Macmillan's entry application, that any particular move towards European integration was but a single step without significant consequences, and was necessary to secure British influence over future EC development, had lost their effectiveness by 1992 (Ridley, 1992, 160 *et passim*).

Hailed by one veteran anti-marketeer and former Leader of the House of Commons as the 'champions of Westminster', rebels were boosted by the gift of Westminster offices by a former national treasurer and over £300 000 from overseas supporters (Biffen, 1993; *Sunday Times*, 18 July 1994). They were also sustained by polling evidence of both public and party opinion, and the covert sympathy of a group of serving ministers (Leigh, 1993). Above all, the rebellion was joined by Thatcher herself and three former party chairpersons, Norman Tebbit, Cecil Parkinson and Kenneth Baker. Tebbit described the Treaty as 'close to treason' and called on Tory MPs to vote with Labour to defeat the Bill. Thatcher declared in Parliament that she would never have signed the treaty, that it was a betrayal of the trust placed in MPs, and voted against the party Whip for the first time in her life. The rebels also had significant support from the Tory press, in particular from the *Sunday Telegraph* and the Murdoch press which villified Major's leadership in *The Times* (Rees-Mogg, 1993).

The rebels were also sustained by their beliefs, but were far from being an ideologically coherent group (Spicer, 1993, 167–85). Some were veteran anti-marketeers like Teddy Taylor who rejected European interference in favour of economic independence. Others, like the rebels' parliamentary draughtsman Bill Cash, were 'constitutionalists' opposed to the further loss of legislative sovereignty from Westminster. Others, like Nicholas Budgen, were neo-liberal Thatcherites more specifically concerned at the loss of independent monetary policy-making implied by economic and monetary union. The European issue always divided those who place the highest priority on the formal sovereignty of the British Parliament from those who regard the pooled sovereignty of the EC as the best guarantee of Britain's international influence and domestic prosperity. Now the Maastricht rebellion illustrated more dramatically than ever the extent to which a sovereignty/interdependence dimension was displacing and cutting across the party's traditional ideological faultline over how interventionist the state should be (D. Baker, Gamble and Ludlam, 1993a, 1994a). The extension of QMV, the pursuit of a single currency and a European Central Bank, and the fear of a Maastricht Mark Two emerging from the 1996 Inter-governmental Conference (IGC) all threatened Conservative unity because of fears over sovereignty.

The general lines of argument took two forms. One concerned the wisdom of pooling sovereignty to maximise the British influence, prosperity and security which were seen as the real purpose of possessing sovereignty. The 'pooling' case had been presented at length by Geoffrey Howe, who argued that by an 'infinite gradation of joint decision making in the EC', the UK was seeking 'to maximize its sovereign power – to the fullest possible extent' (G. Howe, 1990, 678, 687; cf. Heseltine, 1987, 273–4; Gilmour, 1992, 323–5). The opposing rebel point of view was put simply by Michael Spicer: 'I do not understand the concept of pooling sovereignty. One either has or does not have sovereignty' (Commons Hansard, 24 March 1993, Col. 1174). A related argument stressed the impact of pooling sovereignty on British parliamentary democracy and liberty. Tebbit warned a fringe meeting at the 1994 party conference that, 'Those essential bulwarks of British democratic self-government, government in Parliament, administration by impartial civil servants, accountability through Parliament, law-making open to scrutiny, justice dispensed by an independent judiciary under the statute and common law, are being swiftly eroded.' (European Foundation, 1994b, 7–8; cf. Minogue, 1990, 20; Hill, 1993).

The defence of sovereignty was rarely absolute, however. Membership always meant subordination of Westminster law to Community law, and very few rebels any longer called for withdrawal. When Norman Lamont floated the possibility during the party conference in 1994, he was disowned by Euro-rebel leaders, most damningly by Tebbit. This second form of the sovereignty argument surfaces over QMV. Ambivalence is displayed by rebels who defend the use of QMV to create the single market, pooling sovereignty in pursuit of economic liberalism, but attack the new uses of QMV in the Maastricht Treaty as undermining national sovereignty. On currency control and independent central banking, older divisions over state intervention are crisscrossed by new disputes within the 'monetarist' camp of the early 1980s over whether discretion in monetary policy should be retained by the

British government or whether it should be 'privatised' at a European level. 'Fixers v Floaters', a chapter title in Thatcher's memoirs, reflects a *laissez-faire* antagonism to all fixed exchange rate mechanisms that unites Thatcher and her adviser Alan Walters with other Euro-rebels happy even to invoke Keynes's opposition to Churchill's return to the Gold Standard in 1925 (Walters, 1989; Ridley, 1991, 194 *et passim*; Spicer, 1992, 96, 100). This antagonism combined with a view of exchange rate management as a treacherous denial of money supply-targeted monetarism. The neo-liberal position was most bluntly put by rebel Teresa Gorman: 'I wish with all my heart we could be an offshore island like Hong Kong, a free trade area with the minimum of government intervention and the maximum of business activity' (Gorman, 1993, 190).

The Maastricht Treaty united such neo-liberals with other Euro-dissenters into a formidable parliamentary rebellion. Heath did not lose a vote on Europe, unlike Major. The difference is not accounted for by the size of the two leaders' majorities, they were similarly small when opposition was most fierce. One crucial change was the discipline of the Labour Party. On key votes in the 1970s, Heath could rely on Labour cross-voters to carry the pro-European line. In the 1990s Labour was officially pro-European and the large number of Labour Euro-sceptics were prepared to support the official line to defeat Major's government. An alliance was struck between opposition parties who believed Major would adopt the treaty's Social Chapter rather than abandon the treaty, and rebels who hoped Major would rather abandon the treaty, resulting in humiliating government U-turns on Labour's Social Chapter amendments, which were accepted in exchange for postponing the vote until after the Bill's passage. The government resorted to ducking votes and conceding other amendments it thought it would lose. The rebels' unofficial whipping system was effective, and enraged the Whips (Gorman 1993, 197–209). Major finally played the 'orange card', concluding a pact with the Ulster Unionists to survive the postponed Social Chapter votes on 22 July 1993, but still lost. He called a vote of confidence and all but one of the rebels capitulated. Mutually assured electoral destruction and a pro-integration Labour government was the alternative. There was no parliamentary party to the right of the Conservatives that could provide the rebels with the sort of platform that the far-right parties gave their European counterparts. The only indisputable consequence of bringing down Major's government would have been to bring into office a government committed to the whole Treaty and to further integration.

The collapse of the ERM in August 1993 eased tensions. In a much-cited *Economist* article in September 1993, Major insisted the EU should 'remain a union of sovereign national states' and 'resist the temptation to recite the mantra of full economic and monetary union as if nothing had changed' (Major, 1993). More tensions were eased at the party conference in October 1993. Though rebel motions were suppressed, rebels used the conference fringe to launch a book about the rebellion (Gorman 1993), and Bill Cash launched the European Foundation to carry on the campaign. The conference cheered Brussels-bashing platform speeches by Cabinet ministers, and Major's own speech promised that the party would fight the 1994 European Parliament (EP) election as 'the only mainstream party not prepared to move towards a centralised Europe'. Tebbit said Major was now 'singing the sceptics' tune'. Fears that divisions would nevertheless explode during the EP election campaign were heightened in March 1994 when Major performed a dramatic U-turn on the reform of QMV (Ludlam, 1995). To the delight of his backbench sceptics, Major had called Labour leader John Smith 'Monsieur Oui, the poodle of Brussels', so the climbdown that followed sparked bitter recriminations and universal speculation that Major could not survive the summer. Few backbenchers dissented from the sentiment expressed in a special rebel statement entitled 'The British Capitulation on the Blocking Minority' (European Foundation, 1994b).

The rebels issued a fierce manifesto ahead of the EP election, but the demand for unity in the campaign succeeded, if only because the rebels did not wish to be blamed for the anticipated electoral disaster. The party fought the campaign as the enemies of a 'socialist superstate' run from Brussels and as defenders of the 'national veto' on unspecified 'issues of vital national interest' (Conservative Party, 1994a; George and Ludlam, 1994). 'Europe right or left not Europe right or wrong' was the slogan aimed at winning over both voters and parliamentary dissidents. It appeared to win over the latter, but failed spectacularly to win over the former. The result was the worst for the party in a national election this century (Chapter 3). It was reduced to 18 MEPs in the 'deep south' as the Liberal Democrats won their first two seats and Labour took 62 seats.

Somewhat to the surprise of commentators, Major survived the election results relatively unscathed. The party's losses were less dramatic than had been widely predicted. Most importantly, Major's veto at the Corfu EU Summit of Jean-Luc Dehaene's succession to Jacques Delors as President of the European Commission was received on his backbenches as a long-overdue act of defiance. In the run-up to the 1994 party conference Major responded to German Christian Democratic Union (CDU) proposals to form a two-tier Europe, as opposed to a single-tiered multi-track Europe in which all members participated in all policy-making, by declaring in Leiden that, 'I recoil from ideas for a Union in which some would be more equal than others' (Major, 1994a). The conference again feasted on anti-European Commission jibes, delivered to noisy cheers by Michael Portillo, whose ovation eclipsed the traditional platform favourite (but pro-European) Heseltine. An academic survey of Conservative MPs during 1994 found, as Table 6.2 shows, that the conference's scepticism was more widely shared on the backbenches than the numerical strength of the Euro-rebellions in 1993 had revealed (D. Baker, Fountain, Gamble and Ludlam, 1994b, 1995). Convinced of the advantages of membership, the attitudes of majorities of Tory MPs were nevertheless clearly sceptical, and closer to the rebels on some issues such as a single currency referendum, cohesion funds and the Commission's right to initiate legislation. Any moves to further integration at the IGC in 1996 seemed bound to produce more turmoil. In terms of party management, the sizes of the minorities of either Euro-enthusiasts or Euro-sceptics demonstrated the depth of divisions in the PCP, and were arguably as serious a sign for party leaders as was the sympathy for rebel positions. Minorities of just 20 per cent represent about 50 backbenchers, and minorities of 30 per cent nearer 80. On the referendum issue, there appeared to be over 100 backbenchers on both sides of the divide, though opinion later shifted as even more MPs came to see the referendum more as a device to save the party than to protect British sovereignty.

The explicit sanction by party leaders of the pro-European cause throughout most of the period discussed here was a crucial factor in the behaviour of pro-Europeans. During the Maastricht rebellion, leaders of pro-European groups in the party like the Conservative Group for Europe (founded 1970) and the new (1993) Positive European group of around 90 MPs concentrated on parliamentary activity against the rebels, organising no equivalent of the rebels' public Maastricht Referendum Campaign. The Conservative Group for Europe published *The Positive Europe* to 'redress the balance' disturbed by 'a

TABLE 6.2   *Backbench Conservative MPs' attitudes in 1994 to European integration*

Statement	Strongly agree or agree %	Neither %	Disagree or strongly disagree %
The disadvantages of EC membership have been outweighed by the benefits	59	9	32
An Act of Parliament should be passed to establish explicitly the ultimate supremacy of Parliament over EU legislation	56	16	28
Britain should block the use of QMV in the areas of foreign and defence policy	87	6	7
The establishment of a single EU currency would signal the end of the UK as a sovereign nation	51	11	38
Britain should never rejoin the ERM	52	15	33
There should be a national referendum before the UK enters a single currency	55	4	41
Britain should adopt the Social Protocol	5	2	93
Cohesion funds should be phased out	66	18	16
The 1996 IGC should not increase the supranational powers of EU institutions	88	5	7
The Commission should lose the right to initiate legislation	61	4	35

Source: University of Sheffield Parliament Project Survey, conducted April to June 1994 (D. Baker, Fountain, Gamble and Ludlam, 1995).

small but determined group of . . . Europhobes . . . chasing phantoms of its own creation' (I. Taylor, 1993). A sign of increasing pro-European discontent came in 1994 with the launch of the Action Centre for Europe (ACE) to combat the 'wave of anti-European sentiment' unleashed by right-wing intellectuals and 'influential elements of the press' (ACE, 1995). With Lord Whitelaw as Patron, Lord Howe as President, and Cabinet Ministers Kenneth Clarke and David Hunt on the Advisory Council, it listed prominent leaders of existing Conservative pro-European groups as well as the Confederation of British Industry and other prominent City and business interests among its supporters and contacts. Howe published an appeal to

Cabinet pro-Europeans to fight back against the sceptical direction of policy into 'a ghetto of sentimentality and self-delusion' (G. Howe, 1995).

A Wider Thatcherite Rebellion?

Surveys of ideological groupings in the PCP in the 1980s and 1990s have tended to draw two conclusions in common, whether based on methodical academic research (Norton, 1990) or on close journalistic observation (Riddell, 1992). The largest grouping of Tory MPs is said to be that of the 'loyalist', shapeless mass of backbenchers with no strong general ideological commitments. Second, ideologically defined groupings that can be identified are said to be indistinct and rarely engage in factional rebellions across a range of issues. One of the most interesting questions asked about the Euro-rebellion is whether it forms the core of a broader factional phenomenon. The evidence is not strong. Reports after the ratification of the Maastricht Treaty that the 'Fresh Start' group of sceptics was forming itself into a general purpose faction proved premature. Under Heath there had been some evidence that Europe was an arithmetical common factor among persistent rebels, but the clearly identifiable neo-liberal grouping that reacted against Heath's economic policy U-turn never raised its dissident vote above 13 (Norton, 1978, 122). It is clear that under Major disappointed supporters of Mrs Thatcher did focus their discontent on Europe, but that was in part precisely because they found it difficult to specify a general platform from which to oppose Major. He did, after all, extend the 'Thatcher revolution' in education, health and the civil service far beyond Thatcher's own achievements in these fields (Chapter 11), and tackled the long-delayed privatisations of the rail and coal industries. In spite of their chorus of more spending cuts and lower taxes, the right-wing of the PCP, including its Euro-rebels, could have little doubt that cuts in public expenditure by the mid-1990s, especially in social spending, went further than Thatcher ever attempted. Even on Europe, it was Major, not Thatcher, who had finally confronted the single currency and the Social Chapter by negotiating the opt-outs.

Thatcher did not assume the party leadership or the premiership on the crest of a broad wave of Thatcherite party or public opinion (Crewe and Searing, 1988). If anything, public opinion moved against the key tenets of Thatcherism (Crewe, 1989). Neither, even by 1990, was more than around a fifth of the PCP identifiably Thatcherite (Norton, 1990). This made the presence of known Thatcherites in key government departments crucial. Hence one source of factional discontent was the justified perception that the balance of influence within Major's governments and Cabinets swung against Thatcherite ministers (D. Baker, Gamble and Ludlam, 1992b; Ludlam, 1993). Major's small majority and the impact of the Maastricht rebellion narrowed his room for manoeuvre, and this was the real significance of his famous off-air remark after the July 1993 confidence vote,

> The real problem is one of a tiny majority. . . . You have three right-wing members of the Cabinet who actually resign. What happens in the parliamentary party? . . . I could bring in other people. But where do you think most of this poison is coming from? From the dispossessed and the never-possessed. You can think of ex-ministers who are going round causing all sorts of trouble. We don't want another three more of the bastards out there.

An attempt in 1994 by the main Thatcherite faction, the Conservative Way Forward group (president, Margaret Thatcher), to influence Major's choice of ministers ended in humiliation when its delegation was ejected from Downing Street without delivering their submission. But unlike Thatcher, who was able to get rid of her Cabinet 'wets' over time, Major remained stuck with Cabinet members who issued open calls for a rightward change of course to put 'clear blue water' between the party and its opponents (Portillo, 1994b).

Rebellions under Major on non-European issues did not present evidence of broader factional behaviour in parliamentary votes of disgruntled Thatcherites. The most widely forecast and publicised rebellions forced a review that postponed the pit closure programme for a while, and a compensation package for the elderly at the time of the original decision to put VAT on domestic fuel. But such issues were always more likely to mobilise the party's left, the numbers involved were in single figures, and the involvement of Euro-rebels was marginal. If anything disparate frustrations over unconnected policy issues found a common focus over Europe, which cut across so many tendentious issues. This seemed to be the case as frustration over the collapse of Post Office privatisation in November 1994 stiffened the resolve of the Euro-rebellion against the Community budget increases that Major made a vote of confidence, from which eight MPs abstained, though this coincided with widespread backbench fury over new revelations of the level of fraudulent expenditure of Community funds.

The eight abstainers lost the Whip and were joined by another protester to form a 'Gang of Nine'. Ironically, Major appeared to have created a voting faction where none had previously existed. Freed from the whip, eight of the nine then withheld support from the government on a non-European issue as the second stage of the unpopular VAT on fuel decision was thrown out in the Commons. They rebelled again over a European Common Fishery Policy reform. Pressed later to vote with the 'minority' government to maintain its right to the majority of the seats on standing committees so crucial to its legislative programme, only five of the nine obliged. Facing disaster in the May 1995 local elections (Chapter 3), Major felt obliged to re-unite the parliamentary party. The Whip was restored to the expelled rebels, with no strings attached. The rebels gloated, and Major and his Chief Whip were portrayed as humiliated.

The proportion of backbenchers willing to engage in repeated rebellion over Europe grew to unprecedented levels under Major (Table 6.1). The main general factors explaining this trend were the right-wing alarm over Thatcher's sacking that undermined appeals to loyalty and unity at Westminster, the acceleration of apparently irrevocable European integration set out in the Maastricht Treaty, the public denunciation of such developments by Thatcher and other former senior leaders, dismay at the effect of Britain's membership of ERM and the manner of its expulsion, financial support from wealthy Tories, the encouragement of crucial sections of the Tory press and of public and party opinion. The rebels' attitudes, if not their behaviour, were supported by a majority of their less rebellious backbench colleagues (Table 6.2). Analysis of party members' attitudes revealed them also to be closer to the party's rebels on key issues. A 1992 survey of party members conducted before the ERM humiliation found that 53 per cent agreed that 'Conservatives should resist further moves towards European integration', and 57 per cent that 'A future Conservative government should not agree to a single European currency' (Whiteley, Seyd and Richardson, 1994, 57). Euro-sceptics have long felt that events and public opinion would inexorably move opinion in their direction (Bulpitt, 1992). By 1995, Major was hoping European integration issues would abate, and was constructing a European policy that he hoped would isolate all but a handful of irreconcilable anti-marketeers. He intended to prevent the 1996 IGC resulting in any constitutional proposals that would ignite his rebels or make a divisive referendum unavoidable. The retirements of Jacques Delors and President Mitterrand gave him hope that his 'British Agenda' would gain more support in Europe, too, and help lessen domestic tensions. In 1995 the government launched a diplomatic offensive to secure French opposition to further integrationist initiatives. The rebels remained cynical. Major's frustration was compounded by angry defiance of his personal authority when he addressed their Fresh Start group in June 1995. He resigned the leadership, demanding his critics 'shut up or put up'. Major wrote that 'One issue above all others created this cauldron: Europe' (*Daily Telegraph*, 3 July 1995). Redwood, one of his cabinet 'bastards', resigned to fight on a platform of outright opposition to the single currency and Major's opt-out strategy. Major resisted calls to buy dissident votes with even the distant promise of a referendum. All but one Tory national paper abandoned him. Major's victory by 218 to 89, with 20 abstentions or spoiled papers, did not clear the air. Members of the 'Gang of Nine' acclaimed the gang of eighty-nine, pointing out that, discounting the 'payroll vote', nearly half the party's backbenchers had apparently deserted Major, and seemed unlikely to 'shut up'. If MPs attitudes demonstrated in Table 6.2 are anything to go by, then almost any acceleration of integration at the 1996 IGC will generate even more rebellion in a PCP that has rarely, if ever, been more damagingly divided by parliamentary dissent. Only the fact that the IGC would take place very close to the next general election gave Major an effective weapon against the rebels: the same fear of electoral annihilation that had forced them, finally, to capitulate in their struggle against the Maastricht Treaty.

Note

The author thanks Martin Smith and Andrew Gamble for comments on an earlier draft, and the ESRC for funding the research on which Table 6.2 is based. The ESRC research was conducted with Imogen Fountain, Andrew Gamble and David Baker.

7

Remaking the Opposition?

ADAM LENT and MATTHEW SOWEMIMO

Introduction

The failure of either the Conservative or Labour parties to deal successfully with Britain's relative economic decline in the post-war decades had a profound impact on party politics. Between 1959 and 1983 neither party won re-election after serving a full term of office. The volatility of the electorate undermined the two-party system as the Liberal and nationalist parties claimed large shares of the vote (Chapter 3). From the 1960s the energies of many disenchanted with the performance of the mainstream parties were directed into single-issue pressure groups from the Child Poverty Action Group and (social security) Claimants Unions to the Vietnam Solidarity Campaign, and broader social movements like the women's liberation movement and the Gay Liberation Front. The inflationary world, deflationary policies and mass unemployment of the 1970s further damaged the cohesion of the main parties, especially Labour (Ludlam, 1994), and created the opportunity for the Thatcherite agenda to capture the Conservative Party (Chapter 2). By the mid-1980s Margaret Thatcher was claiming to have marked out new territory in British politics, and to have forced rival parties to follow her on to it. Her apparent electoral invincibility, virtually guaranteed by the breakaway from the main opposition party of the SDP in 1981, added to the frustration of activists who frequently turned to single-issue campaigns and 'new social movements' in pursuit of political agendas previously monopolised by the main parties, or by trade unions now shackled by Thatcher's reforms (Hinton, 1989;

Church, 1992; Saggar, 1992; Chapter 10; Lovenduski and Randall, 1993). This chapter considers the impact of unbroken Conservative rule from 1979 on the political and organisational coherence of the major opposition parties, and on other forms of political opposition.

The Parties

Both the Labour and Liberal Democrat parties have felt obliged to respond to Conservative dominance. Arguably the most powerful impact of contemporary Conservatism on Labour has been straightforward electoral defeat. This gave potency to Kinnock's regular call for the winning of the next election to be Labour's 'unremitting objective' to which all other activities were to be subordinated. It has been further argued that Kinnock, Smith, Blair and their supporters also set out to imitate the style, ethos and policy of Thatcherism in order to win back lost votes (Heffernan and Marqusee, 1992; Hay, 1994). This is a simplistic analysis. The left-wing agenda of the early 1980s was itself but a short-term deviation from a traditionally moderate and pro-capitalist record, especially when the party found itself in office (M. J. Smith, 1992, 1994b). It is true that many of the reforms were influenced by Thatcherite themes such as low taxation, individualism or material self-advancement. It is true that Labour policy is no longer as distinct from Conservative policy as it was in its 1983 or 1987 manifestos. But Labour is not just a set of policies: it is also a whole range of ideological debates, organisational structures and identities that cannot simply be bolted on to another party's platform. To see the new Labour Party as a paler carbon copy of Thatcherism is to ignore such factors.

The same general argument applies also to the Liberal Democrats, whose very emergence from the wreckage of the Liberal/SDP Alliance is testimony to the significance of organisational factors. The Liberal Democrats subsequent response to Conservative dominance in the 1988–94 period had two main features. In the 1988–92 period, when the newly formed party was attempting to establish an identity, its leadership developed a post-Thatcherite programme seeking to utilise market disciplines in order to achieve traditional Liberal Democrat objectives. After 1992, in the aftermath of a fourth consecutive Tory victory, the Liberal Democrat leader, Paddy Ashdown, sought to capitalise on popular disaffection with what he claimed was a stagnant political system and a discredited political class. In this phase the

Liberal Democrats took on a far more populist stance, drawing on the experience of other 'anti-politics' movements in Western Europe and America.

Changes in Policy

The pace of major policy shifts in the main opposition parties differed, but had in common an apparent accommodation with neo-liberal economic policy objectives and mechanisms. Labour in the early 1980s was characterised by confused and limited shifts on policy (Benn, 1980; Whiteley, 1983; Pimlott, 1984). An earlier attempt to form a social democratic breakaway had floundered (Taverne, 1974), but the SDP split (Bradley, 1981) galvanised Labour's remaining social democratic wing. The first four years of Kinnock's leadership saw some major policy developments: acceptance of Britain's EC membership, the right to buy council houses and the dropping of commitments to repeal all Tory anti-trade union legislation and to renationalise all privatised firms. However, such shifts were often unclear in a period when other major antagonisms like the miners' strike, the rate-capping rebellions and the *Militant* issue overshadowed, and even defined, much that the party did (Crick, 1986; Seyd, 1987; Wainwright, 1987). It was not until 1987 that the inner core of the leadership was able to utilise its most persuasive argument for a policy overhaul, namely the party's unexpectedly poor showing in its third successive general election defeat (Hughes and Wintour, 1990; M. J. Smith and Spear, 1992; Shaw, 1994) .

The policy review, which began shortly after the 1987 conference, set the tone for further development of policy into the 1990s. Membership of the EC, the principal issue that produced the SDP split (Owen, 1992), was wholeheartedly embraced. Support for the Social Chapter, membership of the ERM, and the extension of monetary and political integration would become key features of party policy. After unilateral disarmament was officially dropped in the review, there followed a policy of strong support for multilateral arms negotiations and membership of NATO, alongside limited criticism of NATO strategy and Tory defence policy, specifically the purchase of Trident nuclear missiles. The review also proposed constitutional reforms, including a freedom of information Act, Scottish and Welsh assemblies, a ministry for women, and an elected second chamber.

Most fundamental were the indications of major shifts in economic policy. Nationalisation as the key policy commitment was rejected in favour of renationalisation only of those industries regarded as more efficient and fair under public control such as water and electricity, as well as British Rail and the Post Office. Instead there was an emphasis on regulation of private concerns in the interests of the environment and good industrial relations. Large-scale public spending to end unemployment was replaced by a partnership between the government, the public sector and business to ensure investment and training in order to make Britain internationally competitive. Trade union activity would still be legally controlled but by less harsh legislation. Unions would no longer play more than a consultative role in a Labour government's economic policy. The vestiges of a universalist welfare benefits policy were threatened by the expected impact of the report of Social Justice Commission (Commission on Social Justice, 1994).

Policy reform was a direct response to the catastrophic loss of votes to the Conservative Party. As Kinnock pointed out in an interview in *New Socialist*, if Labour had won the 1987 election there would not have been a 'great rethink of policy because you get elected on those policies [that won the election] and then you attempt to implement them' (Mortimer, 1988, 6).

Many of the most significant disputes over reform were thus influenced or shaped in some way by Conservative policy: the dropping of the commitment to renationalisation in response to large-scale privatisation; internal party conflict over the repeal of Conservative trade union legislation; the changing economic agenda, moving away from Keynesianism towards tight spending control with knock-on effects on welfare and public sector policy. It is worth noting, however, that much of the Thatcherite economic policy agenda had in turn been prefigured under Labour in the mid-1970s (Ludlam, 1992).

Given the consumer-orientation of much post-war Liberal Party economic policy, the main shifts in Liberal Democrat economic policy were on macro-economic policy. The new economic policy initiated by Ashdown and Alan Beith (the parliamentary Treasury spokesman) showed the impact of Conservative dominance. The reshaping of the party's economic policy occurred during 1991–2 and was later to face a backlash from a disquieted party membership. The key policy positions were contained in macro-economic and competition policy.

The Liberal Democrats' initial economic policy paper, *Britain's Industrial Future*, had supported a centralised system of pay bargaining including a corporatist-style annual assessment and public discussion of wage increases (Liberal Democrats, 1989, 12). Its successor policy document, *Economics for the Future*, turned full-circle on this issue and supported a further decentralisation of pay bargaining. It repudiated legally-enforced incomes policy, a long-time commitment of the Liberals and the Alliance. This document adopted an almost fatalistic accommodation with Thatcherite labour market deregulation, arguing, 'It is also difficult to reconcile centralisation of pay bargaining with the increasing contractual complexity of the labour market as firms tend towards the structure of the small core staff controlling a floating population of temporary part time or fixed term contract employees' (Liberal Democrats, 1991).

More fundamental was the Liberal Democrats' support for an independent Bank of England committed to maintain price stability. *Economics for the Future* argued that the historical record showed that politicians could not be trusted to conduct a consistent counter-inflationary monetary policy. The document criticised the Thatcherite Medium Term Financial Strategy as being too lax, and supported strict rules in setting macroeconomic policy. The arguments used by Beith and Ashdown in support of an independent Bank of England are very similar to the positions of those neo-liberal economists who have advocated constitutionally entrenching the price stability objective through an independent central bank, in order to constrain politicians in their management of economic policy.

The Thatcherite stress on sound money and anti-inflationary policy induced a defensiveness in Liberal Democrat economic policy. Support for an independent Bank of England showed how far they were prepared to circumscribe their traditional policy objectives of public investment and redistribution in order to achieve respectability. An independent Bank of England would have been free to instigate a tight monetary policy that might negate precisely the sort of fiscal stimulus which the Liberal Democrats proposed in their 1992 manifesto. Ashdown's chief policy advisers argued that this policy helped to engender party self-discipline because continual Conservative attacks on opposition profligacy required lowering party members' expectations of additional public expenditure. Central bank independence was designed to reassure both the electorate and the financial markets that the party could deliver on its chosen expenditure priorities.

On competition policy the Liberal Democrats actually sought to outflank the Conservatives, supporting government objectives such as consumer choice and the liberation of markets, but arguing that the reality of the operation of privatised utilities had failed to live up to the promise of Tory rhetoric. In *After Privatisation* the Liberal Democrats endorsed the break-up of the BT and British Gas private monopolies (Liberal Democrats, 1992). Further proposals to sell off parts of British Rail and open the rail network to competitors were defeated by the 1992 party conference, signalling that the neo-liberal direction of Ashdown's policy was going to encounter resistance.

Even on environmental protection free market economics is also in evidence. The Liberal Democrats' environment spokesman, Simon Hughes, advocated 'sustainable economics' where economic growth was harmonised with environmental responsibility. However, in setting stringent targets for carbon dioxide emissions and pollution control, Hughes disavowed interventionist methods to achieve them. Instead the Liberal Democrats advocated environmental taxes, to penalise market behaviour which contravened their environmental objectives. This reliance on the market rather than state regulation to encourage responsible behaviour by industrial companies drew on the neo-liberalism of the party's economic policy.

Changes in Strategy and Organisation

As with policy, the timing of serious organisational change in the main opposition parties varied, but in both parties a desire to improve the effectiveness of party activity, both external campaigning and internal policy-making, was manifested in organisation reforms aimed at strengthening the discipline of party members and the authority of their leaders.

Four objectives, all aimed at restoring Labour's public popularity, influenced the changes in Labour Party organisation during Conservative rule: overhauling the machinery for making policy, improving the impact of campaigns, downplaying trade union influence, and asserting the leadership's political authority over the left, especially the Marxist 'Militant tendency'. As leader, Kinnock soon established bodies for policy development that were more responsible to his office than to the National Executive Committee (NEC) or its sub-committees. New bodies included the Joint Policy Committees and the Campaign Strategy Committee. This initiative reached its logical conclusion with the establishment of the machinery for the policy review. With the backing of the union bloc vote Kinnock was able prevent the annual conference from challenging the review's recommendations. In the 1990s, the policy initiative has shifted somewhat to Labour's front-bench again, with individual spokesperson's offices making policy decisions in consultation with policy development groups such as the Social Justice Commission and the Policy Forums, always subject to the leader's approval. The NEC, like the conference, no longer plays the central role in policy initiative or development.

Following the amateurism of the 1983 campaign and the breakdown of party hierarchies in the preceding years, different groups within Labour, including the conference, called for a professionalisation of campaigning strategy. There were associated demands for a major reorganisation of party headquarters, culminating in the establishment in 1985 of three new directorates of policy, organisation, and campaigns and communications to replace the ten existing departments. The campaigns and communications directorate achieved the highest public profile. Run by Peter Mandelson, it came to symbolise the new 'yuppie' slickness of Labour's campaign style derided by many party figures, including John Prescott. As part of the campaign reorganisation, Peter Mandelson and Patricia Hewitt (Kinnock's press officer until she was made director of policy in 1987) helped establish the Shadow Communications Agency, a body made up of advertising specialists, pollsters and media workers. As many gave their services voluntarily, Labour gained cut-price access to the apparently sophisticated methods of media manipulation and polling which the Conservatives had bought at great cost from Saatchi & Saatchi. The key to the new style was strict coordination and centralisation, especially during general elections. Hewitt and Mandelson have written that, 'The chief feature was the coherence and discipline of the campaign day . . . this disciplined execution was essential in creating an image – a much-needed image in the case of the Labour Party – of a united party, fit to govern. It is a lesson, indeed, which applies not only in election time' (Hewitt and Mandelson, 1989, 53).

Throughout the 1980s the Conservatives made great gain out of the contrast between their self-portrayal as a party implacably united behind Margaret Thatcher and the Labour Party as riven by the disloyalty and indiscipline of its extremists. These extremists, in the imagination of the Tories and the media, took a number of forms: Militant 'infiltrators', rates rebels, striking miners, the 'loony left', black sections and unilateralists. Partly in response, the Labour leadership set about incrementally strengthening the discipline of the party. Most famously this involved the expulsion of Militant members for which a new machinery of investigation and discipline was set up, the National Constitutional Committee (Shaw, 1988). However, stricter discipline was applied in many other areas (Seyd, 1993). Almost unanimous NECs, passive conferences and centralised campaigning have similarly ensured that serious disunity and rebellion now very rarely play a significant public role for Labour. Survey evidence of party members' attitudes to such controversial party issues suggested that they remained close to public opinion generally. Party activists were not 'extremist', in the sense of being out of line with members in general or with the public at large (Seyd and Whiteley, 1992).

However, the most important factor in ending the image of disunity and rebellion has been the almost total marginalisation of the radical left. This has enormously reduced any fundamental ideological or policy disputes, as well as ending the possibility of serious political challenges to the party leadership. The multiple reasons for this marginalisation are outside the scope of this essay (Seyd, 1987, 1993), although clearly the changing economic, social and political conditions of the last 20 years, of which Thatcherism was both symptom and cause, have played an important role. One such change was the declining potential of the trade unions as a vehicle for left-wing policy advancement. From 1983 onwards there were moves to limit the influence of the unions: at conference through the bloc vote, in Constituency Labour Parties (CLP) over the selection of parliamentary candidates, and in the electoral college that chooses the leader and deputy leader. All these were areas in which it was argued that not only the unions, but the union leadership themselves, had too much power. A series of antagonisms and compromises finally led to a major reform of the trade unions' position. The 1993 conference agreed that unions should hold ballots of levy-paying members for leadership elections. The same conference also accepted, by a very narrow vote, that a combination of a ballot of local union branches and CLP members should be used for the selection of Labour's parliamentary candidates. Moves have also been made to limit the bloc-voting of union delegations at conferences by giving union delegates individual votes, removing the discipline of mandates from their union or its executive. However, the implementation of this measure has proved problematic, with senior union figures attempting to defy it at the 1994 conference (Minkin, 1992).

Major changes in Liberal Party organisation followed the Liberal Party/SDP merger into the Liberal (originally Social and Liberal) Democrats, and, like Kinnock's Labour reforms, were motivated by the leadership's desire to create a more disciplined and cohesive party. During the period of Alliance politics the Conservatives had continually drawn attention to the ill-disciplined nature of the Liberal Party conference, and portrayed the Liberals as an ill-assorted group of single issue lobbies and regional factions. The Liberal Democrats' SDP activists were acutely sensitive to these charges and, under their former leader, Robert Maclennan, sought to draw up a constitution which would create a disciplined national party. The Maclennan constitution replaced the old Liberal Assembly model with a policy-making conference composed of elected representatives. This was designed to create safeguards against the recurrence of the Liberal leadership's defeat at the 1986 Eastbourne assembly on the replacement of the Polaris nuclear deterrent. Many former SDP activists attributed this defeat to the unelected composition of the Eastbourne Assembly. Accompanying the new conference rules was a more centralised policy-making system of Green and White papers, giving delegates a 'fixed diet' of proposals from the party policy committee (Stevenson, 1993, 115).

After the 1992 General Election defeat and the return of a fourth Conservative government, Ashdown adopted a new political strategy, refocusing on the new mood of anti-politics developing in Western democracies. He abandoned his earlier ambition to realign the left and reverted to stressing the Liberal Democrats' distinctiveness and independence. The issue which he seized on to pursue this revised strategy was disaffection with the political system itself and the whole political class. Within months of their re-election in 1992, the Tories were thrown into crisis by the ejection of sterling from the ERM and then by the protracted ratification of the Maastricht Treaty (Chapters 9 and 6). After its fourth defeat, Labour was in a weak position to capitalise on the disarray of the government. Ashdown reinvented himself, attempting to become the focus of popular disillusionment with politics and the Westminster system, assuming the mantle of Ross Perot (Wintour, 1993, 36). Ashdown was fascinated by the mood of anti-politics in Western democracies but wanted to turn this phenomenon to constructive use.

In policy terms, Ashdown embellished the Liberal Democrats' traditional constitutional reform agenda to move into the anti-politics electoral marketplace. In a speech to the Charter 88 pressure group in

July 1993, he floated ideas for hypothecated taxation and the recruitment of ministers from outside Parliament in order to reinvigorate the political elite (Ashdown, 1993). The future direction of strategy was, however, severely shaken by the election of Tony Blair to the Labour leadership in 1994. Ashdown wished to portray his party as the sole focus for non-Labourist progressive politics on the centre/left. The Chard speech was based on the belief that it would be the Liberal Democrats who would be the focal point for a realignment of politics on the centre-left.

Blair had a record of being a 'moderniser', consistently advocating a strategy which sought to expand Labour's electoral appeal to groups alienated from the party during the 1980s. Blair was closely associated with the drive to adopt the one-member one-vote (OMOV) system for selecting parliamentary candidates. He has sought to reposition his party to attract the disillusioned middle-class Tory voters who protested against the government in 1993–4 in by-elections and European elections. On macro-economic and social policy, Blair has already shifted Labour towards the centre ground, making it increasingly difficult for the Liberal Democrats to find a distinctive political space.

At the same time, members of the SDP 'Gang of Three' have warmly welcomed Blair's election, with Bill Rodgers declaring Blair to be the best candidate for Prime Minister. All this has posed an awkward question for Paddy Ashdown: 'Why do the Liberal Democrats need to exist in the aftermath of Blair's election?' Former SDP activists within the Liberal Democrats have argued that Blair's election actually helps both electorally and politically. Alan Leaman, Ashdown's chief policy adviser until 1993, argues that a more electable Labour Party will remove the 'fear factor' amongst potential Tory defectors, thus enabling the Liberal Democrats to win seats in the South West of England (Leaman, 1994, 12). Ashdown has subsequently adopted this line himself (*The Guardian*, 15 September 1994). While there is agreement on the 'electability' issue, Ashdown has been criticised for hurriedly seeking to articulate artificial differences with Labour following Blair's election, arguing that, 'The real radical alternative to forced differentiation is to stand our ground. We should welcome Labour's shift towards our values but point out where it doesn't come up to the mark . . . We should avoid differentiation for its own sake' (*The Reformer*, 1994, 3).

On the 'differentiation issue', such criticism has also led to Ashdown revising his position. The leadership now welcomes Labour's conversion to Liberal Democrat policies and values, but argues that it remains incomplete. At the 1994 conference Ashdown refused to abandon the traditional stance of maintaining 'equidistance' between Labour and Conservative parties until Labour's leadership is able to demonstrate that its modernisation is completed. Nevertheless the Liberal Democrats, after initially moving further towards post-Thatcherite revisionism, now seem to have lost the initiative in opposition politics as Labour's modernisation intensifies. Blair's decision to replace Clause Four of the Labour constitution has central symbolic importance in this respect. It may well be that the Liberal Democrats' future role can realistically only be to become an external regional appendage to a Labour-led coalition government.

Changes in Ideology

When the Labour Party was founded, it defined its ideological territory largely by its opposition to the *laissez-faire* liberalism of a Liberal Party portrayed as heavily influenced by industrialists. The Liberal Party responded to the challenge of labour by adopting a modified 'new liberalism' offering government action to deal with the 'social question'. The ideological impact of Thatcherism on the descendants of the old parties appeared to be to send them both back towards the simpler verities of liberal individualism (Greenleaf, 1983b).

The central aspect of the Labour Party's ideology influenced by Conservative domination over the last 15 years, was the attitude to the capitalist values of economic prosperity and individualism, and their relationship to the Socialist goals of freedom and equality. Thatcherism's ideological emphasis was on the value of personal wealth through individual enterprise in the free market, and the positive effect this supposedly has on the prosperity of the nation as a whole by the encouragement of economic growth and hence employment and wealth (Chapter 2). It was also a philosophy that appeared to win the votes of a critical selection of the electorate for the Conservative Party, backed up as it was by material encouragement to adopt capitalist and individualist values through the sale of council houses and of shares in privatised industries (Chapter 3). It was therefore highly unlikely that the Labour Party, in a period of massive overhaul, would not be influenced by these much-trumpeted values. An observer wrote soon after the 1983 election that:

> A dominant theme within Labour's election campaign, echoed from Foot to Hattersley and Benn, was a call for a return to 1945, to Attleeism, with the implicit message that this was the golden age of socialism in power . . . it is tempting to share the golden age myth, to draw on its sense of past collective achievements to defend the welfare services from the present unbridled individualism of Thatcherism. (H. Rose, 1983)

However, as the 1980s progressed the notion that individualism and materialism were not wholly bad gained respectability in the party, and this has played an increasingly influential role in policy development. These values gained acceptance by regular attempts on the part of the parliamentary leadership, and by writers and thinkers on the 'soft left' effectively arguing that these new values of the 1980s were not incompatible with the traditional Socialist goals of freedom and equality. A typical contribution from the one-time intellectual stan- dard-bearer of this ideological initiative, Bryan Gould, stated that the party must not:

> be so mesmerised by the importance of the collective interest that we denigrate the validity of individual aspiration, nor should we overlook the fact that the only way in which economic success, or any other benefit can be delivered effectively, and enjoyed in human experience, is when it is delivered and enjoyed by individuals. (Gould, 1989, 77)

The Labour leadership gradually began to portray itself as an efficient organiser of a market system, which would enhance freedom and welfare through a careful balance of market and public enterprise (Hattersley, 1987). Kinnock stated in an interview with Tribune:

> There are areas which can be the subject of market operations, provided that the environment is safeguarded, the consumers are not exploited, there isn't sweated labour, and there is fair competition. By regulation we try to get markets to meet human need. That's a very basic socialist proposition. It isn't tossing everything over to the market, it's saying that there are areas in which the market can do the job, there are many areas in which it can't; what we want to see is the job done. (cited in P. Kelly, 1988)

The move to link the objectives of freedom and equality to the encouragement of an efficient market has gathered pace for a number of years now, the clearest policy effect being the downgrading of Labour's nationalisation plans. Tony Blair has made the efficient management of the market, so as to encourage national and individual prosperity and thus enhance the freedom and well-being of the populace, the centrepiece of Labour's appeal to the electorate. Blair argued in a high profile relaunch of Labour's economic policy in September 1994 that the difference between Labour and the Conservatives was not disagreement about the importance of the market but over the Tory preference for a *laissez-faire* market dominated by short-term objectives and Labour's goal of a market based on investment in industry and education. Such a policy, Blair argued, 'did not alter the left's traditional commitment to social justice. On the contrary, most of us would not be in politics without such a commitment. But it is the insight of the left that efficiency and social justice go hand in hand' (*The Guardian*, 28 September 1994).

It was also during this relaunch that Gordon Brown, the shadow chancellor, indicated more clearly than ever before how he regarded this new ideological-policy leaning as a break from the past:

> Past Labour governments tried to counter the injustice and failings of the free market forces by substituting government for market, and often saw tax, spend and borrow policies as the isolationist quick fix for national decline. The fact is that these policies cannot work in the highly-integrated world economic environment in which we live. (*The Guardian*, 28 September 1994)

This shift has been confirmed and looks likely to be taken even further by Blair's plans to drop the Clause IV commitment to 'common ownership of the means of production, distribution and exchange'. Much of the new approach looks likely to emanate from Blair's own vision of a progressive ideology which he labelled in his 1994 conference speech as 'Social-ism' and defined as:

> Working together, solidarity, co-operation, partnership. These are our words. This is my socialism. And we should stop apologising for using the word. It is not the socialism of Marx or state control. It is rooted in a straightforward view of society, in the understanding that the individual does best in a strong and decent community of people with principles and standards and common aims and values. (*The Guardian*, 5 October 1994)

It is important to recognise that this fundamental ideological shift is a response not solely to the ideas and popularity of Thatcherism, but is also a response to the failures of the Labour governments of the 1970s and the economic situation that they and the Thatcher administrations both helped to create. Labour's 'new realist' intellectual supporters in the 1980s were conditioned by this legacy, as one has acknowledged:

In the absence of an innovative left, the economic sphere has been serviced
by a new Labourist intelligentsia unschooled in the buoyant language of
socialism and solidarity . . . That generation has known only permanent
mass unemployment. It has watched the decline and fall of Labourism, the
rise and rise of street chic, of women's expectations . . . What completed the
process was the election defeat of 1983 and the horrible discovery that not
even the agony of Thatcherism could make old-style leftism popular.
(B. Campbell, 1985)

The apparent success of the Thatcherite attack on the collectivist
past – most clearly displayed in the propaganda mileage the Government dragged out of the 'Winter of Discontent' well into the 1990s –
also prompted the discarding of symbolic representations of a proud
lineage of past struggles and movements. The most famous of these was
the dropping of the red flag in favour of the thornless red rose logo.
This change exemplified a range of alterations to symbolic elements of
the party which aimed to signal modernity and a break with the past:
from the careful grooming and dressing of leading Labour politicians
to look more like businessmen and women, to the use of a pop song to
promote the policy review document in 1989.

Less conscious, but perhaps more significant, were the enormous
changes in the role and nature of Labour's self-defining history. The
ideological imperatives, the solidarity of the party, the policies, and
Labour's organisational form were all developed in large part by a
certain reading of labour history and British history. Just as a reading
of Victorian Britain helped construct certain types of Conservatism, so
accounts of the Tolpuddle martyrs and the General Strike had been
cause and effect of a certain type of Labourism. The 1980s more than
any other era, saw a re-reading, and even a jettisoning, of these
histories in the light of the new events of the decade. This re-reading
was complex and is to a large extent uncharted. One potent example is
the eclipse of the legend of the NUM's industrial action in the early
1970s by a particular reading of the miners' strike of 1984–5. For many
party members and supporters the disputes of the 1970s had upheld a
radical vision of how a campaigning political trade unionism can
vanquish Tory governments. The 1980s strike usurped this vision,
often being read and presented as a narrative of utter defeat caused
by extremist and autocratic trade union leadership. Similarly the
election victories of 1945 and 1964, when relatively radical policies
were convincingly presented as having won popular support, were
removed as significant reference points by the 1983 election, when left-

sponsored disunity and radicalism were blamed for utter electoral collapse.

A leading Labour advocate of traditional aims and methods charged in 1986 that Labour was becoming an SDP Mark 2 (Heffer, 1986). Some labour leaders had long since responded to the ideological call of Thatcherism. As early as 1983, at the Salford SDP conference, the party leader David Owen, called for a coupling of market forces and social justice in 'the social market'. He attempted to popularise this concept by describing it as a mixture of toughness and tenderness. Commentators at the time interpreted the social market as a shift to the right. The significance of Owen's approach for long-term Liberal Democrat ideological development was that he insisted that the centre-left had to clearly repudiate the corporatism and state interventionism of the 1960s and 1970s if it was to win political power. Owen argued more explicitly for a neo-liberal policy programme after the 1987 election, calling for the dismantling of public monopolies and the rejection of income policies (Owen, 1987).

Although Owen's social market approach has been criticised as vacillating and merely dictated by a desire to present the SDP as 'new and exciting' (Brack, 1989, 66–7, 18–26) its broader themes left a legacy which the Liberal Democrats later embraced. Initially other SDP and Liberal leaders rejected Owen's approach (Jenkins, 1987, 354; Brack, 1989, 47). Indeed the question of how the centre-left should respond to Thatcherism was integral to the merger conflict inside the SDP in 1987–8. Although Owen himself did not join the Liberal Democrats his revisionist contribution was taken up by its party leadership. As Robin Oakley of *The Times* argued in 1987, the merged party looked as if it would become 'an Owenite party without Dr Owen' (Oakley, 1987).

Ashdown's leadership campaign stated that the Alliance had failed to respond effectively to Thatcherism. All the assumptions in his policy positions at this time were centred on a belief that the Conservative government had introduced profound structural changes in the economy and society which had to be either built on or confronted by an equally powerful and reformist vision. Whilst the Alliance had continually emphasised community and the need to combine individual freedom and social justice, Ashdown switched emphasis to the goal of individual freedom. In the revisionist climate of 1987–8 his stress on individualism signalled a move to recapture territory from Thatcher. Ashdown argued that Liberal Democrats should pursue a better form of individualism than the 'impoverished' conception of the Tories, rather than seeking to build a better form of collectivism than that of Labour (Ashdown, 1987).

Since Major's victory in the 1992 General Election, the extent to which the Labour Party has changed over a decade and a half of Conservative rule became apparent. Despite being a man unambiguously from the right of the party, John Smith won an overwhelming victory in the leadership election of 1992, and faced no serious divisions within Labour except over OMOV, and even this ultimately went his way. Never before had a figure from the right been able to command such unity and even popularity. Centre-leaning leaders and deputy leaders such as Hugh Gaitskell, George Brown, Denis Healey and Roy Hattersley were usually at the heart of major disputes within the party, and were inevitably demonised by one or other faction or grouping.

However, the election of Blair, and the hope that many of the party's members and supporters seem to have invested in him, indicate even more clearly the changes in Labour. While Smith was from the 'social democratic' wing of the party, he remained a cautious leader with close links to the trade union movement and the traditions of Scottish Labourism. Blair, however, has managed to construct for himself an image as Labour's bright new hope despite being from the unapologetic modernising wing of the party with none of the traditional associations of Smith. It is indicative of the degree to which Labour has changed when a figure who may bring with him the possibility of even more internal reform, further policy refinement and increasingly slick media manipulation and image-building cannot fail to win a commanding vote in a leadership election as long as he looks likely to win constituencies such as Dudley in the Midlands, and to make real gains in the South. Such a phenomenon has only been made possible by the traumatic experience of the loss of four successive general elections to a virulently anti-Socialist brand of politics.

The General Election of 1992 was a particular shock for Labour because despite a skilful campaign fought around reformed policies and against an uncharismatic prime minister, the party still failed to dent the Tories' consistent 42–3 per cent share of the vote (Chapter 3). All Kinnock's reforms and reviews had done little to quell the hostility of the press, and did not prevent the Conservative Party's successful stigmatisation of Labour as a high-tax, high-spending party. This last feature encouraged Smith to re-emphasies the moderate nature of the party's financial plans, a policy that reached its logical conclusion in September 1994 when Blair and Brown signalled that a Labour government would not aim to raise taxes but only to make the system fairer.

The onus is on Blair to convince voters, the media and his own party that an ideological commitment to the poor and to a fairer society can really co-exist alongside a policy commitment to limited levels of taxation, restrained spending and limited public ownership. While the balancing of these ideology/policy and taxation/spending equations might be possible in opposition, the severest test of the Blair approach will come if Labour win the next election. This test may be made even more severe by the fact that an election win for Labour will probably throw into relief differences over policy and ideology in the party that are at present muted because Blair appears so close to electoral victory. Once this imperative is gone, and under the stress of governing, some old and some new disputes may yet appear. Indeed recent clashes over plans to reform Clause IV display how conflict in the Labour Party still resides just below the calm surface of a smooth-running electoral machine.

The Liberal Democrat 1992 election manifesto, *Changing Britain for Good*, highlighted the party's problem in establishing a clear and cohesive identity. Although it had distinctive and radical policies in areas such as housing finance, environmental policy and constitutional reform, the heterogeneity of the party's programme – to the right on economics and yet egalitarian on the issue of poverty – militated against the development of a definable ideology. This heterogeneity made it difficult for the electorate to comprehend where the party stood in terms of the traditional left/right polarisation (Stevenson, 1993, 138). To a great extent this ambiguity stemmed from the party's desire to respond to the Thatcherite legacy: the economic policy was directed at the need to reassure soft Tory voters about the party's economic responsibility.

However, one clear theme ran through the 1992 programme: the emphasis on decentralisation of power. Decentralisation is integral to policy towards the public services, regional government and in economic policy. The Liberal Democrats show a suspicion of concentrations of power, whether in the market economy or in the political system. Decentralisation was a direct response to the growing Left consensus that the Conservative government had concentrated power in the central state, weakening local government and intermediary institutions in the process. In this area the Liberal Democrats pursued policies which were antithetical to Thatcherism.

Liberal Democrat policy on monetary affairs, competition and environmental policy can be characterised as post-Thatcherite. It sought to use market disciplines rather than state intervention to achieve improved standards in the private utilities, better environmental standards and low inflation. The Liberal Democrat ideology shows that Thatcherism had succeeded in forcing a paradigm shift in the opposition parties. The Liberal Democrats moved away from using state power to achieve egalitarianism and instead sought to use the free market.

A New Diverse Opposition Politics

The decade and a half of Conservative rule has irrevocably changed the nature of British opposition politics. Opposition is now characterised by a far greater diversity of means and ends. Neither the Labour movement nor Liberal 'neighbourhood politics' are any longer the most obvious choices for those wishing to challenge the establishment. Outside parliamentary opposition, there now exist three increasingly influential spheres of campaigning pressure politics, self-help network politics and a new eco-cultural politics. It must be emphasised that these come far closer to constituting modes of political activity than types of organisation. At any one time an organisation or ad hoc campaign might straddle all three spheres, while at another it might draw only on the methods and goals of one. This suggests that one new feature of opposition politics is that the traditional types of organisation and modes of activity have declined in popularity and efficacy, and we do not yet have an analytical language with which to describe the new.

In the early and mid-1980s both the Anti-Apartheid Movement's campaign for sanctions against South Africa and the Campaign for Nuclear Disarmament's activity against Cruise and Pershing missiles involved hundreds of thousands of people in pressure group work, ranging from lobbying Parliament and party conferences to some of the largest street demonstrations in British history. Environmental pressure groups, especially Greenpeace and Friends of the Earth (Church, 1992), have changed public attitudes, influenced government and commercial policy, and changed the news priorities of the media.

Greenpeace is an exemplar of the changing nature of opposition politics, having built a British membership base almost twice the size of the Labour Party's, and enjoying an income equivalent to a successful medium-sized company. Attempts to mobilise environmental activism in a formalised Green party, on the other hand, have been undermined by divisions engendered by advocacy of forms of protest that can happily co-exist in campaign pressure groups, but not with the permanent internal discipline a party needs. Other campaigning pressure groups such as Stonewall, Outrage and disability rights groups have also followed Greenpeace's example, using imaginative and sophisticated methods to influence opinion.

The second sphere of new oppositional politics which has mushroomed is the self-help network. Some of the campaigning pressure groups are also involved in such networks. Pensioners' groups and disabled people's groups, like People First, act as bodies which not only give support to individuals but also aim (through collective activities) to provide a sense of dignity to individuals traditionally subordinated in society. A prominent example is the Pride march and festival organised by gay groups to counter the shame historically associated with homosexuality by the most blatant, public and proud display of individual sexuality. *The Big Issue* homelessness initiative presents probably the most successful example of self-help networks. This form of activity is an attempt to alter power relations in society by challenging perceptions of oneself by oneself and by others. More practical forms of self-help have also developed with the growth of local exchange and trading (LET) Schemes, credit unions and formal and informal consumer and producer cooperatives.

The third sphere of new opposition politics to have developed under Conservative rule is that of eco-cultural politics. This incorporates both certain social, cultural and political values as well as a series of challenging forms of behaviour and life-style. Often associated with youth culture and politics, the sphere is dispersed and fragmented. Eco-cultural politics indicates a growing concern with ecological issues, animal rights and anti-materialist values, sometimes reflected in an interest in mystical and religious interpretations of the world. However, it also indicates new socio-cultural forms such as rave culture, which has its origins in the late 1980s, the mass use of recreational drugs such as ecstasy and marijuana, the increasing commonness and acceptability of squatting, and the new communities of travellers which have grown over the last decade.

How such a diverse range of issues has come to be bound together is difficult to say except to note that it may be a new political deepening and sophistication of a type of rebellious and disaffected youth culture that has probably always existed but which became a mass affair in the post-war period. Although a large section of those who attend raves care nothing for animal rights, and many who actively oppose vivisection have never heard rave music, there appears to be a growing intersection of the personnel involved in these different areas of eco-cultural belief and activity which is effectively articulating the issues and life-styles. This process of articulation has, if anything, been assisted by legislation such as the Criminal Justice and Public Order Act, and government encouragement of aggressive police mobilisations against travellers and unlicensed raves. Such actions have resulted in the establishment of decentralised bodies such as the anti-Poll Tax campaigns and the Freedom Network. Of course these new forms of oppositional politics cannot be said to have replaced parliamentary politics or to have eclipsed the labour movement, far from it. Both the Labour Party and the Liberal Democrats are still a prime focus for opposition, while trades unions remain enormous organisations with resources way beyond other bodies. But it cannot be denied that a new diversification has occurred and that maybe some of the vitality and imagination once associated with the labour movement has now switched to the new oppositional forms.

The reasons for this diversification are multiple and obviously have their origin in circumstances beyond and prior to the environment created by Conservative rule. However, the trend has been accelerated by Conservative dominance. First, the electoral success of the Conservative Party has encouraged a now dominant stream in the Labour Party which prizes political and policy moderation above all things. As a result, movements which generally receive a hostile press, and are commonly accepted to run counter to public opinion (such as gay rights, travellers' rights and militant anti-racism), have had to campaign outside Labour. At no time was this development clearer than in the mid-1980s, when the Labour leadership regularly clashed with those arguing for black sections in the party, and in 1986–7 when the leadership launched an assault on Labour local authorities carrying out equal opportunities policies. Individuals concerned with such issues are more likely to look to groups such as Outrage, the Anti-Racist Alliance or the Freedom Network.

A second reason is that increased centralisation of political power in the hands of a right-wing central government, and cuts in local authority spending, have meant that official policies designed to provide support networks have declined. As a result, people have been forced to act on their own initiative to discover personal and material support by creating their own networks. This is also true of the recession. Organisations such as cooperatives, credit unions, LET schemes and homeless groups are obviously predicated upon the existence of impoverishment and destitution. Furthermore while the circumstances for opposition politics have been harsh, radical consciousness has been raised by governmental and media assaults without political groups facing the ultimate sanction of being outlawed or broken up. As a result, a series of recent issues and legislation has provided the focus for new oppositional politics to develop its organisational sophistication and grow in numbers: Chernobyl and the ecological awareness that followed, the Poll Tax, the closing down of raves, attacks on travellers, the Criminal Justice and Public Order Act, the government's road-building programme, and the export of live animals for slaughter. Interestingly, the most important of these events are issues that usually drew on all three spheres of activity described above. In early 1995 the extraordinary and successful protests in quiet south-eastern harbour towns against the export of live animals not only combined such spheres, but also drew in active mass support from local residents. A third of the population of one such town joined a protest meeting. Far from being discouraged by government attacks on the tactics of animal rights activists, Tory-voting residents continued to blockade harbours and broadcast their indignation at police tactics more commonly deployed against travellers and ravers, adding to the government's severe embarrassment.

Conclusions

Both of Labour and the Liberal Democrats made similar accommodations to the apparently irreversible changes introduced by Conservative governments. Most obviously this entailed an acceptance that major extensions of public ownership were no longer viable. Council house sales would not be reversed. Both parties repudiated any return to the high income tax rates levied on wealthy individuals during the 1970s.

This repudiation reflected the political hegemony Thatcherism had achieved in British politics by the late 1980s: the paradigm shift from collective to individual rights. Labour and Liberal Democrats constantly rejustified their policies in terms of individual rights and opportunities. Both parties attempted to wrest back some of the ideological initiative from the Conservatives, deploying a social democratic critique of Thatcherism as an impoverished form of rampant individualism which had destroyed notions of community and responsibility. After the collapse of the Lawson boom (Chapter 9), the parties were able to argue that excessive consumption had been caused by the reckless pursuit of individual choice in areas such as financial deregulation, taxation and environmental protection. Labour under Kinnock particularly sought to stigmatise Thatcherism in highly moral terms as creating a 'me first' society. The policy review had not only abandoned baggage from the 1960s and 1970s, but also reasserted the virtues of public purpose as opposed to unrestrained individualism.

Although the two parties agreed on their analysis of Thatcherism's failures, they diverged on many policy prescriptions. Labour's institutional links to the trade unions meant that they resisted proposals for labour market flexibility, which the Liberal Democrat leadership embraced. Labour also relied more on public regulation to curb abuses by the privatised utilities. The Liberal Democrats became more enthusiastically committed to free market economics, with proposals to subject the utilities to more competition in order to reduce price, and improve consumer choice. The areas where the two opposition parties differed in their approach to post-Thatcherite revisionism flow directly from the difference in their respective cultures. Paddy Ashdown could claim that free market policies were a reaffirmation of his party's Liberal traditions; whereas Labour, representing strong public sector and trade union producer interests, was more resistant to an accommodation with market disciplines.

The detailed future of the new opposition politics, brighter than the grim claims of depoliticisation would have us believe (see Mulgan, 1994), is impossible to predict, relying as it does on the complex interaction between the different spheres and the different groups. Much will depend on the next general election. Whatever the result, it seems unlikely that the growth of new forms of opposition will be stemmed, or that their growth will be deeply affected by the degree and nature of the responsiveness of any future government, be it Conservative, Labour, or Lib–Lab Coalition.

8

Reforming the State

MARTIN J. SMITH

The modernisation of the state has long been a theme of parties in government. Sclerosis of the institutions of central government has been seen as a cause of Britain's economic and political failure by both the left and the right (Anderson, 1963; Barnett, 1986). Consequently, governments of both parties have attempted to deal with these problems through either piecemeal reforms or attempts at more fundamental change. Piecemeal change has often taken the form of the abolition, merging and creation of new departments. Sometimes these changes represented the priorities of the Prime Minister such as Labour's establishment of a Ministry of Technology, and sometimes changing realities, as with the amalgamation of the ministries of Admiralty, War and Air into Defence (see R. Clarke, 1975).

Before Margaret Thatcher's premiership, strategic attempts at reform had been made by Winston Churchill, Harold Wilson and Edward Heath. Churchill attempted to streamline the lines of management and improve central coordination by creating 'overlords' with responsibility for a cluster of departments (Hennessy, 1986). Problems of accountability and coordination ended the experiment after two years.

Wilson attempted to reform both the structure of government and the civil service. He established ministries such as the Department of Economic Affairs with the aim of challenging Treasury dominance and of modernising the British economy. With the establishment of the Fulton Committee he initiated the most fundamental review of the role of the civil service since Northcote Trevelyan in 1854. The report made important recommendations concerning the staffing, management, structure and professionalism of the civil service. Much of the report was not implemented, but a Civil Service Department was established, a unified structure created, and there was a gradual increase in the number of technical experts used (Hennessy, 1990).

Heath was concerned with continuing the modernisation process initiated by Wilson. Heath's White Paper, *The Reorganisation of Central Government*, introduced major changes aimed at improving the management and efficiency of central government through the creation of super departments such as the Department of Trade and Industry (DTI) and the Department of the Environment (Radcliffe, 1991). The giant departments were intended to improve coordination and provide clearer objectives. In addition, the reforms aimed at providing better management systems and expenditure controls (Hennessy, 1986; Hogwood, 1992). Heath also reformed local government by introducing two tier local authorities made up of county and district councils and, in the large cities, the metropolitan councils and districts (Byrne, 1986).

What unites these attempts at reforms is a pragmatic response to the political and economic crises seen as weakening the post-war state. Both Wilson and Heath wanted to modernise the state. Under the Conservatives since 1979 reform of the state has continued. According to Michael Portillo, 'A revolution is taking place in public management' (Portillo, 1994a, 1). Undoubtedly the years after 1979 saw a fundamental, and probably permanent, change in the nature and role of the state. The question that arises is whether this reform is a continuation of the pragmatic modernisation or a more ideologically-driven attempt to reduce the role of the state and the power of bureaucrats?

Conservatives frequently deny that they have a theory or ideology of the state. 'Other parties may be wedded to fixed and unalterable theories of the state. For better or worse the Conservative Party is not' (Hogg, 1947, 14). Despite such disclaimers, within Conservatism there are a number of conceptions concerning the role and boundaries of the state. This chapter will briefly examine the key Conservative state theories, what changes have occurred, and assess the extent to which Conservative reform of central government has been informed by a particular state theory. It will show that the distinctive Thatcherite view of the state had a limited influence on the reform that occurred.

Conservative Theories of the State

Most commentators on Conservative ideology identify libertarian and collectivist traditions within Conservative thought (see Greenleaf, 1973; Gamble, 1974; Eccleshall, 1984; Willetts, 1992). For libertarianism, the most important goal is liberty and the state must not 'tell individuals how to run their lives but maintain the framework of public order within which individuals may pursue their own ends and interests' (Greenleaf, 1973, 181). For collectivists the primary goal is order and social harmony. The state intervenes in order to achieve social rather than individual goals. For collectivist, or organic Conservatives, society is not made up of sovereign individuals but is 'an interconnected whole bound by a network of reciprocal rights and obligations'. Those with wealth and privilege have a duty to make collective provision for the disadvantaged (Eccleshall, 1984, 86). In reality most strands of conservatism contain elements of both traditions (Greenleaf, 1973).

Within these traditions there are differing conceptions of what the state should do. Some Conservatives are pre-modernists rejecting the notion that the state should attempt to achieve grand plans or large social goals. For Oakeshott, politics should be driven by political experience and an understanding of the traditions of the nation. Rationalism in politics is rejected because of the imperfectability of human behaviour and the likelihood that plans lead to new problems, not solutions (Oakeshott, 1962).

However, in the post-war period the dominant Conservative conception of the state has been modernist: the belief that the state can achieve specified goals and improve the lives of ordinary people. Macmillan, Heath and Thatcher, despite different views on what the state should achieve, had ideologically derived goals, and accepted the necessity for a rationalist approach to political problems. The state is an organisation for achieving political, economic and social ends. Although Thatcher might have rhetorically rejected the idea that the state could be used positively, it is undoubtedly the case that she had specific aims – say, for example, trade union reform – which could only be resolved through state action.

Within Conservative thought there is a range of criteria on which to judge the state. Nevertheless, there are certain conceptions concerning the role and nature of the state that are shared by all Conservatives. First, all Conservatives, even those on the libertarian wing, are concerned with the maintenance of state authority and social order. Second, central to maintaining order is the rule of law. For Conservatives, if a law is legitimately passed it must be obeyed by all people or society will descend into anarchy. No one is above the law and it must be applied equally to all. For,

> the rule of law to which Conservatives pay such respect is as real and solid as the table in the House of Commons. It is no metaphysical conception of natural law, no philosophers' abstraction like the laws of Plato's Republic. It is a body of actual law, imperfect as all actual things must be, but none the less sufficiently embodying the eternal principles to command and exact respect as such. (Hogg, 1947, 76)

Third, the fundamental goal of maintaining order and the rule of law is to protect private property. All Conservatives, even the most collectivist who might accept some nationalisation, maintain the absolute priority of private property. Fourth, the notion of private property is tied in with the idea that there is an autonomous civil society which is clearly distinct from the state. This pluralist conception of the state sees autonomous institutions within civil society as mechanisms for limiting state power (see Hogg, 1947; J. Gray, 1993). Fifth, an important source of constraining the state is constitutionalism. This is not constitutionalism in the sense of developing written and codified rules of government, rather it means government working within the boundaries of tradition. The English constitution is 'the accumulated and sifted experience of our predecessors as embodied in traditional institutions, laws and customs' (quoted in Honderich, 1990, 136). It is much better to regulate government through these traditions than through a new set of formalised rules.

Within the confines of these general perceptions of what the state should do, Conservatism encompasses very different state theories influenced by both libertarian and collectivist thought. At one extreme are the Conservatives who see the fundamental role of the state as maintaining order and the integrity of the nation state. Ideally, this would be achieved by aristocratic government which has the wealth, breeding and education to know how to rule in the national, rather than sectional, interest. Hence, 'In politics, the conservative seeks above all for government, and regards no citizen as possessed of a natural right that transcends his obligation to be ruled' (Scruton, 1984, 16). However, Conservatives realise that with the growth of working-class organisations some democracy is necessary to prevent revolution. Consequently, Conservatives of this disposition can countenance corporatism, economic intervention and the collective provision of welfare as a means of maintaining order (see Honderich, 1990).

At the other extreme is the libertarian position which sees the state's role as maintaining the conditions for the maintenance of a free market. The state should be limited to an absolute minimum of maintaining negative rights: the right to pursue one's goals without interference. However, as Gray has pointed out, this view of the state is not in reality Conservative. It takes no account of the historical context and traditions of the British state, which has never been minimalist, and for Conservatives the role of the state could never be solely protecting liberty (J. Gray, 1993, 5–7). For Gray there should be limited, rather than *laissez-faire*, government: 'Government activity should be confined to the production of public goods' (J. Gray, 1993, 13). The main public good is peace but peace cannot just rely on law and order; it requires some sort of social provision for the poorest in society. The market is essential for maintaining a just society, but sometimes people need to be provided with resources to participate in the market (J. Gray, 1993).

The conceptions of the state which have guided the actions of postwar politicians have come within these two extremes, and to an extent have combined elements of both the liberal and collective, with one dominant (Gamble, 1994, 154). Until 1975 the 'progressive right' dominated post-war Conservative theory of the state (Gamble, 1974). They explicitly rejected *laissez-faire* notions of the state (Eccleshall, 1984, 105), and reconciled themselves to it having an enlarged and interventionist role (Gamble, 1974, 124). The progressive right theory of the state maintains the importance of pluralism by recognising the necessity of intermediate institutions (Hogg, 1947) but it is also rationalist and modernist, seeing the state as a means of achieving social goals. From 1951 most Conservatives accepted that 'the state sector was to be administered not dismantled' (Gamble, 1974, 63).

For the progressive right, which reached its apex under Edward Heath, the key role of the state is to maintain order by preventing conflict between labour and capital. They accepted that the state should provide welfare and even maintain full employment as a means of ensuring the unity of the nation (Gilmour, 1978). They increasingly saw the need to modernise the British state, economy and society in order to provide the wealth to prevent class conflict. At times of economic crisis they were prepared both to intervene substantially in the economy and to incorporate key class actors into corporatist policy mechanisms such as the NEDC and incomes policies. They were prepared to accept some limited public ownership recognising that the market is not the best means to provide all goods (Hogg, 1947, 108–14). For the progressives, 'a state kept within bounds is not an enemy' (Gilmour, 1978, 151).

The dominant theory of the state since the late 1970s has been the Thatcherite view, which grew partly as a critique of Heath's modernism. For Thatcherism the ultimate goal of the state was still order, but the welfare state was a cause of disorder and the declining authority of the state (Gamble, 1994). The state should disengage from certain policy areas. The Thatcherite theory of the state is a complex synthesis of New Right theory, authoritarian and mainstream Conservatism. The rhetoric of Thatcherism focused on limiting the role of government, especially in the economy but also in areas such as welfare. However, despite this rhetoric of disengagement, Thatcherism contained a high degree of authoritarianism, as Gamble makes clear: 'the New Right wanted a new approach to the nation, based on the fundamental principles of the one nation strategy – strong national leadership, a new national consensus, and avoiding the drift between politics being seen in class or interest groups terms' (Gamble, 1974, 103). Thatcherism had a clear agenda which required direct state action. Whilst some state intervention was deemed necessary to dismantle the social democratic state, much was positive and concerned with reasserting authority (Gamble, 1994). Moreover, Thatcherism rejects the pluralism of traditional Conservatism, taking from Enoch Powell the supreme importance of Parliament as the sovereign decision-maker, with the elected executive at its pinnacle. Institutions that challenge Parliament, even an executive-dominated one, threatened the rule of law and the will of the nation. Within Thatcherism is a deep distrust of intermediate institutions such as local government, pressure groups, trade unions and even the media, and so it is proper to weaken these groups. For Thatcherism, the contract of governance is between the parliamentary state and the individual.

This emphasis on Parliamentarianism made Thatcherism very open to the New Right critique of bureaucracy because the civil service is another obstacle to the will of Parliament. The New Right saw civil servants as self-interested budget maximisers, not concerned with serving the voters but with ensuring that the budgets of their agencies were as large as possible. They were a major source of high public expenditure and increased government programmes. They were likely to establish close relationships with interest groups whom they could use to press for larger government programmes (Dunleavy and O'Leary, 1987). For Thatcher, bureaucrats were imbued with the social democratic consensus, open to sectional interests and interested only in increasing public expenditure.

Despite the *laissez-faire* rhetoric there was very little sign of limited government under Thatcher, who believed in the authority of Parliament to pursue its goals unconstrained by groups within civil society. As John Gray points out, from a Conservative perspective, 'the present Government, contrary to its professed intentions, is abandoning the projects of a limited state, and in arrogating to itself evermore discretionary powers, is creating the machinery through which a new political struggle for resources is to be fought' (J. Gray, 1993, 13).

The Thatcherite theory of the state with its concern for authority, order and the rule of law contained much from traditional Conservatism. However, with its anti-pluralism, its emphasis on markets as unquestionable solutions, anti-collectivism and critique of the civil service, it was very different from the progressive Conservative state theory.

Major seems to draw on elements of traditional, progressive and Thatcherite Conservativism in his understanding of the state. He has identified as important the need to cut back the size of the state: 'At all levels my ambition is smaller government, efficient government, responsive government.' However he confirms the traditional Conservative view 'that government has a vital indispensable role to play' and it should 'provide high quality education and health and security for the old, sick and others who depend on our welfare' (Major, 1994b, 2–3) Major emphasises the traditional Conservative concerns in order and nation, progressive Conservatism's commitment to a role for the state in welfare, and the Thatcherite concern with limiting the role of the state.

It is clear that within Conservatism there are competing conceptions of the state. Thatcher challenged the dominant Conservative theory of the state and distrusted state organisation outside the executive, so she embarked on a major reform of government. The next section will assess the changes that have occurred and assess the degree to which they were influenced by Conservative state theory.

The Reform of Central Government

Since 1979 Conservative administrations have reformed the state through shifting the boundaries of the state and by reforming the structure and organisation of central government. Changes in the boundaries of the state are most clearly seen in privatisation. As Marsh highlights,

> The scale of privatisation is immense. In fact, by 1991: over 50 per cent of the public sector had been transferred to the private sector; 650 000 workers had changed sectors, of whom 90 per cent had become shareholders, which represented 20 per cent of the population as compared with 7 per cent in 1979; the nationalised sector accounted for less than 5 per cent of the UK output compared with 9 per cent in 1979; about 125 000 council houses have been sold, most to sitting tenants under the right to buy provisions; and contracting-out was well established in the NHS and the local authority sector. (Marsh, 1991, 463)

Privatisation was one of the flagship policies of the Thatcher period and it has been continued with vigour by the Major administration with the selling of the final BT shares and commitments to sell off British Rail and the few remaining mines, plus a review of the Post Office. However, whilst privatisation has shifted the boundaries of the state, it has not necessarily reduced the role of the state. The government has continued to regulate the privatised monopolies; there has been little reduction in the level of public expenditure, and it has intervened greatly in its reforms of health and education (Chapter 11; Richardson, 1993).

There is also an increasing perception that the government is shifting functions of the state unelected 'extra-governmental' organisations: 'a third of all public expenditure – some £46.6 billion in 1993 – is now being channelled through the appointed contracted out state. There are some 5 521 quangos and over 70 000 quangocrats put there by ministerial appointments' (Weir and Hall, 1994). The central state might be doing less but public bodies are still carrying out many functions.

The government has also attempted to reduce the size of the state by reducing the civil service to under 500 000 workers. The civil service has been reduced from 748 000 in 1976 to 533 350 on 1 April 1994 (Cmnd 2627, 1994, 11). However, much of this reduction was not the result of tasks disappearing but because of privatisation and contracting-out

(Drewry and Butcher, 1991). In addition, the fall in non-industrial civil servants has only been from 565 815 in 1979 to 487 435 in 1994, and at the same time there has been an increase in casual staff employed (from 6862 in 1979 to 19 005 in 1994: HM Treasury, 1994).

Thatcher also saw it as her goal to 'deprivilege' the civil service. Civil service pay increases were limited, and more recently there has been a dramatic shift away from centralised pay and grading systems and the introduction of performance-related pay and individual contracts of employment. Now about 60 per cent of civil servants are covered by 'delegated pay bargaining arrangements' (Cmnd 2627, 1994, 26). Public competition was introduced for certain high-level civil service jobs.

The combination of a long period of Conservative government and civil service reform raised a number of ethical questions. Even a former Conservative Cabinet minister, Lord Prior, has talked of a 'rather cloistered familiarity' between civil servants and ministers (HC 390–i, 1992/3, 16). Several recent cases, such as the paying of some of Norman Lamont's legal fees and the Matrix Churchill affair, have highlighted questions about the relationships that exist between ministers and civil servants (see also HC 390-I, 1992/93). It has been suggested that there is an increasing danger of politicisation through ministers picking civil servants who support their views, civil servants not having experience of a Labour government and by civil servants 'second-guessing ministers' (HC 390-i, 1992/3, 18). However, Peter Hennessy argues that there are very few overt examples of politicisation (HC 390-iv, 1992/3, 82), and the government's civil service White Paper was committed to maintaining the traditional values of permanency and neutrality. The government wants a unified, but not uniform, civil service. Perhaps the greatest changes that have occurred are not in the size and functions of the civil service, but in the structure of government and the introduction of management techniques which were central to Thatcher's initial reforms of the state.

Thatcher and the Reform of Central Government

The revolution in Whitehall gathered momentum under successive Conservative administrations. Despite Thatcher's alternative theory of the state, for a long period she appeared uninterested in the machinery of government (A. Gray and Jenkins, 1993). Before 1988 she did very little. She amalgamated the departments of Industry and

Trade, abolished the Central Policy Review Staff and the Civil Service Department, and in 1988 split the Department of Health and Social Security into its health, and social security (DSS), components. Such changes often resulted from prejudice or political expediency rather than strategic thinking, and were seen as cosmetic rather than substantive (Painter, 1989).

Perhaps her most significant changes were in the Prime Minister's Office, with an increased staff, greater use of external advisers, and greater intervention by the Prime Minister in departmental policy (Hennessy, 1986; A. Gray and Jenkins, 1987). Under Major the size of the Number Ten Policy Unit continued to grow. The staff working directly for the Prime Minister increased from 66 in 1983 to 107 in 1993 (HC 390–i, 1992/3, 8). Partly to by-pass the civil service and to overcome departmental inertia, Thatcher also increased the role of think tanks, but Major has been less willing to give privileged access to these groups.

Early on in her administration, Thatcher was concerned with government efficiency and value for money. In 1979 she appointed Sir Derek Rayner to introduce efficiency audits into departments, leading to the creation of the Efficiency Unit. The aims of the unit were to scrutinise departmental policies and activities, and to find ways of saving public money. Between 1979 and 1985 there were about 300 reviews saving an estimated £300 million a year. There were problems with departments carrying out reviews and setting up the required performance indicators but the Unit did introduce better management techniques into departments and force departments to think about how they operated (Warner, 1984; Collins, 1987).

The work carried out by Rayner and the Efficiency Unit was systematised through the Financial Management Initiative (Richards, 1987). The FMI was intended to promote better information and management in government by providing departmental managers with:

- a clear view of their objectives; and assess and wherever possible measure outputs or performance in relation to those objectives;
- well-defined responsibility for making the best use of their resources including critical scrutiny of output and value for money; and
- the information (including particularly about costs) training and access to expert advice which they need to exercise their responsibilities effectively (Cmnd 8616, 1982 cited Zifcak, 1994, 28).

As a result each department was obliged to implement a management system which would ensure that they had the information to assess the mechanisms for achieving their objectives. This change did produce some savings, but results were variable and it introduced confusion into the roles of ministers and Permanent Secretaries (Zifcak, 1994). However, departments were given a clearer idea about their costs, and the initiatives contributed to a change in culture with the introduction of managerialism into Whitehall (Richards, 1987). According to a former head of the civil service, 'It was a kind of turning point: at once a crystallization of the changes in the management culture of the civil service which had been evolving since at least 1969 (and indeed well before that), and as the starting points of many of the reforms that were to come later' (Armstrong, 1988). Indeed, the FMI was to lay the foundation of the greatest changes to occur in central government this century: the creation of Next Steps Agencies.

The Next Steps

Although Raynerism and the FMI clearly indicated a major change in the culture of Whitehall, the impact was limited by the traditional departmental structure of central government. Consequently, in 1987 the head of the Efficiency Unit, Sir Robin Ibbs, produced the Next Steps report in order to allow for a real delegation of financial and management authority (Hennessy, 1990).

The Ibbs Report, *The Next Steps*, proposed a division in departments between those who are policy advisers and makers at the core of a department, and those concerned with service delivery (in other words, the implementation of policy), be it providing road tax discs, printing government publications or making social security payments. The parts of departments responsible for service delivery were to be hived off into management agencies which would have much greater freedom to determine how services were to be delivered, to control budgets and to hire and fire staff. The intention was to 'clarify the divide between operational responsibility and policy responsibility' (BBC, 1994).

This proposal would effectively dismantle the apparently monolithic and unified civil service established in the nineteenth century, and develop a model where a 'loose federation of many smaller agencies, units and cores predominates' (Kemp, 1993, 8). However, when Mrs Thatcher first announced the Next Steps initiative, it appeared that the changes would be relatively minor. According to Hennessy, 'constitutional changes in ministerial responsibility were out as were any attempts to end Treasury control over budgets, manpower and national pay bargaining. Furthermore, the initial list of candidates for executive agency treatment left the big tax-raising and benefit paying empires intact' (Hennessy, 1990, 621).

The initial Treasury and Civil Service Committees reports were critical of the slow progress in the establishment of new agencies (HC 481, 1989/90, vi). The programme produced inter-departmental conflict, with the Treasury attempting to maintain its control over budgets and manpower (Painter, 1989). However, from late 1989 the speed of reform accelerated greatly. In the third year of the programme 19 new agencies were created, with a further 24 under active consideration. This took the total number of agencies to 50, employing over 180 000 civil servants (Kemp, 1990; HC 496, 1990/1). This was the beginning of the explosion in agencies. By July 1994 there were 97 executive agencies covering 340 000 civil servants (Cmnd 2627, 1994, 13). A further 20 per cent are confirmed agency candidates with the aim of launching the rest of the agencies by mid-1995, although in reality it is likely to be 1996.

There are a number of reasons for the sudden progress in the initiative. First, there was a high degree of prime ministerial authority behind the initiative. Major saw the improvement of public service as an essential part of his programme, and it had broad support within the party. Second, Sir Peter Kemp, a Whitehall outsider, was put in charge of the implementation of the programme. He provided very dynamic leadership and was prepared to spend a lot of time highlighting the benefits of the agencies and showing departments how to create agencies (Greer, 1994). Third, although departments were initially cautious, once they saw how successful the first agencies were they were soon prepared to join the bandwagon. The agencies seemed to have two obvious benefits: they improved the delivery of services, and allowed departments to hive off certain political problems.

The aim of the Next Steps programmes is to release departments and agencies from uniformity: 'The notion of a service-wide system appropriate to everyone is becoming increasingly a fiction' (HC 496, 1990/1, 48). This is a major change in the nature of Whitehall and the modern state. The traditional hierarchical bureaucracy has been replaced by an almost federal system of a core and periphery, with the periphery not being directly controlled by the centre. This raises important questions concerning the role of the agencies and their relationships with departments and the Treasury.

Most agencies are concerned with delivering services, or regulation, or are trading concerns (Dunleavy and Francis, 1990). The agencies are intended to concentrate on service delivery and to a have 'a clear quasi-contractual relationship with the core department' (HC 496, 1990/1, vii). By being semi-autonomous they have the freedom to decide how services can best be delivered. Certain agencies, like the Benefits Agency, which are central to their department's role also have an input into policy advice (HC 496, 1990/1, xv). Consequently the size and function of agencies varies greatly, with the largest having a staff of 72 000 and the smallest under 50 (Dunleavy and Francis, 1990).

The specific goals and functions of the agencies are set out in framework agreements which are negotiated between each agency and the responsible department:

> All new executive agencies have a framework document with five main ingredients: the aims and objectives of the agency; the nature of its relations with Parliament, ministers and the parent department, other departments and other agencies; the agency's financial responsibilities, how performance is to be measured; the agency's delegated personnel responsibilities and the agency's role and flexibilities for pay, training and industrial relations arrangements. (Greer, 1994, 60)

Rather than the relationship between the department and agency being one of command, it is one of a bargained contract specifying tasks and targets. Within that framework considerable freedom is allowed.

With so much work being hived off, departments should, in theory, be reduced in size by about 25 per cent (Efficiency Unit, 1991). The DSS has seen its headquarters staff reduced from about 2500 to 1200 (HC 550-i, 1990/1, 1). However 88 per cent of chief executives 'reported no significance reduction in headquarters financial or personnel staff' (Price Waterhouse, 1994, 8). The key role of departments is now to support ministers by advising them on achieving government goals and coordinating the agencies (Kemp, 1993.6, 390-iv). This will allow them to concentrate on 'policy making, legislation, resource allocation, essential finance and personnel functions, and the procurement of services from agencies or on contract' (Efficiency Unit, 1991; Mottram, 1994).

The agencies also raise important questions about the role of central departments such as the Treasury. The Treasury was initially resistant to the agencies because it feared a loss of financial control. Delegated management means that the Treasury has much less control over how money is spent because detailed management of resources has to be left to chief executives. Instead, the role of the Treasury should be to focus on measuring outcomes and concentrating on 'strategic issues, resource allocation and facilitating best practice' (Efficiency Unit, 1991).

These changes in the structure of government have created difficulties for departments and agencies. Chief executives feel that departments are intervening too much in their work (Efficiency Unit, 1994), partly because of the difficulty in distinguishing policy-making, implementation and day-to-day operational matter. For example, there is debate within the prison service over whether decisions on the level of security in prisons are policy or operational matters. The overall level of security is a policy matter, but ensuring the measures are in place is operational (BBC, 1994). In practice, there is difficulty determining the boundary.

The nature of the relationship also raises issues of accountability. Officially, agencies should improve accountability. Ministerial accountability still exists and the minister is answerable to Parliament for activities of the department. In addition, the chief executive is answerable for the delivery of services, and his or her contract can be terminated if targets are not met. The setting of explicit targets is said to produce genuine accountability, and not the accountability of constitutional myth (Painter, 1994, 244). Graham Mather has argued that Ros Hepplewhite of the Child Support Agency (CSA) and John Wilby of the London Ambulance Service have accepted responsibility for the policy of their agencies:

No Whitehall mandarins with unlimited tenure contract have accepted responsibility for policy disasters. It is now becoming essential, rather than optional that there should be some attempt to tackle the systematic malfunction of Britain's lawmaking and the shocking lack of definition of who is responsible for what in the implementation of policy, and who and in what circumstances will be held to account. (Mather, 1994, 1)

The chief executive also has to answer MPs' letters and appear before Select Committees (Greer, 1994). The new agencies demolish the old myth that a minister can be responsible for everything and delineates clear lines of responsibility: the minister for policy and the chief executive for implementation. According to William Waldegrave, 'there is now a clear distinction between "responsibility, which can be delegated, and accountability, which remains firmly with the Minister"' (see HC 390-I, 1992/3, xi; HC 390-i, 1992/3, 14).

However, as ministers, chief executives and civil servants admit, the distinction between policy and implementation is not always clear. There is evidence that 'the precise division of responsibilities between ministers and civil servants . . . has become more uncertain in recent years' (HC 390–I, 1992/3, xii). How policy is implemented is a policy decision that is taken by the chief executive.

Two clear examples of the ambiguities in this area are the cases of the CSA and the prison service. The CSA was set up to ensure that absent fathers paid maintenance. However, the policy became associated very much with the civil servant in charge, who was consistently criticised for the policy. There were undoubted failures within the CSA. It appeared to be concerned with crude cost saving, it created a range of anomalies, and it failed to meet its targets (*The Guardian*, 3 September 1994). It was unclear whether these were operational or policy failures, but it was civil servant Ros Hepplewhite who resigned and very little criticism was aimed at the minister in charge, Peter Lilley. The change to executive status seemed to have undermined the anonymity of a civil servant, and the lines of responsibility for a policy shifted away from the minister.

In the case of the prison service, there seems to be a debate over who should take responsibility for the attempted escape by IRA prisoners in Cambridgeshire in September 1994. In 1991 when IRA prisoners escaped from Brixton prison, responsibility was laid directly at the door of the Home Secretary, Kenneth Baker. In 1994, the media focused attention on a civil servant, Derek Lewis, to account for the escape. However, when asked who was responsible, Derek Lewis replied that,

> It was quite wrong to be speculating on these issue at this stage. The [Woodcock] enquiry only got under way a few days ago. There is a lot of work to be gone through . . . Until all of that has been put together no one can draw any conclusion as to what action is needed. (BBC, 1994)

Responsibility for the escape is no longer clear cut. It was not until an inquiry was completed by the Prison Inspector, Sir John Woodcock, that responsibility could be apportioned. Even then the report concluded: 'There exists some confusion as to the respective roles of the ministers, the agency headquarters and individual prison governors . . .

The inquiry identified the difficulty of determining what is an operational matter and what is policy, leading to confusion as to where responsibility lies' (*The Guardian*, 20 December 1994). The Home Secretary argued that the escape was not the result of policy failure. The Prison Officers Association felt was that 'Mr Lewis was put there to deflect things from the Home Secretary' (BBC, 1994). The Treasury and Civil Service Select Committee points to occasions where ministers have referred questions to chief executives that they should have answered (HC 496, 1990/1). Whilst the accountability of certain civil servants may have increased, the accountability of ministers is unclear and is further obfuscated by the establishment of agencies (Mather, 1994).

The targets that are supposed to increase accountability have also created problems. Organisation may be directed to achieving targets rather than delivering services, and can produce a 'massaging of figures' (Painter, 1994, 259). Time and resources not budgeted for in business plans are used to supply monitory data to departments (Price Waterhouse, 1994). Conflict over performance objectives may result from mistrust between the agency and the Treasury. Concern persists that because of the Treasury's desire to control, delegation is rhetorical rather than real (Mellon, 1990, 101–2).

Despite the problems with the new agencies and the possibility that departments exercise more control than is at first apparent, a very radical change has undoubtedly occurred in the structure and culture of Whitehall. A uniform hierarchy has been replaced by a core-periphery model, distinguishing between policy-making and policy execution (Kemp, 1993a). As a result there is greater delegation of decision-making and the culture of management has entered Whitehall. Although these changes were initiated by the Thatcher administration, to some extent they contradict Thatcher's Parliamentarianism. They establish a new set of intermediate institutions that are not easily controlled by the executive.

The parliamentary conception of the state, combined with the influence of New Right ideology, also led to a major restructuring of the relationship between the central state and local government. The administration was critical of local government as bodies, often Labour-controlled, that could hinder the implementation of government policy. New Right ideology created the perception that local authorities were hotbeds of waste and unaccountability. The Thatcher administration had three main aims in regard to local government: to control public expenditure, to strengthen local accountability, and to 'bury socialism' (Rhodes, 1992, 51).

The government introduced a range of legislation intended to control local government expenditure and cap rate increases. In the mid-1980s the government abolished the Labour-controlled metropolitan counties and the Greater London Council, which were seen as centres of left-wing opposition. Finally the government introduced the Poll Tax, ostensibly as a mechanism for increasing local accountability. The Thatcher administration reduced local autonomy and forced authorities to become much more managerial (J. Gray, 1994). However, the government failed to reduce local expenditure, increase accountability, or, in terms of electoral results, bury Socialism (Rhodes, 1992). Local authorities have lost functions both to quangos and to central government, but these changes have not made control of local government expenditure significantly easier.

John Major and the Reform of Central Government

Major was prepared to build on the reforms initiated by Thatcher and to make reform a distinctive element of his administration. In 1992 he established the Office of Public Service and Science, with direct responsibility for the civil service and further reform. The department has responsibility for the Citizen's Charter, efficiency, and a new reform, 'market testing' (HC 390–i, 1992/3).

Many elements of the Next Steps programme, such as increased accountability better service delivery, and greater responsiveness to the consumer, were built into a central aspect of Major's programme: the Citizen's Charter. The aim of the Citizen's Charter was to increase the efficiency of public services and to make them answerable to the consumer by providing information on the cost and running of services, and by setting targets for the delivery of services (Cmnd 1599, 1991). Within Whitehall a Citizen's Charter Unit was established which 'should be engaged in constant dialogue with the departments responsible for the delivery of their own services to check that the Charter principles are being carried through in the policy of those departments and to interrogate them as to why they are not if they are not' (HC 390-i, 1992/3, 9).

Most departments have established their own charters with targets for services and means of public redress. For example, in the Employment Service the Job Seekers' Charter specifies the importance of name badges, politeness and consideration, and providing information; there are also targets for the number of people found jobs, time taken for people to be seen, and time for answering phones (Doern, 1993). In the health service the Citizen's Charter seems to be having important, even if symbolic, effects on the way nurses relate to patients, and plan and carry out their care. There is more emphasis on meeting the needs of the patient rather than the hospitals' organisational requirements.

The impact of the charters seems to be variable. They do not give specific legal rights and therefore appear more symbolic than real. Moreover, they sometimes focus on the relatively trivial rather than key questions of levels of provision. However, Doern has some evidence that the Charters have at least made agencies think about how they deliver services and whether they are taking enough account of the needs of their consumers (Doern, 1993). Under the Citizen's Charter, agencies are aware of errors in the delivery of services and have targets for reducing those errors.

The Major administration has also attempted to extend the reforms through the concept of market testing. Developing from the Citizen's Charter came the Competing for Quality initiative. The aims of this programme were:

- to concentrate activity on those things for which the civil service has to be responsible;
- to introduce more competition and choice into the provision of service;
- to improve the quality of service delivery to the citizen. (Oughton, 1994)

Where possible it was thought that tasks still provided by the public sector should be 'market tested' to see whether the service could be provided more cheaply by the private sector. Over 130 000 civil servants had to compete for their own jobs in areas such as typing and payroll services (Butcher, 1993). Initially the plan was to market test £1.5 billion of government services. By December 1993 £1.1 billion of government services had been market tested:

Of nearly 400 tests completed, 25 resulted in a decision to abolish all or a substantial part of the activity; 3 activities were privatised; 113 were contracted out; 229 were subject to competition between in-house teams and outside suppliers (of which in-house teams won 147 and outsiders 82); 6 activities were restructured without a formal test; and 13 tests were withdrawn and efficiency gains made internally. (Oughton, 1994, 7)

The problem with market testing is that it appears to be moving even further from a unified civil service, with certain public servants working in very different conditions from others. It has also been argued that the whole process of 'market testing' has placed agencies under great strain in actually preparing their tenders, and that time has been spent on this task rather than delivering services. More importantly, by forcing chief executives of agencies to undergo 'market testing' the promised autonomy has been undermined.

'Market testing' is pushing government much closer to 'contract government' (Harden, 1992). The state no longer provides services but is responsible for drawing up contracts for the development of services. The government's role is to decide what services are delivered, award the contract to the most efficient provider, and draw up a contract that specifies the rights and duties of the producer and the consumer (Harden, 1992). Accountability exists through the contract and not through parliamentary procedures. This may provide better accountability, but again little thought has been given to its constitutionality.

The consequences of Next Steps and 'market testing' were apparent in a radical report on restructuring the Treasury, published in October 1994. The report recognised that the recent reforms reduce the work of the Treasury, and recommended that a quarter of its senior civil servants should go by April 1995. Chancellor Kenneth Clarke wanted the Treasury's economic forecasting functions to be 'market tested'. With greater delegation of management to agencies and departments, the role of the Treasury in public expenditure could be reduced to setting spending parameters rather than detailed scrutiny (*Financial Times*, 10 October 1994). Consequently, the Treasury could be reduced to a small core, and other departments could be forced to follow.

The last 15 years have seen a major change in the organisation and the form of the state. The state is no longer a hierarchical bureaucracy. There is an increasing division between the policy makers and the suppliers of services, and services are increasingly provided by a range of bodies. More often the provision of services is governed by contract rather than constitutional convention. There has also been a move to greater openness, with departments providing more information on what they are doing and how they are performing. Have these reforms produced a Thatcherite form of limited government?

Assessment of Reform

The nature of the state has changed during the period of Conservative government since 1979. Rhodes (1994) refers to the 'Hollowing out of the State' as functions shift from the centre to agencies, quangos, the private sector and Europe. Harden talks of the 'Contracting State' as state provision has been replaced by contracts. New Right thought can be clearly identified in many changes, such as reducing the size of government and the civil service, managerialism, privatisation and 'market testing'. Nevertheless to see these reforms purely as a response to the New Right is to oversimplify.

For example, many of the changes introduce by Thatcher and Major can be seen to be the implementation of reforms suggested by the Fulton Report of 1968. Fulton proposed a more managerial civil service, creating organisations for the task at hand; and more open recruitment (Kemp, 1990). The reforms are part of a lineage of reform that stretches back to Fulton and Heath's managerialism in the 1970s. Pragmatism remains a strong element in reform.

New Right conceptions of the state were only one of a range of influences on reform. First, economic decline and the unwillingness of people to pay more in taxation forced the government to provide better public services with less resources (R. Butler, 1994). Second, these pressures have been felt world-wide. The government has been strongly influenced by reform programmes in the USA, Australia and New Zealand. A book published in the USA, Osborne and Gaebler's *Reinventing Government*, has become a bible to many British reformers (R. Butler, 1994; Painter, 1994). Third, reform has been particularly effective because it has been in the interest of politicians and officials. For politicians it has been a way of devolving political problems. In a number of highly-publicised cases politicians have succeeded in avoiding the blame for policy failure. When IRA prisoners were transferred to Northern Ireland hours after the IRA announced a ceasefire, the Home Secretary publicly blamed Derek Lewis for the timing of the transfer, even though he had apparently signed the papers. As Alan

Travis points out, 'By allowing him to be used as the public whipping boy for all the riots, breakouts and blunders that plague the prison service, Mr Howard can distance himself from the traditional rock on which many other top politicians' careers have founded' (*The Guardian*, 13 September 1994).

Agencies are also in the interest of officials because they have greater freedom from politicial control over their budgets and administration. This also reduces the hitherto rigid control of the Treasury, allowing departments more autonomy. Consequently, with a high level of political will, the degree of reform has been much greater than commentators would have predicted a few years ago. Fourth, the changes are a result of what many people might call the introduction of post-Fordist techniques into government. Social, technological and economic change, combined with new ways of handling information, mean that there is a rejection of the belief that a uniform hierarchical bureaucracy is the best mechanism for delivering public services. Osborne and Gaebler argue that government bureaucracy developed at a time of mass markets, shared needs and slower rates of change. It could cope at times of crisis and where there were clear goals. In an environment of increasingly free markets, globalisation and information technology, we need flexible and adaptable bureaucracies (Osborne and Gabler, 1992). The watchwords in the 1990s have become disaggregation, differentiation and making the organisation meet the task. The changes in Britain are partly a reaction to these new conditions.

This policy area provides a good measure of the impact of Thatcherism on Conservative politics. The language of managerialism has come to dominate the Conservative attitude to the state. Through the 'market testing' programme and contracting out, many of the principles of Thatcherism have been pursued much further. Moreover, the initial reform was inspired by the New Right critique of bureaucracy, and Thatcher's Parliamentarianism which did not want bureaucratic constraints on the power of the executive.

However, there is some indication that these reforms had unintended consequences (Marsh and Rhodes, 1992). In terms of expenditure and functions, the state is still very large. Contracts and private provision may have increased, but this is still paid for by public money and is formally under public control. Moreover, by creating semi-autonomous agencies and more quangos, the government's ability to control policy may be weakened. Indeed, to some degree Major's reforms aim not solely to reduce the size of the state, but genuinely to improve public services (Doern, 1993).

Major has taken Thatcher's reforms much further, partly influenced by Thatcherite ideology but also in response to long-term trends and to his own commitment to improved public service. This has led to a debate within his party over the future role of the state. Major sees the state as having a role in solving problems of social change, and providing services such as education and health (Major, 1994b) and Kenneth Clarke has reasserted the Conservatives' commitment to the public sector. Michael Portillo, on the other hand, seems to support a much more limited government view of the state, arguing that the state has no role in the economy: 'the State now seeks to do only the things that it alone can do, or that it does best at least for the time being' (Portillo, 1994a).

These changes also have important implications for the distribution of power within central government. The creation of the Next Steps agencies seems to be a move away from Thatcher's concept of a parliamentary limited state. As the agencies become more established, the ability of the executive may decline even further. The central British state has long suffered problems of coordination because of the strength of departments. With the further devolution of power to agencies the problems of coordination may become even greater. Already there are signs that the Treasury – one of the key coordinators – is losing some of its control. This increased fragmentation may make it more difficult for politicians to control the policy process. This conflict between agencies and Parliament highlights a contradiction within Thatcherism. Whilst wanting to improve the authority of Parliament, Thatcher also wanted to ensure that the reforms could not be easily reversed: the changing form of the state is a mechanism for preventing an in-coming Labour government easily reversing Thatcherite reforms.

The other power shift is from professional power to managerial power. In the past the key officials in the government were the professional policy advisers, and it was these professionals who managed the departments from the top to the delivery of services. Increasingly, Permanent Secretaries are becoming policy managers rather than policy advisers. Simultaneously, in the delivery of services it is now a distinct set of managers, the chief executives, who are in control. It is an interesting indication of this shift that several chief executives now earn more than Permanent Secretaries.

Conclusion

The form of the state has shifted greatly since 1979. Managerial criteria have been given much more emphasis, the cost of government is much clearer than before, and there is a concerted attempt to reduce spending. The civil service has been reduced in numbers, and has become much more organisationally diversified with different rates of pay and more open recruitment at higher levels. Most importantly, the structure of government has changed with the division between policy making and the delivery of service. There is, as a consequence, greater concern with the users of the service rather than the producers. Despite the fact that many of these changes may be more rhetorical rather than substantial, it cannot be doubted that there has been a radical change in the organisation and ethos of Whitehall.

Although ideology was the impetus behind the initial reforms, it is difficult to see that Conservative conceptions of the state have influenced them. Certainly, New Right thinking has been important in the introduction of management techniques, 'market testing' and the purchaser provider split. However, the form of the state today hardly meets New Right models. It is still extremely large and ultimately responsible for a whole range of functions including the collective provision of welfare services. In a sense Major has united elements of progressive and New Right Conservatism, continuing the commitment to public service whilst subjecting it to a management ethos and competition from the private sector.

Note

I would like to thank Fiona Devine and Steve Ludlam for comments on earlier drafts of this chapter.

9

Economic Policy under Thatcher and Major

HELEN THOMPSON

In the immediate post-war period the Conservative Party portrayed its
economic policies as a free market bulwark against oppressive Socialist
planning, and popular irritation with the legacy of wartime controls
and with Labour's 'austerity' budgets helped carry the Tories into
government in 1951 (Shonfield, 1958). In office, they broadly accepted
the post-war aims of full employment, stable prices, a healthy balance
of payments, and economic growth to pay for the welfare state. The
Tories were, of course, more attached to free markets and budget
surpluses, much less keen on physical controls or anything else that
smacked of rationing or planning, and preferred to develop monetary
policy as the key instrument of demand management (Cairncross,
1992).

By the 1960s, however, the Tories under Macmillan sought to avoid
'stop–go' responses to chronic balance of payments problems by
embracing incomes policies and indicative planning (Brittan, 1964).
Labour's failure to make progress along the same lines led Heath to
launch the short-lived 'Selsdon Man' economic liberalisation programme in 1970 that collapsed two years later in the U-turn which
ignited the neo-liberal rebellion in his ranks (Gamble, 1990a). Not only
did he introduce an interventionist Industry Act that Tony Benn was
later happy to deploy, but his return to compulsory incomes policy
ended in humiliation, first at the hands of trade unionists and then of
the electorate. The neo-liberal rebellion turned into the ideological

insurrection that captured leading figues in the party and carried Thatcher into the leadership and then into office (Ranelagh, 1992; G. Howe, 1994).

Although the Thatcher governments earned a reputation as being the most ideological of post-war British governments, their economic policy was also frequently marked by U-turns and inconsistencies. In 1979–80 policy was organised around a sterling M3 (£M3) target and sterling was allowed to float. Ten years later £M3 was a forgotten memory and sterling was fixed against the Deutschmark in the ERM. Similarly, the Thatcher administrations' record on intervention in the economy ranged from support for Britain's information technology industry from 1982 to the mid-1980s to indifference to the demise of the traditional manufacturing sector. Whilst Thatcher and her ministers often talked the ideology of free market economics (and, in the early days, of monetarism), these considerations were only rarely reflected in their policy decisions. We cannot take the ideological language of the Thatcher governments as the fundamental precepts of Thatcherite economic policy to compare with the Major record (Bulpitt, 1986).

Indeed, it is highly unlikely that any British government will be motivated by ideology in economic policy-making beyond the very short term. Given the volatile international environment in which economic policy is made, and sterling's perennial weakness, British policy-makers are frequently reduced to crisis management. At the same time, economic management is a crucial determinant of electoral performance and the British political system gives full scope to managing economic policy in an electoral cycle. Consequently, any government's economic policy is best examined within an electoral context.

This is not to suggest that ministers will simply accommodate the preferences of the median voter in a simple political-business cycle, or that ministers will not seek to sell their decisions on ideological grounds; rather, ministers are motivated by a range of considerations defined by the electoral cycle. These include: the provision of material benefits to voters, particularly in policy areas where they are claiming a comparative advantage over opposition parties; strengthening the economic position of their political constituencies *vis-à-vis* other groups; delivering an economic policy package to the electorate which can be sold effectively by the rhetorical ideology ministers have adopted; and pursuing policies which they can implement effectively and which do not pose problems of party management.

Within this framework any precepts of Thatcherite economic policy are best understood as the strategies of the Thatcher governments to manage the economy so as to retain office. Seen in this way, the contrast between floating, a £M3 target and ERM membership does not necessarily mean that the Thatcher governments' economic policies were nothing more than an incoherent mixed bag. The continuity between the Major government's economic policies and the Thatcherite past can then be assessed in terms of whether the new government pursued policies which were determined by the same electoral strategy as its predecessors. At the same time, it is possible to consider the continuity in the ideological rhetoric which the two administrations used to sell their policies to the electorate. The remainder of the chapter is divided into two parts. The first part gives an overview of the Thatcher government's economic policy and outlines some constant themes in their policy approach. The second part examines the policies of the Major government in context of the overall Thatcherite approach and draws some conclusions about the respective economic strategies and problems.

The Thatcher Record

Although the first Thatcher government experimented with a range of economic policy options, the successes, mistakes and assumptions of that administration defined the context of subsequent Thatcherite economic strategy. On entering office in 1979, the government wanted to deliver three broad economic ends: namely, lower inflation achieved by monetary means, cuts in income tax and an ideological presentation of itself as a successful alternative to 1970s corporatist and interventionist economic failure. Ministers soon discovered the difficulties of achieving this particular package of benefits. Income tax cuts were inflationary in themselves and the government was forced to finance them with an inflationary increase in indirect taxation. Neither could the government reduce inflation by monetary targets without the ensuing appreciation in sterling destroying a quarter of the manufacturing sector of the economy, and sending unemployment towards the 3 million mark. In 1981 ministers reversed policy, abandoning the monetary targets first for an old-fashioned fiscal squeeze to reduce inflation and then for a counter-inflationary framework based on exchange rate stability. The Conservatives' subsequent election victory in 1983 demonstrated to Thatcher that, given a divided opposition and the British electoral system, there were sufficient benefits for sufficient voters in low inflation and falling interest rates to offset the poor productive performance of the economy and high unemployment.

After 1983 the Thatcher government rebuilt its economic strategy both on its success on inflation and in surviving the inadvertent decimation of the manufacturing sector of the economy. Having identified a clear constituency to which it could deliver specific economic benefits, ministers now sought to provide consumptive and productive advantages for that constituency, aligned with reasonably low inflation. It is within this context that the specifics of the government's economic policy, in terms of monetary policy, exchange rate management, fiscal policy and intervention in the economy, can best be understood. The following discussion examines in more detail the Thatcher government's perspective on inflation, how it tried to create benefits in terms of production and consumption for its core constituency, and the consistent problems which beset its economic management.

Inflation as a Monetary Phenomenon

There is a simple paradox about the Thatcher governments' approach to inflation: they wanted to deliver low inflation but, from the first adminstration onwards, they repudiated most of the available counter-inflationary weapons. First, despite the evidence that wage increases have been a consistent source of inflationary pressure in Britain, from 1979 the Thatcher government was adamant that it would not practise formal wage restraint. Second, ministers effectively removed credit controls. During the first administration Geoffrey Howe abolished exchange controls which made the corset (which limited bank lending) redundant, and later abolished hire purchase controls. In the mid-1980s financial deregulation and the suspension of broad monetary targets removed the last effective control of the growth of credit in the economy. Finally, after the deflationary 1981 budget, the Thatcher governments never again accepted that fiscal policy could be used to reduce inflation through either public expenditure cuts or tax increases.

Indeed, by the start of the second term the Thatcher governments were only prepared to use high interest rates and the exchange rate as counter-inflationary policies. Nigel Lawson justified this stance on the grounds that 'inflation is pre-eminently a monetary phenomenon [and] interest rates the essential instrument of monetary policy' (*Financial Times*, 8 July 1988). However, by denying the relationships between consumer demand, wage costs and credit and inflation, the third Thatcher government created an inflationary boom from 1987 to 1989 which it could only cure with high interest rates and an appreciation in sterling resulting in recession. The electoral strategy required low inflation because it was the ministers' one claim to economic success between 1979 and 1983, but low inflation would only be delivered by means which could not be labelled a return to 1970s corporatism and interventionism. In this sense the Thatcher governments became 'one-club golfers' with interest rates as their central macro-economic tool, whilst publicly arguing that credit expansion and wages should be left to market forces.

Production and Consumption Constituencies

The Thatcher government's free market rhetoric was betrayed by their frequent willingness to intervene in the economy according to their own ends. After their 1983 General Election victory, Conservative ministers developed a strategy to encourage certain sites of production which were to their electoral benefit, at the same time as allowing market forces to operate in the manufacturing sector. At the heart of the government's strategy lay the financial service sector and a project to recreate London as the prime European financial centre. During the mid-1980s ministers intervened to start deregulating and modernising City practices, as a result of which the City became an unparalleled site for international capital operations. By 1989 the broad financial service sector was the engine of growth of the UK economy, employing 2.6 million people. It represented 19.8 per cent of gross domestic product (GDP) in 1989 compared to 11.6 per cent in 1979. At the same time, the Thatcher government was prepared to intervene to support growth in the nonfinancial service sector. For example, in 1984 the Treasury made services eligible for Regional Development grants for the first time, despite the general move towards selective rather than automatic assistance in regional aid. In this climate, the service sector's share of GDP increased by 2.1 per cent as a proportion of GDP between 1979 and 1984, and by 6.8 per cent between 1984 and 1989.

    With ministers in effect using interventionist policies only in those sectors of the economy dominated by potential Conservative voters, the manufacturing sector was left to fend for itself and served as a symbol of their free market ideological rhetoric. With the government cutting industrial subsidies, real expenditure on trade, industry and energy fell by 40 per cent in real terms from 1978–9 to 1990–1. At the macro-economic level, ministers tended not to consider the question of industrial competitiveness in managing the exchange rate. As 'one-club golfers', Thatcher and her Chancellors were always prepared to engineer an appreciation in sterling when it suited them, whatever the consequences for the competititiveness of British goods.

Privatisation was to many the culmination of the Thatcherite free market approach to industrial production, with most nationalised industries sold to private ownership. However, a government genuinely motivated by a free market ideology would not have created the private monopolies that resulted, and privatisation was at least as important in the revenues it offered minsters to increase consumption for their electoral constituencies. Allied with North Sea Oil revenue, privatisation financed income tax cuts in 1986, 1987 and 1988 on a scale which would usually be dependent on high growth generating new revenues or huge-scale borrowing. These cumulative income tax cuts were crucial to the Thatcher governments' electoral strategy since they were such a significant boost to disposable income, and exploited the Conservatives' general comparative advantage over Labour on the taxation issue. The government further boosted the consumption of its key constituencies by deregulating bank and building society lending and, hence, hugely stimulating the credit and housing markets. As with privatisation, the government was using one-off reforms to create prosperity for consumers and mortgage holders which was not dependent on growth among British producers.

In sum, after 1983 the Thatcher governments made no effort to reverse the decline of the manufacturing sector to enable Britain to pay its way in the international economy without relying on short-term inflows of interest-sensitive capital. Rather, ministers pursued an economic policy which created new cleavages of production and consumption. If British economic decline could not be reversed, then the Thatcher governments ensured that they increased the relative and immediate advantage of particular social and economic groups.

The Problem of Sterling and Europe

Although economic policy helped secure the Conservatives a relatively easy re-election in 1987, the Thatcher governments' economic management was riddled with problems in relation to sterling. These problems were encapsulated in the ongoing ministerial wrangling over ERM membership. From 1982 Thatcher was at odds with successive Chancellors and Foreign Secretaries over whether sterling should participate in the system (Chapter 13). By vetoing ERM membership, Thatcher made it extremely difficult for the government to pursue either a coherent policy for sterling or an effective European policy. Politically, there was no alternative to the EC and Britain's influence on economic issues in the EC (such as monetary union) was diminished once outside the ERM. Economically, the government's reliance on monetary policy and the exchange rate as its central policy tools left it particularly dependent on maintaining international confidence, which could not ultimately be divorced from ongoing openness towards Europe. Outside the ERM, and with Thatcher and Lawson publicly feuding on the issue, the government was left to manage a series of sterling crises and maintain a real interest rate premium over most of the ERM states.

At the same time, those of Thatcher's ministers who supported ERM membership, such as Lawson and later John Major himself, never addressed the question of how Britain could be a successful member of a fixed exchange rate system without a broad counter-inflationary framework and with a large balance of payments deficit. By 1989 the balance of payments deficit was a manifest constraint against the government's ability to pursue exchange rate stability as a policy. Despite evidence that the deficit would become more difficult to finance, Major pushed for an appreciation of sterling in 1990, and then secured Thatcher's acceptance of membership without examining just how membership was supposed to work. The combined effect of these problems was that the Thatcher government's exchange rate policies were dominated by short term and *ad hoc* policy-making, in which one policy was quickly superseded by the next whenever a new crisis arose.

The Thatcher governments' problems in handling sterling were the heart of the troubled legacy which Thatcher bequeathed to Major in November 1990. Seven weeks before Major became Prime Minister, Thatcher had finally agreed to British membership of the ERM and replaced the previous *ad hoc* exchange rate policy with a commitment to the discipline of a fixed exchange rate system. However, whilst Thatcher perceived membership as a short-term necessity to stabilise sterling and cut interest rates, the decision contained the seeds of medium-term disaster for the government (Thompson, 1994). With the

British economy in recession, ERM membership would make the ability to cut interest rates beyond the immediate future dependent on the actions of the Bundesbank. Yet in October 1990 German interest rates were rising, and likely to continue to do so as the Bundesbank sought to contain the inflationary pressure ignited by German reunification. The DM2.95 rate of entry to ERM would only compound Major's problem, since a balance of payments deficit for 1990 of £13.8 billion suggested that sterling was already overvalued. If the foreign exchange markets came to believe that Britain would have to devalue to deal with the problem, there was a risk that interest rate would actually have to be increased despite the recession.

The Major Government

The Major governments' approach to economic policy can best be divided into three periods: first, from November 1990 to April 1992; second, from the Conservatives' General Election victory to Black Wednesday in September 1992; and, finally, from the autumn of 1992 into 1994. The following discussion will examine each of these periods in turn and demonstrate how, slowly and somewhat inadvertently, the Major government took tentative steps away from some of the precepts of Thatcherite economic policy without developing a real alternative strategy.

The Recession and Election Victory

Although both Major and Norman Lamont were relative latecomers to the Thatcher Cabinet, there was little early evidence that either man wanted to depart significantly from the Thatcher–Lawson and Thatcher-Major approach to economic policy. Major and Lamont clearly believed that controlling inflation was crucial if the Conservatives were to be reelected. Lamont told the House of Commons that rising unemployment and business failures were a 'price worth paying' for the defeat of inflation. Meanwhile, both the Prime Minister and Chancellor continuously stressed that sterling's participation in the ERM at a central rate of DM2.95 would remain the counter-inflationary lynchpin of economic policy. This commitment came despite the government's inability to loosen monetary policy during the first three months of Major's premiership because of sterling's weakness within the ERM. Fortunately for Major, he did not have to confront the latent contradiction between sterling's membership of the ERM and the government's rather bare counter-inflationary cupboard. Despite the fact that Britain entered the ERM with an inflation rate above 10 per cent (significantly higher than the other ERM states), the speed with which output fell from the second half of 1990 ensured a sharp drop in inflation in 1991–2.

The overwhelming problem for the government was the recession. Although Lamont was able to cut interest rates by 3.5 per cent from February to September 1991, thereafter there was no scope for any further loosening of monetary policy. With British interest rates at 10.5 per cent, they were now within a fraction of the effective floor of German rates; the next move by the Bundesbank would inevitably mean a further tightening of German policy. Deprived of a monetary stimulus to the economy, the Major government showed itself to be as wedded to one-club golf as its predecessor albeit in a different economic context. Whilst the Thatcher governments insisted inflation was only a monetary phenomenon, Major and Lamont ignored non-monetary stimuli to growth. In the 1991 budget Lamont explicitly ruled out using an expansionary fiscal policy to assist recovery and, indeed, actually tightened policy for 1991–2. Rather than taking action to stimulate the housing market, the government abolished mortgage tax relief against the 40 per cent rate of tax. Despite incontrovertible evidence that massive levels of personal and corporate debt were a huge contributor to the depth of the recession, Major and Lamont were no more prepared to engage with banks and building societies to promote new lending than were the Thatcher governments to restrict credit. Without a policy framework which extended beyond the exchange rate and interest rates, Major and Lamont were left looking to ERM membership to deliver a recovery which it was extraordinarily unlikely to produce.

In terms of the framework for generating production and consumption benefits, there was both continuity and some shift in emphasis in Major's premiership up to April 1992. Certainly, Major retained the non-interventionist approach to the manufacturing sector which Thatcher had exercised after 1983. With the right-wing Peter Lilley remaining Trade and Industry Secretary, leaders of industry regularly complained about the lack of government support as the recession took its toll (Wilkes, 1993). At the same time, Major's approach to the Maastricht Treaty indicated that the competitive position of the British financial services sector remained an important priority. Whilst many interpreted Major as negotiating an 'opt-out' of the monetary union treaty, his actions are better seen as giving Britain the right to 'opt in' to a single currency. The treaty set outs a three-stage timetable to reach a single currency, and Britain's position is unique only in that it will not be obliged to move to the final stage without a separate decision to do so by its government and Parliament. By negotiating such an opt-in to a single currency, Major appeared to want to stall the wrath of Conservative Europhobes and sceptics whilst ensuring that the British financial service sector need not be isolated in the medium to long term.

By contrast, the Major government initially demonstrated slightly different priorities on consumption issues from its predecessor. Although both taxation and the interests of mortgage holders were central to Thatcherite strategy, the Major adminstration's early actions indicated that the former was now more significant than the latter. In the 1991 budget Lamont abolished mortgage relief against the higher rate of tax. This stood in sharp contrast to Thatcher's absolute insistence that mortgage tax relief was sacred for the Conservatives. Meanwhile, income tax cuts remained fundamentally important. By the spring of 1992, the toll of the recession on the Public Sector Borrowing Requirement (PSBR) meant that income tax cuts before a general election were impossible. Yet Major and Lamont still did their utmost to exploit the issue in their pre-election budget, creating a new 20 per cent tax band on the first £2000 of income and declaring that their objective for the next Parliament was to reduce the basic rate from 25 to 20 per cent. During the election campaign, the Conservatives almost exclusively focused their agenda on Labour's expenditure and taxation plans, claiming that a Labour government would deliver a tax bombshell for everybody.

From Zero Inflation to Black Wednesday

Given the severity of the recession and the government's inability to offer a clear programme for recovery, the Conservatives' election victory in 1992 was a let-off for Major. Nevertheless, having won a victory in his own right, Major now had a greater freedom to reformulate his government's economic strategy, albeit within the contours of ERM membership and the recession. The first indication of a possible change in policy came with the appointment of Michael Heseltine as Secretary of State for Trade and Industry. As a backbencher from 1986 to 1990, Heseltine distanced himself from the Thatcher government's approach to questions of production and campaigned for an active and interventionist policy towards the manufacturing sector. Major now appeared to have given Heseltine the chance to lead a systematic effort to rebuild that sector of the economy. In July 1992 Heseltine announced a fundamental reorganisation of the DTI to strengthen its capacity for industrial intervention The reformed DTI would now operate on a sectoral basis with officials required open to an informed dialogue and constructive partnership with industry in direct contrast to its function for most of the Thatcher years (Wilkes, 1993, 242).

Nevertheless, whatever reorientation in policy the new Major government had planned for the medium term, the immediate problem was the recession and the constraints imposed by ERM membership. Major and Lamont appeared to believe that the Conservatives' election victory would produce the necessary boost to confidence to stimulate an economic recovery and strengthen sterling which was trading towards the bottom end of its ERM bands. By June they faced an economic crisis. There was no evidence that the recession was ending despite a 0.5 per cent cut in interest rates during the previous month. On 2 June the Danes narrowly rejected the Maastricht Treaty in a referendum. The next day the French government announced that it too would hold a referendum on Maastricht, believing that the likely 'yes' vote would add legitimacy to the now embattled treaty. The foreign exchange markets concluded that, if the monetary union project were forestalled, then the ERM states would have less incentive to hold their currency parities against the Deutschmark and avoid realignments. As a result the Deutschmark appreciated, pushing most of the other ERM currencies, including sterling, towards the bottom floor of their bands.

Major and Lamont responded to the crisis by declaring that the government's aim was now to achieve zero inflation and that the central means to achieving that was the DM2.95 parity. Major affirmed on several occasions that not only would he not devalue sterling but that he intended to make sterling the hardest currency in Europe, whatever the other economic costs of doing so. Although these pronouncements could be interpreted as pure rhetoric designed only to secure the short-term confidence of the foreign exchange market, Major's words were backed by action; at least on fiscal policy. In July the Cabinet agreed to a new system of public expenditure control in which a Treasury planning total would be sacrosanct in all negotiations. Major and Lamont apparently saw this new fiscal discipline as a vital counter-inflationary control both for its own sake and to protect sterling's counter-inflationary credibility inside ERM.

The public commitment to zero inflation and the rigid system of public expenditure control represented a potentially significant departure from the Thatcherite approach in several respects. First, there is no evidence that the Thatcher governments were ever interested in zero inflation. In 1979 Conservative ministers entered office proclaiming that inflation was the number one evil, but within a few months decided to cut income tax, increase VAT, implement the Clegg Commission recommendation on public sector pay awards and cut subsidies to nationalised industries, all of which had inflationary consequences. In 1986 Thatcher and Lawson had the opportunity to push for zero inflation when the price of oil fell significantly. Instead, they chose an expansionary fiscal policy and a depreciation in sterling to stimulate growth.

Second, the July decision on public expenditure control was a small step towards reintroducing fiscal policy as a counter-inflationary instrument. Implementing a restrictive fiscal policy at the time of a deep recession can hardly be labelled formal demand management. Nevertheless, by placing fiscal policy firmly within the context of exchange rate management, the Major government distinguished itself from the Thatcherite approach in which fiscal and exchange rate objectives rarely operated in tandem. For example, when the Thatcher government was seeking an appreciation in sterling in 1988–90, it was never prepared to tighten fiscal policy as a means to achieve that end.

Meanwhile, in dealing with the crisis of Britain's ERM membership, Major and Lamont demonstrated the same propensity to take short-term decisions without a clear rationale as had Thatcher and her successive Chancellors. Although the Deutschmark rose against almost all ERM currencies from June to September 1992, sterling and the lira were clearly the two currencies under the most severe pressure. The heavy selling of these currencies was not an incidental whim of the foreign exchange markets but reflected an accurate judgement that, in fundamental economic terms, the two parities were unsustainable. In sterling's case, Britain was in a deep recession which meant that any possible increase in interest rates would be disastrous, and the DM2.95 parity flew in the face of the continuing external deficit. Yet Major and Lamont acted throughout the summer of 1992 as if sterling was neither in absolute danger of falling out of its ERM bands nor as if there were any relative difference between an overvalued sterling and an undervalued franc.

Despite the intense pressure on sterling, Lamont ordered the Bank of England not to intervene in the foreign exchange markets in the three months prior to September. He maintained this stance even when sterling fell through its ERM divergent indicator, at which point reserve intervention should have been imperative. At the same time, Major and Lamont refused to countenance any broad realignment of ERM currencies against the Deutschmark which included sterling but not the franc. With the French referendum looming on 20 September, Lamont chaired a meeting of EC finance ministers and central bank governors on 5 September in Bath. The German finance minster and the Bundesbank chief went to Bath hoping to persuade as many states as possible to participate in a realignment to which Italy had already agreed, in exchange for a cut in German interest rates. At the meeting, Lamont effectively ruled out any open discussion of the subject and pointedly refused to admit to sterling's weakness. Instead, he concentrated his energies on a futile effort to bulldoze the Bundesbank chief into a unilateral interest rate cut.

On 16 September, in what came to be known as Black Wednesday, the Major government paid the price of the *ad hoc* and short-term policy which had characterised both the Thatcher and Major administrations' approach to sterling. Despite a 0.5 per cent cut in the German discount rate, the foreign exchange markets turned in an onslaught against sterling which could not be withstood by either massive reserve intervention or a 5 per cent hike in interest rates. On the evening of Black Wednesday, Lamont was forced to announce that Britain was suspending its membership of ERM and that sterling would now float outside the system.

The Search for a New Policy

Black Wednesday left the Major government without a macro-economic policy. Outside the ERM the government's proclaimed commitment to exchange rate stability and zero inflation was obsolete. In the wake of the Black Wednesday disaster ministers could be seen visibly groping for a new policy. Whilst Major declared that 'a growth strategy is what the country wants and a growth strategy is what we are going to get', his

Chancellor was busy trumpeting a return to the monetary targets of the early Thatcher years (*The Guardian*, 31 December 1992). Eventually, Major ordered a cut in interest rates, allowing the depreciation of sterling to continue and hoping that both the monetary stimulus and the boost to industrial competitiveness would generate an economic recovery.

Nevertheless, cutting interest rates and hoping that the inevitable depreciation in sterling could be contained was far from a complete economic strategy. Consequently, in preparing the 1992 Autumn Statement, the government was forced to do far more than make the traditional judgements about public expenditure. Instead, it needed to set out an entire new economic policy both in terms of ends and means. In practice ministers concentrated their efforts in two areas, namely the issue of economic recovery and creating a new counter-inflationary framework.

When the Autumn Statement came, Lamont announced a £4 billion recovery package aimed at industry, housing and capital investment, and expressed hope that recovery could be led by a new partnership between government and industry. At the same time, he outlined a new counter-inflationary framework built around public expenditure control and a formal inflation target to be monitored by the Bank of England. In order to meet the overall public expenditure control figure for 1992–3 set the previous July, Lamont announced significant public expenditure cuts in defence and transport and a ceiling for increases in public sector pay of 1.5 per cent.

The 1992 Autumn Statement certainly represented a different approach from that practised by any of the Thatcher governments. Having placed fiscal policy in the context of exchange rate management in July 1992, Major and Lamont redefined the issue. They now believed both that fiscal policy had a role in stimulating industrial production (as opposed to consumption through income tax cuts), and that it could serve as a central counter-inflationary anchor. Meanwhile, the public sector pay ceiling was a departure from the Thatcherite belief that government could not and should not implement any kind of formal wage restraint. Overall, the new policy was a recognition that managing the macro-economy required more than one-club golf. If interest rates were going to be used as a stimulus to growth, they could not be used to control inflation. Like its predecessors, the Major government saw controlling inflation as an important electoral priority. Unlike the Thatcher governments, the Major adminstration believed that it needed more than interest rates and sterling to achieve that end.

Yet if Major and Lamont did indeed hope for a fresh start in the autumn of 1992, then developments over the next 18 months indicated that the Conservative leadership would not so easily escape from the past across a range of policy areas. On the fiscal front the government faced a new problems in 1993 in the form of the PSBR. By March 1993 the Treasury was predicting a PSBR of £50 billion for the year with no evidence that a firm recovery was yet taking place. This caused a dilemma for Major and Lamont who had made fiscal restraint their counter-inflationary anchor, but who did not want to jeopardise what was at best a fragile recovery with a further tightening of policy. Within this context the 1993 budget was a compromise between the impera- tives of deficit reduction and encouraging growth. Lamont announced a package of indirect and direct tax increases to come into effect from April 1994 which included the imposition of VAT on fuel; an increase in National Insurance contributions and excise duties; and restrictions on mortgage tax relief and the married couples' allowance. He also held out the prospect of a further fiscal squeeze later in the year in a new unified budget in which taxation and expenditure decisions would be taken together. By the time of that budget in November 1993, Kenneth Clarke had replaced Lamont as Chancellor and duly tightened fiscal policy again, not just for 1994 but into 1996. Clarke's first budget froze the income tax allowance and the basic rate limit from April 1994; increased excise duties again, further restricting mortgage tax relief and the married couples allowance from April 1995 with the aim of phasing out the former by 2000; and introduced two new taxes on air travel and insurance premiums. The combined tax increases of the two budgets represented the biggest post-war increase in taxes, taking the equivalent of 3 per cent of GDP out of the economy. At the same time, Clarke announced a cut of 1.3 per cent in public expenditure in real terms for 1994–5 and then smaller increases in 1995–6 and 1996–7 from that lower base. Central to achieving the expenditure targets would be a public sector pay freeze. Given such fiscal restriction, Clarke predicted that the PSBR would fall to £38 billion for 1994–5 and be eliminated by the end of the decade.

In terms of specific detail the 1993 budgets seemed to be a continuation of the counter-inflationary fiscal priorities established in the autumn of 1992. By being tough on public expenditure control and budget deficit reduction, the government was using fiscal policy both as a deflationary weapon in itself and as a symbol of discipline for the foreign exchange markets. It was a commitment which went far beyond the use of fiscal policy as a counter-inflationary weapon deployed by Thatcher and Howe in 1981. Then, a deflationary budget was a one-off action and not scheduled to continue for several years. Moreover, it was designed to allow a loosening of monetary policy with the specific intention of encouraging a depreciation in sterling and not to hold it steady.

Yet if fiscal policy was undeniably a central part of the Major governments' counter-inflationary armoury, the suspicion lingered in 1993 and into 1994 that Major and Clarke had not given up on income tax cuts as part of their electoral strategy. With such a tight fiscal squeeze in the middle years of a Parliament and the possibility of new revenues from the privatisation of British Rail, British Coal and the Post Office, the Prime Minister and Chancellor left the way open for income tax cuts in the run-up to the next general election. In this sense such a restrictive fiscal policy was simply a means of making low inflation and income tax cuts compatible again.

The mixture of the old with the new was further evident in the government's policy towards incomes. By extending the public sector pay ceiling of 1992 into a three-year freeze, Clarke showed that he did not accept Thatcher's view that no Conservative government should practise formal wage restraint. Nevertheless, Clarke was projecting a public sector pay policy to last beyond any wage policy successively implemented by a post-war British government without any policy towards the private sector. If the Major government was accepting that wage restraint had a part to play in controlling inflation, then why were private sector wage increases not considered as a potential inflationary source? At the same time, the 'half a pay policy' begged the question of how the government was actually going to be able to control public sector pay whilst allowing 'market driven' wage increases elsewhere. In sum, whilst the Major government accepted a public sector pay policy to reduce the PSBR, the spectre of a full incomes policy remained too much for a Conservative government to bear.

On industrial policy the potential new start of autumn 1992 proved even more of a mirage. Neither Heseltine's reorganisation of the DTI nor the lofty post-Black Wednesday talk of a new industrial partnership resulted in any innovative policies in 1993. Rather, the government's industrial agenda was dominated by the pit closure fiasco. In the following year, ministers indicated within the space of a few months that they did indeed wish to encourage the growth of the manufacturing sector, but that they were not prepared to develop any resources-backed policy to make that possible. In March the Treasury announced a review of the financial system which would include a comprehensive assessment of the relationship between industry and finance. Treasury ministers encouraged industry to enter a dialogue with the government over the problems of firms finding funding on terms comparable with overseas competitors. Yet, two months later, Heseltine delivered a White Paper on competitiveness which flatly ruled out any interventionist approach to rebuilding the manufacturing sector as an engine of growth, and concentrated instead on a series of educational proposals. The paper explicitly stated that business could best be helped to help itself by the delivery of low inflation and the control of public expenditure by government. Rather than an industrial strategy, Heseltine offered further deregulation of business workplace practice and the privatisation of the air traffic control service to go with the existing commitments to privatise British Rail, British Coal and the Post Office.

Despite occasional bursts of alternative aspiration, the Major government retains the view of its predecessors that a Conservative government can deliver sufficient economic benefits to a big enough constituency without being dependent on Britain's manufacturing, and hence trading, performance. Indeed, in many ways, the Major government has extended the Thatcherite free market approach to the manufacturing sector into a more general tenet of economic policy. Whilst the second and third Thatcher governments actively helped the service sector, the Major government has not intervened to help the sector recover from the particularly heavy toll of the recession. Whether Major and his ministers have failed to understand the complexity of Thatcherite economic practice or whether they simply believe there is benefit in policy consistency, they have been more true to free market rhetoric than the Thatcher administration ever was.

At the same time, the old problems of formulating a coherent and effective exchange rate policy remained in 1993 and 1994. As part of the post-Black Wednesday counter-inflationary framework, Clarke strengthened the position of the Bank of England again. First, he gave the Bank control over the precise timing of interest rate changes, and then he started to publish the minutes of Chancellor–Governor discussions six weeks after their monthly meeting. Nevertheless, whilst the Major government recognised that the foreign exchange markets needed to be impressed with something, partial autonomy for the Bank was insufficient to protect the government from old problems with sterling. In October 1993 sterling fell significantly amid Conservative discontent with John Major's leadership. Between February and April 1994 there were three further bouts of sterling depreciation because of uncertainty about Major's position.

Although on each occasion sterling stabilised without the government having to take corrective action, the threat of a full-scale sterling crisis hangs over Major and Clarke. They were merely fortunate in 1993 that floating was so painless since history suggests that monetary policy can only be detached from the exchange rate for relatively short periods of time. At the same time, the government's attitude towards the European dimension of exchange rate management remains riddled with contradiction. Whilst the government made no response to the rebirth by stealth of the ERM in early 1994, it has set targets for reducing the PSBR and national debt explicitly to comply with the Maastricht convergence criteria for monetary union. These are just the kind of mixed signals to the foreign exchange markets which the Thatcher governments were punished for so heavily in the past.

Conclusions

After the short-lived experiment with a form of monetarism, the Thatcher governments aimed to deliver a range of economic benefits to a core constituency of the electorate, and sold those policies in terms of a free market ideology. The specific ends of policy were reasonably low inflation achieved by monetary means, income tax cuts, increasing prosperity for mortgage holders and selective intervention to assist the service and financial service sectors. At different times, and most particularly after Black Wednesday, the Major government's economic policy has been a critique of aspects of the Thatcher governments' strategy whilst maintaining the rhetoric of a free market approach to policy. There has been an explicit recognition that low inflation requires policies other than high interest rates and an appreciating exchange rate. Ministers have also implicitly accepted that there has to be a careful trade-off between the ongoing priorities of consumption benefits and controlling inflation.

Nevertheless, Major and his Chancellors have essentially sought to deliver the same kind of benefits to the same constituencies as did the Thatcher governments. The rationale of Major's policy lies in the hope that, come the next general election, the traditional Thatcherite constituency of voters will appreciate low inflation and income tax cuts, or at least the promise of them, whatever costs to the contrary they endured from 1992–6. Whilst the Major government has practised a rather un-Thatcherite fiscal and overall counter-inflationary discipline, in many ways this was the inevitable consequence of the problems of exchange rate management both within and outside the ERM, particularly as the PSBR grew. Economic circumstances and the ebbs and flows of the economic cycle almost always restrict the policy options for ministers and mean that only overall policy ends can be sacrosanct. To try to offer the same ultimate economic benefits as the Thatcher governments did, Major and his Chancellors have been forced by the recession and the international financial environment to pursue some economic policies that differ from those of the previous leadership. Thus, although the Major government has pursued some policies which resemble pre-Thatcherite policy, namely a more multipurpose approach towards fiscal policy and a public sector pay policy, these decisions are best understood as means to recreate the old Thatcherite economic order.

The Major government has given several indications that it would like to find a new policy framework which would generate benefits to voters through sustained growth and a strong manufacturing sector. However, the government is inhibited from any change in policy both because it is still seeking to sell its overall policy package in terms of a free market ideological approach and because it flinches from the interventionist policies and European dimension to policy which a new policy framework would require. If the Thatcher governments were essentially a reaction against the politically disastrous modernisation project of the Heath government, then Major has been no more willing to return to an interventionist and explicitly European state to try to reverse British economic decline.

10
Whatever Happened to the 'Enemy Within'? Contemporary Conservatism and Trade Unionism

BEN ROSAMOND

Introduction

Anyone even vaguely acquainted with British politics since the late 1960s or so will be aware of the centrality of the 'trade union question'. Governments, so it seemed, succeeded or (more usually) failed according to the extent to which they were able to manage 'trade union power'. Even eminent academics were given to express their concerns in the most hyperbolic terms. 'This trade union power', wrote Samuel Finer 'which has brought successive governments to a standstill in recent years . . . is manifestly a political power' (Finer, 1973, 391). Various aspects of union activity came to be seen as causes of Britain's economic malaise: their tendency to induce crippling industrial stoppages; their ability to create inflationary wage settlements; their increasing role in decision-making in Westminster and Whitehall; and their privileged access to the Labour Party.

The politicisation of matters relating to unions and employment played right into the hands of the young, pamphlet-writing Turks of Thatcherism. Elected in the aftermath of the wave of industrial action which became known as the 'Winter of Discontent' (1978–9), the

Conservative administrations of Margaret Thatcher embarked upon an unprecedented legislative bombardment in the areas of trade union and employment law reform. Government rhetoric demonised unions. One writer dubbed it 'the industrial cold war' (Carty, 1991). The issue of union power seemed to be enormously salient. In January 1979, 84 per cent of a sample polled by Gallup felt that unions were becoming too powerful (R. Taylor, 1993, 370). The analysis of the relationship between Thatcherism and trade unions became an academic growth industry, attracting a host of contributions from political scientists, lawyers and industrial relations specialists.

Yet, a decade and a half later, the anti-union rhetoric seems to have died. In August 1992 only 21 per cent of Gallup's sample thought that unions were becoming too powerful; 54 per cent thought that the level of union power was 'about right' (cited in R. Taylor, 1993, 370). The trade union question no longer seemed to preoccupy politicians, policy-makers and leader writers. This raises several intriguing questions. Does it mean that Thatcherism solved the 'union problem'? Alternatively, did the Conservative Party under John Major shift its position on unions to a more moderate posture? Has Britain arrived at a new industrial relations consensus? In short, whatever happened to the 'enemy within'?

Conservatives and Unions

Before reviewing the approaches of the Thatcher and Major governments to trade unions, it is useful to pay some attention to the place of unions within British Conservative discourse. There is no clear 'Conservative view' of trade unions. It might be possible to argue that Conservatives would naturally incline towards hostility to trade unionism on the grounds that it emphasises both sectional class divisions at variance with the supposed organic unity of the nation and collectivist forms of action. Nevertheless a 'contextual' approach is more desirable since Conservative attitudes to unions have tended to follow the dominant intellectual tendencies in the party. They have also been formulated within the context of the prevailing political, economic and industrial circumstances.

Following the Second World War, the mainstream of British Conservatism seemed to have become reconciled with the idea that effective trade unionism was a necessary component of British prosperity. For instance, Quintin Hogg (who later became Lord Hailsham), writing in 1947, felt able to argue the following:

> Trade unions are good, and the Trade Union Movement is an essential and valuable part of the industrial machinery of this country. I tend to regard those who refuse to join unions in factories as eccentric perverse, or possibly wanting in public spirit. In short I do not agree with their point of view, but I defend with my life their right to hold it and act on it. (Hogg, 1947, 128)

Such sentiments would seem to be remote from the more zealous outpourings of Thatcherite anti-trade unionist discourse, especially if we agree with Taylor's view that '[t]he world that Mrs Thatcher and John Major have sought to create has no obvious role for trade unions at all' (R. Taylor, 1993, 319). Hailsham's views were characteristic of 'right progressive' Conservative thinking at the time, with its emphasis upon intervention, planning and conciliation. There were intra-party disagreements, but broadly speaking Gamble's summation of the one nation, consensual position of the likes of R. A. Butler and Harold Macmillan reflected the dominant perspective of the post-war British Conservative Party: 'Conservatives' faith in their ability to suspend the laws of capitalist economics by a magical infusion of goodwill and co-operation into industrial relations led them naturally to the belief that they rather than the socialists were the best *protectors* of trade unionism under the new political order (Gamble, 1974, 146).

There is considerable evidence of conciliatory attitudes amongst leading Conservatives. Addison shows how the front bench of the party welcomed the wartime coalition government's 1944 *White Paper on Employment Policy* (Addison, 1994, 244). This document offered a guide to post-war governments by suggesting in its famous opening phrase that the state should seek to maintain 'a high and stable level of employment', thereby sanctioning at least a degree of government intervention to secure and create jobs and to monitor wage levels in industry. In 1947 the Conservatives, as part of a thoroughgoing review of policy, published *The Industrial Charter*. The primary aim of the document seems to have been the portrayal of the Conservatives not as a collection of brutal, free market zealots, but as a party committed to the prevailing ethos of economic management and social justice. It emphasised the role played by Conservative governments in the legal protection of unions and welcomed the involvement of union leaders in the formulation of public policy (R. Taylor, 1993, 69–72).

The Conservatives regained office in 1951 under Churchill. The attempt to create a climate of appeasement in industrial relations was best symbolised by the appointment of the ultra-conciliatory Walter Monckton as Minister of Labour. This strategy was certainly in tune with the broadly Keynesian intellectual tendencies which governed the framework of public policy at the time, but it also reflected the electoral calculus of Conservatives in the 1950s which suggested that proposals for trade union reform would be detrimental to a centre-seeking approach (Gamble, 1974, 148). Indeed with a climate of economic prosperity, the notion that Britain was in need of a radical economic overhaul – and, for that matter, the view that unions were the central cause of decline – were ideas which materialised around a decade or so later.

Britain's economic plight became visible to the political class at the turn of the 1960s. This signified the beginning of the notion that there might be a 'trade union problem' in the UK as rises in wage costs allegedly contributed to the poor competitiveness of British industry. Amongst policy-makers this provoked not aggressive employment law reform packages, but what Marquand has called the 'planning strand in Keynesian social democracy' (Marquand, 1988, 45). For Macmillan's Conservative government – and its Labour successors – this meant looking for ways in which the two sides of industry could be brought together in search of collective solutions, most notably in the form of incomes policies. The creation of the NEDC in 1962, bringing together representatives of capital, labour and the state to discuss growth strategies, was emblematic of the accompanying drift towards 'corporatist' approaches to the big questions of economic management (Middlemas, 1979). Such techniques clearly understood unions to be legitimate partners in the nation's public life. Rather than seeking to crush the power of organised labour, governments (Conservative and Labour alike) sought to harness this power on behalf of industrial recovery.

However, from the late 1950s a debate about trade union power had begun to take shape within the Conservative Party. This reflected the wider public debate about the state of British industry which took place beneath the banner of 'modernisation'. More Conservatives were prepared to argue for the creation of a new legal framework for the regulation of phenomena such as the closed shop, secondary action, unofficial strikes and the susceptibility of union funds to civil action (R. Taylor, 1993, 118–24). The idea that the British system of industrial relations was in urgent need of reform became conspicuous in the 1960s. Harold Wilson's Labour government set up the Donovan Commission to report on the state of British industrial relations and then tabled its own ill-fated proposals for reform in the White Paper, *In Place of Strife*. Meanwhile under the new leadership of Edward Heath, the Conservatives turned their attention to devising policy which would stimulate industrial efficiency through the effective regulation of the labour market. The broad thrust of these ideas emerged in the 1968 policy statement *Fair Deal at Work*, and reached maturity in the 1971 Industrial Relations Act. The Act attempted to place industrial relations within a regulatory framework which compelled unions to undergo formal registration, insisted that collective agreements should be legally binding, restricted trade union immunities, the closed shop and secondary action and created a National Industrial Relations Court. The legislation was part of a wider macro-economic strategy which also disowned incomes policies and state intervention in industry generally (Gamble, 1990a, 121–6). While partly reflecting a neo-liberal emphasis on the need to restrict the capability of unions to take industrial action, the Industrial Relations Act also sought formally to recognise the legitimacy of trade unions (Marsh, 1992, 12–13). The legislation suffered from this contradiction and failed to win the compliance not only of unions, but also many employers. In addition, as subsequent research found, the Act had very little impact on British industrial relations (Weekes, 1975). The government also found itself entangled in the British version of the escalation of industrial conflict which characterised advanced economies at the time (Crouch and Pizzorno, 1978), notably in the mining industry. As far as some Conservatives were concerned, the Heath experience offered a formative lesson on the dilemmas of trade union reform. The drift of academic opinion was migrating from the view that incomes policies and the incorporation of union leaderships into the state were the most appropriate ways of solving the problem of inflation and tempering union power. Legislative regulation became a desirable solution in Conservative opinion, yet the union movement appeared powerful enough to resist changes to the law.

The Thatcherite Approach

The Thatcher government took office in 1979 without detailed plans for reform of the trade union movement. Unlike the party under Heath in the 1960s, Conservative leaders did not spend the years of opposition drawing up a meticulous legislative agenda for the reform of the British system of industrial relations (Moran, 1979; Marsh, 1992, 54–9). The lack of a blueprint is explained by the fact that the Conservative Party, while united in its antipathy to union power, was undoubtedly divided at the highest level on the most effective way to deal with the problem. Broadly, the likes of Margaret Thatcher saw the solution in terms of a neo-liberal, anti-collectivist approach which would use labour law as a partial means to reassert the sovereignty of the market mechanism. James Prior, who became Thatcher's first Employment Secretary, represented the alternative view, which argued that minimal legal change would be sufficient to restore a balanced, 'voluntary collectivism' in the labour market (Prior, 1980). This raised party management issues, but also allowed elements in the Conservative leadership to develop the populist theme of trade union power as part of what Stuart Hall has called 'the great moving right show' (Hall, 1988, 39–56).

Despite the initial reticence and the lack of overt manifesto commitments, one of the most striking features of the Thatcher period was the sheer quantity of trade union reform sponsored by the governments of the 1980s. Figure 10.1 shows the scale of legislative activity undertaken by the Thatcher governments in the area of trade union and employment law reform.

The literature on the legislation is considerable (MacInnes, 1987; Auerbach, 1990; Hanson, 1991; Marsh, 1992). Several features of the legislation are worthy of note. The most obvious facet of the laws is their incremental character as evidenced by the progressive restriction of trade union immunities, the gradual erosion of the lawfulness of the closed shop and secondary action, and the ongoing tightening of union ballot regulations. Indeed, several commentators have noted the increasing arrogance of each legislative package. Auerbach shows how the Green Papers at the root of each Act evolved from broadly consultative documents into assertive polemics as the decade progressed (Auerbach, 1990, 159–60). Marsh maintains that the initial incrementalism owed much to fears that governments of the 1980s might suffer from the problems of compliance faced by the Heath government in the early 1970s. Once compliance was not deemed to be a problem, the Conservatives' pragmatic concerns converged with their ideological precepts (Marsh, 1992, 74–80).

FIGURE 10.1 *Summary of trade union and employment legislation, 1979–90*

Employment Act 1980

- Picketing restricted to striker's place of work
- Restrictions on 'sympathy' strikes
- Future 100 per cent union membership agreements (closed shops) to require 80 per cent ballots in favour
- Government funds made available to unions on voluntary basis for ballots on strikes

Employment Act 1982

- Unions cease to be immune from civil action and may be fined by the courts if found liable of undertaking unlawful action in disputes
- Definition of 'trade dispute' narrowed so that legal immunities only applicable in strikes involving employees and their own employer
- Existing closed shops not approved in last five years require 80 per cent ballot in favour (or 85 per cent if a secret ballot)
- Dismissal for refusal to join closed shop deemed unfair
- Unlawful for non-union companies to be excluded from tender lists
- Employers allowed to chose which employees to re-employ following a strike

Trade Union Act 1984

- Secret ballots on industrial action required if unions to retain immunities
- Secret ballots to elect union executive committees every five years
- Unions operating political funds to ballot members on retention of fund every 10 years

Employment Act 1988

- Abolition of protections for post-entry closed shop
- Right to postal rather than workplace secret ballots on election of leaders and maintenance of political funds
- Right not to be called out on strike without secret ballot
- Legal protection to union members refusing to go on strike or cross picket line even if dispute is lawful
- Establishment of Commissioner for the Rights of Trade Union Members to assist members with legal action against their unions
- Reduction of TUC's influence over employment policy via reorientation of Manpower Services Commission

Employment Act 1989

- Restriction of rights for union lay officials' paid time off

Employment Act 1990

- Closed shop effectively outlawed as right of complaint provided for anyone refused employment on grounds of union membership
- Unions liable for civil damages unless they repudiate unofficial stoppages
- Removal of immunity for those organising secondary action
- Allowance for the selective dismissal of unofficial strikers

The content of the laws is summed up well by Fosh, Morris, Martin, Smith and Undy in their consideration of the basis of the 1980s legislation:

> The Conservatives appear to have had two aims in their legislative activity for the reform of industrial relations and the reshaping of the labour market. These were the deregulation of the labour market (regulation of terms and conditions by statute or by collective bargaining must be reduced as 'a burden on business') and individual freedom (the individual must be free to enter into those contracts which seem to him/her appropriate or necessary). (Fosh *et al.*, 1993, 14)

Beyond these two pillars of the legislation, other writers have identified certain threads which ran through the Thatcherite union legislation. For instance, Miller and Steele point to the ways in which the legislation attacked collective bargaining via decentralisation and 'enterprise confinement'. The narrowing of the definition of a trade dispute so that single employers only are involved might be seen as an attempt to shift bargaining away from the national and the industrial levels. In addition Miller and Steele identify the themes of union democracy, most notably in the 1984 Trade Union Act, the importance of the dissenting union member, the reduction of union influence generally and the progressive intricacy of the law which places additional burdens on unions (for example, in balloting requirements: see K. Miller and Steele, 1993, 230–2).

There is much debate in the literature about the motivations behind the legislation. The discussion centres on the extent to which the Thatcher governments followed a New Right programme with commentators dividing more or less into the general 'radical' and 'sceptic' camps distinguished by Gamble (Gamble, 1990b). Radicals, such as the distinguished labour law scholar Lord Wedderburn, detect a marked similarity between the legislative path of the Thatcher government and the ideas of F.A. Hayek (Wedderburn, 1989). Wedderburn interprets the legislation as consisting in total of a characteristically Hayekian cocktail of deregulation and individualisation presided over by a strong state. To think otherwise would amount to being 'juridically tone-deaf' (Wedderburn, 1989, 15). Hayek's works, notably *The Constitution of Liberty* (1960) and *Law, Legislation and Liberty* (completed in 1979) contained several passages on trade unionism which had undeniable echoes in Thatcherite rhetoric and legislation. For Hayek, unions – particularly in the UK – had accrued powers and privileges (especially through legal immunities) which took them well beyond their appropriate role as voluntary associations or friendly societies. The granting of tort immunity meant that unions had been extracted from the rule of law. In effect they had become monopolistic threats to personal freedom in the labour market through their recourse to secondary action and the use of the closed shop. Industrial and national-level trade unionism further jeopardised economic prosperity as they interfered with the workings of the market and distorted real wage levels. What was necessary, claimed Hayek, was the removal of all 'privileges' which denied the law access to trade unions and institutions, such as the closed shop.

The sceptical position is taken by Auerbach (1990; 1993) who recognises the similarity between New Right thinking and the legislation, but argues that the Thatcherite approach – like much policy making – was a response to circumstances, notably the volatile industrial relations climate of the late 1970s and early 1980s. As such, trade union policy making was *ad hoc* and pragmatic and geared towards the goal of keeping the Tories in office. Fredman (1992) contends that the consistent use of the language of individual rights and freedom by the Conservatives provided an effective justification for the changes in labour law, but in no way were they reflective of a clearly worked out strategic approach.

With such a profusion of legislation it is easy to forget the other aspects of the Thatcherite approach which had a direct bearing upon unions. Two areas merit attention: the political exclusion of unions and the implications for unions of macro-economic policy. In terms of political exclusion, the Thatcher governments downgraded both quantitatively and qualitatively the contacts between union leaders and ministers (Mitchell, 1987). Combined with the abolition or reorientation of various tripartite institutions this has meant, as Marsh argues, that, 'Unions have had virtually no influence on legislation since 1979' (Marsh, 1992, 138).

Conservative macro-economic policy, with its emphasis upon deregulation, liberalisation and rolling back the state, also held important implications for trade unionism. The market-led approach of Thatcherism explicitly revoked the 1944 pledge to pursue the goal of full employment and put in serious doubt the legitimacy of collective bargaining as an appropriate way of organising affairs in the labour market. Moreover, the global processes of de-industrialisation (the decline in manufacturing employment) and 'flexiblisation', which were stimulated if not actually created by Thatcherism, posed serious challenges to the ability of unions to organise and operate in traditional ways (Marsh, 1992).

The Major Approach: Constrained Thatcherism?

In his exhaustive analysis of relations between trade unions and the state since 1945 Robert Taylor cites a number of notable journalists and academics writing from the late 1980s or so who were prepared to claim a substantial victory for Thatcherism in its battle with British trade unionism (R. Taylor, 1993, 265–7). The period of transition between Thatcher and Major seemed to mark both a dwindling of anti-union rhetoric from the Conservatives and the sense that there was little else to be done. The Conservatives' manifesto for the 1992 General Election provides a case in point. The section on 'Workers and Unions' amounted to five short paragraphs plus a series of short policy proposals which foreshadow some of the legislation which was to follow (Conservative Party, 1992, 20).

The key question here is whether the policies of the 1980s led to a radical alteration in the balance of power in the labour market. If they did induce significant change, then it would be possible to accept that further reform along Thatcherite lines might not be necessary. Unfortunately, for at least two reasons, this is a fiendishly difficult question to answer. First, 'radicals' and 'sceptics' would no doubt disagree about what constitutes 'success' in this context. Second, the premise of the question assumes that the Major government toned down the Conservative assault on trade unions. The accuracy of this assumption will be questioned below.

There is a substantial debate about the effectiveness of the legislation. The work done by Millward, Stevens, Smart and Hawes (1993) argues that the 1980s saw quite radical changes in the fabric of British industrial relations, the most notable of which was the degeneration of trade union representation in the workplace. However, a changed legal environment is but one of several putative reasons for such changes. Indeed, as Marsh (1992) emphasises, while the law undoubtedly shifted the balance towards employers, the legal changes of the 1980s did not automatically produce an employers' onslaught on the union movement. While this point is accepted by Taylor, he prefers to understand the key change of the 1980s as an alteration in the 'climate' of industrial relations towards greater individualisation and a diminished culture of industrial militancy (R. Taylor, 1993).

A further possible explanation for the less politicised nature of industrial relations and trade union questions is offered by Marsh in his review of opinion poll data. Noting the tendency for the public to continue to regard trade unions as a 'good thing', he suggests that 'the public has been given the sort of unions they wanted: politically less involved, and strategically and economically constrained' (Marsh, 1990, 63–4). The logic of this argument would lead to the conclusion that the significance of the trade union question has waned, and politicians now see little political advantage in the use of demonising rhetoric about union power.

An alternative explanation lies in the value for the Conservative Party of maintaining a high level of salience for the trade union issue. As suggested above, enmity towards the excesses of unionism provided a key populist component in the construction of the new Conservative coalition in the late 1970s. It is a lot less easy to conjure up the spectre of powerful unionism after a decade and a half in government, especially having claimed to have altered the terrain so radically. Consider the incompatibility of these two propositions:

Government Proposition 1: We have successfully curbed trade union power and transformed British industrial relations.

Government Proposition 2: Further trade union reform is necessary to restore Britain to economic health.

To articulate proposition 2 is tantamount to admitting the inaccuracy of proposition 1. Therefore, as a device in Conservative statecraft, anti-union rhetoric has become devalued.

Legislation under Major

In spite of the downgrading of anti-union rhetoric, the Conservatives under John Major continued to make laws in the areas of trade union and employment law reform. Figure 10.2 summarises the legislation which had both its origins and its ratification in the Major period.

FIGURE 10.2   *Summary of trade union and employment legislation since 1990*

Trade Union and Labour Relations (Consolidation) Act 1992

- Amalgamation of collective employment rights legislation

Trade Union Reform and Employment Rights Act 1993

- Rights for users of public services to seek injunctions to prevent disruption of those services by unlawful industrial action
- Automatic deduction of union dues by employer rendered unlawful unless each employee provides written authorisation every three years
- Workers have right to join unions of their choice
- All ballots for industrial action to be postal and subject to independent scrutiny
- Employers to be given seven days' notice in advance of strike action approved by ballots
- Lawful for employers to offer inducements to employees to transfer to non-union contracts
- Abolition of Wages Councils
- Advisory, Conciliation and Arbitration Service's terms of reference amended so that it no longer encourages collective bargaining
- Series of rights relating to maternity leave, unfair dismissal on grounds of pregnancy, victimisation following health on safety complaints and job descriptions

The most significant piece of legislation, by some distance, was the 1993 Trade Union Reform and Employment Rights Act (TURERA). The official Conservative view of this legislation demonstrated the new taciturn rhetoric. In 1992 Gillian Shephard, then Employment Secretary, described the legislation proposed in the advance White Paper as signifying the end of the Conservative government's long-running 'war' with the trade union movement. This was a 'tidying up' exercise only (*European Industrial Relations Review*, 223, August 1992, 12). A more cynical view might be that the Conservatives were concluding the war by patrolling the battlefield and bayoneting the wounded. True, TURERA did possess a Majorite inflection, notably with its allusions to the Citizens Charter idea, but several of its provisions followed a decidedly Thatcherite trajectory. Smith and Morton, for instance, are adamant about the continuities revealed by this piece of legislation: 'The TURERA is another step in the evolution of the Conservative government's project to diminish union power, and one which marks a new confidence and a willingness to jettison past inhibitions' (P. Smith and Morton, 1994, 6).

The 1993 Act further restricted trade union immunities. It made yet more detailed specifications concerning the membership and government of trade unions, and allowed for the investigation of union finances without a complaint from an individual member. The Act also eradicated the last supports for minimum wage legislation in the UK by abolishing the Wages Councils. It further discouraged collective bargaining by altering the terms of reference of the Advisory, Conciliation and Arbitration Service (ACAS), and it allowed employers to offer workers inducements to shift to non-union individual contracts of employment, a provision of a late amendment in which the government sought to overrule a Court of Appeal decision which held that the 1992 Trade Union and Labour Relations (Consolidation) Act outlawed 'sweeteners' to employees in exchange for the relinquishment of trade union rights (*European Industrial Relations Review*, 234, July 1993, 11–12). The Major government was also responsible for the abolition of the tripartite NEDC which had been set up under the auspices of Harold Macmillan's Conservative government in 1962.

The public sector pay policy of the Major government provided further evidence of both continuity and a certain degree of statecraft. After 1979 the government used its role as employer to set tight limits on wage rises in the public sector on the grounds that this would be one effective curb on the roots of inflation. The clear message of the Major government was similar. In September 1993, the Chancellor of the Exchequer announced a virtual pay freeze in the public sector. Any changes in pay would have to be offset by greater productivity. To increase pay bills would threaten both economic recovery and the prospects for reducing unemployment (*European Industrial Relations Review*, 237, October 1993, 13). While it may be true that the Major government did not involve itself in detailed negotiations, its reminder to Railtrack in 1994 that the 5.7 per cent pay offer to signal workers contravened the wage freeze policy provided evidence of the fear of the 'inflationary psychology' of negotiated wage rises, even in a concern that was due for impending privatisation. However, it has been suggested that the Major government did operate in a pragmatic manner in this area when necessary. Its second successive acceptance of the recommendations of the public sector pay review bodies implied that the Conservative leadership was eager to avoid any confrontation with public sector unions in the run-up to local and European elections (*European Industrial Relations Review*, 242, March 1994).

At one level it is possible to maintain, in terms of the substance of policy on trade unions, that Conservative governments since 1990 continued to follow the principles of Thatcherism. At another level, this sort of argument threatens to obscure the important ways in which the context of Conservative attitudes to unions has altered, most notably with respect to various aspects of what might be called the 'European dimension'.

European Dilemmas

The final two years of Margaret Thatcher's premiership saw the matter of European integration move to the centre of the political agenda in the UK. The stimulus provided by the project to complete the EC's internal market and the associated Commission-inspired social dimension quickly drew new battle lines of debate in an area of direct relevance to industrial relations and trade unions. Unions became enthusiastic supporters of the 'social dimension' in general and the proposed Social Chapter in particular (Rosamond, 1993). The Social Chapter's emphasis on a set of European-level statutory rights for individual workers contributed significantly to the transition in union and Labour Party policy away from a defence of the pre-1979 status quo towards the view that a combination of social partnership and positive rights was the most appropriate way ahead (Rosamond, 1992). Therefore, the first important aspect of the emerging European dimension was the contribution that it made to the changed parameters of debate on industrial relations.

Even more serious for the Major government was the way in which issues stemming from and related to the social dimension came to be the key issue in British politics. The successful negotiation of the Maastricht Treaty on European Union in December 1991 was utterly dependent upon the other 11 member states agreeing to remove the so-called Social Chapter from the text of the treaty at Britain's insistence. The Social Chapter had emphasised the notion of 'social partnership' and had provided for the extension of QMV into areas such as equal opportunities, worker consultation and working conditions. Instead the member states minus the UK signed a 'social protocol' which meant that the 11 would use the EC's institutions to debate and legislate in the area of social policy and workers' rights. The official position of the Conservative Party was that the Social Chapter would impose costs on British industry which would threaten competitiveness and destroy jobs. It was founded on a collectivist and corporatist ethos which ran against the grain of the government's thinking which favoured, in the words of the 1992 White Paper *People, Jobs and Opportunities*, 'a lightly regulated, decentralised and flexible approach to employment and social affairs' (cited in K. Miller and Steele, 1993, 233).

This position was perfectly acceptable to all but the most Europhile of Major's backbenchers. However, the issue of the Social Chapter did reappear during the ratification crisis of 1993 which seemed to endanger both the fabric of the Conservative Party (D. Baker, Gamble and Ludlam, 1993b) and the survival of the government. The Labour Party in Parliament tried to link acceptance of the Social Chapter with ratification of the Maastricht Treaty. With a backbench rebellion in full swing, the government was forced to call for a vote of confidence on the back of the treaty ratification vote. This ensured that the UK was not compelled to participate in the new 'social community' devised by the other 11 EC states, but it did show how the issue of European-level social legislation could be used to exploit fundamental divisions in the Conservative Party. In this context the Major leadership was forced to play a difficult intra-party management game (Chapter 6).

The Major government also found itself obliged to incorporate EC directives which had a direct bearing on employment law into UK legislation. For example, Part II of TURERA amended a number of individual employment rights, most of which owe their presence in UK law to a series of EC Directives dating as far back as 1975 (*European Industrial Relations Review*, 238, November 1993, 24). In other words, there can be little doubt that the legislative activity of Conservative governments on unions and industrial relations became increasingly subject to external constraint. Following the SEA (1986), the addition of articles 100A and 118A to the Treaty of Rome meant that matters relating to workers' rights and social matters generally could be subject to QMV in the Council of Ministers.

However, a government is always likely to respond to European level legislation and jurisprudence in ways which suit both its priorities and the political and legal framework of its country. One pair of commentators note the minimalist way in which the Major government chose to enact these directives and point to other measures in TURERA which restrict union activity 'thereby hindering collective action to protect those who avail themselves of these rights' (P. Smith and Morton, 1994, 6). Indeed there is some debate amongst industrial relations and legal scholars about the nature of the UK government's adoption of EC social legislation. Wedderburn sees little inconsistency between the

Conservatives' acceptance of health and safety directives and the Hayekian endorsement of minimal controls on working conditions (Wedderburn, 1989, 33). However, other aspects of European law would appear to protect non-Thatcherite aspects of the British industrial relations system. Miller and Steele maintain that 'the few remaining statutory supports to collective bargaining (consultation on redundancies and on the transfer of an undertaking) owe their continued existence to the fact that they are based on European directives' (K. Miller and Steele, 1993, 233).

Conclusions

The attitude of the Major government to trade unions displayed continuity with the previous Thatcher administrations as well as change. Surprisingly, perhaps, the legislative agenda pursued in the area of trade unions and industrial relations after 1990 clearly continued some of the major themes of Thatcherite labour law, but was not accompanied by the kind of public effusion of anti-union discourse characteristic of the defining legislative moments of the Thatcher period. This matter offers an interesting case study of the politics of support. In some key senses, it was no longer a viable strategy for Conservatives to accentuate the 'union problem', in spite of the fact that the assumptions which defined union policy under Thatcherism had become deeply ingrained. Beyond the philosophical underpinnings of labour law, ideas concerned with the deregulation of the labour market and the reduction of union-induced burdens on employers were still clearly central to Conservative strategies for economic renewal. There was no urgent need for the Conservative leadership to take a cautious approach to union reform as it would no longer ignite public or intra-party opposition of any substance. Yet the diminished salience of the union issue, combined with the changes in industrial relations, meant that there was less political capital to be gained than in the early 1980s from overt 'union bashing'.

There might be a temptation to interpret both the changes in trade union potency and outlook and the transformation of industrial relations culture in the UK solely to the policies of British Conservative governments since 1979. There are, however, powerful arguments from at least two sources to suggest that such changes have been – and will continue to be – driven by forces beyond the control of governments.

First, it would be perfectly plausible to locate the foregoing discussion in the context of radical shifts in the organisation of the global economy. Thus the de-industrialisation of the British economy, combined with rises in the service sector of the economy and a general casualisation of the workforce, might well be seen as more crucial determinants of patterns of employee relations and union power. It might be argued that governments, such as those of Margaret Thatcher, have accelerated this type of industrial restructuring (MacInnes, 1987, 79–80), but a global perspective places philosophies and patterns of labour law in a proper context. The examination of trade union legislation under the Conservatives does, nevertheless, reveal a lot about the British mediation of these global changes and is illustrative of the domestic and intra-party constraints on policy change.

Second, as shown above, by the time of the Major administration, trade union reform was providing a vivid illustration of the importance of the European dimension for an understanding of British politics. Indeed it is the European dimension which is most likely to lead to a greater politicisation of issues surrounding work, employment and unionism as the 1990s progress. The incorporation of EU legislation on workers' rights into British law is a possible stimulus for divisions on this issue to re-emerge in the Conservative Party. This will simply add a new lens through which the party views the union issue. Perhaps the 'enemy within' might still be around. It might just need a little help from the 'enemy without'.

11

Social Policy under Thatcher and Major

CHRIS PIERSON

As the leader of the wartime coalition, the Conservative Party entered the post-war era committed to the introduction of progressive social policies to tackle poverty, healthcare, and education provision (Addison, 1994). In opposition after the shock of the 1945 election defeat, Rab Butler coordinated an even more fundamental review of party social policy, and called for 'a total reorganisation of the social structure on which our party rested, an acceptance of redistributive taxation to reduce the extremes of poverty and wealth, and a repudiation of laissez-faire economics' (Butler, 1971, 133). Throughout the 1950s and 1960s Conservative governments increased expenditure on health, welfare and social policy, and sought to maintain full employment. Heath experimented with neo-liberal economic policies, but pledged to improve public services, 'abolishing poverty and squalor and raising standards of care for the old and sick' (J. Campbell, 1993, 376). In the Cabinet, future monetarists Keith Joseph at Health and Social Security, and Margaret Thatcher at Education, presided over expanding budgets. Both were very effective at squeezing additional money out of the Treasury, with Thatcher's White Paper, *A Framework for Expansion*, promising 'an extra £1000 million per year for education by 1981' (J. Campbell, 1993, 388). Even as the welfare state was subjected to financial pressure and increasing political criticism in the 1970s, the commitment to universal welfare continued to be proclaimed. As one senior Tory frontbencher wrote at the time, 'Only

202

Liberal ideologues, not Conservatives, see something fundamentally wrong with the welfare state. State provision for welfare is fully in accordance with Conservative principles. The welfare state is a thoroughly Conservative institution, which is why conservatives did so much to bring it into existence' (Gilmour, 1978, 162).

The subsequent rejection of the post-war social policy consensus is regarded as one of the central features of Thatcherism (Chapter 2). Recent scholarship, however, has seriously challenged claims both about the ubiquity of consensus before 1979 and its abandonment thereafter (Pierson, 1991; Butler, 1994). As one of her closest Cabinet collaborators and an originator of Thatcherism was later to lament, 'Margaret Thatcher's Government did not, in fact, succeed in controlling, let alone cutting, expenditure on the public services. The spending grew strongly in real terms' (Ridley, 1992, 85). None the less, it is clear that the rhetoric and policy ambitions of the Thatcher administrations were quite different from what had gone before, as was the external environment in which they operated. It was left to Thatcher's third administration, after 1987, to set out the direction of a radical restructuring of the welfare state. Thatcher's own involvement was famously cut short by her removal from office and the inauguration of John Major's premiership.

In discussion of the welfare state, as elsewhere, two contrasting views have come to dominate explanations of Major's administration and its relationship to the preceding period of governance under Thatcher. The first has tended to see Major's administration as a return towards traditional Conservatism, a more consensual and pragmatic politics that abandons the further-flung, ideological outposts of Thatcherism. A second view sees Major as the authentic inheritor of the radical neo-liberal mantle, carrying through the agenda of his predecessor with a zeal which is sometimes seen to have 'out-Thatchered Thatcher'.

In fact, neither of these accounts is wholly convincing. The idea of a 'return to consensus' is doubly confusing. The problem begins with the mis-specification of the Thatcher era. Thatcher came to power in 1979 fired by the conviction that Britain's long-term decline could only be reversed by 'rolling back the frontiers of the state'. Britain's citizens had become too dependent upon a state which eroded individual responsibility, stifled economic initiative and suppressed choice. Her ambition was to reverse the direction of post-war development, to restore economic incentives and disciplines, and to direct a much reduced welfare budget towards those in 'real need'. For all the rhetoric, however, the social policy record of the Thatcher governments was actually marked as much by continuity as by change. But if the Thatcher premiership was not one of unqualified radicalism, it has also to be said that evidence of a subsequent change in policy, to bring the Conservative Party back on to 'the centre ground', is strictly limited. Perhaps the nearest we come to such a 'return to consensus' is the seemingly unambiguous commitment in the 1992 Conservative manifesto to the retention and upgrading of Child Benefit, and with it an implicit endorsement of at least some element of welfare universalism. In fact, if there was a consensus re-emerging in the early 1990s, it probably had more to do with the Labour Party moving 'rightwards', or even with all parties coming to terms with Britain's changed position within a distinctively new and increasingly globalised international economy (Chapter 7).

On the other hand, the alternative view, which sees Major as 'the man who out-Thatchered Thatcher', has also to be treated with considerable caution. Certainly, since Major took over leadership of the Conservative Party, the Thatcherite policy agenda has been pressed further forward and this has sometimes given the impression that the Major government has rushed in where even Thatcher feared to tread (for example on privatisation of coal, rail, and postal services). But in this context it is really more appropriate to see the role of the Major government as implementing rather than originating policy change. Thus, whilst the Major government has not been particularly innovative, this does not mean that it has been an administration of consolidation. In the realm of social policy, Major's government has been putting in place, sometimes against fierce opposition, the most profound institutional changes for a half a century, notably in the process of implementation which is, in many ways, the decisive stage in policy elaboration. But the 'grand strategy' of reform is still Thatcher's, and to understand this process we have to go back to the policy changes of the Thatcher era, and especially of her third administration from 1987.

Setting the Social Policy Agenda: The Thatcher Legacy

Almost every policy initiative of government is likely to have a social dimension, but social policy is conventionally taken to describe the activities of the welfare state: measures for the provision of key welfare services, often confined to health, education, housing, income maintenance and pensions, and personal social services. There are very real problems with defining the welfare state in this rather narrow and institutional way (Pierson, 1991, 6–7). It draws attention away, as Thatcherites have often argued, from the relationship between social and other policy areas, especially economic policy. None the less, the welfare state thus narrowly defined covers a vast area of government activity. It is an employer to millions, and the principal, even sole source of income for many millions more; in 1992–3 it consumed some £60 billion of public expenditure and accounted for two-thirds of all government spending and over a quarter of national income (Hills, 1993, 8).

From the very earliest days of the first Thatcher government, Conservatives were deeply concerned about the way in which the welfare state had developed throughout the post-war period, but more especially during the 1970s. They argued that many of Britain's problems at the end of the 1970s, especially economic underperformance and social indiscipline, were directly attributable to the growth of the welfare state. It displaced the necessary disciplines and incentives of the marketplace, undermining the incentive to invest and the incentive to work. It encouraged the rapid growth of an 'unproductive' public bureaucracy, and the monopoly of state provision entrenched the position of public sector workers and their trade unions, enabling them to command inflationary wage increases. The welfare state was portrayed as inefficient and geared to the interests of organised producers rather than disaggregated consumers. Its compulsory provision of welfare services denied the individual freedom of choice, whilst its progressive tax regime had become positively punitive. Yet, despite the huge and growing resources devoted to it, the welfare state was failing to meet its policy objectives. It had not only failed to eliminate deprivation, it had actually made the position worse by displacing traditional community- and family-based forms of support, entrapping the poorest in a 'cycle of dependence'.

Given these multiple vices of the welfare state, and despite the voices of doom on both right and left, it is remarkable that so little welfare reform was undertaken by the first two Thatcher governments. Certainly, there was the major, and electorally rather successful, right to buy public housing, entrenched in the 1980 Housing Act. The 1980 Education Act legislated for an element of parental choice in selection of schools, and introduced the Assisted Places Scheme to provide state support for some children to attend selected private schools. Through-out the early 1980s there was a succession of minor changes to social security entitlements designed to make being a welfare claimant even less attractive and/or to shift the burden of provision towards individuals or their employers. Since 1982, pensions have been uprated in line with prices rather than, as previously (and more generously), in line with average incomes. This has had a profound cumulative effect upon pensioners, with the basic old-age pension now worth less, relative to average disposable incomes, than it was in 1948. Yet overall welfare spending continued to rise through the first half of the 1980s, largely to fund semi-permanent mass unemployment (Hills, 1993, 51).

It was left to the third Thatcher administration to initiate a process of wholesale reform in the welfare state and the public services more generally (Chapter 8). As well as the implementation of the Social Security Act of 1986, these years witnessed the passage of the Education Reform Act (1988), the Housing Act (1988), the National Health and Community Care Act (1990) and the implementation of wholesale reform of the NHS following the White Paper, *Working for Patients*, in 1989 (Department of Health, 1989). Cutting across this was the more general strategy for the reform of the public services contained in the Next Steps initiative (N. Lewis, 1993; Connolly, Mckeown and Milligan-Byrne, 1994). Major's social policy agenda has been dominated by the implementation and amplification of this burst of reforming legislation. There were important reforms in all of the five areas identified above as making up the welfare state, but in this discussion I shall concentrate upon the three most important sectors: education, health and social security.

Education Reform

The Education Reform Act (1988) has been described as 'the most important and far-reaching piece of educational law-making for England and Wales since the Education Act of 1944', (Maclure, 1989, v). Discussion here is confined to England and Wales. The experience in Scotland and Northern Ireland has been rather different. For example, by mid-1994 Scotland had just one opted-out school, a total that seemed as likely to go down as up! The Education Reform Act (1988) provided for the following changes:

- the inauguration of a national curriculum for all maintained schools;
- a policy of open enrolment under which parents are free to choose schools for their children;
- under the local management of schools (LMS), responsibility for the running of schools was transferred from Local Education Authorities (LEAs) to schools' own governing bodies;
- all secondary schools and larger primary schools might seek to opt out of local authority control and become grant-maintained (GM) schools, directly funded by central government;
- new funding and planning arrangements were established for both universities and polytechnics;
- provision was made for the establishment of City Technology Colleges;
- the Inner London Education Authority (ILEA) was abolished.

This process was further developed under Education Acts in 1992 and 1993. As well as changing aspects of the national curriculum and encouraging specialisation within particular schools, these made provision for the publication of comparative league tables indicating pupils' performance in National Curriculum assessments and public examinations, as well as school truancy records. Responsibility for inspection of schools passed from Her Majesty's Inspectors of Schools to the Office for Standards in Education (Ofsted). The Secretary of State has also been given new powers to put a 'hit squad', an 'Education Association', into schools which he or she deems to be 'failing'. The government sought to hasten the move towards a system of 'decentralised' GM schools by simplifying the process of opting out, and transferring further local authority powers to a new regional Funding Agency for Schools. The division between polytechnics and universities was abolished, virtually doubling the number of Britain's universities overnight.

Implementation of Educational Reform

The reforms were greeted by admirers and critics as radical innovations. The government insisted that educational standards could be raised by increasing parental choice and encouraging inter-school competition, while at the same time centralising control of the school curriculum. Its intention was to marginalise the power and influence of local government and their LEAs, of the teachers and their unions, and of the 'educational establishment' held responsible for a largely unproven long-term decline in standards. The aim is a system of opted-out, self-managed schools, directly funded by central government, operating their own selection criteria and competing with other schools for students. The most popular schools will expand, while competition will encourage less successful schools to make themselves more attractive to parents. Increased competition is also to be the watchword in higher education, with funding reflecting the capacity of institutions to attract students and provide courses at lowest cost.

Implementing the reforms has proved difficult. Whilst the principle of a national curriculum now finds broad political support, the content has been controversial, with criticism focused on controversial areas such as sex education, religious instruction and the content of history teaching. The original curriculum proved to be too large and too detailed. The government was greatly indebted to Sir Ron Dearing, former Post Office chairman, whose recommendations for a simplified and streamlined curriculum it was happy to accept. The government had always anticipated opposition from teachers and other education professionals: it was not disappointed. It was perhaps rather more surprised at the level of parental resistance. Although the teaching unions were sometimes divided, the opposition of the largest of them, the National Union of Teachers (NUT), with the at least tacit support of a significant number of parents, made it extremely difficult for the government to press ahead with testing. League tables of schools' performances were published, but the criticism that these were a measure not of the value added by schools but rather of the social composition of their intakes found substantial support.

Seemingly the cornerstone of the government's policy, at least in terms of the rhetoric of choice and quasi-market diversity, was the move towards a system of GM schools outside LEA control. John MacGregor, former Secretary of State for Education, claimed that GM schools were 'the Jewel in the Crown of parental power' (cited in Power, Halpin and Fitz, 1994, 210). The government's long-term ambition is to see virtually all schools opt for GM status. Funding arrangements, the rights to curricular 'specialisation' and the mechanics of parental ballots all seem to favour opting out. The White Paper *Choice and Diversity* anticipated that 'there could be over 1500 GM schools by April 1994. By 1996 most of the 3600 maintained secondary schools, as well as a significant proportion of the 19 000 maintained primary schools, could be grant-maintained' (Department for Education, or DFE, 1992, 19). Such projections now look wildly optimistic. By April 1994, 928 schools, rather than 1500, had opted for GM status, while the overall number of ballots, and the numbers of ballot votes to opt out, were falling *(Times Educational Supplement,* June 1994). There was also evidence that many opted out not to free themselves from local government control but to prevent school closures or amalgamations. Meanwhile, the oversupply of school places, perhaps as many as 1.5 million, remained a substantial problem (DFE, 1992, 24).

For all the talk of decentralisation and the empowerment of parents, the education reforms actually place unprecedented powers in the hands of the Secretary of State, including discretionary powers to intervene when the decentralised process is 'not working'. Under these circumstances, it was unfortunate for the government that one of Major's least successful Cabinet appointments was that of John Patten as Education Secretary. He managed to give offence in most corners of the educational world, described parents opposed to testing as 'ncan- derthal', and finally paid £100 000 in libel damages and costs to Birmingham's Director of Educational Services after calling him 'a nutter'. In the 1994 Cabinet reshuffle he was replaced by Gillian Shephard, a former teacher, who promised a more conciliatory line.

Some parts of the agenda have met with success. The programme to double the numbers entering higher education by the year 2000 was largely met within three years, and the principle of a national curriculum enjoyed very widespread political support, but in the strategic areas of testing and GM status the government has had enormous difficulty. Despite new alternatives to the traditional A-level and initiatives in the DFE, the DTI and the Department of Employ- ment, there is also a lingering suspicion that 'vocational training' remains substantially underdeveloped.

Health Reform

In the late 1980s, the government embarked upon a still more controversial and high-risk strategy in reforming public health care. The NHS had been at the heart of the welfare consensus, and even after 1983 ministers were anxious to stress that the NHS was 'safe in their hands'. However, while the principle of public health care free at the point of use and funded from general taxation remained very popular (Chapter 3), by 1987 there was evidence of growing dissatisfaction with the perfomance of the NHS (Bosanquet, 1988). Although NHS funding increased in real terms by nearly 30 per cent between 1979 and 1987, the government was widely criticised for underfunding public health-care. The government determined that a better use of NHS resources, estimated at £30.7 billion for 1993–4, could be secured by wholesale reorganisation. After a rather faltering review process, the government's proposals emerged in the White Paper, *Working for Patients*, in 1989. It stipulated the following changes:

1. Delegation of decision-making to district, hospital or individual general practitioner (GP) level.
2. Hospitals and other units could seek to opt out of local health authority control and acquire the status of self-governing trusts. Trusts have the freedom to sell their services to other health authorities, to budget-holding GPs, and to the private sector, they may establish their own management structures and determine their own terms and conditions of employment.
3. Health authorities are free to buy services from within their own area, from other health authority areas, from opted-out hospitals and from the private sector.
4. GP fundholding: larger practices will have their own budgets.
5. GPs' contracts were redrafted to give greater financial incentives, to stipulate certain statutory requirements and to limit the prescription of certain drugs.
6. The NHS was restructured along more business managerial lines.
7. Greater auditing of quality and value for money.
8. Encouragement of greater cooperation with the private sector.

As with education, so in the health service; the government's reforms concentrate upon dividing the purchasers of health services from their providers. While insisting that 'NHS services are available to all, paid for mainly out of general taxation; and mostly free at the point of use', the government looked to the introduction of competition and choice to deliver more effective care without a major increase in resources. The remit is to make the health service more responsive to the consumer: the patient, or more normally the patient's surrogate, the GP or the health authority as purchaser. As with schools, the government has encouraged the expansion of trust status and argued that 'in time, Trust status will become the natural organisational model for units providing patient care' (NHS Management Executive, 1990, 3).

Implementing Health Reform

Making trust status the norm in the provision of healthcare other than primary care is one of the few uncontroversial claims made about the reforms of the past five years. There was reluctance to move towards trust status before 1992, given Labour's commitment to reverse many of the changes, but the election result ushered in a new round of applications for trust status. By April 1994, more than 90 per cent of hospitals had either applied for, or had already attained, trust status; and more than one-third of all GPs, covering 40 per cent of patients, were in fundholding practices (*Financial Times*, 26 August 1993; *The Economist*, 28 May 1994). The consequences of these changes are vigorously contested.

The government hails the reforms as an enormous success. Their response to the first report on NHS Trusts of the Select Committee on Health, published in 1993, celebrated an average of 600 000 more patients treated per year, a reduction of over half in the numbers of patients waiting more than a year for hospital treatment, 'greater patient choice' and 'better value for money' (HM Government, 1993). The government argues that its 'internal market' for health care has brought enhanced competition, better auditing, more effective management and more healthcare output from a limited resource. The highly publicised publication in 1994 of league tables of trusts' performance was taken as a further landmark in generating the information which would allow patients to choose effectively. In part, the hostility of health professionals is taken as evidence of the government's success.

Despite, or perhaps because of, the ubiquity of the government's changes, they continue to generate intense hostility. One of the bitterest confrontations in the 1992 election campaign focused on Labour's claim that the Conservatives were seeking to 'privatise' the NHS. At one level, this would appear to be plainly untrue. The Tories did not propose to dispose of the assets of the NHS in a public share flotation. The 1992 manifesto retained a commitment that 'need, and not ability to pay, is and will remain the basis on which care is offered to all by the NHS' (Conservative Party, 1992, 27). Yet critics sought to justify their claims about privatisation by pointing to the autonomy of individual trusts, to the introduction of private-sector management and techniques in the trusts, and to the further blurring of the boundaries of public provision given that trusts could now purchase services from private sources. Some argued that trusts would make it easier to move towards wholesale privatisation at some later date.

It is perhaps more appropriate to suggest that what critics have identified here is not so much the privatisation as the 'commodification' of healthcare: that is, making healthcare something that is bought and sold on a market. In part this is precisely what the government intends, and certainly it is the case that the internal market does not create healthcare rationing: it simply makes it more explicit. Yet there is evidence that the new structure can create circumstances in which treatment is determined not by clinically judged need but by the healthcare purchaser's capacity to pay (*The Independent*, 4 July 1994). This has been the central contention of those who argue that the new system creates a two-tier service in which patients of contract-holding GPs may be treated ahead of patients of non-fundholders. Even some enthusiastic supporters of the reform process acknowledge that there is a problem of two-tierism, but insist that this is an inevitable part of the transition, maintaining that the remedy is to ensure a health service in which all GPs become fundholders (*The Economist*, 28 May 1994). This would eliminate the two tiers, but would not address the more fundamental objection that the decision to treat patients would still be made on contractual/financial rather than clinical grounds. If one concentrates upon the objections of healthcare professionals rather than those of politicians and commentators, perhaps the most frequently-voiced objection to the reforms is that they destroy the ethos of public service, and introduce an element of competition which is simply inappropriate. Of course, this may be dismissed as the response of professionals who find their monopolistic powers being challenged, but the sense that healthcare should not be the object of economic competition undoubtedly strikes a chord in public opinion (Chapter 3).

A second set of objections relates to the loss of public accountability. The move from a consensual to a more managerialist administration, the downgrading of the influence of locally-elected councillors and the concentration of powers in the hands of the Secretary of State's appointees (predominantly people with a background in private sector business), all suggest a service that is less accountable to local populations and with more powers concentrated in central government. Opponents insist that trusts have been packed with Conservative

Party supporters. Power may have been relocated but it has not passed into the hands of the immediate consumers of healthcare, or to their elected representatives. Public accountability is also said to have been weakened by 'gagging' clauses in the contracts of trust employees, which prevent them bringing matters of concern to wider attention.

It is extremely difficult to adjudicate on these competing views of the NHS reform process. There is no shortage of often contradictory anecdotal evidence, and the air is thick with partisan statistical evidence. We are looking at a reform process which is only partially completed, and we must be cautious in deciding which are permanent features of the new regime and which are transitory. At this stage, the following comments seem in order. First, the fundamental problem is one of resources. In comparison with other developed states, Britain devotes a low proportion of its GDP to healthcare and at an unusually low administrative cost. In 1993, Britain devoted just over 6 per cent of GDP to healthcare compared with over 12 per cent in the USA and a European average much closer to 8 per cent (Hills, 1993, 56). Of this expenditure, as little as 3 per cent was officially attributed to administrative costs in the pre-reform NHS (Le Grand, 1990, 99). There is already evidence that administration will be significantly costlier under the reformed system (perhaps closer to 5 per cent in the case of GP fundholders). This has fuelled complaints that the NHS is top-heavy with managers whose salaries might be better spent on clinical care (*The Economist*, 28 May 1994). However much efficiency the reforms may inject, it is difficult to see that they can redress problems that arise from underspending. Second, it has long been recognised that ill health has a social class and regional component, with higher rates of mortality and morbidity amongst manual workers and their families and in the less prosperous regions of the country, and that middle-class patients often gain better access to healthcare resources (Goodin and Le Grand, 1987). There has apparently been some success in addressing this inequality over the past 20 years through the national redistribution of health service spending (Le Grand, 1990). Given the devolution of decision-making and the government's overriding concern with efficiency in the reform process, it is not clear that the trend towards greater equity in health care can be sustained.

Third, it remains notoriously difficult to measure health outcomes. The government's reforms, and particularly its measures for medical audit, are meant to get past the barrier of simply measuring spending and to look at outcomes: how many patients are treated, for what conditions, and at what cost. Yet such data are still a surrogate for measuring the nation's health and well-being. There is still a suspicion that the NHS is primarily a national medical service rather than an integrated service for the promotion and maintenance of good health. Given that so much of the improvement in the nation's health over the last century has been gained through improved diet, better housing and improved working conditions, it may be that the most important contribution that the government could make to improving the nation's health is to address the problems of mass poverty and mass unemployment. Whilst the 1992 White Paper, *The Health of the Nation*, recognised the importance of preventative measures and the impact of 'life style', there was little attempt to address these social aspects of public health (Department of Health, 1992). The White Paper set out commendable targets for improvements in the nation's health but did not adequately specify the mechanisms and resources through which these could be realised. Early evidence of unmet targets came with the failure to make any impression on levels of school-age smoking (*The Guardian*, 28 July 1994).

Finally, those who are anxious about the long-term integrity of the NHS will see a cautionary tale in the experience of public dental services. It is no longer clear that, in dental care, the government can sustain its central commitment to 'a comprehensive health service available to all, largely free at the point of delivery and financed mainly from general taxation' (HM Government, 1993, 3). The dental profession has been in long-standing dispute with the government over treatment fees. In many areas of the country, it became impossible to register with an NHS dentist, treatment was not free at the point of delivery for very substantial numbers of non-exempt adults, and a system of dental care based on private insurance became the norm in affluent districts. As a result, the existing regional/social class division in standards of dental health was likely to become still more pronounced (*The Times*, 28 June 1994).

The Reform of Social Security

The Conservatives' reform of social security provision is of rather longer standing than its attention to education and healthcare. In general, policy has been less innovative and more incremental. The policy objectives have also been different. The first attempt at a systematic reappraisal came in 1985–6 with the government's White Paper and subsequent legislation on *The Reform of Social Security*, the 'Fowler Reviews', trailed as 'the most fundamental examination of our social security system since the Second World War' (Department of Health and Social Security, 1985). The legislative changes that followed, however, were rather less dramatic. There was a downgrading of future entitlements under the state earnings-related pension scheme (SERPS), limited inducements to opt out of state provision and a deterioration in the welfare services for the least privileged. The changes reflected the characteristic concerns to cut costs, seen most clearly in the introduction of cash-limited Social Fund loans, to offset the labour market consequences of welfare benefits by improving the incentives to take low paid employment, and to encourage the private welfare sector by offering financial inducements.

The reforms of 1985–6 reflected what have continued to be the overriding concerns of government in this area. The government wished to achieve 'value for money', but even more than in the other areas of welfare spending its dominant concern has been to constrain absolute levels of spending. This is unsurprising. The social security budget constitutes the single largest item of public expenditure, projected at £80 billion for 1995–6, nearly one-third of all public spending (DSS, 1993, 7). The vast bulk of this money goes on benefits and pensions and is widely regarded as 'consumption' expenditure, contrasting with what is seen as an element of 'investment' in health and education spending.

An increasingly important secondary theme has been the impact of benefit levels and entitlements upon the labour market. Thatcher's first government was wedded to the idea that benefits had become too generous and were eroding the willingness to work, especially for low wages. Indeed, the welfare state was seen to be complicit in a more general erosion of of individual responsibility and self-discipline, underwriting not just idleness but also immoral and even unlawful behaviour (Murray, 1990). A continuing ambition of Conservative governments has been to create greater labour market flexibility, not least by making it more attractive to be in low-paid work rather than in receipt of unemployment benefit or income support. The carrot has been some form of income supplement for families with a low-waged breadwinner, while the sticks have been repeated tightening of entitlement to state support, and constraint upon the level of improvement in benefit rates. On pensions, the government has stressed 'affordability' (levels must be set according to the capacity of the economy to pay), and the importance of individuals making their own welfare arrangements (especially by encouraging private pension provision).

These themes have continued under Major's government. 'Strategic priorities', according to the Social Security Departmental Report for 1993 (DSS, 1993, 2) are to:

- focus benefits on the most needy;
- minimise disincentive effects;
- simplify the benefit system;
- ensure that the system adapts to the differing needs of people it is intended to benefit;
- bear down on abuse and fraud;
- encourage personal responsibility;

In 1994, *The Growth of Social Security* echoed the paramount concern of the earlier 'Fowler Reviews' with the potentially unsustainable long-term costs of public welfare provision (DSS, 1994).

Implementing Social Security Reform

It is hard to see that the government's social security reforms of the last five (or indeed, 15) years can be counted as one of its greatest policy successes. The growth of social security spending has been controlled, but it now stands significantly higher than in 1979. Between 1990 and 1993, the proportion of GDP accounted for by welfare spending actually rose by 5 per cent, whilst the adequacy of benefits had actually fallen since 1979 for the unemployed and pensioners. Meanwhile, income inequality has become more pronounced, with the poorest tenth of the population more than 10 per cent worse off in real terms by 1994 than they had been in 1979. All this comes from a government whose tax take from the economy was higher than under the last Labour government (Hills, 1993, 4, 36, 45, 51).

To some extent, the government is the victim of changes in the external environment and/or of its own policy incompetence in other areas. It is extremely expensive to run a welfare system with an ageing population and permanent mass unemployment, but its attempts to address this challenge have not met with unqualified success. One of the most-publicised of these was the establishment in April 1993 of the CSA, which was to ensure that proper maintenance for dependent children was paid by their absent fathers. There is considerable public and political support for ensuring that absent fathers contribute to the support of their children, though the initiative has been widely criticised for the extent to which any funds recovered would go not to deserving children but to defray the Treasury's social security costs. In practice, the CSA created enormous hostility, both because of the way it has conducted its business and because it has tended to target not the least responsible fathers but those who already supported their children. In its first year of operation, the CSA fell significantly short of its projected financial targets (*Financial Times*, 5 May 1994).

Of rather longer standing has been the encouragement of private pension provision as a supplement to (or, where possible, a replacement of) state provision. Encouraging private pensions by financial inducements and reducing state benefits has been a recurrent feature of policy, at least since the 1986 Social Security Act. By 1991–2, there were more than 5 million men and women in personal pension schemes (Campling, 1994, 406). But this strategy came under increasing attack following the growing evidence of extensive malpractice in the private pensions industry. Most notorious has been the Maxwell pensions scandal, but almost as shocking has been the astonishingly widespread professional misconduct, in which many of the country's leading pension companies have been found knowingly to have misled clients into taking out private pensions when their interests were much better served by staying in the public scheme. As a result, the government has been forced to legislate for rather tighter control of the private pensions industry (*The Guardian*, 25 July 1994).

Meanwhile, the government continued the long-standing policy of tightening the conditions under which benefits are paid. Recently this has included the replacement of unemployment benefits and income support by a more stringently administered Job Seeker's Allowance, and closer medical supervision of entitlement to Invalidity Benefit. The government's priorities are reflected in the increasing attention and money devoted to the detection of social security fraud, and in the much-publicised criticism made by the Secretary of State at the 1993 Conservative Party conference of 'benefit tourism', in which he condemned European citizens who came to the UK to abuse the *largesse* of our social security provision. Yet for all the Conservatives' ambition to encourage self-reliance, the number of those dependent upon the state for an income has grown substantially over the past 15 years, with the numbers of those claiming means-tested Income

Support, for example, having doubled since the mid-1980s (Hills, 1993, 41).

Charter Man

We have seen that the Major government's record on social policy has been dominated by the implementation of the agenda of his predecessor, but there is one area in which the Major administration could claim to have originated policy, and that was in the inauguration and promotion of the Citizen's Charter, an initiative strongly identified with the Prime Minister. Introduced in the summer of 1991, it was trumpeted in the 1992 Conservative manifesto as 'the most far-reaching programme ever devised to improve quality in public services' (Conservative Party, 1992, 13). The many Charters for particular public services are said to be about promoting 'quality, choice, standards and value' in the public sector (*The Citizen's Charter*, Cmnd 1599, 1991). The Charters for particular public services (early initiatives included the Taxpayer's Charter, the Parent's Charter and the Patient's Charter) sought to provide performance targets, set explicit standards, define the customer-citizen's rights and introduce tougher and more effective complaints procedures under the scrutiny of independent inspectorates. The initiative also provided for the award of a 'Chartermark' to especially meritorious public organisations. And, in keeping with the spirit of the age, a 'Charterline' to handle citizens' questions or complaints by telephone. Some have been persuaded that 'there is a very Big Idea at the heart of government, of which the Citizen's Charter may be used as a flagship'. This 'Big Idea' is that public administration should be reoriented around the interests and aspirations of its consumers rather than it producers using, so far as is possible, the incentives and techniques of the private sector (Chapter 8; N. Lewis, 1993, 316).

In general, the response has been more sceptical. First, it is argued that the Charter understands the citizen too narrowly, leaving us with what is 'not really a citizen's but a consumer's charter' (Connolly, Mckeown and Milligan-Byrne, 1994, 30). Critics also insist that the 'new' guarantees written into the Charters often do not enhance existing rights and are not legally binding. Also at issue is whether consumers of public services are truly analogous to private sector consumers. Is the applicant for Income Support really in a position to take her custom elsewhere if she is dissatisfied with the way in which the Benefits Agency handles her case? Conspicuously, the Charter made no commitment to increase resources in public services. In the words of the Liberal Democrat MP, Malcolm Bruce: 'it is no consolation to people who go into the housing department [of the local authority] to be told politely, quickly, efficiently and courteously that there are no houses available to meet their demands' (cited in Connolly, Mckeown and Milligan-Byrne, 1994, 28). Finally, some are not even persuaded that the Charter is really all that new (J. Wilson, 1994, 151).

The Charter has been given great prominence by the Prime Minister, including his infamous guarantee in the 1992 Conservative manifesto to develop more but less obtrusive, motorway service stations. Most of the great public services and many of the minor ones now have their own Charters, and the Charter has its own Cabinet minister. But it is still unclear just how much difference the Charter makes to the delivery of public services and, whatever may have been its real impact, it is hard to see it as the central principle in the current transformation of Britain's public services.

Conclusions

Much of the reforming zeal of the Major administration has been focused upon the public services, and it has substantially changed the structure of Britain's welfare state. Whilst some of the themes of the Thatcher era persist, there has been some shading of the rhetoric. The grander claims of the 'heroic' phase of Thatcherism, and its promise to 'roll back the frontiers of the state', have given way to the more mellow promise of greater choice, diversity and standards within the public services. In reality, the ambition of the reform process has been to extract a greater welfare output from a welfare input which could not rise in line with either social expectations or demographically-driven need. The preferred vehicle of improved efficiency has been the introduction of market disciplines. The centrepiece of reforms in both health and education has been to separate the purchasers from the providers of public services, and in this way to reallocate power from producers of these services to their consumers. The reforms have also seen the introduction of private sector practices and personnel into the public services, in the confident belief that this will improve overall efficiency. In the realms of social security and community care the overriding concern with cost is still more directly expressed. Growth in the social security budget has been a reflection of an increase in the number of claimants (in part the product of an ageing population), rather than of their more generous treatment. Indeed, if the primary goal of the social security system is the prevention of poverty, policy has increasingly failed over the past 15 years. A further recurring theme of the reform process has been the reallocation of responsibility for welfare away from the state and back to individuals and their families. In part, this has been expressed in the transfer of welfare activities (such as pensions and housing) into the private sector, and exposing individuals to the vagaries of the market (not an entirely comfortable experience for the new owner-occupiers in the recession of the early 1990s). It has also meant shifting responsibility for caring services from low-paid women workers in the public services towards unpaid women relatives in the home.

Within the Cabinet in 1995 there was an evident division of opinion between those who, like Peter Lilley at Social Security and Michael Portillo at Employment, saw the Thatcherite agenda as still very partially fulfilled and those, like the Chancellor Kenneth Clarke, whose position was rather closer to that of a European Christian Democrat: pro-EU, pro-market economy, but also committed to a substantial and continuing state provision of welfare. Outside the Cabinet, there is a wing of Conservative opinion, well represented by the 'No Turning Back' group, which would wish to see the privatisation of welfare activity carried much further, and the example of dental services shows that residualisation may come about without any very radical initiative, but simply through a process of 'benign neglect'. Yet, given the constraints within which policy makers operate, it seems unlikely that the direction of reform will change very radically in the foreseeable future. Mass state provision of healthcare, education and pensions is still electorally popular and, whatever the longer-term ambitions of some Conservative politicians, wholesale withdrawal does not look a likely political option in the near future. Of course, the election of a non-Conservative government would make a difference, but it is clear that an incoming centre-left administration would not seek to reverse all of the changes made since 1979: its ambitions would anyway be severely constrained by considerations of cost. It is also possible that the hand of the British government may be forced by the development of social policy at an EU level, including adjudications of the European Courts. Amongst some politicians and policy-makers, there is perhaps even now a dawning realisation that the welfare state cannot be understood solely as a cost and a constraint upon economic growth. Welfare states have never been simply an expression of (decreasing) social generosity towards the 'less fortunate'. Some politicians are relearning that parts of the welfare state have an efficiency effect, and that the failure to invest in education and healthcare may actually depress the prospects of long-term economic growth. The capacity to act upon such an insight, however, is likely to be limited by the structural weaknesses of the British economy and the electoral logic of Britain's archaic political institutions. For all the rhetoric of choice and empowerment, the single most important political consideration surrounding the welfare state over the last 20 years has been its cost. Not just the recent past but also the foreseeable future of British social policy looks likely to be dominated by the constraint of cost in a context of comparative economic decline.

12

Foreign and Defence Policy under Thatcher and Major

JIM BULLER

Introduction

In understanding Conservative foreign policy it can be difficult to distinguish between party policy and British policy, in that post-war British foreign policy has been largely bipartisan. However, it is true to say that the sense of nation and empire has been so important to Conservative thought (Chapter 2) that the issues facing British external relations have had special resonance for the Conservative Party (Bulpitt, 1986). The post-war Conservative Party has been faced with the tensions of maintaining Britain's world role and readjusting to Britain's political and economic decline. In the years following the Second World War the central aim of Conservative, and British, policy was to maintain Britain's centrality in the three circles of influence: the USA, the Empire/Commonwealth, and Europe.

Yet, by the mid-1950s it was clear that Britain was facing relative economic and political decline. The 1955 Suez crisis was indicative of Britain's changing position. It demonstrated that Britain's world role was not so much the result of partnership with the USA, but of dependence on US support. The shock of Suez resulted in a rapid reassesment of British foreign and defence policy. Britain no longer had the capacity to maintain an imperial role, and the Conservatives under Macmillan accepted the need for withdrawal from the vestiges of empire (Sanders, 1990, 104). Suez also created problems for the relationship between Britain and the USA, and the Macmillan governments tried hard to re-establish the alliance. The alliance was increasingly based around security issues through Britain's role in NATO. With the cancellation of the British Blue Streak missile came the final realisation that Britain's nuclear capability was dependent on US support and expertise (C. J. Bartlett, 1992). At the same time Britain's 'out of area' defence commitments were gradually reduced, with the Conservative Party doing nothing to overturn the Labour's withdrawal from East of Suez in the 1960s.

The long-term impact of these events was to push Britain closer to Europe, despite initial reluctance to become involved. In 1960 Macmillan started the process of persuading the Cabinet that Britain should join the EEC, the beginning of a long process of applications and rejections that ended with entry under Heath in 1973. Heath's attitude represented a significant change in the Conservative policy on Europe. Under Macmillan membership was seen as the best way of retaining a close partnership with the USA (Reynolds, 1991). For Heath it was more a recognition that Britain's future was tied to Europe and that its future world role would only be through an 'ever closer union' (Campbell, 1993, 397). Consequently, post-war Conservative policy seemed to be a pragmatic adjustment to Britain's new position in the world. Nevertheless, it was a readjustment constantly constrained and tortured by the spirt of Britain's imperial past. The view of Britain's position in the world and its defence capabilities often did not coincide with the realities of pragmatic British foreign policy. It has been suggested that to some extent foreign policy under Thatcher was an attempt to return to past glories (Barnett, 1986).

It is often argued that the Conservative Party implemented a radical ideological programme in domestic policy after 1979. A question less often asked is whether this happened in the areas of British foreign and defence policy. Many authors now question the distinction between foreign and defence policy, arguing that given economic interdependence (Chapter 9) and 20 years of EC membership (Chapter 13), issues such as exchange rate management, trade policy and aid to the former Soviet Union are likely to be just as important as traditional concerns with diplomacy and war. This chapter will be concerned with the more traditional content of foreign and defence policy, and in this sense the distinction between foreign and domestic policy is still legitimate.

Those authors who look for a distinct, coherent ideological programme in these areas point to a number of features: Thatcher's strident nationalism and emphasis on reversing Britain's decline from great power status; her attempt to rejuvenate the 'special relationship' with the USA; her anti-Communist rhetoric; and her renewed emphasis on defence spending, notably on the purchase of Trident. This chapter will argue that the Conservative governments after 1979 did not implement any radical programme in foreign and defence policy. The Conservative leadership has often seemed content to follow previous policy practices. In other areas policy has broadly followed the existing concerns of the Foreign Office and the Ministry of Defence (MoD), although it is also argued here that this bureaucratic lead has not been incompatible with the interests of the Conservative leadership. After 1987, even where structural changes at the international level have encouraged the Conservative leadership to radically revise policy, it has shown reluctance. Policy has reflected a mixture of inactivity and cautious pragmatism.

There are several initial reasons for arguing that any Conservative administration might only have a limited impact in this policy area. As Rose argues, parties can make a difference in British politics, but for limited reasons. Any party intending to implement fresh manifesto commitments will first have to deal with problems and policy programmes left over from previous administrations. These policy programmes may frustrate attempts by the party leadership to pursue its own policies. More seriously, existing policy trends may run counter to manifesto commitments, forcing substantial revision or abandonment. Even if a party can overcome inertia in Whitehall, policy change can frequently confront 'structural constraints' within the economy or society. Finally, parties will always be constrained by electoral considerations. In this sense, the leadership will pay attention not only to whether a policy is popular, but whether it is feasible. In short, because of these constraints policy will exhibit great continuity with past practices, and change will be incremental (R. Rose, 1980).

Although many disagree with Rose's argument, it might be particularly useful for understanding the conduct of British foreign and defence policy since 1945. First, policy in this area is noted particularly for its resistance to radical change. The foreign policy equivalent of legislation is embodied in treaties, communiqués and international regulations, most of which are long term. A good example is the open-ended commitment undertaken by Eden to provide four army divisions and the 2nd Tactical Air Force for the joint defence of Western Europe (Sanders, 1990, 64–5; Wallace and Wallace, 1990). Moreover, many policy programmes at the MoD have time frames of ten years or more and are difficult to reverse. A good example is Labour's decision in the 1970s to continue with the secret 'Chevaline' programme to update the Polaris warhead (McGrew, 1988).

Second, the structural constraints facing foreign and defence policy-makers often leave less room for innovation. At the domestic level, commentators have noted the large policy influence of the armed services and defence contractors, who have privileged relations with the MoD. Perhaps more important, with the increasing 'internationa-lisation' of policy, are external structural constraints. Whitehall has no jurisdiction over foreign governments. Powerful international lobbies, pressure groups and supranational organisations can be even more difficult to control. In short, establishing a coalition of agencies at the external level for the implementation of 'second order' decisions, let alone radical policies, is likely to be very problematic (S. Smith and Clarke, 1985).

Finally, as with domestic policy, foreign and defence policy will always be constrained by electoral considerations. Many commentators have noted that successful initiatives, particularly the resolution of conflicts, can have positive electoral spin-offs. Although there is disagreement among academics about its importance, the so-called 'Falklands factor' is an obvious example (Sanders *et al.*, 1987; Thatcher, 1993). However, opportunities for conflict resolution are rare. A more important consideration for party leaders is to try to prevent external problems that might adversely influence domestic politics from reaching Westminster. This may be unavoidable. External events can explode without warning, directly challenging government policy at an electo-rally sensitive time (e.g. the Reykjavik Summit, 1986). Alternatively problems can be intractable and not susceptible to short-term solutions, but have the capacity to upset domestic party management (Bulpitt, 1988); examples discussed below are Rhodesia, Northern Ireland, Hong Kong and Bosnia.

To conclude, structural constraints, electoral considerations and the inertia of Whitehall all initially suggest that Conservative foreign and defence policy after 1979 was likely to demonstrate continuity rather than radical change. Finally, it is worth recalling that since the mid-nineteenth century Britain has been a status quo power, benefiting from the existing international order. Instead of promoting radical initiatives, British leaders since 1945 have been more concerned with promoting an international order that optimises their international influence (S. Smith and Clarke, 1985, 170; McGrew, 1988, 101).

Leaving the EU aside, two features of this international order, or 'external support system' (Bulpitt, 1983), will be discussed below: the promotion of a 'special relationship' with the USA, and the attempt to forge a new Commonwealth out of the remnants of the British Empire. Although this international order implied some costs for British party leaders, it allowed them to preserve some great power status, at least until the late 1960s.

Historical Perspective

The central foreign policy task facing British leaders since 1945 has commonly been portrayed as reversing or disguising the extent of Britain's absolute decline in great power status (Kennedy, 1981; Gamble, 1990a). Here the special relationship with the USA had a number of benefits, including allowing Britain to acquire a defence capability unrivalled in Western Europe. Although cooperation with the Americans in the atomic energy field had continued after 1945, Britain's attempt to develop her own nuclear deterrent was boosted by the repeal of the McMahon Act in 1958. Under this agreement, Britain alone had access to US information on the design and production of warheads. When work on Britain's Blue Streak missile was abandoned, Macmillan eventually purchased Polaris at a price said to have been less than 2 per cent of the defence budget (Baylis, 1981, 59–62; Horne, 1989, 432–43). Finally, US forces in Europe and their arsenal of strategic nuclear weapons guaranteed a level of defence against the Soviet Union that Britain could not afford unilaterally.

This defence capability conferred on British leaders a status and prestige which set them apart from their European counterparts. Britain's efforts to develop her own nuclear deterrent and her continuing military and diplomatic presence East of Suez ensured a pivotal role as Washington's second-in-command at NATO. This further guaranteed London's prominent involvement in general discussions with the Americans over strategy to contain Communism (Gowing, 1986). British statesmen clearly felt that this junior role alongside the USA gave them some licence to play the role of wise counsel to this often impulsive superpower. Two considerations seemed to have been important when explaining the desire of every British leader from Attlee (over Korea) to Wilson (over Vietnam) to play this part: first, there was genuine fear in London that a regional conflict involving the superpowers would escalate into a nuclear war; second, as was often noted by contemporary biographers and diarists, these statesmen rarely overlooked the possible electoral spin-offs from sitting at the 'top table' of international affairs (Castle, 1984, 237; Horne, 1989, 231).

Alongside the 'special relationship', it was hoped that the new Commonwealth would allow British foreign policy-makers to carry on 'punching above their weight' in the world. As Leopold Amery speculated in 1953, 'Other nations now outside it may very well decide to join it in the course of time . . . who knows but that it may yet become the nucleus around which a future world order will crystalise' (Porter, 1975, 336). However, by the early 1960s it became apparent that the Commonwealth was not going to play this role. The Commonwealth failed to develop into a united forum exerting international influence. Instead, members fought with each other (wars between India and Pakistan, Malaysia and Indonesia) and expelled each other (South Africa in 1960). More disturbing was the realisation by the new African members that they could use the Commonwealth as a platform to attack British policy, particularly towards Rhodesia and South Africa (H. Wilson, 1971, 180, 277; J. Campbell, 1993, 338).

Although this international order helped to disguise Britain's decline, it carried costs. First, it consumed large amounts of time, energy and diplomatic resources, often distracting leaders from sensitive domestic concerns. American foreign policy, under pressure from Congress, could oscillate between isolationism and provocation towards the Soviet Union (Baylis, 1981, 43–8; Horne, 1989, 43–5, 93–8, 116–33, 226–33; Sanders, 1990, 60–5). As for the 'empire circle', the point is best illustrated by Macmillan's own reflection that, 'The complications, confusions and conflicts of Central Africa seemed never to be absent from our minds and were destined to absorb an immense amount of effort with little corresponding result' (H. Wilson, 1971, 287, 558; Horne, 1989, 193; 389).

Second, this external support system could be a source of dissent within both Conservative and Labour parties. The stationing of American missiles on British soil was one continual source of problems. Both Colonel Zinc's claim to have 'in his hands' full operational control of Britain's Thor missiles, and the RB47 incident, caused major rows in the Commons (Baylis, 1981, 65–6). Furthermore, the effectiveness with which the Rhodesian leadership could exploit their contacts with the Conservative right wing to obstruct moves towards majority rule proved a continual frustration for Conservative leaders. Similarly,

Wilson found himself continually berated by his backbenchers for supplying arms to the federal government during the Nigerian civil war in the late 1960s (H. Wilson, 1971, 557–8; Horne, 1989, 188, 205, 394–7). The influx of large numbers of immigrants from former colonies in the 1950s produced another domestic political headache.

For the purposes of comparison with the period 1979–94, it is worth digressing to note one or two of the methods used before 1979 by party leaders to stop external problems producing adverse domestic political consequences. In this sense, party policy was often as concerned with 'rational inactivity' as with dramatic policy initiatives (Bulpitt, 1988). Both Macmillan and Wilson sought a frontbench consensus on the Rhodesia issue in order to contain backbench dissent (H. Wilson, 1971, 181; Horne, 1989, 180–5). When Heath showed a willingness to break this consensus and deliberately politicise the issue in order to unite his party, Wilson refused to countenance military action in Rhodesia for the very same reason that it would help unite the opposition (H. Wilson, 1971, 207–8). Finally, even when there was no real chance of a breakthrough, Wilson began another round of negotiations with the Smith regime in 1968, arguing that even if they failed at least it would be harder for Heath to exploit it at the 1970 election (H. Wilson, 1971, 567).

By the end of the 1960s, several longer-term trends made this external support system more difficult to sustain. America's threat to de-couple from the defence of Western Europe now seemed serious. Détente, and the emergence of a US–Soviet condominium over nuclear proliferation led to a fear that the USA would reach an agreement 'over the head' of Britain which would be detrimental to British security interests. In particular, Whitehall continued to worry that the Strategic Arms Limitation Talks (SALT) agreements in the 1970s would nullify Europe's option to acquire Cruise missiles (Baylis, 1981, 102).

At the same time, London's special relationship with Washington appeared to be in terminal decline. Wilson's decision to relinquish Britain's commitments East of Suez, and Heath's decision not to resurrect this role, meant that Britain became less important strategically. Second, the reduction of British defence expenditure under all governments until the late 1970s probably sent the wrong signals, especially when the USA was urging European governments to make greater efforts to guarantee their own security (Baylis, 1981, 101; Chichester and Wilkinson, 1982, 35–54). Third, Heath's decision not to have a special relationship with Nixon, while clearly a temporary anomaly in the conduct of British policy, did nothing to reverse this trend. Finally, it is important not to forget that since the 1950s much of the US foreign policy establishment had always preferred to deal with Europe as a whole. Thus pressure was maintained on European leaders to develop a common foreign and security policy, to the detriment of bilateral ties (Kissinger, 1979).

Foreign and Defence Policy under the Conservative Party, 1979–94

So how has the Conservative Party responded since 1979? This chapter will argue that in the areas surveyed below policy has demonstrated a large amount of continuity, both between Thatcher and Major, and with the period before 1979. First it will be argued that Thatcher's resurrection of the special US relationship represented one last attempt to patch up what was left of the old external support system. Furthermore, after 1987, where structural changes seem to signal an end to this strategy, the Conservative leadership was reluctant to revise policy radically. Instead, policy has reflected a mixture of inactivity and cautious pragmatism, although more recently Major seems to be showing signs of falling back on pre-1939 methods of foreign policy management in response to this 'new world order'.

A couple of general observations about foreign and defence policy under Thatcher point to continuity. It is generally accepted that Thatcher had little experience of, and devoted very little thought to foreign and defence policy before 1979. Compared with previous Conservative leaders, she rarely travelled abroad, and her previous frontbench jobs had all been in areas of domestic policy. More importantly, she spent little time developing a coherent approach to the plethora of problems and issues of foreign affairs. Her world-view was one-dimensional, consisting of anti-Communism presented in rhetoric that had changed little from her statements on the subject in the 1950s (H. Young and Sloman, 1986, 97–9). If there was a radical departure after 1979, it did not derive from a coherent blueprint developed in the years of opposition.

Second, any Thatcherite revolution in Whitehall seems to have stopped short of the Foreign Office and the MoD. Apart from John Nott's short tenure at the MoD in the the early 1980s, these two departments remained in control of the 'wets' or 'whigs'. Furthermore, neither the Centre for Policy Studies nor the Number Ten Policy Unit was ever given much of a brief to investigate foreign and defence policy (Coker, 1988).

It would nevertheless be wrong to suggest that Thatcher had no interest in or influence on foreign and defence policy after 1979. Some commentators have noted how she quickly became interested in foreign affairs, dominating policy in areas of greatest concern. It is possible to detect a rough division of labour in the management of foreign policy under Thatcher. On matters which held little interest to her, she was prepared to grant the Foreign Office a certain amount of autonomy. Leaving aside South Africa, such issues included management of the last vestiges of the 'imperial hangover' such as the Rhodesia/Zimbabwe issue, Hong Kong, and relations with the Commonwealth in general. When it came to relations with the superpowers, however, she often ignored the Foreign Office, although, even when this was the case, Thatcher seemed more concerned with following pre-1979 foreign policy concerns than charting a new course for British policy.

Thatcher between the Superpowers

In the introduction, one possible candidate for a coherent, ideological foreign policy programme was suggested: Thatcher's 'resolute approach' which included her strident nationalism and continuing emphasis on the importance of reversing Britain's decline from great power status (Parsons, 1989; Riddell, 1989, 184–86), the attempt to rejuvenate the 'special relationship', her anti-Communist rhetoric (Cooke, 1989, 29–39), and finally a renewed emphasis on defence spending, the decision to purchase Trident, and the continual pressure from Thatcher to upgrade NATO's intermediate-nuclear forces (INF: Wheeler, 1991; Thatcher, 1993, 239–44). Commentators noted that Thatcher seemed consciously to disown the traditional concern of British policy-makers to balance a policy of deterrence with détente in their relations with the Soviet Union (B. White, 1988).

This argument has a number of flaws, and no writer surveyed here seriously claims that Thatcher's renewed relationship with Reagan and return to Cold War values represented a radical or distinctive foreign policy. Whilst it is plausible to argue that Thatcher's reliance on a Cold War strategy was pursued up to 1983, evidence suggests that it was reconsidered and dropped after the election victory. Thatcher recalls the adoption of a new approach at a Chequers seminar in September

1983, leading to Howe embarking on a number of official visits to Eastern Europe and the Soviet Union, where he stressed the need to develop high level contacts with a new generation of more moderate Soviet leaders. At the same time, both he and Heseltine called for measures to develop an East–West dialogue (B. White, 1988, 151–2; Thatcher, 1993, 450–1). In short, it was a return to the old strategy of balancing deterrence and détente.

Second, it should be noted that this renewed Atlanticism reflected a continuity of strategic interests and domestic political concerns. One of the dominant concerns of Thatcher's memoirs was the preservation of Western unity in the face of constant Soviet attempts to isolate Western Europe. In the early 1980s, Thatcher testifies to a certain amount of 'wobbling' among Britain's European allies over the decision to modernise its INF under the 'dual-track' agreement (Thatcher, 1993, 236–42). At the same time, Reagan's enthusiasm for the Strategic Defense Initiative again raised the possibility that the USA might withdraw prematurely from the defence of Western Europe (Byrd, 1991, 29). Behind Thatcher's concern was a deeply held belief that Western Europe would be unable to survive a Soviet attack without the commitment of American forces (Allen, 1988, 49–50; Thatcher, 1993, 814).

This policy also reflected domestic political calculations similar to those that had motivated earlier British leaders. Although her Atlanticism did not always enjoy uncritical public support, as over her decision to support the bombing of Libya from British bases in 1986 (M. Smith, 1988, 21; H. Young, 1990, 477), Thatcher is adamant that if she had let the alliance decline, the party would have suffered at the polls. The British public may not have universally approved of specific features of the American nuclear guarantee, such as the nuclear bases at Greenham Common, but they understood the desirability of the general policy, especially when faced with the general disarray of the Labour Party on the subject (D. Dunn, 1991, 14; Thatcher, 1993, 445–9).

Moreover, this renewed emphasis on the special relationship, NATO and the new approach after 1984 of cultivating relations with the Soviet Union allowed Thatcher to resume the role of counsel to the superpowers which had been so popular with her predecessors. Although her influence in Washington was patchy (note the failures over Lebanon and Grenada), some commentators observed the beneficial domestic political spin-offs Thatcher enjoyed from this role, especially during the negotiations before the INF Agreement in 1987 (M. Smith, 1988; H.

Young, 1990, 394 and 512–14). In short, the second Cold War between 1979 and 1987 presented a fortuitous set of circumstances for Thatcher to make one final attempt to patch up part of the old external support system which had proved so useful in allowing Britain to maintain an influence out of proportion with any objective measure of her economic and military might.

However, it seems reasonable to argue that since 1987 this international system has been falling into a state of terminal decline. This has led to suggestions that British foreign policy-makers face a new critical 'historical juncture' (Coker, 1988; McGrew, 1988; *The Economist*, 1990a; Croft, 1991; Sanders, 1993a). Before assessing how Major's government responded, it is necessary to note a number of features of this 'new world order'.

First, despite Thatcher's efforts, the special relationship has continued to develop such that many American policies now impinge awkwardly on British foreign and security policy. The regeneration by the mid-1980s of the superpower condominium on the issue of nuclear arms reductions produced renewed fears that the US would arrive at an agreement over the heads of Conservative leaders. One obvious example here was the INF negotiations at Reykjavik in 1986, where Reagan's apparent willingness to negotiate away all strategic nuclear weapons in ten years led Thatcher to recall, 'it was as if there had been an earthquake beneath my feet' (Thatcher, 1993, 471). The completion of the START treaty and the continuation of the Strategic Arms Reduction Talks START II talks revived fears that the USA was de-coupling from the defence of Western Europe, raising new questions about the future of Britain's independent nuclear deterrent (Hoffman, 1991; *Financial Times*, 19 February, 1993, 27 March 1993). The despatch of two advisers from Conservative Central Office to advise George Bush's Presidential campaign in 1992 apparently did nothing to reverse these broader trends (*Financial Times*, 7 December 1992).

The rise of a new American–German alliance not only destroyed Britain's claim to a special relationship with Washington, but also impinged awkwardly on the external strategy of the Conservative leadership. Most worrying was Bush's support for German calls to downgrade NATO's policy of 'flexible response'. This led to a willingness to negotiate reducing the level of short-range nuclear forces in Europe, the cancellation of the Follow-on-to-Lance missile, and the acceptance that NATO's remaining nuclear forces would be 'weapons of the last resort'. If that were not enough, Washington's support for

German reunification and closer European integration, and Clinton's enthusiasm for a common European foreign and security policy, produced a chilly response from Whitehall (Thatcher, 1993, 790–812; *Financial Times* 17 November 1993).

With the break-up of the Soviet Union and the Warsaw Pact, euphoric talk of a 'new world order' evaporated. Instead the West found itself faced with new and perplexing regional problems in southern and eastern Europe. Much public attention has been devoted to the conflict in former Yugoslavia (see below). However, just as important are the simmering regional conflicts within the former Soviet Union, in particular the rivalry between Russia and the Ukraine. In short, this new external environment posed a severe challenge to British strategic thinking. So how did the Major government respond?

The Major Administration and the New World Order

Again there is a powerful case for pointing to continuity. Thatcher's initial response provided an unapologetic statement of inactivity: 'the world of the "new world order" was turning out to be a dangerous, uncertain place in which the Conservative virtues of hardened Cold Warriors were again in demand' (Thatcher, 1993, 770). After 1990, policy under Major was best described as cautious pragmatism. One good illustration of this was Whitehall's response to attempts to strengthen a European common foreign and security policy.

There have been recent reports that the Major government has become more relaxed about plans to expand the role of the Western European Union (WEU). Two points of caution are in order. Any evidence of equanimity on the part of the British may soon lead to a resurfacing of tension with the European partners. The Major government still sees the growth of common foreign and security structures as something which should be compatible with NATO. However, France sees an expanded role for the WEU through the newly formed 'Eurocorps' as part of the EU and separate from NATO (Sanders, 1993a; *Financial Times*, 27 January 1994). Second, it is likely that any British desire to play a more active role in plans to expand the WEU is motivated by a concern not to be marginalised by a Franco-German axis on this issue. Recent reports suggest that Whitehall does not have any genuine enthusiasm for the project, and it should also be remembered that NATO's institutional structure confers on Britain a status far out of proportion to its power (Allen, 1988; *Financial Times*, 25 January 1994).

More interestingly, in response to this fluid external environment, the Major government has recently shown signs of falling back on pre-1939 methods of foreign policy management. The parallels between the international system today and that before 1939 are not hard to see. With the unification of Germany, the emergence of an unstable Russia from the ashes of the old Soviet Union and the reappearance of ethnic rivalry in southern and eastern Europe, Whitehall is once again preoccupied with managing a new balance of power. This is illustrated by Thatcher in the section of her memoir devoted to 'The German Problem and the Balance of Power'. Here she expresses a need to balance the power of a united Germany which, 'by its very nature [is] a destabilising rather than [a] stabilising force in Europe' (Thatcher, 1993, 791). Such concerns have continued under Major's leadership.

On the one hand, there has been an attempt to revive the Anglo-French *entente* as a counter-balance to Germany. Some commentators have noted a 'springtime' in relations, pointing to recent cooperation over agricultural subsidies in the General Agreement on Tariffs and Trade (GATT) negotiations. There is a similarity of interests over the Bosnian conflict, where both countries have troops on the ground. This said, there is little evidence that either Thatcher or Major has been able to wean France off its preference for close cooperation with Germany, particularly over the institutional development of the EU after 1996 (Buchan, 1993; Thatcher, 1993, 796–8).

At the same time Whitehall has been concerned not to isolate or provoke Russia, given the uncertain security situation in Eastern Europe. Some senior Conservatives including David Howell, Chairman of the Commons Foreign Affairs Select Committee, have criticised the Partnership for Peace proposals as a 'dangerous fudge'. However, a concern not to undermine Yeltsin's fragile domestic political position has meant that these agreements, promising more military cooperation between NATO and the emerging states in Eastern Europe without giving firm security guarantees, were probably the most that the Major administration was prepared to contemplate. To quote then Foreign Secretary, Douglas Hurd, 'Are the US Congress, the House of Commons, the French Assembly, the Bundestag, solemnly ready to guarantee with the lives of their citizens, the frontiers of Slovakia? If not . . . then it would be a deceit to pretend otherwise' (D. White, 1994).

Finally, Whitehall's concern with this new balance of power is evident in responses to the crisis in the former Yugoslavia. Put bluntly, the endgame of policy has not been to solve this intractable problem. Instead, policy seems to reflect the more limited objective of preserving the alliance of the 'contact group', comprising the USA, Russia, Britain and France. Whilst providing reluctant support for unilateral US air strikes on Serbian supply lines, Whitehall opposed calls to lift the arms embargo (*Financial Times* 14 April 1993). In London's view, if the West were seen to be arming the Moslems, not only would it exacerbate the conflict and endanger the lives of British troops on the ground, but it runs the risk of putting Yeltsin under intolerable pressure to arm the Serbs. As Hurd has noted, defending the apparent impotence of the EU in the face of this conflict, 'what it [the EU] did do was what it was capable of doing, which is to prevent individual countries starting to back individual horses in Yugoslavia' (*Financial Times*, 21 April 1993; House of Commons Debates, 29 April 1993). In short, policy has been concerned to prevent a re-run of 1914 or 1939.

Defence Priorities and Expenditure: Keeping Up Appearances

So far, then, it can be argued that Conservative foreign policy up to 1987 largely reflected pre-1979 concerns. The renewal of the Cold War provided an opportunity for Thatcher to shore up an international order which exaggerated Britain's influence. Since the decline of this order after 1987, and the rise of an unpredictable environment, policy has reflected a mixture of inactivity, cautious pragmatism and a willingness to fall back on past practices. It should come as no real surprise that these general conclusions are also applicable to the approach of the Conservatives towards defence planning and expenditure. However, it will be further argued that such inactivity and cautious pragmatism can be viewed as rational from the viewpoint of Conservative governments.

First, there is a strong case for arguing that there was no Thatcherite revolution at the MoD. In the beginning, with a renewed emphasis on increasing expenditure, and the first comprehensive review of British defence priorities since 1957, there was reason to expect a new approach. However, whilst the Nott Review in 1981 did recommend radical measures to reduce the Royal Navy, these conclusions were overtaken by the Falklands War. Instead, the government announced that HMS Fearless and HMS Intrepid were to be maintained, and five new frigates and a logistic landing ship were to be ordered (Laurent, 1991). Moreover, Nott's proposals, as well as his admission that Britain could no longer afford all her defence commitments provoked so much controversy that another review was avoided until *Options For Change* in 1990. The emphasis on a 'strong state' came to an end in 1985, when Britain's commitment to a NATO agreement to increase defence spending by 3 per cent per annum in real terms ran out. Since then, it has fallen to the lowest levels since 1945 (Byrd, 1991, 23; *Financial Times*, 5 July 1993).

From 1983 to 1990, policy can best be characterised as 'keeping up appearances' (Greenwood, 1991). Whilst the 'funding gap' between resources and commitments continued, the Thatcher regime adopted new techniques to avoid and disguise the problem. First, there was Heseltine's new emphasis on more effective resource management. The argument was that the funding gap could be bridged by better use of existing resources. Hence there was reform of the procurement process, contracting-out of support services, privatisation of the Royal Ordnance Factories and Her Majesty's dockyards, and a greater willingness to collaborate with other countries to cut research and development costs (Laurent, 1991). After 1986, under Younger, the MoD fell back on the even older technique of 'cheese-paring' to disguise the funding gap. All three services were asked to economise on operations and maintenance, whilst the MoD stretched out construction schedules on existing procurement projects and imposed a moratorium on payments to contractors (Greenwood, 1991).

Since 1990 policy has shown strong continuity, although opinions differ on whether this is a result of ideological sclerosis or rational inactivity. *Options For Change* did not challenge any single component of military capacity, instead, it shared out the cost-cutting relatively equally among all three services (Sanders, 1993a, 294–5). The inability of Tom King to provide a detailed strategic rationale for the cuts led to revival of those criticisms of *Options* as being another Treasury exercise in cheese-paring (Defence Committee 1991: 394; *Financial Times*, 24 February 1994, 27 April 1994). Moreover, the drive for further savings in procurement and support services, under the 'Front Line First' programme, seems like a return to the Heseltine strategy of dismissing any talk of a funding gap by highlighting resource management (*Financial Times*, 15 July 1994). In short, continuity equals ideological sclerosis.

Some writers take a more sympathetic view, arguing that this inactivity is rational in the light of two real problems facing Major. First, the problem with those who argue that there is no strategic rationale behind *Options* is that they assume that there is a clear strategic rational for the future size and shape of British defence forces; yet with the ending of the Cold War there are few reliable benchmarks to guide defence planners. It is no longer clear what threat is to be overcome, or what mission is to be achieved. Now military contingencies arise at very short notice, and often on several fronts (for example, Bosnia, Somalia and Rwanda). This raises awkward questions: who and where is the primary future threat to British security interests? How flexible should future defence forces be? Which countries can Britain count on for help, and what is Britain's most appropriate role in any military alliance (see Rifkind's comments on this subject, *Financial Times*, 15 February 1993). Moreover, when there is no consensus over the answers to these questions, inactivity, cautious pragmatism and a willingness to fall back on past practices may not be such an irrational approach (Sabin, 1993).

The second point to note when asserting this argument about rational inactivity is that defence policy now generates a good deal of domestic controversy. Senior ministers have to work very hard to calm backbench fears that British forces are dangerously overstretched. Pressure from the Commons Defence Committee is said to be one of the reasons for the decision in February 1993 to cancel two regimental mergers, and add to this the row that erupted in October 1993, showing a group of 14 Tory MPs threatening to vote against substantial future defence cuts, risking the government's narrow majority. There is even evidence to suggest that Rifkind had taken to mobilising this backbench pressure against future Treasury demands for defence cuts (*Financial Times*, 10 November, 1993). In short, with no clear choices about future defence strategy, and facing awkward questions with potentially adverse domestic consequences, the temptation for Conservative leaders will be to move cautiously.

Imperial Hangovers

As well as having to deal with a new external environment, the Conservative Party since 1979 has also had to cope with a number of persistent 'imperial hangovers'. Once again policy has displayed a large degree of continuity, both between Thatcher and Major, and also with policy before 1979. More specifically, policy towards these problems has broadly followed Foreign Office concerns, although it is further argued that such a lead was broadly in line with the objectives and interests of Conservative leaders. In this policy area, there has been a concern to maintain Britain's image abroad and to stop these problems having an adverse impact on domestic politics.

The argument that there was a Thatcherite revolution in this policy area can be dismissed relatively quickly. Although prone to sporadic initiatives – for example, on Hong Kong (see below) or Rhodesia, where Thatcher argued for the early acceptance of the Muzorewa government and the lifting of sanctions – in the end policy broadly followed Foreign Office concerns (H. Young, 1990, 175–83; Gilmour, 1992, 227–32; Thatcher, 1993, 72–8). It could be argued that one possible exception to this rule was Thatcher's dominance over the Falklands issue. She was largely responsible for resisting Ridley's proposals for 'lease-back' of the islands. In Gilmour's view, this policy was likely to be the most effective in preventing a war with Argentina (Gilmour, 1992, 244). Second, the support that Thatcher gave to Nott's insistence on the withdrawal of 'Endurance' almost certainly sent the wrong signals at a politically sensitive time. Finally, once war broke out, Thatcher took control of policy and dominated the decisions taken thereafter. However, the argument here is that the evidence above reflects little more than a case study of malign neglect and crisis management. Whitehall failed to predict the invasion, and were very lucky to win the ensuing battle (H. Young, 1990, 258–79; Gilmour, 1992, 241–51). Furthermore, since 1982, there are no signs that the conflict is anywhere near resolution (Little, 1988). In short, there has not been anything approaching a revolution of ideas in this area.

Has Major's approach to this area differed from that of his predecessor? One of the ways to tackle this question is to look at an imperial hangover which has spanned both the Thatcher and Major administrations: namely the problem of Hong Kong. When answering this question, the first point to note is that there seems to have been little party political input into Britain's policy. Thatcher describes how she drew up proposals in 1983 to inject some democratic reform into the colony's political structure, but admits these proposals were dismissed as unworkable by the Foreign Office. From then on, her memoirs indicate that she toed the officials' line, accepting both China's claim to sovereignty and its desire to take over the colony's administration after 1997 (Thatcher, 1993, 488–94). Since then, British policy has been concerned to ensure that the existing legal, economic and social system would be preserved in Hong Kong under the 'one country, two systems' principle. According to the Joint Declaration signed in December 1984, this would be achieved by gradually strengthening democracy in the colony. However, by the time she left office, Thatcher admits that progress in this area had been negligible (Thatcher, 1993, 494; *The Economist*, 1990b).

The second point to note is that this policy seems to have reflected similar calculations to those that drove general policy towards remnants of the Empire before 1979. First, maintaining international support for Britain's last colonial outpost remained an important consideration. Both Conservative leaders and Foreign Office officials want to be seen to be honouring the Joint Declaration. Second, if gradually strengthening democracy was about shoring up confidence in the colony, there was an additional (more cynical) domestic political reason behind this strategy. Democratic reforms might also help stem the threat of large-scale immigration from Hong Kong. Put bluntly, at times it seems that policy is just as concerned with keeping the Hong Kong issue at arms length from Westminster and domestic politics (House of Commons Debates, 20 February 1989, cols 368–70; *The Economist*, 3 June 1989).

If little progress was made in implementing this policy before 1990, at first glance Chris Patten's proposals to strengthen democracy in time for Hong Kong's 1995 legislative elections looked like quite a dramatic break with past practice (*Financial Times*, 8 October 1992). The most controversial part of Patten's package was his proposals for the conduct of the legislative elections to be held in 1995. The reforms were announced without any prior consultation with Peking. They were criticised as too radical and provocative by many including Sir Percy Cradock, Britain's former chief negotiator on the Hong Kong issue (*Financial Times*, 9 December 1993). However, it can be argued that these differences boil down to style rather than substance. Patten's proposals aim to maximise democracy within the constraints of Chinese Basic Law. During negotiations, Britain offered to make a number of concessions which would have furthered watered down the proposals (*The Guardian*, 1 October 1993).

Finally, these proposals continued to reflect the underlying considerations outlined above. The decision in 1989 to offer the right of abode to 50 000 Hong Kong households after the Tiananmen Square massacre has not stemmed the number of emigrants leaving the colony and the threat of large-scale immigration remains a concern for British leaders (*Financial Times*, 18 March 1993, 25 February 1994). Meanwhile on hearing that China had formally confirmed that it would dismantle all the colony's electoral bodies after 1997, a British Embassy spokesman is reported to have reacted by saying: 'those who have to take responsibility, will have to explain themselves to six million people here in Hong Kong' (*The Independent*, 1 September 1994). In other words, let China face the wrath of international opinion if it dares; British consciences are clear.

Northern Ireland

One final external problem worth mentioning briefly in this context is the Northern Ireland problem. Again, evidence seems to point to broad continuity between Conservative policy after 1979 and that of earlier administrations. This continuity reflects similar calculations to those behind the management of Britain's last remnants of empire. On the one hand, since 1969, policy has reflected short-term crisis management, with a continual attempt by London to fulfil the first element of civil government by providing effective law and order (R. Rose, 1976a, 26). At the same time, in the absence of devolved local administration, policy has been concerned to ensure that the conflict does not spread to Westminster and upset domestic politics.

Even a superficial glance at the history of the Northern Ireland problem shows why these concerns have been persistent. Providing an account of the Labour Government's policy towards Northern Ireland between 1974–6, Wilson comments that the problem has had a deleterious effect on the careers of at least four Prime Ministers before him (H. Wilson, 1979, 66). Both Callaghan and Thatcher testify that the problem has to be 'carefully managed' and 'given constant attention' (Callaghan, 1987, 498; Thatcher, 1993, 384). Finally, there is every reason to think that if Major writes his memoirs, he will make similar comments. Before the cease-fire, the IRA's bombing campaign of the City of London was producing a number of awkward domestic political spin-offs. The refusal of insurance companies to provide cover against terrorist attacks led to the Treasury underwriting the liability. More generally, Major had to consider the unquantifiable effect on the

City's reputation as a top-class provider of financial services (*Financial Times*, 12 December 1992, 27 April 1993).

In the absence of any 'solution' to the problem of Northern Ireland, three methods have been used by the Thatcher and Major administrations to stop the conflict having an adverse impact on domestic politics. First, irrespective of whether policy reflects a new political initiative or rational inactivity, all British governments since 1969 have shown concern to maintain a frontbench consensus. In his memoirs, Wilson explicitly mentions the desirability of bipartisanship and notes that this was an objective of policy in itself between 1974–6 (H. Wilson, 1979, 67–71). Although there is a keen debate concerning the motives and consequences of the 1985 Anglo-Irish Agreement (AIA), writers are generally agreed that it conferred one major benefit on the Thatcher government: it enjoyed massive cross-party support in the Commons as well as general public support (Kenny, 1986; O'Leary, 1987, 17; Guelke, 1988, 100). Finally, Tony Blair's recent support for the government's call to the Irish Republican Army (IRA) to clarify whether their cease-fire was permanent, as well as his denunciation of Tony Benn's invitation to Gerry Adams to speak at Labour's conference in October, suggests that Major still enjoys this consensus.

A second consideration of all Conservative administrations since 1979 has been to maintain the support of the international community. This policy does not just reflect the Foreign Office's traditional predisposition to avoid offending foreign governments; it is also broadly in line with the interests of party leaders in office. Implementing a policy which has a broad measure of support at the international as well the domestic level can be an effective way of insulating the domestic political process. Although clearly disappointed that the AIA made little contribution to enhancing security in the Province, Thatcher refrained from pulling out because of broader international opinion' (Thatcher, 1993, 413). Others have noted how, unlike the Sunningdale Agreement, the AIA survived Unionist attempts to sabotage it, thus effectively quarantining the problem (O'Leary, 1987; Guelke, 1988, 100). Finally, although it is too soon to speculate over the long-term implications of the recent IRA cease-fire, it clearly has the support of international opinion (that is, the Americans), and seems to be having the effect of isolating and further detaching the increasingly intransigent Democratic Unionist Party DUP from the Ulster Unionists (*The Independent*, 1 September 1994).

Finally, pacifying the conflict is a pre-requisite for the longer-term British strategy of gradually off-loading responsibility for the problem onto the Irish government. An Irish dimension to the problem was officially recognised by the Heath government in 1973 and, although progress has been slow, a number of important developments have occurred under Conservative administrations since 1979. The essence of the AIA was the institutionalisation of this Irish dimension, through the creation of the IGC. Under this proposal, the Thatcher government accepted Dublin's right to put forward proposals on 'political' matters that were not the responsibility of a future devolved administration in Northern Ireland. As some commentators have noted, an agenda covering such political matters could be very wide-ranging (Kenny, 1986, 105–6; O'Leary, 1987, 7).

Since 1990, developments have continued in this direction. The Irish government became involved in intensive bilateral talks with London aimed at kick-starting the roundtable talks on the province's constitutional future. The publication of these proposals was continually delayed. However, there was speculation that Dublin was prepared to drop its adherence to articles 2 and 3 of its constitution, which assert reunification as the constitutional goal of the Republic. In return, reports suggest that London was willing to grant Dublin an increased role in the province through the creation of a number of all-Ireland Executive Boards.

Conclusions

Although this chapter has stressed continuity, it would be wrong to suggest that there were no differences between Thatcher and Major, or between them and the period before 1979. Many commentators are fond of noting Thatcher's assertive style towards foreign affairs, which was something that had not been seen in Downing Street for some years. With this went a new emphasis on nation, as Thatcher publicly stated that it was her intention to reverse Britain's decline in great power status. However, if this new assertive style represented a break with previous practice, Major has reverted to a less strident approach than that of his predecessor, most notably over relations with the EU. The argument here is that, although there may have been differences in the way it has been presented, it is the substance of policy that is important, and this has demonstrated substantial continuity.

Two main conclusions are applicable in this context. First, up to 1987 all party leaders, Thatcher included, have attempted to promote and preserve an external environment which exaggerated Britain's international influence, and provided beneficial domestic political spin-offs. Since the decline of this strategy after 1987, policy under both Thatcher and Major has demonstrated cautious pragmatism. On the one hand, this can be interpreted as ideological sclerosis. However, with future policy almost certainly involving difficult choices with possible adverse domestic political consequences, rational inactivity may be a better way of explaining the present approach of the Major leadership.

Second, if policy has been broadly continuous from 1945–94, it also seems to have reflected similar domestic political calculations. In short, both Labour and Conservative governments have been concerned to manage policy so that it is of some benefit, or at least does not adversely affect their domestic political position. Of particular interest here is the approach to managing the awkward issue of Britain's declining imperial concerns. Although, all party leaders, including the Conservative leadership since 1979, have displayed a keen awareness that if handled badly, these grim, intractable policy issues could have an awkward impact on domestic politics. Hence policy has been just as concerned with keeping these problems at arms length from Westminster, as with any attempt to implement policy solutions.

13

Conservative Foreign Policy towards the European Union

STEPHEN GEORGE and MATHEW SOWEMIMO

Since the nineteenth century, in terms of both its electoral programme and its self-image, the Conservative Party was the party of nation and empire. In the twentieth century it had to adjust to the disintegration of empire. Like Britain, the Conservative Party lost an Empire and had to search for a new role. One candidate for that role was Europe: the Conservatives might have become the party of European integration as had the Christian Democratic parties in the original six member states of the EC. That it did not work out like that owed something to problems of internal party management (Chapter 6). However, it also owed a great deal to the realities of Britain's position in relation to Europe and the rest of the world as perceived by Conservative politicians.

Conservative Policy before Thatcher

Winston Churchill posed as a great champion of European integration during the post-war years when the Conservatives were in opposition to the Attlee government but, when he became Prime Minister, he did nothing to live up to the expectations that he had raised on the continent. The Conservative government that came into office in 1951 took no steps to change the decision of its Labour predecessor not to participate in the European Coal and Steel Community (ECSC); and hopes of British support for the transformation of the Council of

Europe into a body with real supranational powers to bind national governments were also soon quashed.

When the six ECSC states began to discuss the formation of a general EEC, the Conservative government of Eden sent an observer to the negotiations in Messina, but he was withdrawn when it became apparent that what was being discussed was an organisation that would demand some surrender of sovereignty by the member states.

At this stage Conservative policy was driven by a belief which was shared across the political spectrum: namely, that Britain remained a world power both politically and economically, and neither needed to join, nor would benefit from joining such a supranational organisation as the EEC. These considerations of what was in the national interest were reinforced by the party's self-image as the party of nation and empire. Neither nationalism nor imperialism was compatible with tying the country's future to that of the European continent.

Some disquiet was privately expressed by Harold Macmillan who, at the time of the EEC negotiations, was the Chancellor of the Exchequer. He was concerned at 'the prospect of a world divided into the Russian sphere, the American sphere and a united Europe of which we were not a member' (Macmillan, 1971, 73).

After Macmillan became Prime Minister in 1957, he gradually came round to the view that Britain ought to apply to join the EC. Three main factors seem to have carried weight in this decision. First, it was obvious that, despite predictions to the contrary, the EEC was tremendously successful in promoting mutual trade between the members; it was the world's fastest-growing trading group, and economic growth rates in the six were outstripping Britain's. Against this, the Commonwealth was proving a declining asset for Britain, and the European Free Trade Association, which the British had set up as an alternative to a trade relationship with the six, was too small a grouping to provide much of a stimulus to the British economy.

More important, though, than the economic considerations were the political considerations. Following the emergence of Charles de Gaulle as President of France, the six were considering a scheme for cooperation on foreign policy. This concerned Britain's Conservative leaders because de Gaulle was notoriously opposed to Anglo-American domination of the capitalist world, and in favour of Europe following an independent line in world affairs. British policy since the war had been concerned above all with forming a solid bloc against Communism, and in the eyes of both Labour and Conservative governments this had involved ensuring that the USA would accept its responsibilities as the leader of the capitalist world, with Britain exercising influence through the maintenance of the 'special relationship'.

Following consultations with the US President, John F. Kennedy, during which Kennedy urged him to take Britain into the EEC, Macmillan decided to go ahead with an application with the primary aim of heading off French domination and the emergence of a third force in world affairs. Yet despite the essentially political motives for the application, it was presented to the Conservative Party and to Parliament as a move made for essentially economic reasons.

De Gaulle's veto of the Macmillan application, and later of the application by Harold Wilson's Labour government, prevented British membership until 1973, when it was achieved by the Conservative government of Edward Heath. Personally, Heath was convinced of the necessity of Britain being in the EC, and of the merits of closer unity between all the member states. However, he did not convey his personal convictions to the party as a whole. For most Conservatives membership remained a pragmatic necessity rather than a principled commitment. It was perhaps only because the Labour Party came out in opposition to membership of the EC that Heath was able so easily to carry his party with him despite serious doubts about the implications for traditional Conservatives.

Two important principles that guided Conservative policy towards Europe come out of this brief review of the pre-Thatcher years. First, with the partial exception of the Heath government, Conservative policy towards Europe was informed by a political objective – to prevent the emergence of a separate European political entity that would undermine the basis of global order – and this meant ensuring that the EC did not undermine the hegemonic position of the USA. Second, the commitment to membership was presented to the party by the leadership as a pragmatic necessity rather than as a principled commitment.

The Thatcher Governments, 1979–84

As leader of the opposition, Margaret Thatcher repeatedly described the Conservatives as 'the party of Europe'. This stressed continuity with the previous leadership, and allowed the Conservatives to attack the unenthusiastic position towards the EC taken by the Callaghan government.

However, soon after the Conservatives returned to office the new Chancellor, Geoffrey Howe, signalled that the problem which the Labour government had identified with respect to British contributions to the EC budget was far worse than the Conservatives had realised while in opposition. As it came to the end of its transitional period of membership, Britain was about to become one of only two net contributors to the budget (along with Germany) despite being only the seventh wealthiest member state in terms of GDP per head.

The existence of the problem was acknowledged by the European Commission, and by Britain's European partners; and at her first European Council meeting, in Strasbourg in June 1979, Thatcher put her case very reasonably. However, by the time of the second European Council in Dublin in November 1979 her tone had hardened, and she became involved in an unseemly squabble with the German and French leaders. Her tone subsequently became increasingly strident, as a settlement proved difficult to find.

A number of reasons contributed to the unpleasant nature of the budgetary dispute, which dominated Britain's relations with the rest of the EC until 1984. First, there was certainly fault on both sides. The French government in particular indicated at Dublin that it would be unwilling to concede any rebate in excess of the £350 million initially proposed by the Commission, and held to this as adamantly as Thatcher did to her insistence that she could not accept less than £1000 million. These entrenched and publicly proclaimed positions inevitably made negotiation and compromise very difficult.

Second, solutions to the problem that tried to resolve it by increasing the overall size of the budget, allowing more to be spent in Britain, were not acceptable to a Conservative government that was committed to reducing overall public expenditure. On the other hand, any solution that reduced the benefits to other member states was unacceptable to their governments; and structural reform of the budget to shift the pattern of expenditure within existing ceilings would have involved reforming the CAP, which was a symbol for all the original six of the success of the EC. Hence the dispute came to revolve around the payment of a budgetary rebate to Britain, which was also difficult terrain, because there was no agreement on how the contributions, and therefore the deficit, should be calculated.

However, the problem was undoubtedly made worse, and the dispute prolonged, by the intransigent tone adopted by the Prime Minister. Here the explanation is partly reduced to personality: it was Margaret Thatcher's nature to speak bluntly and to argue fiercely, an approach well adapted to the adversarial nature of British domestic politics but unusual in European politics, where coalition governments based on deals, concessions and guarded diplomatic language are the norm.

In addition to the personal predisposition of the British Prime Minister, domestic considerations of party management were important. During her first period in office Thatcher was far from secure in her position as Prime Minister and leader of the party. She was under constant criticism from the Heath wing of the party, and had yet to win the total confidence of the right wing. Her performance at the Dublin European Council, which was probably provoked by what she saw as the intransigence of the other participants, produced a large measure of support within the party for her resolute defence of the national interest. It was not a performance that Heath or his followers could support, as they were committed to a positive stance towards the EC; but on this issue the old totems of nationalism and suspicion of the foreigners in Europe proved stronger sentiments within the party than the more recent and half-hearted adoption of the title 'the European party'. In terms of the internal party struggle, Thatcher discovered that to be a sceptic about the benefits of belonging to the EC put her in a stronger position than her opponents.

Her intransigence in this arena also added to an image that she began to develop for herself as 'the iron lady', 'the conviction politician', and the lady who was 'not for turning'. As she invented her own image, so Thatcher's performances in the EC became driven more by this determination to show herself to be consistent, principled and tough than by any simple determination to achieve a settlement of the budgetary dispute. The problem could have been resolved much earlier had Thatcher been prepared to accept a compromise on her somewhat arbitrary demand for a rebate of £1000 million. Favourable deals were on the table some months before the final settlement.

This attitude changed as a result of the consolidation of Thatcher's position following her second election victory in 1983, and the increasing concern of the Foreign Office at moves among the other member states to push ahead towards further integration, without Britain if necessary. This determination was fed by the realisation that in the recovery from the 1979 oil crisis, Europe was lagging well behind both Japan and the USA, and risked coming a permanent third in the economic league-tables behind an increasingly dominant Japan, which would have the USA as its only realistic competitor. In response to this challenge, proposals were being made for far-reaching initiatives that would not be welcome to the British government, but which it was in no position to deflect so long as it remained isolated because of the budgetary dispute.

Thatcher's intransigent stance over the budget, and the rhetoric that she adopted in defining and defending her position, served to reinforce the nationalist and anti-European strands in the self-image of the Conservatives. The Heathite, pro-European view, always something of a minority position, was driven to the margins of the party. This fed into later discussion of the direction of policy towards the EC, and proved to be an unhelpful factor when the government tried to adopt a more positive stance.

The Single Market Negotiations

After the resolution of the budgetary issue, Britain's relations with the EC entered a period where the direction of policy seemed quite favourable for the Conservative Party's free-market orientation. In 1986 the government managed to secure the adoption of many of its policy priorities in the SEA, which seemed to hold out the prospect that the Conservatives' neo-liberal economic agenda would be institutionalised across the whole of Europe.

This success followed a change in the government's negotiating tactics, with both Thatcher and Howe (by then Foreign Secretary) showing pragmatism about how they achieved their policy objectives and being prepared to make compromises.

The path to the signing of the SEA started with Howe's initiative in presenting a meeting of European foreign ministers at Stresa with a paper entitled, *Europe – The Future*. Howe's analysis converged with that of other national governments on the strategic challenges that Europe faced, such as the environment. The Stresa Paper also noted the importance of political cooperation in external affairs (George, 1994, 175–6).

At the ensuing European Council in Milan the British analysis was received favourably, but there seemed to be momentum behind institutional reform involving an expansion of supranationalism. The

Italian presidency backed Treaty revision and an IGC was called to discuss this. Both Thatcher and Howe were extremely annoyed at being bulldozed into an IGC. Thatcher was also publicly hostile to any new institutional reforms (*The Times*, 1 July 1985). Nevertheless she responded by resolving to make the best of an unwelcome development (Thatcher, 1993, 551).

At the IGC, the key document was the White Paper on freeing the internal market, written by the British Commissioner, Lord Cockfield (1994), which laid out a timetable for freeing the movement of goods, services, capital and labour. It was a move towards 'deep free trade' whereby a product or service which met the requirements of any EC state could then be sold in any other member state. The single market thus involved mutual trust in regulatory standards (Willetts, 1992, 172).

It was at this juncture that Thatcher was persuaded that the prize of achieving a genuine common market, the dismantling of non-tariff barriers, was great enough to justify a compromise on institutional reform. She had previously been opposed on principle to the use of QMV in the Council of Ministers; but in the past, market liberalisation had been blocked by governments who opposed initiatives that threatened national vested interests. The requirement for unanimity meant that progress towards the single market had effectively gone at the pace of the slowest member. In particular, Howe and David Williamson, Thatcher's adviser on EC affairs, were able to convince her that unless she supported QMV to implement the single market directives, the Greek government would veto them.

So, having entered the IGC with a rejectionist stance, Thatcher was prepared to compromise once she was persuaded that QMV would be a means of exerting national leverage for Conservative policy priorities (Taylor, 1989, 12). In particular, the government was determined to gain access to the German market for British banking, insurance and general financial services; QMV was the means to achieve this. Once supranational reform was inextricably linked in Thatcher's mind with the pursuit of Britain's national interest, she was prepared to endorse it.

Subsequently, Thatcher publicly regretted ceding the national veto. In the light of the operation of QMV, especially the European Commission's application of it to push for a European-wide 48–hour week, Thatcher argued that the powers had been abused. This retrospective regret was shared by many Conservative MPs, Euro-sceptics who believed the concession on QMV fuelled the ambitions of the federalists for an expansion of the EC's competence into areas such as employment law and industrial policy. The link between QMV and British policy objectives was soon broken: Conservatives came to see it as a route towards the interventionist policies of Jacques Delors, and of Socialist and Christian Democratic governments in other member states.

In addition to its free-trade aspects, the SEA also incorporated into a treaty for the first time another aspect of the EC of which the British approved, political cooperation in external affairs. European Political Cooperation (EPC) was an inter-governmental procedure established to allow member states to consult one another on foreign policy and to attempt to move towards common views on specific issues and regions. EPC suited the British because it was inter-governmental; it was an evolutionary path towards a stronger identity for the EC in international affairs without compromising the foreign policy prerogatives of member states. As such the government did not see why it needed to be written into a treaty at all, but was relieved that it appeared as a separate article of the SEA, and remained clearly apart from the formal procedures of the EC itself.

The Delors Report

At the beginning of June 1988 the Germans took over the Presidency of the Council of Ministers. They immediately moved to support the French government in pressing for further institutional reform and for moves to EMU, a goal that had been reaffirmed in the preamble to the SEA. Nigel Lawson, the then Chancellor, later argued that Thatcher's concession of this point in the SEA was a critical mistake (Lawson, 1992, 904).

The renewal of the Franco-German drive towards federalism was given additional impetus by the second term of office of the Commission President, Jacques Delors. His speech to the British Trade Union Congress in July 1988, arguing for a 'social Europe', alarmed Thatcher. She was even more disquieted by Delors' speech to the EP, also in July 1988, when he predicted that in ten years 80 per cent of economic legislation, and perhaps tax and social legislation, would be directed from the Community.

It was at this juncture that Thatcher decided to make a pre-emptive intervention in the debate over European federalism. She did so in the now infamous Bruges speech in October 1988. In that speech she stressed the enduring importance of nationhood and national sovereignty. She also tied these themes to a rejection of an interventionist Europe.

Much of the speech was an anodyne reworking of timeworn British themes, like the need for reform of the CAP, and the importance of completing the single market. However, in a strikingly doctrinal passage of the speech, Thatcher warned that the EC's trajectory of development was bringing it into conflict with Britain's free market policies: 'We have not successfully rolled back the frontiers of the state in Britain only to see them reimposed at a European level, with a European super-state exercising a new dominance from Brussels' (Thatcher, 1988).

Diplomatically, the speech produced a hostile reaction from the governments of several member states, particularly as it was made not to a domestic British audience, but on the continent itself. It was perceived as an intervention in the internal politics of other member states. The neo-Gaullist tone of the speech was the first indication that Thatcher was going to take an uncompromising stance on the next stage of European political integration.

The Dispute over the European Monetary System

At this stage divisions emerged within the British government over how it should respond to the challenge of EMU. The central dispute involved Thatcher, her Foreign Secretary, Howe, and the Chancellor of the Exchequer, Lawson.

Lawson shared Thatcher's opposition to EMU and adopted the same doctrinal attitude on the issue of a single currency. However, Lawson and Howe disagreed with Thatcher's attitude to the ERM of the European Monetary System (EMS). Both these ministers had become convinced of the economic case for sterling's membership of the ERM, although they supported membership primarily for diplomatic reasons. Thatcher, strongly influenced by her economics adviser Sir Alan Walters, was adamantly opposed to ERM membership and resisted the pragmatism of her senior ministers.

The Delors Report, published in April 1989, laid out a three-stage route to full EMU. Stage one was to ensure that all member states had joined the ERM, with stages two and three being the establishment of a European Central Bank and a single currency. This report encouraged the financial markets and governments to view the ERM as a stage in the development towards a single currency. As a result the ERM became invested with much greater political significance. It was no longer merely a device to achieve exchange-rate stability and anti-inflationary discipline. From 1988 onwards there were no further realignments in the system, and the ERM bands became fixed rather than adjustable.

In the light of this development, the Foreign Office's objective, shared by Lawson and Howe, was to detach stage one of the Delors plan from stages two and three. They hoped that a British concession here would forestall the drive towards EMU, and allow the government to unravel the coalition in favour of monetary union by stressing the pitfalls. Lawson hoped that accession to the ERM would achieve this in two respects. First, ERM membership could be regarded as a 'goodwill diplomatic concession' to the other member states. Second, the government would then be in a stronger position to argue for a separation of the stages. From the spring of 1989 onwards, Lawson repeatedly made the case for separation of stage one from stages two and three: 'The ERM is an agreement between independent sovereign states . . . Economic and Monetary Union by contrast, is incompatible with independent sovereign states with control over their own fiscal and monetary policies' (Lawson, 1992, 910). However, Lawson subsequently resigned in a dispute over the public criticism of his policies by Walters, whom Thatcher refused to repudiate in Parliament.

European Policy in 1989–90

Although Thatcher had broken up the Lawson/Howe axis, the divisions within the government continued because her new Chancellor, John Major, also urged her to adopt a pragmatic approach to European integration. Major put forward an initiative that would enable the government to maintain Conservative Party unity and which would be interpreted as a constructive contribution towards the achievement of monetary union.

The 'hard ECU' (European Currency Unit) proposal was the British counter-initiative to the single currency on the Delors model. It was not simply a plan dictated by the demands of party management. Major hoped to shift debate away from the simple political objective of a single currency and on to the questions of the degree of economic convergence between member states that would be necessary, and the possible deflationary impact of too precipitate a move towards EMU. The hard ECU embodied this evolutionary approach. It centred on a proposal for a thirteenth currency available to all EC citizens and companies to use if they so wished. If in time the market so developed in the ECU, then this *common* currency could become the basis for a *single* currency.

This gradualist approach stressed the free market as a route towards a single currency and therefore found favour with Conservative back-benchers. Its proposal for a new supranational body, a European Monetary Fund, to control the supply of the ECU meant that it also enlisted some early support on the continent. However, as it became clear that Thatcher's attitude was steadfastly negative, the hard ECU was taken less and less seriously in the rest of Europe. It came to be seen as a spoiling tactic, designed to obstruct rather than facilitate monetary union. These fears were confirmed when, in her statement on the Athens European Council in 1990, Thatcher declared that she did not think that anyone would use the ECU anyway. She thereby subverted the purpose of her Chancellor's proposal within months of its announcement.

Thatcher also sent out signals to the Community that she was resolutely opposed to federalism and that she considered Britain's link with the USA to be of greater value than its membership of the EC. On 5 August 1990, in a speech at the Aspen Institute in Colorado, she put forward an alternative political and economic project to federalism, calling for a free trade area encompassing North America and Europe (Thatcher, 1993, 720).

Thatcher had been disquieted by the Bush administration's tilt towards Germany in 1989, with the implied message that the USA now regarded Germany as the key actor in Europe (Thatcher, 1993, 783). The Aspen speech was a public expression of her resistance to the Foreign Office's wish to give the European link pre-eminence over the Atlantic link. Thatcher was also privately annoyed with both France and the USA for failing to support her opposition to German unification. Subsequently, she was to endorse the sentiments of Nicholas Ridley, that European federalism had become the new vehicle for German dominance. This prospect reinforced her determination to seek a continuing American role in Western Europe:

> A united Europe would augment, not check, the power of a united Germany. Germany would pursue its interests inside or outside such a Europe – while a

Europe built on corporatist and protectionist lines implicit in the Franco-German alliance would certainly be more antipathetic to the Americans than the looser Europe I preferred. (Thatcher, 1993, 784)

The Aspen speech is another example of Thatcher's consistent linkage of security, political, and economic issues within the Atlantic relationship. Her conception of the relationship saw the USA as the most reliable upholder of a liberal world-trading order. She feared that a federal Europe would develop marked protectionist tendencies, thus encouraging a global trend towards regional trading blocs. She also feared that a federal EC would lead to the eventual withdrawal of the US security guarantee to Europe.

In October 1990, Major and Douglas Hurd, then the new Foreign Secretary, finally prevailed on Thatcher to join the ERM. Central to the PCP's approval of this move was the expectation that the ERM would provide the basis for a rapid reduction in interest rates in the run-up to the general election. However Britain's membership came at a particularly unpropitious time. On the one hand, the nature of the system had changed because of the political factors discussed above; but, in addition to this, a new inflexibility had arisen in the system, due to the historically high level of German interest rates.

The Rome European Council in October 1990 triggered the series of events that led to the fall of Margaret Thatcher and a reappraisal of European policy by the British government. At the summit, Thatcher's obduracy provoked the other member states into setting a date for the beginning of the second stage of EMU. Thatcher reacted intemperately, saying that the other 11 were 'living in cloud cuckoo land' (K. Baker, 1993, 377).

In her Commons statement on the European Council meeting, Thatcher dramatically departed from the Foreign Office script and asserted that she would not 'hand over sterling and the powers of this House to Europe' (Hansard, 30 October 1990, col. 873), and that the government's policy was to support the creation of a hard ECU as a parallel currency; but in her view there was little chance of it being widely used in place of national currencies.

This performance led to the resignation of Howe as Deputy Prime Minister. He had publicly maintained the line that in the past, as with the SEA, Thatcher had taken an uncompromising stance but had signed up in the end. He now feared that Thatcher could not be persuaded to compromise and that she was opposed to further

European integration in principle. He envisaged the prospect that Thatcher would veto a new treaty at the IGC, and believed that her doctrinal opposition to further integration risked Britain losing decisive influence in the development of the Community:

> How on earth are the Chancellor and the Governor of the Bank of England, commending the hard ECU as they strive to, to be taken as serious participants in the debate against that kind of background noise? . . . It is rather like sending your opening batsmen to the crease only to find the moment the first balls are bowled, that their bats have been broken before the game by the team captain. (Hansard, 13 Nov. 1990, col. 464)

The ensuing leadership challenge to Thatcher led to her replacement by John Major and the rejection of the doctrinal stance of the former Prime Minister.

The IGCs and the Maastricht Treaty

In the run-up to the IGCs, Major abandoned Thatcher's confrontational rhetoric, adopted a conciliatory tone, and went on a 'charm offensive' in European capitals. This was best reflected in his declaration, during a visit to Chancellor Kohl in Germany, that Britain should be 'at the very heart of Europe' (*The Guardian*, 12 March 1991). Although such bland and relatively uncontentious statements were devoid of policy content, they signalled that the British government wished to seek allies for its negotiating objectives rather than to polarise the argument on institutional reform.

The treaty that emerged from the IGC was a significant diplomatic triumph for the government. The bulk of the proposals in an earlier, more federalist, draft (put forward by the Dutch presidency) were rejected, especially in the field of political union. Of great symbolic importance for Conservative MPs, the government secured the deletion from the Preamble of a declaration that the EU which the Treaty created had a federal goal, and its replacement by the traditional phrase 'an ever closer union'. But the most significant concessions to the British position were what the opposition dubbed the 'dual opt-out' provisions for monetary union and social policy.

In the IGC on monetary union, the British government argued for all member states to have the right to decide whether to proceed to the third stage of full union at the time that the step was about to be taken, rather than having to sign up in advance for all stages. This condition was, however, unacceptable to the other member states because they feared that the German Parliament might decide at the last moment not to abandon the Deutschmark in favour of a common currency, and without German participation monetary union would be a meaningless exercise. Instead the other states agreed to a Protocol to the Treaty allowing the British Parliament the right to decide at the later stage on Britain's participation (Denmark subsequently negotiated a similar concession), but binding the others to proceed.

Similarly, the British government opposed the inclusion of a chapter on social policy in the treaty. On this issue it was successful, although it agreed to allow the other 11 to append a separate protocol on social policy, and agreed that decisions could be made by the other 11 under this protocol as though it were part of the Treaty. The decisions taken under the protocol would be binding on the 11, but not on Britain.

On CFSP, the government resisted pressure from some other member states to make agreement on joint action subject to QMV. Instead Title Five of the Treaty set out a framework for the formulation of common positions and the pursuit of joint action in foreign policy on the basis of unanimity. If the Council of Ministers wished to introduce QMV in CFSP, then it must also decide to do so unanimously. In this area the government had sacrificed no sovereignty but had made a series of *communautaire* concessions.

The Treaty also made a number of concessions to those who argued for an expansion of the powers of the EP. The EP was granted co-decision powers with the Council of Ministers in a wide range of areas. However, the British government, along with the French, resisted the federalist preference of giving it the right to initiate legislation.

The most positive case that the government made for the inter-governmental nature of the Treaty was in relation to the subsidiarity provisions of article 3b. Ministers had begun to use this term since the signing of the SEA to present a coherent and intellectually sustainable case that the Community should be involved in a policy area only when national governments could not achieve desired ends by themselves. The government posed the issue as, 'What policy areas is it appropriate for the Community to be involved in?' The Conservatives' consistent desire to curb the Commission could now be articulated in terminology that was drawn from continental theories of federalism, and was therefore very difficult for federalists to argue against. For example, in responding to the Social Chapter the government argued that it was completely unnecessary for the Community to become involved in areas such as employment law at all.

Government ministers were addressing two audiences when they expounded the doctrine of subsidiarity. When addressing other EC governments, they hoped to portray British objections to further integration as not being motivated by sheer obstinacy. They also deployed this term in order to reassure Conservative MPs that the government did not envisage the Community developing inexorably into a federal state. The government's tactic here was to try to redefine Britain's relations with the Community through the use of language that would both pacify its domestic constituency and strike a less confrontational note on the continent.

The problem with the concept of subsidiarity was the ambiguity about how it could be applied in practice. The government constantly insisted to opponents of the treaty that article 3b meant that many of their concerns were being addressed and that in future there would be a reversal of the integrationist trend. The government seized the initiative after the Danish and French referendums to make the case that the popular disaffection with the EC, as revealed in these results, reinforced the need to put subsidiarity into practice.

At the Edinburgh summit in December 1992 the Commission undertook to justify explicitly all legislative proposals on subsidiarity grounds, both in the Preamble and in accompanying memoranda. However, the treaty language in 3b is couched in quite subjective terms and makes no attempt to set objective standards or criteria for defining areas which are most appropriately dealt with at a national or European level (Teasdale, 1993, 191).

Given the legal ambiguity of 3b, the government found a more secure basis for achieving its objectives in the new political mood in the Community that resulted from the shock of the Danish and French referendum results. This mood led the government to argue that the debate in the Community was now at last going Britain's way. In an article in *The Economist*, Major was keen to state the government's belief in this new realism: 'Maastricht changed all that. For the first time, the sort of questions that Britain had been asking were asked in other Community countries as well' (*The Economist*, 1993, 23).

The government was hopeful that in this new climate the Commission would exercise greater self-restraint and discontinue its past practice of bringing forward proposals that had dubious legal bases in European treaties, the most infamous example (often quoted by

Conservative MPs) being the 48–hour week legislation, brought forward by the Commission under the health and safety at work provisions of the SEA.

The Government's European Strategy after Ratification

After the ratification of the Treaty the government hoped to shift attention away from institutional questions and monetary union and on to its ambitions for an extension of deregulation in Europe. The break-up of the ERM in July 1993 added weight to the government's arguments that the economic conditions in Europe had pushed the achievement of EMU into a remote future.

The government was encouraged that a new mood was developing in Europe which would be more receptive to British ideas in the sphere of economic policy. German economists and politicians, including the Economics Minister, Gunter Rexrodt, had begun to reappraise the country's high social costs of production and the corporatist structure of German industry. Increasingly the signs seemed to be that Germany would embrace aspects of Britain's deregulatory model.

The new conservative French government began a series of large privatisation programmes in 1993. Within the Gaullist Party many leading figures, like Phillipe Seguin and Jacques Chirac, had moved away from the federal position. This movement on the right was given further impetus by the success of the 'Other Europe' list of Philippe de Villiers in the 1994 European parliamentary elections in France. This campaign showed the extent of popular opposition to further EU integration and seemed likely to encourage Prime Minister Balladur to move on to this terrain in the run-up to the 1995 presidential elections.

In this climate of 'new realism' the European Commission published its White Paper, *Growth, Competitiveness and Employment* in December 1993. The government seized on the paper as reflecting the increasing convergence between the Commission's economic thinking and Conservative policy. The paper did indeed accept much of the British economic analysis of Europe's malaise in relation to high levels of structural unemployment.

The White Paper adopted the government's language of labour-market flexibility and made accommodations with Conservative free-market views. It conceded that 'social protection schemes have – in part at least – had a negative impact on employment' and called for greater flexibility in the organisation of work (European Commission, 1993, p. 124). In the debate on the paper in the House of Commons, the Chancellor and the Foreign Secretary struck an almost triumphalist tone in their remarks:

> We now have a document that bears the stamp of this government's policies . . . People in Europe are listening to the British and the Conservative experience. They are privatising, they are deregulating, they are going for competitive open markets. (Kenneth Clarke, MP, Hansard, 9 December 1993, cols 581 and 583)

> The Commission has moved a long way in the past year or so. It has moved well beyond the British Labour Party in analysing why Europe has failed to create jobs to the same extent as the United States and Japan, let alone the new Asian competitors. (Douglas Hurd, Hansard, 9 December 1993, col. 508)

In the discussions that followed the publication of the White Paper, Britain found that the German government was an ally on the issue of faster deregulation within the EU. Rexrodt argued in May 1994 that a task-force of experts should be formed to root out unnecessary Euro-legislation. The German Economics Minister's remarks provoked a strong counter-attack from Delors who accused him of wishing to gut the Maastricht Treaty of the Social Chapter (*Financial Times*, 17 May 1994).

The British government also began to develop its earlier tactic of redefining Britain's position in the Community through the use of language. Previously ministers had responded defensively to opposition allegations that the Maastricht opt-outs had created a two-speed Europe, with Britain in the slow lane. They now sought to regain the initiative.

From the spring of 1994 onwards, Hurd and Major began to talk of a multi-speed Europe and 'variable geometry'. They wished to make Britain's position in the post-Maastricht and post-enlargement EU appear to be less aberrant and more normal. The multi-speed outline which Hurd began to develop did not depart from an objective description of the constitutional and economic dynamics of the EU in the 1990s.

A multi-speed Europe was the natural consequence of the 'pillar' structure in the Maastricht Treaty, the convergence criteria for EMU, the Schengen agreement, and the prospective accession of Eastern Europe states. If the EU broadened its membership to incorporate

Eastern Europe, then it was widely accepted that it would be impossible for those states to participate in monetary union.

The convergence criteria made it likely that only an inner core of states would satisfy the criteria on inflation, budget deficits and interest rates, in order to form a currency union. Britain had already reserved for itself the right not to participate in EMU even if all other states did so. Therefore the government's new multi-speed vision, like subsidiarity, was directed at breaking down the simplistic interpretation of Britain's continental allies surging ahead towards further integration, while Britain languished in isolation and obduracy.

John Major's Ellesmere Port speech on variable geometry during the European elections did not then signify a change in government policy towards either EMU or political union (Major, 1994c). Ellesmere Port represented only the government's exposition of the developing reality of the EU.

Continuities between the European Policies of the Thatcher and Major Governments

Although Major changed the government's diplomatic approach towards Europe, his policy showed important continuities with his predecessor. In her Bruges speech of 1988 Margaret Thatcher identified five guiding principles for the future of the EC. These were: that willing and active cooperation between independent sovereign states was the best way to build a successful EC; that Community policies should tackle present problems in a practical way; that Community policies should encourage enterprise; that Europe should not be protectionist; and that the defence of Europe should be achieved through NATO (Thatcher, 1988) The arguments developed by John Major in his *Economist* article were remarkably similar. He said:

It is for nations to build Europe, not for Europe to supercede [sic] nations. (Major, 1993, 27)

Unless the Community is seen to be tackling the problems which affect [the electorates of Europe] now, rather than arguing over abstract concepts, it will lose its credibility. (Major, 1993, 23)

I want to see a competitive and confident Europe, generating jobs for its citizens and choice for its consumers. (Major, 1993, 27)

He also called for a successful outcome to the GATT negotiations and the removal of barriers to trade with Eastern Europe (Major, 1993, 24 and 27); and for 'common security arrangements firmly linked to NATO' (Major, 1993, 27).

The other policy principle with which Thatcher was particularly associated, but which was noticeably not mentioned in the Bruges speech, was monetary union. On this Major stated forthrightly that in the light of the effective collapse of the ERM in July 1993, 'economic and monetary union is not realisable in present circumstances' (Major, 1993, 24).

The objectives outlined by John Major in this article clearly did not differ substantially from those of the Thatcher governments. While maintaining the essential objectives of its policy in the EC, what the new government tried to do in the 1990s was change the tone in which relations with Brussels, and with the other member states, were conducted.

Conclusions

It is a mistake to see Conservative policy towards the EU as driven purely by considerations of internal party management. The Conservative Party has always prided itself on being a pragmatic party of government, and its policies to Europe whilst in office have generally been driven by a pragmatic response to what was perceived as being in the national interest, in the context of a rapidly changing world. The biggest exception to this pragmatism was the attitude of Margaret Thatcher when Prime Minister, which became increasingly dogmatic. In particular, Thatcher clung to two fundamentals of past Conservative policy. One was attachment to the USA and the Atlantic Alliance as Britain's primary international partnership; the other was an attachment to sovereignty, especially in monetary matters.

Unfortunately for Thatcher, the basis for both of these positions shifted beneath her. The Bush administration in the USA showed itself to be more interested in developing a partnership with Germany than with Britain, largely because Britain was seen as being on the sidelines of European developments (George, 1992). This was a US policy priority that continued with the Clinton administration after the end of the Thatcher premiership.

Second, Thatcher's opposition to monetary union, when it looked as though the other member states were intent on going ahead regardless of whether Britain joined in, caused increasing concern amongst British industry and in financial circles in the City of London. This was the basis of Howe's condemnation of Thatcher in his resignation speech.

In many respects the Major government remained loyal to the economic programme of the Thatcher governments, but in the context of accepting that the debate was no longer about whether there would be closer European cooperation in the future; it was now about what sort of EU would emerge from that closer cooperation. If Britain wished to influence the nature of the EU, especially on such important issues as how much intervention there would be in the workings of the free market, and the closely related issue of whether the EU remained an outward-looking organisation or became inward-looking and protectionist, then it had to be at the centre of the debate, not standing on the side-lines sulkily protesting at everything that the others proposed.

It was the realism of the recognition that Britain had no future outside Europe that drove the policy of the Major government towards the EU, an approach expected to survive Hurd's retirement and replacement by Malcolm Rifkind in July 1995. However, that policy was frequently deflected by the strength of domestic opposition to it from within the Conservative Party, a phenomenon that is analysed elsewhere in this volume.

14

The Character of Contemporary Conservatism

STEVE LUDLAM and MARTIN J. SMITH

> The talk of the 'English disease' has been replaced by wonder at the 'Thatcher miracle'. Britain the laggard has become Britain the world leader. Our policies have become the standard against which others are measured. There has been a revolution whose chief casualties have been socialism and the weak complacent Conservatism of the sixties and early seventies. (Tebbit, 1988, 267)

> Perhaps all creeds need a mythical golden age to which their adherents long to return. But neither economically nor socially does the Victorian age produce an acceptable model for contemporary Britain. Hence Thatcherite neo-liberalism – misleadingly called radicalism – was doomed to failure. The giddy dance of dogma has now halted, but the Conservative Party has not yet regained its balance. It still has to choose between the nineteenth and the twentieth centuries, between two-nation Thatcherism and one-nation Toryism. The Record of Thatcherism – and also the Conservative tradition – should be its guide. Britain's sudden swing to the right under Mrs Thatcher might have been defensible had it transformed the economy . . . But the sacrifice imposed upon the poor produced nothing miraculous, except for the rich. Instead of experiencing an economic miracle, Britain experienced the lowest growth rate since the war. The lunge to the right caused social retreat without economic advance. (Gilmour, 1992, 337)

As the comments of two of Thatcher's Cabinet ministers cited above illustrate, the impact on contemporary Conservatism of the years since 1975 remains violently contested even within the highest ranks of the party she led. In the introduction to this book, we undertook to reconsider in this chapter the general state of the party, the main interpretations of Thatcherism, and the principal hypotheses offered about Major's stewardship. What conclusions can we draw on the basis of the contributions to this volume?

Party

Several chapters have demonstrated the extent of the multiple crises afflicting the Conservative Party. The collapse in the party's electoral performance, so formidable for a decade after 1979, was revealed in local, European and by-elections after 1992 (Chapter 3). Major's electoral appeal is clearly and deliberately different from Thatcher's, even if his instinctive reaction to electoral set-backs is increasingly to wrap himself in the Union Jack. But economic recession in the South of England is now the Tories' key problem because of three factors. The regional basis of its support in the populous and prosperous South has enabled the party to take office on modest national shares of the popular vote, but is now at risk. Second, the opposition parties have enjoyed an associated recovery in the South that has previously eluded them. Third, the convincing evidence that economic voting models best explain fluctuations in the party's electoral support undermines hopes of the Tories' southern vote reviving on the basis of an intensified appeal to nationalism against Europeanism and Scottish separatism.

In spite of 15 years of Conservative domination, the British electorate have not become increasingly Thatcherite since 1979; rather the reverse (Chapter 3). Similar conclusions can be drawn about the party's members. In spite of a limited shift in party members' attitudes towards Thatcherite ideas, the evidence suggests that Thatcher responded to attitudes in the party but did not change them a great deal, and there remain a considerable number of 'progressive' Conservatives in the party's membership. Most striking is the finding that the party's membership is falling dramatically. Disillusion at the party's economic policy failure helps explain the decline in membership, and the ideological drive of Thatcherism within the party may have disturbed the balance of party culture, alienating non-Thatcherites but not replacing them with new long-term members (Chapter 4). The importance of party members in raising funds, acting as party ambassadors in their communities, and helping to win election campaigns, all make the reversal of this legacy of the Thatcher era an urgent problem for Major.

Nicholas Ridley insisted that although Thatcher put reliable allies into key posts, such as the Treasury, she did not in general promote MPs into government on ideological grounds (Ridley, 1992, 25, 162). Neither, apparently, did she take steps to transform the Parliamentary party as a whole into a Thatcherite party. If the resulting social profile of successful candidates is anything to go by, the distinctly minority position of Thatcherites on her benches, back and front, was apparently not addressed by any systematic strategy to change the pattern of candidate selection (Chapter 5). Comparing the social composition of the Parliamentary elite of the party with the profile of its members (Chapter 4), it is clear that Thatcher's leadership has not made the party's MPs significantly more socially representative even of the party's own members, any more than the members are representative of the party's voters. The long-term changes in the social composition of new MPs and ministers did not accelerate under Thatcher or Major; indeed, they appeared to have stopped and gone into reverse since the mid-1980s. Certainly the suggestion that Thatcherism reflected or heralded the invasion of Parliament by Tory estate agents can be rejected without hesitation.

The cohesion of the Parliamentary party has declined dramatically under Major (Chapter 6). In part this has been a result of factors he inherited, in part the result of external pressures arising from the desire of other European governments to make progress towards EMU. It is difficult to argue that Major's change of leadership style has weakened party unity. Thatcher's leadership style helped weaken it to the point where it cost her job. As one of her allies has put it, Thatcher's Parliamentary party chose Major to succeed her 'because it wanted a broad continuation of Thatcherite polices and also a change of style' (K. Baker, 1993, 421). Thatcher herself compared her party management style to that of her successor, writing that, 'John Major – perhaps because he had made his name as a whip, or perhaps because he is unexcited by the sorts of concepts which people like Nigel [Lawson] and I saw as central to politics – had one great objective: this was to keep the party together' (Thatcher, 1993, 719). In 1993 Major prevented one of the most serious rebellions of the century from splitting the party or destroying the government. It is difficult to imagine Thatcher doing less damage to unity at Westminster than Major has suffered. His image of indecisiveness conceals some skilful manoeuvring given such a small and diminishing majority in Parliament, underpinned by a willingness, in the last resort, to confront his Euro-rebels with the threat of electoral annihilation. Considering the extent of sceptical attitudes among MPs (Chapter 6), this was a considerable achievement. In his first five years of leadership, he lost two Cabinet colleagues over Europe, Lamont in 1993 and Redwood in 1995, who resigned to contest the leadership election Major called to call the rebels' bluff. In her last five years, Thatcher lost five Cabinet colleagues over Europe. Thatcher intensified Conservative alarm over sovereignty, which certainly imposed a constraint on Major's party management. But Major's reshuffle after defeating Redwood did not suggest he was appeasing irreconcilable Thatcherites.

Whatever the inconsistencies of policy management, the free market economic stance of Thatcherism has been a principal feature of Thatcherism (Chapters 2 and 9). Both parties are reported to have shifted, apparently irreversibly, towards neo-liberal macro-economic policy and indeed social policy (Chapter 7). If anything, the process has hardened since Major became leader and won the 1992 election, which is another indirect indication that he has maintained the ideological impetus of Thatcherism. Although particular new opposition movements have done great damage to the Conservatives, notably over the Poll Tax and the export of live animals, their more profound impact has been on the ability of the Labour and Liberal Democrats to recruit energetic political activists who are broadly left-of-centre. Insofar as this alienation from Parliamentary opposition politics reflects the unbroken longevity of Tory rule, and the removal of so many policy arenas from the direct control of Parliament (Chapter 8), it is an important achievement of Thatcher that has also been sustained and intensified by Major.

We can conclude that, by the mid-1990s, the Conservative Party had succeeded in drawing its main opponents on to its policy terrain, but was becoming less able to exploit its advantages. The bases of its electoral triumphs were visibly weakening, its membership and funding were falling alarmingly, and its reputation for unity in defence of the British state lay in tatters as it divided from top to bottom over Europe and national sovereignty. Had Thatcherism, triumphant and triumphalist for so long, failed after all?

Interpretations of Thatcherism

We had to stress continually that, however difficult the road might be and however long it took us to reach our destination, we intended to achieve a fundamental change of direction. We stood for a new beginning, not more of the same. I was again asking the Conservative Party to put its faith in freedom and free markets, limited government and a strong national defence. (Thatcher, 1993, 15)

> Much of the economic achievement will remain and is unlikely to be reversed by any government in the future. That is what is so unique about Margaret Thatcher's record. She forced the Labour Party to abandon, one by one, the basic policies of socialism . . . She forced the political debate in Britain onto the ground of who can best run a market economy in Britain; it is no longer about whether we have a market economy or a socialist one. (Ridley, 1991, 254–5)

The complexity of the phenomenon of Thatcherism has been in evidence throughout the chapters of this book. The five interpretations identified in the introduction were: that Thatcherism was a matter of leadership style and personality; that it was a continuation of Tory statecraft whose ideological direction was mainly a secondary device deployed to achieve the main aims of restoring the authority of the British state and of the Conservative Party as the natural party of government in British politics; that it was a self-conscious ideological strategy to construct a socially authoritarian but economically liberal consensus in British politics; that it was a project aimed at the reconstruction of British political economy as a post-Fordist regime; and finally that it was in reality a muddled mixture of inconsistent policy initiatives whose general direction was conditioned mainly by difficulties of implementation of policy goals (Marsh, 1994). What general conclusions does this permit us to offer?

In the early 1980s politics undergraduates were invariably confronted with exam questions that asked whether Thatcherism was 'style or substance'? Such a question now seems utterly anachronistic. The evidence of Thatcher's impact on public policy, notably on economic policy and latterly on social policy, including the influence on other parties' stances, is overwhelming, however inconsistent or occasionally tentative the formation or implementation of policy may have been. Ironically, how substantial her long-term ideological impact has been on Conservative Party members and MPs is more disputable, judging by some of the evidence we have examined.

Yet there are areas where Thatcher's style has been identified as a significant element of contemporary Conservatism. The most important policy arenas, noted in Chapters 12 and 13, where this was the case were foreign policy and, most prominently, policy on Europe. In spite of inheriting, and apparently supporting, a policy of keeping Britain at the heart of Europe, Thatcher's personal style became increasingly significant, first in setting the tone of Britain's budgetary dispute in the EC in the early 1980s, and then in manouevres over the SEA, EMU, and, of course, the ERM. This had real consequences for negotiating outcomes, as well as for party cohesion, and was a legacy that Major could not circumvent easily by his very different style. 'The lady vanishes', one headline put it in 1993, 'but the handbag will haunt Major'. On the other hand, her iron lady style of prosecuting the Cold War changed dramatically once the opportunity to do business with Gorbachev presented itself (Chapter 12). Here though, it is worth considering how much more difficult Thatcher's promotion of *glasnost* might have been had she not enjoyed the reputation for anti-Communism that the iron lady style had given her. Furthermore, as insiders' memoirs have confirmed, her style had important effects on her management of the party, not least on its cohesion at the highest levels. As one of her early lieutenants (but ultimate destroyers) put it, 'Margaret Thatcher was beyond argument a great Prime Minister. Her tragedy is that she may be remembered less for the brilliance of her many achievements than for the recklessness with which she later sought to impose her own increasingly uncompromising views' (G. Howe, 1994, 691).

The appearance that Thatcher was thus uniquely driven by ideological imperatives has informed some of the most influential work on Thatcherism, but these have been increasing challenged in the light of the inconsistencies in her record. The conflicting interpretations of Thatcherism as either a hegemonic ideological project or the conduct of statecraft designed to restore the fortunes of state and party can often be assessed by the same evidence. For example, although clearly presented as an ideological alternative to Keynesianism, Thatcher's economic policy emerges as far too inconsistent and *ad hoc* to be portrayed as being driven by precise ideological guidelines (Chapter 9). For example, the private monopolies resulting from privatisation do not suggest a simple picture of ideological commitment to maximum free competition. The almost accidental emergence of the privatisation policy, and the early resistance of Thatcher's government to privatisation ideas faced by its proponents (Redwood, 1995), also testify to the absence of an ideological slide rule from which policy initiatives could be read off. Indeed, a strong argument can be made for viewing

Thatcherite economic policy as being mainly concerned with satisfying the short-term demands of key sections of her electoral constituencies (Chapter 9). This is consistent with the statecraft approach, suggesting a government driven by the 'vote motive' rather than driving it out of party political calculation to satisfy the requirements of neo-liberalism.

Thatcher's industrial relations reforms were similarly justified using strongly ideological rhetoric, but the actual programme implemented, and the pace of change, attest more to a pragmatic if determined statecraft than to a carefully designed and ideologically inspired strategy (Chapter 10; Marsh, 1992). The succession of attacks on effective trade unionism can be seen as a negative assault on an interest group believed to have embarrassed the party, undermined the authority of business managers, and invaded policy-making areas where they had no legitimate concerns. In other words, what was being pursued was statecraft designed to recover party and state from the assumed humiliations of the Heath government. There may have been a Hayekian desire to cripple unions, but Thatcher's governments moved cautiously and sometimes relied for support on right-wing unions, and even encouraged the formation of such a union in the Nottingham coalfield in their battle to destroy the NUM. Both ideological imperatives and pragmatic statecraft can be discerned in the production and implementation of economic and industrial policy.

What is striking about the reform of the welfare state and of the state itself under Thatcher, considering their centrality to the ideological rhetoric of Thatcherism, is that so little radical reform was undertaken until after the 1987 election (Chapters 8 and 11). Indeed, if Thatcher had lost that election, there would have been little to show in this respect from the first eight of her 10½ years in office. The rapidity with which she disowned an alleged hidden agenda to reform welfare before the 1983 election suggests the pursuit of statecraft, rather than ideas. Even the intellectual standard bearer of the 'hegemonic project' interpretation, Stuart Hall, has subsequently argued that the attack on welfare was most significantly served by her wider legacy and by social change, suggesting that:

> the combination of the public spending deficit and the inevitable long-term increasing cost of delivering social services provides the opportunity for another aspect of the Thatcherite project, not just to erode or undermine the welfare state, but to bring the epoch of what has been known as welfare capitalism to an end (Hall, 1993).

On the other hand, it is important to recognise that a focus on particular social policy areas that were not addressed in detail until Thatcher's third term can be misleading. As she herself has put it, 'My economic policy was also intended to be a social policy. It was a way to a property-owning democracy' (Thatcher, 1993, 698). Some of the consequences of this social engineering for electoral behaviour were real (Chapter 3).

The most unambiguous arguments for treating Thatcherism as statecraft rather than ideology are made in respect of foreign policy, defence policy, and policy on Europe (Chapters 12 and 13). Beyond a crude anti-Communism that chimed well in Washington, Thatcher's foreign policy was characterised by inactivity and cautious pragmatism (Chapter 12). No attempt was made to reform the Foreign Office, the object of so much of Thatcher's scorn, or the MoD. Neither the Thatcherite think tanks nor her Policy Unit in Downing Street devoted much refoming zeal in this direction. On Ireland and Hong Kong, there were no radical departures from traditional British policy under Thatcher. A revival of nationalism had been one ideological shift discernible under Thatcher (Chapter 2) but, even in the arena where this was most apparent, in her negotiations in Europe, a hard-headed pragmatism was at work, for example, in the promotion of the single market programme from the mid-1980s (Chapter 13). In the process she personally argued for the use of the QMV procedure to be used to overrule national sovereignty and clear obstacles to wider free enterprise. This was a sign of a wider ideological purpose, perhaps, but one seriously at odds with her nationalism. And eventually, of course, even after her opposition to it had cost her two senior neo-liberal Cabinet colleagues, she did finally take Britain into the ERM, a move that she signally fails to defend in terms of principle in her memoir (Thatcher, 1993, 723–4).

The post-Fordist analysis is more specific than the general hegemonic approach, in its emphasis on economic and labour market policies. The evidence of this book suggests that, like the general hegemonic view, it ascribes a high degree of strategy, coherence and economic awareness that seems questionable in the light of the pattern of economic failure, changes in policy and inconsistency (Chapter 9). Beyond a rhetorical commitment, still unfulfilled, to reduce the 'burden' of public spending, and apart from a strategy of introducing post-corporatist industrial relations into the public services, the state reforms do not appear to be consciously aimed at an active or detailed post-Fordist economic strategy, except in the negative respect that they appear to be aimed in part at making any revival of social democratic interventionism impossible (Chapter 8). In this respect Thatcher's industrial relations strategy appears to offer evidence of positive post-Fordist strategy, but the succession of attacks on effective trade unionism can equally be seen, as suggested above, as negative reactions to earlier humiliations, thus also fitting the statecraft model of Thatcherism.

The chapters in this book about policy have been primarily about the impact of Thatcher and Major on Conservative ideas and policies, not about the impact of the policies on British society; hence any evaluation of the fifth interpretation of Thatcherism that insisted on measuring the reality of policy outcomes is necessarily constrained. Nevertheless, the evidence of the messiness of policy formation strongly supports the argument that a disaggregated approach to different policy areas, of the kind demanded by the fifth interpretation, is to be recommended (Chapter 2). There is in this book plentiful evidence also of the continuity of Thatcher's policies with those of her predecessors, and of the many unintended effects of policy that undermine consistency and interpretations that rely on evidence of consistency.

Many analysts insist that Thatcherism did not in fact become hegemonic: Thatcher failed to convince the electorate (Crewe, 1988); she did not win over the Conservative Party (Norton, 1990; Gamble, 1991; Whiteley, Seyd and Richardson, 1994); she did not even construct a 'dry'-dominated Cabinet (Ridley, 1992); and many Thatcherite policies were not effectively implemented (Marsh and Rhodes, 1992). This lends force to the representation of Thatcherism as a continuation of traditional Conservative statecraft concerns of governing competently and winning elections. However, what must be acknowledged is that, in crucial areas such as economic and social policy, Thatcher's statecraft was based on different policy preferences from those of previous Conservative administrations. In that sense she did change the policy agenda, and justified the new statecraft by reference to an alternative ideology. From this point of view it makes more sense to see the ideological banner-waving of Thatcherism as providing, beyond a platform from which to attack opponents, a basis for rationalising the outcomes of policy initiatives (Chapter 2). Even Major describes himself as leading a party that is trapped in a Thatcher myth of its own making, 'a party that is harking back to a golden age that never was, and is now invented'.

Conservatism under Major

I agreed neither with John's analysis nor his conclusion. I said that the government could not subscribe to a treaty amendment containing the full Delors definition of EMU . . . I was extremely disturbed to find that the Chancellor [Major] had swallowed so quickly the slogans of the European lobby. At this point, however, I felt that I should hold my fire. John was new to the job. He was right to be searching for a way forward which would attract allies in Europe as well as convince Conservative MPs of our reasonableness. But it was already clear to me that he was thinking in terms of compromises which would not be acceptable to me and that intellectually he was drifting with the tide. (Thatcher, 1993, 721)

As for the three candidates who did put their names forward . . . none of them was a Thatcherite. The fact that Margaret was under the impression that John was one, and backed him accordingly, merely underlined how out of touch she had become. (Lawson 1992, 1002)

Reports of the death of Thatcherism have been greatly exaggerated. The principles of Conservatism are not being killed off or interred. They live on. Thatcherism was not an ideology. It evolved, and was more pragmatic. The idea that the departure of Margaret Thatcher saw a dramatic shift from ideology to pragmatism is a false reading. (Redwood, 1995)

If no single theory explaining the origin and motivation of Thatcherism emerges as superior from the surveys in this book, we must still consider what has been the long-term impact of Thatcherism on contemporary Conservativism. At the time of his election, Major was presented as Janus-faced. One face looked back to the traditions of progressive Conservatism, claiming ideological influences such as Iain Macleod. His policy concerns were said to have been been shaped by his years as a council leader in the deprived borough of Lambeth. But his other face looked forward to continuing the Thatcherite revolution: to making the state more efficient, cutting public expenditure and squeezing inflation out of the economy. Even as he was being elected leader, his closest colleagues were uncertain of what ideological baggage he carried into the post. The three general hypotheses about Major's leadership that were identified in the introduction were first, that he was tightly constrained by the changes that Thatcher had made to the party and to the state; second, that he offered a new mixture of Thatcherite neo-liberalism with elements of socially progressive Conservatism; and third that he, like Thatcher, did not have a strong ideological motive but had simply taken over the task of exercising statecraft. What conclusions can now be drawn?

At one level the problem is that the focus on Major and the constraints of the Thatcher legacy is artificial, a response to the historically extraordinary interest in the person of Thatcher and the analysis of Thatcherism. There are no books on Homeism or Callaghanism, or even on Heathism or Wilsonism. Thatcher's policies, personality, gender and longevity as Prime Minister, and the disarray of opposition politics, have all contributed to a Thatcherism industry. But it is vital in analysing politics to look beyond the leading personalities and not to mistake rhetoric for reality, or intention for policy. Such approaches frequently ignore the fact that all politics takes place within a context, and context shapes and defines the operations of politics. Great shifts in policy in British government have not followed changes of leadership but altered external circumstances. Macmillan shifted from a *laissez-faire* industrial policy to interventionism and planning when confronted with the symptoms of Britain's relative economic decline. Heath abandoned his 'Selsdon Man' free market project when faced with the collapse of important companies, industrial unrest and rising unemployment. The Labour government abandoned full employment Keynesianism before, not after Wilson retired, because of the impact of the oil price shock, the world recession, unprecedented inflation rates and the resulting collapse of confidence in sterling. Policies change within administrations as much as, or more than, between administrations (Gamble and Walkland, 1983).

Both Thatcher and Major had to deal with Britain's changing position in a world economy that has become increasingly international and interdependent, with the deregulation of financial markets and the growth of transnational production. Such changes have further limited the autonomy of all British governments. The adoption of low inflation rather than full employment as the primary objective of macroeconomic policy, and other policies later called Thatcherism, began under Labour, and the continuation of the Thatcherite agenda in economic policy under Major must also be seen in its external context. The European issue is similarly one where long-term constraints and dilemmas are present that limit all leaders, and remove from them control over the content and timing of important policy agendas.

Furthermore, the way that the state is organised, how policy is made, and the nature of the policy networks that exist within central government all shape the nature of policy outcomes. For example, in order to reform health policy, the Thatcher administration had first to reform state structures to circumvent existing health policy networks. The process of reform only began in earnest after 1989 when Thatcher's Health Policy Review created an alternative structure for developing health policy (Chapter 11; M. J. Smith, 1993). Major – or any future prime minister – is constrained by the state structures created by the Thatcher administration, and unless there is a strong political will to change those structures, policy will continue to be shaped by them.

The mere passage of time is an important contextual factor. Fifteen years has allowed the Conservative Party the time to develop and implement policy changes that otherwise may have been modified by alternations of government or restrained by the prospect of Labour taking office. It has been the longest period of single-party domination in the post-war period. Rose has indicated the extent to which it takes a long time to implement policy changes (Rose, 1990). If Thatcher was successful in turning the ship of state around, then it will take a long time for a new administration to do the same. And whereas Thatcher followed a failed Labour government, Major was following 11 years of Thatcherite government.

Major, like any incoming prime minister, was therefore constrained by his economic and political inheritance. The combined consequences of the collapse of the Lawson boom and of ERM membership imposed severe constraints on his early economic policy-making. The size of the public deficit, and the changing demography of Britain, imposed similarly tight limitations on social policy. On the other hand, when the collapse of ERM liberated Major from the early constraints, his economic policy direction appeared to be strongly Thatcherite in purpose, though elements of statecraft designed to reconstruct the party's electoral base are also discernible (Chapter 9). The introduction of explicit inflation targets, carefully avoided by Thatcher's Chancellors, is one example of the return to Thatcherite objectives. The introduction of explicit public sector pay targets is another departure, but once again is intended to achieve the same outcome as Thatcher's implicit policy. In spite of much posturing, there has been no revival of pre-Thatcherite industrial policy under Major.

Severe structural constraints can conceal policy preferences. No such concealment has been necessary in Major's reforms of the state, where structural constraints and ideological preference have pointed in the same direction. Major's acceleration of civil service reform suggests strong commitment rather than inherited constraint. Indeed, he made state reform the key plank of his domestic policy platform. Where Thatcher has been described as unwilling to devolve power from her power base in Parliament, Major has looked more eager to contract out the state. If Thatcher's centralised entrepreneurial state looked like Tesco's, Major's looks more like a chain of Kentucky Fried Chicken franchises. In social policy Major was implementing, rather than originating change (Chapter 11), but the rhetoric of efficiency was being directed at ever more sensitive policy areas in ways that did not suggest reluctance. And in the crucial area of Europe policy, one in which an important change of direction was predicted, the evidence suggests willing continuity (Chapters 13 and 6). Major did not merely sustain the broad rhetoric of Thatcherite nationalism; he implemented it and negotiated the opt-outs from EMU and the Social Chapter.

Within the party, Major has not seemed particularly constrained by his inheritance. He immediately reduced the influence of Thatcherites in his governments, and infuriated them by bringing Heseltine back into the Cabinet. He has humiliated Thatcherite factions seeking to influence his government reshuffles, and in spite of his apparently long retreat during the Maastricht rebellion, finally confronted his rebels with the threat of an election, and they capitulated. Neither the expulsion of Euro-rebels that made his a minority government, nor his extraordinary resignation in June 1995 and the reshuffle that followed his re-election, suggest a leader shackled by an inheritance.

The difficulties that disgruntled Thatcherite right-wingers have had in identifying a broad alternative policy platform, in spite of the opportunity offered by Redwood's manifesto, raises the second hypothesis, that Major has remixed Thatcherism with progressive Conservatism. If there is a return to progressive Conservatism, it is not to be found in core social policy, although on some issues the longer-term trends of political culture have been followed in progressive directions. Who, even ten years ago, could imagine a Conservative government, let alone one committed to get 'back to basics', legislating to lower, if not yet equalise, the age of homosexual consent, and planning to make divorce easier? Ridley feared that the new Major government's 'avowed intent to improve the public services is not so much a repudiation of Thatcherism, as a decision not to embark on the last great Thatcherite reform, to complete Margaret Thatcher's last piece of unfinished business' (Ridley, 1992, 258). It is doubtful whether Ridley would have taken this view in 1995, by which time Major had not only undertaken but accelerated the pace of public service reform. In other respects, Major's persistence with the Thatcherite social policy platform seemed to be creating a risky new mix, but not necessarily a progressive one. By persisting with Thatcher's programme of converting public services into market places in which a rhetoric of individual choice and citizen's charters concealed a reconstruction of pre-war social and material inequalities, and at the same time appearing to weaken Thatcher's defence of the primacy of Parliament and the cohesion of the nation-state, Major seemed to be cutting against the grain of two historic elements of Conservatism: social obligation to Burke's 'hideous phantom' (the mass of the people) and defence of the British state. Hayekian rhetoric about the perverse ineffectiveness of active social policy was not persuading popular opinion that nothing could be done to tackle the social origins of the corrosive crime wave engulfing the Tories' middle-class supporters. The occupational insecurities of middle-class professionals were found by investigators to be a source of misery, rather than of pride in the entrepreneurial uncertainties that ministers proclaimed to be the precondition of prosperity. 'Negative equity' – literally, houses worth less than their purchase prices – seemed to describe the state of a widening range of middle-class educational and social investment. Even the appeal to family values made explicit in the ill-fated back-to-basics campaign, always a risky appeal given the impact of unfettered market forces on real families, came badly unstuck when linked to the CSA's bungling attempts to save the Treasury money by making 'absent' fathers pay more maintenance. Ruined parents and impoverished second families, rather than repentant wastrels, filled the pages of the Tory tabloids.

In domestic industrial relations, Major, like Thatcher, mobilised his state to defeat strikers, and continued the trend of trade union legislation, introducing new laws that were seen by union leaders as striking even deeper at traditional workplace representation. Before Major had served five years as prime minister, trade union leaders had abandoned any strategy of restoring to union activities those legal immunities that even Conservatives once accepted were justified to redress the massive imbalance of private power in the capitalist workplaces which had determined the quality of ordinary workers' lives. Rather than immunity in collective activity, such as strikes or solidarity action by trade unionists, a structure of positive legal rights for individual employees, preferably guaranteed by the European Court, had become the objective of the trade unions' political strategy. There was little sign here of a new admixture of progressive Conservatism either.

Alongside the continued reforms of the state machine, Major and other Conservative leaders continued to debate the proper role of the state along the lines set down by Thatcher. Ministers on different ideological wings of the party could depart from their departmental territory and make general proclamations about the positive or negative effects of state intervention without breaching the protocols of collective responsibility. Unfortunately, taking the moral high ground in this way has helped to highlight the threat to the British Parliamentary state posed by the growing impact of European legislation that UK citizens are obliged to obey, but which have been introduced by politicians acting in legislative forums to which British citizens owe no allegiance, having no opportunity to vote for or against these legislators. The rationales offered for such a retreat from Parliamentary democracy, whether based on promises of prosperity or on warnings about security, remained fundamentally anti-democratic however paternalistic the tone in which they were delivered. The resulting ability of far-right Tory MPs to adopt a populist stance in defence of the rights of the common citizen is no less real for being enormously ironic. The inviolability of the UK itself was apparently being placed at issue by Major's pursuit of an end to the war in Ireland. In the latter case, Major may well have been constrained by his inheritance of a bipartisan traditional policy (Chapter 12). By early 1995 however, his persistent pursuit of the peace process, which threatened to compound his minority government status by undermining the Unionist pact he had secured in 1993 over Europe, did not suggest a Prime Minister wishing to abandon an inherited policy.

Indeed, what is most noticeable about Major's leadership is that it has been precisely in those areas where Thatcherism was incomplete that Major has remained most faithful to the Thatcher project: commercialisation of public services, civil service reform, the formal limitation of the UK commitment to European integration through the opt-outs, and the trickiest privatisations of rail, coal, and, though now stalled, of postal services. Given the public hostility to much of his extension of health and education reform and privatisation, and the hostility of traditional Tory interest groups to his prevarication over single currency membership, it is difficult to see Major as a simple statecraftsman looking only to underpin the electoral base of his party.

As under Thatcher, there is more evidence of statecraft in foreign policy, though insofar as Major appears to be returning to balance of power diplomacy in the face of post-Soviet disorder in Europe, he is returning not to a progressive post-war Conservative ideology but to a pre-war Foreign Office tradition. There is, of course, the very hesitant and ambiguous concern to keep Britain 'at the heart' of the EU, hedged around with qualifications pronounced in a markedly Thatcherite tone. Conclusions here have to be partial, however. At the time of writing the precise details of Major's platform for negotiating at the 1996 IGC is unclear, and the tone of his speeches, so alarming to his hitherto loyal Euro-enthusiastic MPs, may turn out to be aimed more at neutralising the rebellion that threatened the existence of his government than at cutting off negotiating options in 1996. There is no doubt, on the other hand, that his 'confederalism' is genuine. His *Economist* article did not come out of the blue as a sop to his rebels, but was consistent with earlier statements. His high-profile 'variable geometry' speech during the Euro-election campaign did no more than describe the reality of opt-outs, and repeat arguments previously made public by supposed Euro-enthusiast Douglas Hurd. The alarm he sounded in the Leiden speech was not at the prospect of a multi-speed, multi-track Europe, but of a multi-speed Europe in which the UK was excluded from policy-making on some of the main tracks (Chapter 6). The emphasis on the demands of Major's Euro-rebels obscured the extent to which he was leading an attempt to Thatcherise European policy, notably towards deregulation of business and of industrial relations, and towards extreme fiscal conservatism.

The conclusion on the Major hypotheses, then, is that he has not been unwillingly constrained by the key components of the Thatcherite legacy. There is evidence of a continued pursuit of statecraft, but in his mix of Conservatism it is the persistence of Thatcherite objectives that stands out most clearly. There may, as the Cabinet's least restrained Thatcherite has suggested, have been a change of personalities and rhetoric (Redwood, 1995), but in Major's case students may finally be permitted to argue with conviction that as far as political change is concerned 'Majorism' is more style than substance. Faced with changes in the world economy, the collapse of the post-war consensus, the rise of new right ideology and changes in state structures, Major's direction has been one of implementing Thatcherism rather than challenging its key precepts. In policy area after policy area, Major has maintained the Thatcherite agenda.

Conclusion

The two principal policy challenges facing Conservatism at the time of Thatcher's election as leader were how to manage Britain's relative economic decline in an increasingly integrated world economy, and what relationship should Britain have to the growing EC. In general terms Thatcherism created a new ideological consensus around a neo-liberal economic package intended to enable Britain to manage relative decline and come to terms with its changed position in the world economy. This package included: legitimation of an enhanced role for the market in industrial and social policy; prioritising low inflation over full employment; the need to cut income tax; the need to reform the welfare state and to challenge the power of the unions. Disputes naturally continued over the precise level and manner of welfare provision in health, education and social security, the correct monetary policy mechanisms for controlling inflation, and the degree of activism in industrial policy. But by 1990, although most Conservative MPs could not be called Thatcherite (Norton, 1990), only a handful Conservative MPs called explicitly for a return to Keynesianism, or for progressive social and taxation policies, or for an enhanced role for the trade unions.

In spite of the high level of agreement on domestic economic and social policy that Thatcher established and Major has continued, the question of Britain's relationship with Europe has become the main cleavage that divides contemporary Conservatism. Although Thatcher initially remained a pragmatist in foreign and European policy, the impetus to European integration from the SEA and the Maastricht Treaty has made it impossible for the party any longer to evade the fundamental implications for national sovereignty. Senior Thatcherite Cabinet ministers clashed first over membership of the ERM, and then over the Maastricht Treaty. From the Cabinet down, contemporary Conservatism is divided over monetary union and other policies that require the pooling of sovereignty, such as foreign and security policy. Hence, whilst there is near-unanimous Parliamentary support for Major's Social Chapter opt-out, and a majority of his MPs oppose membership of a single currency, there are large minorities, including Cabinet and other ministers, in favour of Britain's full participation in monetary union and other supranational initiatives. In the survey of Conservative MPs cited in Chapter 6, 93 per cent of backbenchers opposed the social chapter. There is not much sign of division along the conventional left–right axis here. But while a majority of 51 per cent of backbench MPs agreed that 'The establishment of a single EU currency would signal the end of the UK as a sovereign nation', a large minority of 38 per cent disagreed. This is a stark division on an issue that will be central to public policy and party debate for some years to come, and provides one measure of the disagreements that were dominating the party by 1995.

The single currency dominated the leadership election in July 1995 that Major called to 'lance the boil' of Euro-rebellion. While Redwood resigned from the Cabinet to denounce the single currency, Major refused even to promise a referendum. Yet Redwood's manifesto otherwise differed little in substance from Major's 'no change' platform, suggesting that Thatcher's neo-liberal legacy remained largely uncontested. And although some Redwood supporters argued for a more extreme anti-welfare agenda, many MPs' support for more radical spending cuts represented a tactic to fund pre-election tax cuts as much as a strategic assault on Britain's so-called dependency culture. Similarly, MPs' votes did not express only policy preferences, but also views on how to save their seats. The leadership crisis highlighted other key problems facing British Conservatives. The party's crucial alliance with business wobbled as the Confederation of British Industry stressed its support for a single currency, while all but one national Tory newspaper turned against the premier. Major's gamble revealed again the toughness of a leadership style so often ridiculed as indecisive. Victory reinforced his image as a skilful party manager, and his immediate reshuffle gave no comfort to his critics. But his survival stemmed largely from the belief that alternative leaders would prove even more divisive: it signalled the fundamentally insoluble nature of party divisions over Europe.

Our final conclusion must therefore be that the period of Thatcher's leadership saw the centre of gravity of economic and social policy shift significantly to the right, where it has remained under Major in spite of continued debate over detail. But contemporary Conservatism has not yet discovered how to reconcile the party's deep-rooted and popular tradition of defending the sovereign British Parliamentary state with the active membership of the EU demanded by British big business and implied by the decline of Britain's diplomatic influence as a former imperial power. By the mid-1990s fundamental issues of national sovereignty raised by European integration and unresolved since the 1950s could no longer be evaded; they produced almost unmanageable divisions inside Parliament, the government and the Cabinet, and threatened to overwhelm Major's disunited party.

Guide to Further Reading

1 Introduction

For general overviews of the history and ideas of the Conservative Party see Blake (1985) and Eccleshall (1990) respectively. On post-war Conservatism see Harris (1972) and Gamble (1974) for academic analyses, and Hogg (1947) for a flavour of the immediate post-war Conservative mood and much else. Surveys of important aspects of the party and its ideas in the post-war period are gathered in Layton-Henry (1980). J. Campbell (1993) provides a fine account of Heath's government. Gamble (1994) is the best single volume on the record and politics of Thatcherism. Marsh and Rhodes (1992), Riddell (1991), and Kavanagh and Seldon (1989) all offer analyses of the impact of Thatcher's policies. The most useful insider accounts of the Thatcher era are listed in the reading guide to Chapter 2. For unique insights into the party's members see Whiteley, Seyd and Richardson (1994). On Major's career Anderson's biography (1991) is most helpful, and Kavanagh and Seldon (1994) collect wide-ranging analyses of his impact on party, government, and policy.

2 Ideology

Annotated documentary overviews of Conservatism are offered in O'Gorman (1986) and Eccleshall (1990). Contrasting participants' accounts of the ideology and policies of Thatcherism can be found in Gilmour (1992), Pym (1985), Tebbit (1988) and Ridley (1992). An update of Hogg's statement of Conservative philosophy (1947) is offered in Willetts (1992). The tensions between individualism and collectivism in British politics are set out in Greenleaf (1983a & b). Hoover and Plant (1989) analyse the ideology of neo-liberal conservatism. Theories of Thatcherism are offered and discussed in Hall (1988), Jessop *et al.*, (1988), Gamble (1994), and Letwin (1992). The political sociology of the Thatcher years is analysed in Edgell and Duke (1991). The impact of Thatcherism on policy is analysed in Marsh and Rhodes (1992) and surveyed in Kavanagh and Seldon (1989). The emergence of division over national sovereignty is discussed in D. Baker, Gamble and Ludlam (1993a). The most important memoirs are Lawson (1992), Thatcher (1993), and G. Howe (1994). Major's succession is assessed in Kavanagh and Seldon (1994).

3 Electoral Performance

The argument that Britain has become a 'dominant one party system' is presented in Crewe (1988). On the impact of electoral geography in a first-past-the-post system see Gudgin and Taylor (1978), and for more recent analysis see Johnston, Pattie and Allsopp (1988). On the influence of the media in campaigns, see W. Miller *et al.*, (1990); on the impact of campaign spending, see Johnston and Pattie (1993a). The suggestion that Labour was becoming the natural party of government is made in the pioneering election study by D. Butler and Stokes (1969). McKenzie and Silver (1968) analyse the phenomenon of working class Conservatism. Contrasting interpretations of electoral volatility can be found in Särlvik and Crewe (1983) and Heath, Jowell and Curtice (1985). The 'economic voting' model is set out in Sanders (1993b). Most of the important academic arguments about electoral behaviour in contemporary Britain are collected in Denver and Hands (1992). The unprecedented collapse of popularity under Major is measured in Crewe (1994).

4 Party Organisation

The party's historic and comparative strength is assessed by Katz and Mair (1992). McKenzie (1964) analyses the party's organisation in its post-war heyday. Whiteley, Seyd and Richardson (1994) present the results of the first full-scale survey of the activism and attitudes of Conservative Party members in the 1990s. R. Kelly (1989) covers the phenomenon of the Conservative Party conference in the 1980s. Tether (1991) discusses recruitment. Pinto-Duschinsky (1981) presents evidence of Conservative Party funding; Fisher (1994) discusses recent trends and problems. Ball (1994) assesses the level and health of local associations' contributions. Morris (1991) sheds light on the Tories as a participant observer. The general dynamics of party support are analysed in Whiteley and Seyd (1996).

5   The Parliamentary Elite

Guttsman (1967) provides an early analysis of the Conservative elite. The most detailed study of post-war trends among MPs up to 1975 is Mellors (1978). More recent updates are in Burch and Moran (1985), D. Baker, Gamble and Ludlam (1992b), and D. Baker, Fountain, Gamble and Ludlam (1994a). The results of the 1992 British Candidate Study are presented in Norris and Lovenduski (1995). On methodology, see Edinger and Searing (1967). Crucial methodological critiques, including Crewe's seminal overview, are collected in Crewe (1974). The significance of unrepresentativeness was discussed in D. Butler and Pinto-Duschinsky (1980).

6   Rebellions and European Integration

For detail and analysis of every rebellion up to 1979 see Norton (1975, 1980). On the 1975 referendum campaign see Goodhart (1976). Norton (1978) focuses on Conservative dissent under Heath. For a survey of Tory divisions on Europe up to 1979 see Ashford (1980). The Poll Tax revolt is recounted in D. Butler, Adonis and Travers (1994). For the inside accounts of the clashes over ERM see Lawson (1992), Thatcher (1993) and G. Howe (1994). For an account of why Thatcherites became disillusioned with Europe in the 1980s see Ridley (1992) and Hill (1993). The Maastricht Rebellion is analysed in D. Baker, Gamble and Ludlam (1994b). The pro-EU position is set out in I. Taylor (1993); the rebel position is presented by Spicer (1992). For results of the 1994 survey of Conservative MPs' attitudes to European integration see D. Baker, Fountain, Gamble and Ludlam (1995).

7   Opposition Politics

Seyd (1987) charts the rise and fall of Labour's left in the early 1980s. Wainwright (1987) describes the tensions between national electoral politics and grassroots campaigning. Contrasting accounts of Labour's 'modernisation' can be found in Hughes and Wintour (1990) and Heffernan and Marqusee (1992). Contrasting visions of Labour's future by leadership contenders are in Heffer (1986) and Hattersley

(1987). M. J. Smith and Spear (1992) offer views of Labour's development in many key areas of policy. Shaw (1994) analyses the whole process of transformation since 1979. Stevenson (1993) surveys third-party politics since 1945. Owen (1992) offers the best insider account of the birth and death of the SDP. Brack (1989) discusses a key ideological concept associated with the SDP. McKee (1994) provides analysis of the politics and leadership of the Liberal Democrats.

8 Reforming the State

Various Conservative views of the state are discussed in J. Gray (1993), Greenleaf (1973) and Honderich (1990). Historical overviews of the reform of central government are provided by Hennessy (1990) and Radcliffe (1991). The most comprehensive reviews of the current reforms are in Greer (1994) and Zifcak (1994). The government's view of reform is outlined in the White Paper (Cmnd 2627, 1994) and a useful source for some of the ideas behind recent changes is Osborne and Gaebler (1992). Questions of accountability are examined in Giddings (1995).

9 Economic Policy

Economic policy and performance across the whole post-war period are surveyed in Cairncross (1992). Dow (1964) and Brittan (1964) cover the 1950s Conservative governments, while Blackaby (1979) covers the Heath government. Useful empirical accounts of the Thatcher governments' economic policy are to be found in Keegan (1984, 1989) and D. Smith (1987). D. Smith (1992) also covers the first year of the Major government. G. Howe (1994) and Lawson (1992) offer the accounts of Thatcher's two long-serving Chancellors of the monetarist and the supply-side 'revolutions'. For the most persuasive explanations of Thatcherism as economic policy see Jessop *et al.*, (1988), Gamble (1994) and Bulpitt (1986). An early effort to analyse Major's approach can be found in Wilkes (1993). For discussion of industrial policy see Grant (1993) and Middlemas (1991). Recent analyses of the overall economic performance of the economy since 1979 include Johnson (1991), and Mitchie (1992).

10   Trade Unions

R. Taylor (1993) provides an historical overview of the 'union question' since 1945, covering all the periods of Conservative government. Moran (1979) examines Heath's clashes with the unions, which helps to explain the ferocity of Thatcher's assault. MacInnes (1987) and Hanson (1991) discuss Thatcher's general industrial relations approach and legislation. Marsh's study (1992) incorporates a measured assessment of the impact of the Thatcher reforms on trade union activity, including the emergence of 'new realism'. Millward *et al.*, (1993) provide the most recent survey evidence of Thatcherism's impact, and much else besides. Rosamond (1993) discusses the meaning of British trade unions' turn to Europe.

11   Social Policy

For a general treatment of British social policy in its theoretical, historical and international context, the most comprehensive and up-to-date source is Pierson (1991). Ideologies and theories of the welfare state and the detail of policy developments since 1945 are dealt with in Lowe (1993). The notion of a post-war consensus informs the overview by Deakin (1994). As good as a snapshot of the current state of welfare and of the future challenges is Hills (1993). Also useful for the background between 1974 and 1989 is Hills (1990). Discussions of the recent changes can be found in Burrows and Loader (1994) and A. Oakley and Williams (1994). On quasi-markets and social policy reform, see Le Grand and Bartlett (1993) and W. Bartlett, Propper, Wilson and Le Grand (1994). Good coverage of a range of contemporary issues in social policy, including the Citizen's Charter, can be found in the journals *Talking Politics, Policy and Politics, Critical Social Policy, Journal of Social Policy* and *Journal of European Social Policy.*

12   Foreign and Defence Policy

Overviews of post-war British foreign policy are provided by Byrd (1988), Reynolds (1991) and Sanders (1990). C. J. Bartlett (1992) surveys the post-war 'special relationship' with the USA, and Gowing

(1986) focuses on its nuclear component. Croft (1991) and Byrd (1991) offer collections that focus on foreign and defence policy under Thatcher; M. Smith, Smith and White (1988) additionally present theoretical analyses. Coker (1988) concentrates on Conservatism and defence policy. Sabin (1993) discusses defence policy in the light of 'Options for Change'. O'Leary (1987) analyses the AIA, while Boyle and Hadden (1994) discuss the position in the wake of the Downing Street Declaration.

13 European Policy

On Conservative policy towards the EEC in its early years, and especially the 1961–3 membership negotiations, Camps (1964) remains the most valuable and detailed source. J. W. Young (1993) analyses the factors that shaped both the Macmillan and Heath applications, and Lord (1993) looks in detail at British entry under Heath. As well as the earlier Conservative governments, the Thatcher and Major governments are covered in George (1994). Nugent (1994) is the best introduction to the institutional development of the EU since the Maastricht Treaty. Cockfield (1994) is a book specifically on the 1992 programme by the man who was responsible for the Commission's White Paper on freeing the internal market. G. Howe (1994), Thatcher (1993) and Lawson (1992) provide insiders' accounts of the arguments surrounding the ERM and monetary union.

References

Abrams, M., Rose, R. and Hinden, R. (1960) *Must Labour Lose?* (Harmondsworth: Penguin).
ACE (1995) *Mission Statement* (Whittle-le-Woods: ACE)
Addison, P. (1994) *The Road to 1945. British Politics and the Second World War* (London: Pimlico).
Alderman, R. and Carter, N. (1991) 'A Very Tory Coup: The Ousting of Mrs. Thatcher' *Parliamentary Affairs*, Vol. 44.
All England Law Reports (1982) (London: Butterworth).
Allen, D. (1988) 'British Foreign Policy and Western European Cooperation', in Byrd, P. (ed.), *British Foreign Policy Under Thatcher* (Oxford: Philip Allan).
Anderson, B. (1991) *John Major: the Making of a Prime Minister* (London: Fourth Estate).
Anderson, B. (1992) *John Major* (London: Headline).
Anderson, P. (1964) 'Origins of the Present Crisis'. New Left Review, Vol. 23.
Armstrong, R. (1988) 'Taking Stock of our Acheivements', in Peat Marwick McLintock, *Future Shape of Reform in Whitehall* (London: Royal Institue of Public Administration).
Ashdown, P. (1987) *After the Alliance* (Hebden Bridge: Hebden Royd).
Ashdown, P. (1993) *Speech to Charter 88, 12 July 1993*, (London: Liberal Democrats).
Ashford, N. (1980) 'The European Economic Community', in Layton-Henry 1980.
Auerbach, S. (1990) *Legislating for Conflict*, (Oxford: Clarendon Press).
Auerbach, S. (1993) 'Mrs Thatcher's Labour Laws, Slouching Towards Utopia' *Political Quarterly*, Vol. 64, No. 1.
Aughey, A. (1978) Conservative Party Attitudes towards the Common Market, Hull Papers in Politics No. 2, (Hull: University of Hull).
Baker, D., Fountain, I., Gamble, A. and Ludlam, S. (1994a) 'Britain's Conservative Elite: Ideological Obstacles to European Integration', Paper presented to the *European Consortium for Political Research Workshop on National Elites and European Integration*, Madrid, April 1994. (Essex: European Consortium for Political Research).
Baker, D., Fountain, I., Gamble, A. and Ludlam, S. (1994b) 'What Tory MPs Think about Europe', *Parliamentary Brief*, Vol. 3 No. 3.
Baker, D., Fountain, I., Gamble, A. and Ludlam, S. (1995) 'The Blue Map of Europe: Conservative Backbencher Attitudes to European Integration', *Political Quarterly*, Vol. 66, No. 2.
Baker, D., Gamble, A. and Ludlam, S. (1992a) 'Conservative MPs: A Response.' *Sociology*, Vol. 26, No 4.
Baker, D., Gamble, A. and Ludlam, S. (1992b) 'More Classless and Less Thatcherite? Conservative Ministers and New Conservative MPs after the 1992 Election', *Parliamentary Affairs*, Vol. 45, No. 4.

Baker, D., Gamble, A., and Ludlam, S. (1993a) '1846 . . . 1906 . . . 1996? Conservative Splits and European Integration', *Political Quarterly*, Vol. 64, No. 4.

Baker, D., Gamble, A., and Ludlam, S. (1993b) 'Whips or Scorpions? Conservative MPs and the Masstricht Paving Motion Vote', *Parliamentary Affairs*, Vol. 46, No. 2.

Baker, D., Gamble, A., and Ludlam, S. (1994a) 'Mapping Conservative Fault Lines: Problems of Typology', in Dunleavy, P. and Stayner, G. (eds), *Contemporary Political Studies 1994* (Exeter: University of Exeter Press).

Baker, D., Gamble, A., and Ludlam, S. (1994b) 'The Parliamentary Siege of Maastricht 1993: Conservative Divisions and British Ratification of the Treaty on European Union', *Parliamentary Affairs*, Vol. 47, No. 1.

Baker, K. (1993) *The Turbulent Years: My Life in Politics* (London: Faber and Faber).

Ball, S. (1994) 'Local Conservatism and the Evolution of the Party Organization', in Seldon and Ball (1994).

Barnes, J. (1994) 'Ideology and Factions', in Seldon and Ball (1994).

Barnett, C. (1986) *The Audit of War*, (London: Macmillan).

Bartlett, C. J. (1992) *'The Special Relationship': A Political History of Anglo-American Relations since 1945* (Harlow: Longman).

Bartlett, W., Propper, C., Wilson, D. and Le Grand, J. (eds) (1994) *Quasi-Markets and the Welfare State* (Bristol, School of Advanced Urban Studies).

Baylis, J. (1981) *Anglo-American Defence Relations, 1939–80* (London: Macmillan).

BBC (1994) *Newsnight*, 13 September 1994.

Bealey, F., Blondel, J. and McCann, W. (1965) *Constituency Politics* (London: Faber & Faber).

Benn, T. (1980) *Arguments for Socialism* (Harmondsworth: Penguin).

Benn, T. (1992) *The End of an Era: Diaries 1980–90* (London: Hutchinson).

Berrington, H. B. (1961) 'The Conservative Party: Pressures and Revolts', *Political Quarterly*, Vol. 32.

Berrington, H. B., (1973) *Backbench Opinion in the House of Commons 1945–55* (Oxford: Pergamon).

Biffen, J. (1993) 'Champions of Westminster', *The Guardian*, 25 February 1993.

Blackaby, F. T. (1979) *British Economic Policy 1960–74: Demand Management* (Cambridge: Cambridge University Press).

Blake, R. (1970) *The Conservative Party to Peel to Churchill* (London: Eyre and Spottiswoode).

Blake, R. (1985) *The Conservative Party from Peel to Thatcher* (London: Fontana).

Blondel, J. (1973) *Voters, Parties and Leaders* (Harmondsworth: Penguin).

Borthwick, G., Ellingworth, D., Bell, C. and Mackenzie, D. (1991) 'Research Note: The Social Background of British MPs', *Sociology*, Vol. 25, No. 4.

Bosanquet, N. (1988) 'An Ailing State of National Health', in Jowell, R. Witherspoon, S. and Brook, L. (eds), *British Social Attitudes: The 5th Report* (Aldershot: Gower).

Boyle, K. and Hadden, T. (1994) *Northern Ireland: The Choice* (Harmondsworth: Penguin).

Brack, D. (1989) *The Myth of the Social Market* (London: Link Publications).

Bradley, I. (1981) *Breaking the Mould: The Birth and Prospects of the Social Democratic Party* (Oxford: Martin Robertson).

Brand, J. (1989) 'Faction as its Own Reward: Groups in the British Parliament 1945–1986', *Parliamentary Affairs*, Vol. 42.

Brittan, S. (1964) *The Treasury under the Tories 1961–1964*, (Harmondsworth: Penguin).

Brittan, S. (1975) 'The Economic Contradictions of Democracy', *British Journal of Political Science*, Vol. 5.

Buchan, D. (1993) 'Springtime in Paris', *Financial Times*, 29 May.

Bulpitt, J. (1983) *Territory and Power in the United Kingdom* (Manchester: Manchester University Press).

Bulpitt, J. (1986) 'The Discipline of the New Democracy, Mrs Thatchers Domestic Statecraft', *Political Studies*, Vol. 34, No. 1.

Bulpitt, J. (1988) 'Rational Politicians and Conservative State Craft' in Byrd, P. (1988).

Bulpitt, J. (1992) 'Conservative Leaders and the "Euro-Ratchet": Five Doses of Scepticism', *Political Quarterly*, Vol. 63, No. 3.

Burch, M. and Moran, M. (1985) 'The Changing British Political Elite, 1945–83', *Parliamentary Affairs*, Vol. 38, No. 1.

Burke, E. (1968) Reflections on the Revolution in France (Harmondsworth: Penguin).

Burrows, R. and Loader, B. (eds) (1994) *Towards a Post-Fordist Welfare State* (London: Routledge).

Butcher, T. (1993) 'Whitehall's Managerial Revolution', *Public Policy Review*, Vol. 1.

Butler, A. (1994) 'The End of Post-War Consensus: Reflections on the Scholarly Uses of Political Rhetoric', *Political Quarterly*, Vol. 64, No. 4.

Butler, D., Adonis, A. and Travers, T. (1994) *Failure in British Government: The Politics of the Poll Tax* (Oxford: Oxford University Press.

Butler, D. and Butler, G. (1994) *British Political Facts 1900–1994* (London: Macmillan).

Butler, D. and Kavanagh, D. (1988) *The British General Election of 1987* (London: Macmillan).

Butler, D. and Kavanagh, D. (1992) *The British General Election of 1992* (London: Macmillan).

Butler, D. and Pinto-Duschinsky, M. (1980) 'The Conservative Elite, 1917–78: Does Unrepresentativeness Matter?', in Layton-Henry 1980.

Butler, D. and Stokes, D. (1969) *Political Change in Britain: The Evolution of Political Choice*, (London: Macmillan).

Butler, R. (1971) *The Art of the Possible* (Hamish Hamilton: London).

Butler, R. (1994) 'Reinventing British Government', *Public Administration*, Vol. 72.

Byrd, P. (1988) British Foreign Policy Under Thatcher (London: Philip Allan).

Byrd, P. (1991) 'Defence Policy, An Historical Overview and a Regime Analysis', in Byrd, P. (ed.) *British Defence Policy, Thatcher and Beyond* (London: Philip Allan).

Byrne, T. (1986) *Local Government in Britain* (Harmondsworth: Penguin).

Cairncross, A. (1992) *The British Economy since 1945* (Oxford: Basil Blackwell).
Callaghan, J. (1987) *Time and Chance* (London: Collins).
Campbell, B. (1985) 'A Leading Role for the New New [sic] Left', *The Times*, 27 September 1985.
Campbell, J. (1993) *Edward Heath* (London: Jonathan Cape).
Campling, J. (1994) 'Social Policy Digest: 91', *Journal of Social Policy*, Vol. 23, No. 3.
Camps, M. (1964) *Britain and the European Community* (London: Oxford University Press).
Carty, H. (1991) 'The Employment Act 1990, Still Fighting the Industrial Cold War' *Industrial Law Journal*, Vol. 20, No. 1.
Cash, W. (1992) *Europe: The Crunch* (London: Duckworth).
Cash, W. (1993) 'Eurosceptics and Eurorealists', *European Journal*, Vol. 1, No. 1.
Castle, B. (1984) *The Castle Diaries, 1964–70* (London: Wieldenfeld & Nicolson).
Charter Movement (1991) *Charter News* (Swanley: The Charter Movement).
Chichester, M. and Wilkinson, J. (1982) *The Uncertain Ally* (Aldershot: Gower).
Church, C. (1992) *Coming of Age: The First Twenty Years of Friends of the Earth in Britain* (London: Gollancz).
Clarke, H., Mishler, W. and Whiteley, P. (1990) 'Recapturing the Falklands, models of Conservative Popularity, 1979–83', *British Journal of Political Science* 20, Vol. 20.
Clarke, K. (1993) 'The Lovable Pooch at Number 11. Kenneth Clarke interviewed by Andrew Hicks', *Crossbow*, October 1993.
Clarke, R. (1975) 'The Machinery of Government', in Thornhill, W. (ed.), *The Modernization of British Government* (London: Pitman).
Cmnd 8616 (1982) *Efficiency and Effectiveness in the Civil Service* (London: HMSO).
Cmnd 1599 (1991) *Citizen's Charter* (London: HMSO).
Cmnd 2627 (1994) *The Civil Service, Continuity and Change* (London: HMSO).
Coates, D. (1989) *The Crisis of Labour* (London: Phillip Allan).
Cockfield, A. (1994) *The European Union: Creating the Single Market* (London: Wiley and Chancery Law).
Coker, C. (1988) *Less Important than Opulence, the Conservatives and Defence* (London: Institute for European Defence and Strategic Studies).
Collins, B. (1987) 'The Rayner Scrutinies', in Harrison, A. and Gretton, J. (eds) *Reshaping Central Government* (Oxford: Transaction Books).
Commission on Social Justice (1994) *Social Justice: Strategies for National Renewal. The Report of the Commission on Social Justice* (London: Vintage).
Connolly, M., McKeown, P. and Milligan-Byrne, G. (1994) 'Making the Public Sector More User Friendly? A Critical Examination of the Citizen's Charter', *Parliamentary Affairs*, Vol. 47, No. 1.
Conservative Party (1977) *The Right Appraoch to the Economy* (London: Conservative Central Office).
Conservative Party (1992) *The Best Future for Britain: The Conservative Manifesto 1992* (London: Conservative Central Office).

292   References

Conservative Party (1994a) *A Strong Britain in a Strong Europe: the Conservative Manifesto for Europe 1994* (London: Conservative Central Office).

Conservative Party (1994b) *The 111th Conservative Conference* (London: Conservative Central Office).

Conservative Party (1994c) *The Conservative and Unionist Central Office Annual Report and Accounts 31 March 1994* (London: Conservative Central Office).

Cooke, A. B. (1989) *Margaret Thatcher, The Revival of Britain* (London: Aurum Press).

Cosgrave, P. (1978) *Margaret Thatcher: A Tory and Her Party* (London: Hutchinson).

Crewe, I. (ed.) (1974) *British Political Sociology Year Book; Elites in Western Democracy* (London: Croom Helm).

Crewe, I. (1988) 'Has the Electorate become Thatcherite?' in Skidelsky, R. (ed.) *Thatcherism* (London: Chatto & Windus).

Crewe, I. (1989) 'Values, the Crusade that Failed' in Kavanagh and Seldon (1989).

Crewe, I. (1994) 'Electoral Behaviour', in Kavanagh and Seldon (1994).

Crewe, I. and Searing, D. (1988) 'Ideological Change in the British Conservative Party', *American Political Science Review*, Vol. 82, No. 2.

Crick, M. (1986) *The March of Militant* (London: Faber and Faber).

Criddle, B. (1994) 'Members of Parliament', in Seldon and Ball (1994).

Critchley, J. (1992) *Some of Us: People who did well under Thatcher* (London: John Murray).

Croft, S. (ed.) (1991) *British Security Policy, the Thatcher Years and the End of the Cold War* (London: Harper Collins).

Crouch, C. and Pizzorno, A. (eds) (1978) *The Resurgence of Class Conflict in Western Europe* (London: Macmillan).

Deakin, N. (1994) *The Politics of Welfare: Continuities and Change* (London: Harvester Wheatsheaf).

Denver, D. and Hands, G. (eds) (1992) *Issues and Controversies in British Electoral Behaviour* (London: Harvester Wheatsheaf).

Department of Health (1989) *Working for Patients* (London: HMSO).

Department of Health (1992) *The Health of the Nation* (London: HMSO).

Department of Health and Social Security (1985) *The Reform of Social Security* Cmnd. 9517 (London: HMSO).

Devine, F. (1992) 'Working Class Evaluations of the Labour Party', in Crewe, I., Norris, P., Denver, D. and Broughton, D. (eds), *British Elections and Parties Yearbook 1992* (London: Harvester Wheatsheaf).

DFE (1992) *Choice and Diversity* (London: HMSO).

Doern, G. B. (1993), 'The UK Citizen's Charter, Origins and Implementation in Three Agencies', *Policy and Politics*, Vol. 21.

Dow, J. C. R. (1964) *The Management of the British Economy 1945–60* (Cambridge: Cambridge University Press).

Drewry, G. and Butcher, T. (1991) *The Civil Service Today* (Oxford: Basil Blackwell).

DSS (1993) *The Government's Expenditure Plans 1993/4 to 1995/6* (London: HMSO).

DSS (1994) *The Growth of Social Security*, (London: HMSO).
Duncan, S. and Goodwin, M. (1988) *The Local State and Uneven Development* (Cambridge: Polity Press).
Dunleavy, P. (1979) 'The Urban Basis of Political Alignment, Social Class, Domestic Property Ownership and State Intervention in Consumption Processes', *British Journal of Political Science*, Vol 9.
Dunleavy, P. (1993) 'The Political Parties' in Dunleavy, P., Gamble, A., Holliday, I. and Peele, G. (eds) *Developments in British Politics 4* (London: Macmillan).
Dunleavy, P. and Francis, A. (1990) 'Memorandum to the Treasury and Civil Service Select Committee' HC 496 (1990/91) *The Next Steps Initiative* (London: HMSO).
Dunleavy, P. and Husbands, C. (1985) *British Democracy at the Crossroads* (London: Allen and Unwin).
Dunleavy, P. and O'Leary, B. (1987) *Theories of the State* (London: Macmillan).
Dunn, D. (1991), 'Challenges to the Nuclear Orthodoxy', in Croft, S. (1991).
Dunn, R., Forrest, R. and Murie, A. (1987) 'The Geography of Council House Sales in England, 1979–85', *Urban Studies*, Vol. 24.
Eccleshall, R. (1984) 'Conservatism' in Eccleshall, R., Geogheyn, V., Jay, R. and Wickford, R. *Political Ideologies* (London: Hutchinson).
Eccleshall, R. (1990) *English Conservatism since the Restoration: An Introduction and Anthology* (London: Unwin Hyman).
The Economist, (1990a) 'Shadows of Gunboats', 17 February 1990.
The Economist, (1990b) 'Surrender', 17 February 1990.
Edgell, S. and Duke, V. (1991) *A Measure of Thatcherism: A Sociology of Britain* (London: Harper Collins).
Edlinger, L. J. and Searing, D. (1967) 'Social Background in Elite Analysis: A Methodological Enquiry' *American Political Science Review*, Vol. 61, No. 2.
Efficiency Unit (1988) *Improving Management in Government, The Next Steps* (London: HMSO).
Efficiency Unit (1991) *Making the Most of the Next Steps: The Management of Ministers' Departments and Executive Agencies* (London: HMSO).
Efficiency Unit (1994) *Next Steps, Moving On* (London: HMSO).
Ellis, W. (1994) *The Oxbridge Conspiracy* (London: Michael Joseph).
European Commission (1993) *Growth, Competitiveness and Employment* (Brussels: European Communities).
European Foundation (1994a) *The Bournemouth Speeches: Bill Cash MP, Sir James Goldsmith MEP, Rt Hon Lord Tebbit* (London: European Foundation).
European Foundation (1994b) *The British Capitulation on the Blocking Minority* (London: European Foundation).
Finer, S. (1973) 'The Political Power of Organised Labour', *Government and Opposition*, 8, 391–406.
Finer, S., Berrington, H. B., and Bartholomew, D. J. (1961) *Backbench Opinion in the House of Commons, 1955–59* (Oxford, Pergamon Press).
Fisher, J. (1994) 'Political Donations to the Conservative Party', *Parliamentary Affairs*, Vol. 47, No. 1.

Fosh, P., Morris, H., Martin, R., Smith, P. and Undy, R. (1993) 'Politics, Pragmatism and Ideology: The "Wellsprings" of Conservative Union Legislation (1979–1992)' *Industrial Law Journal*, Vol. 22, No. 1.

Franklin, M. (1985) *The Decline of Class Voting in Britain* (Oxford: Clarendon Press).

Franklin, M. and Page, E. (1984) 'A Critique of the Consumption Cleavage Approach in British Voting Studies', *Political Studies*, Vol. XXXII.

Fredman, S. (1992) 'The New Rights, Labour Law and Ideology in the Thatcher Years', *Oxford Journal of Legal Studies*, Vol. 12, No. 1.

Friedman, M. and Friedman, R. (1980) *Free to Choose* (Harmondsworth: Penguin).

Gamble, A. (1974) *The Conservative Nation* (London: Routledge and Kegan Paul).

Gamble, A. (1988) *The Free Economy and the Strong State: The Politics of Thatcherism* (London: Macmillan).

Gamble, A. (1990a) *Britain in Decline: Economic Policy, Political Strategy and the British State* (London: Macmillan).

Gamble, A. (1990b) 'The Thatcher Decade in Perspective' in Dunleavy, P., Gamble, A. and Peele, G. (eds), *Developments in British Politics, 3* (London: Macmillan).

Gamble, A. (1991) 'Following the Leader', *Marxism Today*, January.

Gamble, A. (1994) *The Free Economy and the Strong State: The Politics of Thatcherism, (2nd edn)* (London: Macmillan).

Gamble, A. & Walkland, S. A. (1983) *The British Party System and Economic Policy 1945-1983: Studies in Adversary Politics* (Oxford: Oxford University Press).

Garel-Jones, T. (1993) 'Tories must set Agenda for Tomorrow's Europe', *The Times*, 21 June.

George, S. (1990) *An Awkward Partner* (Oxford: Oxford University Press).

George, S. (1992) 'The European Community in the New Europe' in Crouch, C. and Marquand, D. (eds) *Towards Greater Europe? A Continent Without an Iron Curtain* (Oxford: Basil Blackwell).

George, S. (1994) *An Awkward Partner: Britain in the European Community* (Oxford: Oxford University Press).

George, S. and Ludlam, S. (1994) 'The Euro-election Manifestos', *Parliamentary Brief*, June 1994.

Giddings, P. (ed.) (1995) *Parliamentary Accountability: A Study of Parliament and Executive Agencies* (London: Macmillan).

Gilmour, I. (1977) *The Right Approach* (London: Hutchinson).

Gilmour, I. (1978) *Inside Right: Conservatism, Policies and the People* (London: Quartet).

Gilmour, I. (1992) *Dancing with Dogma: Britain under Thatcherism* (London: Simon and Schuster).

Gilmour, I. (1993) *Dancing with Dogma: Britain under Thatcherism* (London: Pocket Books).

Glennerster, H., Power, A. and Travers, T. (1991) 'A New Era for Social Policy: A New Enlightenment or a New Leviathan?', *Journal of Social Policy*, Vol. 20.

GLYC (1969) *Set The Party Free* (London: GLYC).

Goldthorpe, J. H., Lockwood, D., Bechhofer, F. and Platt, J. (1968) *The Affluent Worker, Industrial Attitudes and Behaviour* (Cambridge: Cambridge University Press).

Goodhart, P. (1976) *Full-hearted Consent: The Story of the Referendum Campaign, and the Campaign for the Referendum* (London: Davis-Poynter).

Goodin, R. E. and Le Grand, J. (1987) *Not Only the Poor: The Middle Classes and the Welfare State* (London: Allen & Unwin).

Gorman, T. (1993) *The Bastards: Dirty Tricks and the Challenge to Europe* (London: Pan).

Gould, B. (1989) *A Future For Socialism* (London: Jonathan Cape).

Gowing, M. (1986) 'Nuclear Weapons and the "Special Relationship"', in Louis, W. M. and Bull, H. (eds), *The Special Relationship, Anglo-American Relations since 1945* (Oxford: Clarendon Press).

Grant, W. (1993) *Business and Politics in Britain* (London: Macmillan).

Gray, A. and Jenkins, W. (1987) 'Public Administration and Government in 1986', *Parliamentary Affairs*, Vol. 40.

Gray, A. and Jenkins, W. (1993) 'Public Administration and Government in 1991–2', *Parliamentary Affairs*, Vol. 46.

Gray, C. (1994) *Government Beyond the Centre* (London: Macmillan).

Gray, J. (1993) *Beyond the New Right* (London: Routledge).

Gray, J. (1994) 'Kill the Leviathan', *The Guardian*, 3 October.

Greenleaf, W. H. (1973) 'The Character of Modern British Conservatism', in Benewick, R., Berki, R. N. and Parek, B. (eds), *Knowledge and Belief in Politics* (London: George Allen & Unwin).

Greenleaf, W. H. (1983a) *The British Political Tradition, Vol. I: The Rise of Collectivism* (London: Methuen).

Greenleaf, W. H. (1983b) *The British Political Tradition, Vol. II: The Ideological Heritage* (London: Methuen).

Greenwood, D. (1991) 'Expenditure and Management', in Byrd, P. (ed.), *British Defence Policy, Thatcher and Beyond* (London: Philip Allan).

Greer, P. (1994) *Transforming Central Government* (Milton Keynes: Open University Press).

Gudgin, G. and Taylor, P. (1978) *Seats, Votes and the Spatial Organisation of Elections* (London: Pion).

Guelke, A. (1988) *Northern Ireland: The International Perspective* (Dublin: Gill and Macmillan).

Guttsman, W. (1967) *The British Political Elite* (London: Macmillan).

Habermas, J. (1976) *Legitimation Crisis* (London: Heinemann).

Hall, S. (1988) *The Hard Road to Renewal. Thatcherism and the Crisis of the Left* (London: Verso).

Hall, S. (1993) 'Thatcherism Today', *New Statesman and Society*, 26 November.

Hall, S. and Jacques, M. (eds) (1983) *The Politics of Thatcherism* (London: Lawrence and Wishart).

Hanson, C. (1991) *Taming the Trade Unions, A Guide to the Thatcher Governments' Employment Reforms* (London: Macmillan).

Harden, I. (1992) *The Contracting State* (Milton Keynes: Open University Press).

296   *References*

Harris, N. (1968) *Beliefs in Society: the Problem of Ideology* (Harmondsworth: Penguin).
Harris, N. (1972) *Competition and the Corporate Society: British Conservatives, the State, and Industry* (London: Methuen).
Hattersley, R. (1987) *Choose Freedom: The Future of Democratic Socialism* (Harmondsworth: Penguin).
Haxey, S. (1939) *Tory MP* (London: Gollancz).
Hay, C. (1994) 'Labour's Thatcherite Revisionism: Playing the Politics of Catch-Up', *Political Studies*, Vol. 42, No. 4.
HC 390-1 (1992/3) Treasury and Civil Service Select Committee, *The Role of the Civil Service, Interim Report* (London: HMSO).
HC 390-i (1992/3) Treasury and Civil Service Select Committee, *The Responsibilities and Work of the Office of Public Services* (London: HMSO).
HC 390-iv (1992/3) Treasury and Civil Service Select Committee, *The Role of the Civil Service, Minutes of Evidence* (London: HMSO).
HC 394 (1990/91) House of Commons Defence Committee Report, Statement on the Defence Estimates (London: HMSO).
HC 481 (1989/90) Treasury and Civil Service Select Committee, *Progress in the Next Steps Intiative* (London: HMSO).
HC 496 (1990/1) The Treasury and Civil Service Select Committee, *The Next Steps Initiative* (London: HMSO).
HC 550-i (1990/91) Social Security Committee, *The Organisation and Administration of the Department of Social Security* (London: HMSO).
Heath, A. (1990) 'Class and Partisan Politics', in Clark, J., Modgil, C. and Modgil, S. (eds), *John Goldthorpe, Consensus and Controversy* (London: Falmer Press).
Heath, A., Jowell, R. and Curtice, J. (1985) *How Britain Votes* (Oxford: Pergamon Press).
Heath, A., Jowell, R., Curtice, J., Evans, G., Field, J. and Witherspoon, S. (1991) *Understanding Political Change* (Oxford: Pergamon Press).
Heffer, E. (1986) *Labour's Future: Socialist or SDP Mark 2* (London: Verso).
Heffernan, R. and Marqusee, M. (1992) *Defeat from the Jaws of Victory* (London: Verso).
Hennessy, P. (1986) *Cabinet* (Oxford: Basil Blackwell).
Hennessy, P. (1990), *Whitehall* (London: Fontana).
Heseltine, M. (1987) *Where there's a Will* (London: Hutchinson).
Heseltine, M. (1990) *Where there's a Will* (London: Arrow Books).
Hewitt, P. and Mandelson, P. (1989) 'The Labour Campaign', in Crewe, I. and Harrop, M. (eds), *Political Communications: The General Election Campaign of 1987* (Cambridge: Cambridge University Press).
Hill, S. (ed.) (1993) *Visions of Europe: Summing up Political Choices* (London: Duckworth).
Hills, J. (ed.) (1990) *The State of Welfare*, (Oxford: Clarendon Press).
Hills, J. (1993) *The Future of Welfare: A Guide to the Debate* (York: Joseph Rowntree Foundation).
Hinton, J. (1989) *Protests and Visions, Peace Politics in Twentieth-Century Britain* (London: Hutchinson Radius).

HM Government (1993) *NHS Trusts: Interim Conclusions and Proposals for Future Enquiries* (London: HMSO).

HM Treasury (1994) 'Civil Service Staffing 1979–1994', *Treasury Occasional Paper No 1* (London: HM Treasury).

Hoffman, M. (1991) 'From Conformity to Confrontation, Security and Arms Control in the Thatcher Years', in Croft (1991).

Hogg, Q. (1947) *The Case for Conservatism* (West Drayton: Penguin).

Hollingsworth, M. (1991) *MPs For Hire: The Secret World of Political Lobbying* (London: Bloomsbury).

Home Affairs Committee (1993) *Funding of Political Parties: Minutes of Evidence* (London: HMSO).

Honderich, T. (1990) *Conservatism* (Harmondsworth: Penguin).

Hoover, K. and Plant, R. (1989) *Conservative Capitalism in Britain and the United States: A Critical Appraisal* (London: Routledge).

Horne, A. (1989) *Macmillan, 1957–86* (London: Macmillan).

Howe, G. (1990) 'Sovereignty and Interdependence: Britain's Place in the World', *International Affairs*, Vol. 66, No. 4.

Howe, G. (1994) *Conflict of Loyalty* (London: Macmillan).

Howe, G. (1995) 'A Better European Policy for Britain', *Financial Times*, 30 January.

Howe, M. (1993) *Europe and the Constitution after Maastricht* (Oxford: Nelson and Pollard).

Hudson, R. and Williams, A. (1989) *Divided Britain* (London: Belhaven).

Hughes, C. and Wintour, P. (1990) *Labour Rebuilt: the New Model Party* (London: Fourth Estate).

Jackson, R. (1968) *Whips and Rebels* (London: Macmillan).

Jenkins, P. (1987) *Mrs. Thatcher's Revolution* (London: Jonathan Cape).

Jessop, B. (1989) *Thatcherism: The British Road to Post-Fordism*, Essex Papers in Politics and Government, No. 68 (University of Essex: Department of Government).

Jessop, B., Bonnett, K., Bromley, S. and Ling, T. (1988) *Thatcherism, A Tale of Two Nations* (Cambridge: Polity Press).

Johnson, C. (1991) *The Economy under Mrs Thatcher 1979–1990* (Harmondsworth: Penguin).

Johnston, R.J. (1987) 'A Note on Housing Tenure and Voting in Britain, 1983', *Housing Studies*, Vol. 2.

Johnston, R.J. (1993) The Rise and Decline of the Corporate Welfare State', in Taylor, P.J. (ed.), *Political Geography of the Twentieth Century, A Global Analysis* (London: Belhaven).

Johnston, R.J. and Pattie, C.J. (1989) 'A Nation Dividing?' *Parliamentary Affairs*, Vol. 42.

Johnston, R.J. and Pattie, C.J. (1992a) 'Class Dealignment and the Regional Polarisation of Voting Patterns in Great Britain, 1964–1987', *Political Geography*, Vol. 11.

Johnston, R.J. and Pattie, C.J. (1992b) 'Unemployment, the Poll Tax and the British General Election of 1992', *Government and Policy*, Vol. 10.

Johnston, R.J. and Pattie, C.J. (1993a) 'Great Britain, Twentieth Century Parties Operating under Nineteenth Century Regulations', in Gunlicks, A.

(ed.), *Campaign and Party Finance in North America and Western Europe* (Boulder, Co: Westview).

Johnston, R. J. and Pattie, C. J. (1993b) 'Where the Tories Lost and Won' *Parliamentary Affairs*, Vol. 46.

Johnston, R. J., Pattie, C. J. and Allsopp, J. G. (1988) *A Nation Dividing?* (Harlow: Longman).

Johnston, R. J., Pattie, C. J. and Fieldhouse, E. A. (1994) 'The Geography of Voting and Representation', in Heath, A., Jowell, R. and Curtice, J. (eds), *Labour's Last Chance, the 1992 Election and Beyond* (Aldershot: Dartmouth).

Johnston, R. J., Pattie, C. J. and Johnston, L. C. (1989) 'The Impact of Constituency Spending on the Result of the 1987 British General Election', *Electoral Studies*, Vol. 8.

Johnston, R. J., Pattie, C. J. and Russell, A. P. (1993) 'Dealignment, Spatial Polarisation and Economic Voting: an Explanation of Recent Trends in British Voting Behaviour', *European Journal of Political Research*, Vol. 23.

Jordan, G. and Ashford, N. (eds) (1993) *Public Policy and the Nature of the New Right* (London: Pinter).

Judge, D. (1992) 'Disorder in the "Frustration" Parliaments of Thatcherite Britain', *Political Studies*, Vol. 40, No. 3.

Katz, R. and Mair, P. (1992) *Party Organizations: A Data Handbook* (London: Sage).

Kavanagh, D. (1987) *Thatcherism and British Politics*, (Oxford: Oxford University Press).

Kavanagh, D. (1990) *Thatcherism and British Politics*, 2nd edn (Oxford: Oxford University Press).

Kavanagh, D. (1992) 'Changes in the Political Class and its Culture' *Parliamentary Affairs*, Vol. 45.

Kavanagh, D. and Morris, P. (1989) *Consensus Politics From Attlee to Thatcher* (Oxford: Basil Blackwell).

Kavanagh, D. and Seldon, A. (eds) (1989) *The Thatcher Effect: A Decade of Change*, (Oxford: Oxford University Press).

Kavanagh, D. and Seldon, A., (eds) (1994) *The Major Effect* (London: Macmillan).

Keegan, W. (1984) *Mrs. Thatcher's Economic Experiment*, (Harmondsworth: Penguin).

Keegan, W. (1989) *Mr. Lawson's Economic Gamble* (London: Hodder and Stoughton).

Kelly, P. (1988) 'The Tribune Interview: Neil Kinnock', *Tribune*, 4 March.

Kelly, R. (1989) *Conservative Party Conferences* (Manchester: Manchester University Press).

Kemp, P. (1990) 'Memorandum to the Treasury and Civil Service Select Committee', in HC 496 (1990/91).

Kemp, P. (1993a) *Beyond Next Steps, a Civil Service for the 21st Century* (London: Social Market Foundation).

Kemp, P. (1993b) 'Memorandum to the Treasury and Civil Service Select Committee' (HC 391-iv 1993/4).

Kennedy, P. (1981) *The Realities Behind Diplomacy* (London: Fontana).

Kenny, A. (1986) *The Road to Hillsborough* (Oxford: Pergamon Press).

Keynes, J. M. (1973) *The General Theory of Employment, Interest and Money* (London: Macmillan).

King, A. (1981) 'The Rise of the Career Politician in Britain – and its Consequences', *British Journal of Political Science*, Vol. 11.

King, A. (1985) 'Margaret Thatcher: The Style of a Prime Minister', in King, A. (ed.), *The British Prime Minister* (London: Macmillan).

Kissinger, H. (1979) *The White House Years* (Boston, MA: Little, Brown).

Knapman, R. (1993) 'Bureaucrats Beware', *Parliamentary Brief*, Vol. 2., No. 1.

Lamont, N. (1993) 'The Day I Almost Quit', *The Times*, 16 September.

Lang, I. (1994) *The Swinton Lecture* delivered at the University College of Ripon and York St John, York, 3 July 1994 (London: Conservative Central Office).

Laurent, P. (1991) 'The Costs of Defence', in Croft (1991).

Lawson, N. (1992) *The View from No. 11: Memoirs of a Tory Radical* (London: Bantam).

Layton-Henry, Z. (ed.) (1980) *Conservative Party Politics* (London: Macmillan).

Le Grand, J. (1990) 'The State of Welfare', in Hills (1990).

Le Grand, J. and Bartlett, W. (1993) *Quasi-Markets and Social Policy* (London: Macmillan).

Leaman, A. (1994), 'A Responsible Radicalism', *The Reformer*, Vol. VI, No. 4.

Leigh, E. (1993) 'The Judgement of Others', *The Spectator*, 5 June.

Letwin, S. (1992) *Anatomy of Thatcherism* (London: Fontana).

Lewis, J. and Townsend, A. (eds) (1989) *The North-South Divide* (London: Paul Chapman).

Lewis, N. (1993) 'The Citizen's Charter and Next Steps: A New Way of Governing?', *Political Quarterly*, Vol. 64, No. 3.

Liberal Democrats (1989) *Britain's Industrial Future: Federal Green Paper No. 10*, (Hebden Bridge, Hebden Royd).

Liberal Democrats (1991) *Economics for the Future: Federal White Paper No. 4* (Dorset: Liberal Democrat Publications).

Liberal Democrats (1992) *After Privatisation* (Dorset: Liberal Democrat Publications).

Linton, M. (1994) *Money and Votes* (London: Institute for Public Policy Research).

Little, W. (1988) 'Anglo-Argentine Relations and the Management of the Falklands Question', in Byrd, P. (ed.), *British Foreign Policy Under Thatcher* (Oxford: Philip Allan).

Lord, C. (1993) *British Entry to the European Community Under the Heath Government of 1970–4* (Aldershot: Dartmouth).

Lovenduski, J. and Randall, V. (1993) *Contemporary Feminist Politics: Women and Power in Britain* (Oxford: Oxford University Press).

Lowe, R. (1993) *The Welfare State in Britain since 1945* (London: Macmillan).

Ludlam, S. (1992) 'The Gnomes of Washington: Four Myths of the IMF Crisis of 1976', *Political Studies*, Vol. XL, No. 4.

Ludlam, S. (1993) 'Majorism – Shuffling to the Left?', *Politics Review*, November.

Ludlam, S. (1994) 'The Impact of Sectoral Cleavage and Spending Cuts on Labour Party/Trade Union Relations: The Social Contract Experience', in *British Parties and Elections Yearbook 1994* (London: Frank Cass).

Ludlam, S. (1995) 'Britain and the European Union', in Catterall, P. (ed.), *Contemporary Britain: An Annual Review 1995* (London: Institute of Contemporary British History).

MacInnes, J. (1987) *Thatcherism at Work. Industrial Relations and Economic Change* (Milton Keynes: Open University Press).

Maclure, S. (1989) *Education Re-formed: A Guide to the Education Reform Act* (London: Hodder & Stoughton).

Macmillan, H. (1938) *The Middle Way* (London: Macmillan).

Macmillan, H. (1962) *Britain, the Commonwealth and Europe* (London: Conservative Political Centre).

Macmillan, H. (1971) *Riding the Storm, 1956–1959* (London: Macmillan).

Macmillan, H. (1973) *At the End of the Day 1961–1963* (London: Macmillan).

Major, J. (1993) 'Raise Your Eyes, There is a Land Beyond', *The Economist*, 25 September.

Major, J. (1994a) *Europe: A Future that Works*. William and Mary Lecture given by the Prime Minister the Rt Hon. John Major MP at the University, Leiden, 7 September (London: Downing Street Press Office).

Major, J. (1994b) *The Role and Limits of the State*, Speech to the European Policy Forum QEII Conference Centre, London, 27 July (London: Downing Street Press Office).

Major, J. (1994c) *Variable Geometry*, Speech at Ellesmere Port, 31 May (London: Conservative Central Office).

Marquand, D. (1988) *The Unprincipled Society* (London: Fontana).

Marsh, D. (1990) 'Public Opinion, Trade Unions and Mrs. Thatcher', *British Journal of Industrial Relations*, Vol. 28, No. 1.

Marsh, D. (1991) 'Privatisation under Mrs Thatcher', *Public Administration*, Vol. 69.

Marsh, D. (1992) *The New Politics of British Trade Unionism. Union Power and the Thatcher Legacy* (London: Macmillan).

Marsh, D. (1994) *Explaining Thatcherism: Beyond Uni-Dimensional Explanations* (Glasgow: University of Strathclyde Department of Government).

Marsh, D. and Rhodes R. (eds) (1992) *Implementing Thatcherite Policies: Audit of an Era* (Buckingham: Open University Press).

Marsh, D. & Tant, T. (1994) 'British Politics Post-Thatcher: A Minor Major Effect', in Wale, W., *Developments in Politics: An Annual Review*, Volume 5 (London: Causeway Press).

Marsh, D., Ward, H., Sanders, D. and Price, S. (1992) 'Modelling Government Popularity in Britain 1979–87', in Crewe, I., Norris, P., Denver, D. and Broughton, D. (eds), *British Elections and Parties Yearbook 1991* (London: Harvester Wheatsheaf).

Mather, G. (1994) 'The Market, Accountability and the Civil Service', Paper presented at the Public Administration Conference, University of York, 5–7 September.

McGrew, T. (1988) 'Security and Order, the Military Dimension', in Smith, M., Smith and White (1988).

McKee, V. (1994) 'The Politics of the Liberal Democrats', in Dunleavy, P. and Stayner, G. (eds), *Contemporary Political Studies 1994* (Exeter: University of Exeter Press).

McKenzie, R. (1964) *British Political Parties* (London: Mercury Books).

McKenzie, R. and Silver, A. (1968) *Angels in Marble: Working Class Conservatives in Urban England* (London: Heinemann).

McKie, D. (ed.) (1993) *The Guardian Political Almanac 1993/4* (London: Fourth Estate).

Mellon, E. (1990) 'Memorandum to the Treasury and Civil Service Select Committee', in HC 496 (1990/1).

Mellors, C. (1978) *The British MP: A Socio-Economic Study of the House of Commons* (Farnborough: Saxon House).

Michie, J. (ed.) (1992) *The Economic Legacy 1979–1992* (London: Academic Press).

Middlemas, K. (1979) *Politics in Industrial Society. The Experience of the British System Since 1911* (London: André Deutsch).

Middlemas, K. (1991) *Power, Competition and the State: Volume 3: The End of the Post-war Era* (London: Macmillan).

Miller, K. and Steele, M. (1993) 'Employment Legislation, Thatcher and After' *Industrial Relations Journal*, Vol. 24, No. 3.

Miller, W. (1977) *Electoral Dynamics* (London: Macmillan).

Miller, W., Clarke, H. D., Harrop, M., Leduc, L. and Whiteley, P. (1990) *How Voters Change* (Oxford: Clarendon Press).

Millward, N., Stevens, M., Smart, D., and Hawes, W. (1993) *Workplace Industrial Relations in Transition* (Aldershot: Dartmouth).

Minkin, L. (1992) *The Contentious Alliance: Trade Unions and the Labour Party* (Edinburgh: Edinburgh University Press).

Minogue, K. (1990) 'Is Sovereignty a Big Bad Wolf?', in *Is Sovereignty a Big Bad Wolf?* (London: The Bruges Group).

Mitchell, N. (1987) 'Changing Pressure Group Politics: The Case of the TUC', *British Journal of Political Science*, Vol. 17.

Mitchie, J. (ed.) (1992) *Economic Legacy 1979 to 1992* (London: Academic Press).

Moran, M. (1979) 'The Conservative Party and the Trade Unions since 1974', *Political Studies*, Vol. 27, No. 1.

Morris, R. (1991) *Tories* (Edinburgh: Mainstream).

Mortimer, J. (1988) 'Arguments for Change', *New Socialist*, Summer.

Mottram, R. (1994) 'A Future Shape for the Civil Service – The Positon of HM Government', Paper presented to QMW Public Policy Seminar, A Future Shape for the Civil Service, London: 7 June.

Mulgan, G. (1994) *Politics in an Antipolitical Age* (Cambridge: Polity Press).

Murray, C. (1990) *The Emerging British Underclass* (London: Institute for Economic Affairs).

Newton, K. (1976) *Second City Politics*, Oxford, Oxford University Press).

Newton, K. (1980) *Balancing the Books* (London: Sage).

Newton, K. (1992) 'Do People Read Everything they Believe in the Papers? Newspapers and Voters in the 1983 and 1987 Elections', in Crewe, I., Norris,

P., Denver, D. and Broughton, D. (eds), *British Elections and Parties Yearbook 1991* (London: Harvester Wheatsheaf).

NHS Management Executive (1990) *Working for Patients NHS Trust: A Working Guide* (London: HMSO).

Norris, P. and Lovenduski, J. (1995) *Political Recruitment: Gender, Race and Class in the British Parliament* (Cambridge: Cambridge University Press).

Norton, P. (1975) *Dissension in the House of Commons 1945–1974* (London: Macmillan).

Norton, P. (1978) *Conservative Dissidents: Dissent within the Parliamentary Conservative Party 1970–74* (London: Maurice Temple Smith).

Norton, P. (1980) *Dissension in the House of Commons 1974–1979* (Oxford: Clarendon Press).

Norton, P. (1990) 'The Lady's not for Turning', but what about the Rest? Margaret Thatcher and the Conservative Party 1979–89', *Parliamentary Affairs*, Vol. 43, No. 1.

Norton, P. (1994) 'Sorry, but it's the 1923 Committee', *Parliamentary Brief*, Vol. 3, No. 3.

Norton, P. and Aughey, A. (1981) *Conservatives and Conservatism* (London: Temple Smith).

Nugent, N. (1994) *The Government and Politics of the European Union* (London: Macmillan).

Oakeshott, M. (1962) *Rationalism in Politics* (London: Methuen).

Oakeshott, M. (1973) 'On Being Conservative', in De Crespigny, A. and Cronin, J. *Ideologies of Politics* (Oxford: Oxford University Press).

Oakley, A. and Williams, A.S. (1994) *The Politics of the Welfare State* (London: University College London Press).

Oakley, R. (1987) 'Owen's Merger Imprint,' *The Times*, 19 September.

O'Gorman, F. (1986) *British Conservatism: Conservative Thought from Burke to Thatcher* (Harbour: Longman).

O'Leary, B. (1987) 'The Anglo-Irish Agreement, Folly or Statecraft?' *West European Politics*, Vol. 10, No. 1.

Osborne, D. and Gaebler, T. (1992) *Reinventing Government* (London: Plume).

Oughton, J. (1994) 'Market Testing and the Future of the Civil Service', Paper Presented at the Public Administration Conference, University of York, 5–7 September.

Owen, D. (1987) *Sticking With It*, (London: Social Democrat Publications).

Owen, D. (1992) *Time to Declare* (Harmondsworth: Penguin).

Painter, C. (1989) 'Thatcherite Radicalism and Institutional Conservatism', *Parliamentary Affairs*, Vol. 42.

Painter, C. (1994) 'Public Service Reform, Reinventing or Abandoning Government?', *Political Quarterly*, Vol. 65.

Parsons, A. (1989) 'Britain and the World', in Kavanagh and Seldon (1989).

Pattie, C.J and Johnston, R.J. (1990a) 'One Nation or Two? The Changing Geography of Unemployment in Great Britain 1983–1988', *Professional Geographer*, Vol. 44.

Pattie, C.J. and Johnston, R.J. (1990b) 'Thatcherism – One Nation or Two? An Exploration of British Political Attitudes in the 1980s' *Government and Policy* Vol 8.

Pattie, C. J. and Johnston, R. J. and Fieldhouse, E. A. (1994) 'Gaining on the Swings? The Changing Geography of the Flow of the Vote and Government Fortunes in British General Elections, 1979–1992', *Regional Studies*, Vol. 28.

Pattie, C. J., Whiteley, P., Seyd, P. and Johnston, R. J. (1994) 'Measuring Local Campaign Effects' *Political Studies* Vol. 42.

Peterson, J. (1992) 'The European Community', in Marsh and Rhodes (1992).

Pierson, C. (1991) *Beyond the Welfare State?* (Cambridge: Polity Press).

Pimlott, B. (ed.) (1984) *Fabian Essays in Socialist Thought* (London: Heinemann).

Pinto-Duschinsky, M. (1981) *British Political Finance 1830–1980* (Washington, DC: American Enterprise Institute).

Pinto-Duschinsky, M. (1985) 'Trends in British Political Funding 1979–1983', *Parliamentary Affairs*, Vol. 38.

Pinto-Duschinsky, M. (1989) 'Trends in British Party Funding 1983–1987', *Parliamentary Affairs*, Vol. 42.

Pirie, M. (1988) *Micropolitics* (London: Wildwood House).

Ponting, C. (1990) *1940: Myth and Reality* (London: Cardinal).

Porter, B. (1975) *The Lion's Share* (London: Longman).

Portillo, M. (1994a) 'A Revolution in the Public Sector', A Speech Delivered to Hertford College Deregulation Seminar, Oxford, 7 January.

Portillo, M. (1994b) *Clear Blue Water: A Compendium of Speeches and Interviews by the Rt Hon. Michael Portillo MP* (London: Conservative Way Forward).

Powell, J. E. (1989) 'The Conservative Party', in Kavanagh and Seldon (1989).

Power, S., Halpin, D. and Fitz, J. (1994) 'Parents, Pupils and Grant-maintained Schools', *British Educational Research Journal*, Vol. 20, No. 2.

Price Waterhouse (1994) *Executive Agencies, Survey Report 1994* (London: Price Waterhouse).

Prior, J. (1980) 'Industrial Relations – Approaching the Year 2000' *The Granada Guildhall Lectures 1980. The Role of the Trade Unions* (St Albans: Granada).

Pym, F. (1985) *The Politics of Consent* (London: Sphere Books).

Radcliffe, J. (1991) *The Reorganisation of Central British Government* (Aldershot: Dartmouth).

Ranelagh, J. (1992) *Thatcher's People: an Insiders Account of the Politics, the Power, and the Personalities* (London: Fontana).

Redwood, J. (1995) 'The Flame that Will not Die', *The Guardian*, 16 January.

Rees-Mogg, W. (1993) 'Major Fails the Leadership Test', *The Times*, 10 May.

Reif, K., Cayrol, R., and Niedermayer, O. (1980) 'National Political Parties: Middle Level Elites and European Integration', *European Journal of Political Research*, Vol, 8.

Reynolds, D. (1991) *Britannia Overruled: British Policy and World Power inthe Twentieth Century* (Harlow: Longman).

Rhodes, R. A. W. (1992) 'Local Government Finance', in Marsh and Rhodes (1992).

Rhodes, R. A. W. (1994) 'The Hollowing Out of the State: The Changing Nature of the Public Service in Britain', *Public Quarterly*, Vol. 65.

Richards, S. (1987) 'The Financial Management Initiative', in Harrison, A. and Gretton, J. (eds), *Reshaping Central Government* (Oxford: Transaction Books).

Richardson, J. (1993) 'Doing Less By Doing More: British Government 1979–93', *EPPI Occasional Papers*, No. 93/2, University of Warwick.

Riddell, P. (1983) *The Thatcher Government* (Oxford: Martin Robertson).

Riddell, P. (1989) *The Thatcher Era and its Legacy* (Oxford: Basil Blackwell).

Riddell, P. (1991) *The Thatcher Era and its Legacy* 2nd edn (Oxford: Basil Blackwell).

Riddell, P. (1992) 'The Conservatives after 1992', *Political Quarterly*, Vol. 63, No. 4.

Riddell, P. (1993) Honest Opportunitism: the Rise of the Career Politician.

Ridley, N. (1992) *My Style of Government: The Thatcher Years* (London: Fontana).

Rosamond, B. (1992) 'The Labour Party, Trade Unions and Industrial Relations', in M.J. Smith, and Spear (1992).

Rosamond, B. (1993) 'National Labour Organisations and European Integration, British Trade Unions and "1992"', *Political Studies*, Vol. 41, No. 3.

Rose, H. (1983), 'Property of the Professionals', *The New Statesman*, 30 September 1983.

Rose, R. (1964) 'Parties, Factions and Tendencies in Britain', *Political Studies*, Vol. 12, No. 1.

Rose, R. (1976a) *Northern Ireland, A Time of Choice* (London: Macmillan).

Rose, R. (1976b) *The Problem of Party Government* (Harmondsworth: Penguin).

Rose, R. (1980) *Do Parties Make a Difference?* (London: Macmillan).

Rose, R. (1990) 'Inheritance Before Choice in Public Policy', *Journal of Theoretical Politics*, Vol. 2.

Russel, T. (1978) *The Tory Party: its Policies, Divisions and Future* (Harmondsworth: Penguin).

Russell, A.T., Johnston, R.J. and Pattie, C.J. (1992) 'Thatcher's Children: Exploring the Links between Age and Political Attitudes', *Political Studies*, Vol. XL.

Sabin, P. (1993) 'British Defence Choices Beyond "Options For Change"', *International Affairs*, Vol. 69, No. 2.

Saggar, S. (1992) *Race and Politics in Britain* (London: Harvester Wheatsheaf).

Sanders, D. (1990) *Losing an Empire, Finding a Role* (London: Macmillan).

Sanders, D. (1991) 'Government Popularity and the Next General Election', *Political Quarterly*, Vol. 62.

Sanders, D. (1993a) 'Foreign and Defence Policy', in Dunleavy, P., Gamble, A., Holliday, I. and Peele, G. (eds), *Developments in British Politics, 4* (London: Macmillan).

Sanders, D. (1993b) 'Why the Conservative Party Won – Again', in King, A. (ed.), *Britain at the Polls, 1992* (Chatham, NJ: Chatham House).

Sanders, D., Marsh, D. and Ward, H. (1990) 'A Reply to Clarke, Mishler and Whiteley', *British Journal of Political Science*, Vol. 20.

Sanders, D., Marsh, D. and Ward, H. (1993) 'The Electoral Impact of Press Coverage of the British Economy, 1979–1987', *British Journal of Political Science*, Vol. 23.Sanders, D., Ward, H. and Marsh, D. (1987) 'Government Popularity and the Falklands War: A Reassessment', *British Journal of Political Science*, Vol. 17.

Särlvik, B. and Crewe, I. (1983) *Decade of Dealignment* (Cambridge: Cambridge University Press).

Scruton, R. (1984) *The Meaning of Conservatism* (London: Macmillan).

Seldon, A. and Ball, S. (eds) (1994) *Conservative Century: The Conservative Party since 1900* (Oxford: Oxford University Press).

Semmel, B. (1962) *Imperialism and Social Reform* (London: Allen and Unwin).

Seyd, P. (1972) 'Factionalism within the Conservative Party: the Monday Club' *Government and Opposition*, Autumn.

Seyd, P. (1980) 'Factionalism in the 1970s', in Layton-Henry, (1980).

Seyd, P. (1987) *The Rise and Fall of the Labour Left* (London: Macmillan).

Seyd, P. (1993) 'Labour: the Great Transformation' in King, A. (ed.), *Britain at the Polls, 1992* (Chatham NJ: Chatham House).

Seyd, P. and Whiteley, P. (1992) *Labour's Grassroots: The Politics of Party Membership* (Oxford: Clarendon Press).

Shaw, E. (1988) *Discipline and Discord in the Labour Party: the Politics of Managerial Control in the Labour Party 1951–87* (Manchester: Manchester University Press).

Shaw, E. (1994) *The Labour Party since 1979: Crisis and Transformation* (London: Routledge).

Shonfield, A. (1958) *British Economic Policy since the War* (Harmondsworth: Penguin).

Slack J. and Whitt L. (1992) 'Ethics and Cultural Studies' in Grossberg L., Nelson, C. and Treichler, P. (eds), *Cultural Studies* (New York: Routledge).

Smith, D. (1987) *The Rise and Fall of Monetarism: The Theory and Politics of an Economic Experiment* (Harmondsworth: Penguin).

Smith, D. (1992) *From Boom to Bust: Trial and Error in British Economic Policy* (Harmondsworth: Penguin).

Smith, M. (1988) 'Britain and the US, Beyond the Special Relationship?', in Byrd, P. (ed.) *British Foreign Policy Under Thatcher* (London: Philip Allan).

Smith, M., Smith, S. and White, B. (1988) *British Foreign Policy: Tradition, Change and Transformation* (London: Unwin Hyman).

Smith, M.J. (1992) 'A Return to Revisionism? The Labour Party's Policy Review', in M.J. Smith, and Spear (1992).

Smith, M.J. (1993) *Pressure, Power and Policy: State Autonomy and Policy Networks in Britain and the United States* (Hemel Hempstead: Harvester Wheatsheaf).

Smith, M.J. (1994a) 'The Core Executive and the Resignation of Mrs Thatcher', *Public Administration*, Vol. 72.

Smith, M.J. (1994b) 'Understanding the Politics of Catch-Up: The Modernization of the Labour Party', *Political Studies*, Vol. 42, No. 4.

Smith, M.J. and Spear, J. (eds) (1992) *The Changing Labour Party* (London: Routledge).

Smith, P. and Morton, G. (1994) 'Union Exclusion – Next Steps', *Industrial Relations Journal* Vol. 25 No. 1.

Smith, S. (1991) 'Foreign Policy Analysis and the Study of British Foreign Policy', in Freedman, L. and Clarke, M. (eds), *Britain in the World* (Cambridge: Cambridge University Press).

Smith, S. and Clarke, M. (1985) *Foreign Policy Implementation*, (London: George Allen and Unwin).

Spicer, M. (1992) *A Treaty too Far: A New Policy for Europe* (London: Fourth Estate).

Stevenson, J. (1993) *Third Party Politics Since 1945: Liberals, Alliance and Liberal Democrats* (Oxford: Basil Blackwell).

Studlar, T. and McAllister, I. (1992) 'A Changing Political Agenda? The Structure of Political Attitudes in Britain, 1974–87', *International Journal of Public Opinion Research*, Vol. 4.

Taverne, D. (1974) *The Future of the Left: Lincoln and After* (London: Jonathan Cape).

Taylor, I. (1993) *The Positive Europe* (London: The Conservative Group for Europe).

Taylor, P. (1989) 'The New Dynamics of EC Integration in the 1980s', in Lodge, J. (ed.), *The European Community and the Challenge of the Future*, First Edition (London: Pinter).

Taylor, R. (1993) *The Trade Union Question in British Politics. Government and Unions since 1945* (Oxford: Basil Blackwell).

Teasdale, A. (1993) 'Subsidiarity in Post-Maastricht Europe', *Political Quarterly*, Vol. 64, No. 2.

Tebbit, N. (1988) *Upwardly Mobile* (London: Wiedenfeld & Nicolson).

Tebbit, N. (1991) *Unfinished Business* (London: Wiedenfeld & Nicolson).

Tether, P. (1991) 'Recruiting Conservative Party Members', *Parliamentary Affairs*, Vol. 44, No. 1.

Thatcher, M. (1977) *Europe as I See It* (London: European Conservative Group).

Thatcher, M. (1988) *Britain and Europe*, text of the speech delivered by the Prime Minister on 20 September 1988 (London: Conservative Political Centre).

Thatcher, M. (1993) *The Downing Street Years* (London: Harper Collins).

Thomas, J. A. (1958) *The House of Commons, 1906–1911: An Analysis of its Economic and Social Chararcter* (Cardiff: University of Wales Press).

Thompson, H. (1994) *Joining the ERM, Core Executive Decision-Making in the UK 1979–1990* (Unpublished PhD, LSE).

Veljanovski, C. (1987) *Selling the State* (London: Weidenfeld and Nicolson).

Von Beyme, K. (1985) *Political Parties in Western Democracies* (Aldershot: Gower).

Wainwright, H. (1987) *Labour: A Tale of Two Parties* (London: Hogarth Press).

Wallace, W. and Wallace, H. (1990) 'Strong State or Weak State in Foreign Policy? The Contradictions of Conservative Liberalism, 1979–87', *Public Administration*, Vol. 68, No. 1.

Walters, A. (1989) 'My Deviant Economics', *The Independent*, 26 October 1989.
Warner, N. (1984) 'Raynerism in Practices: Anatomy of a Rayner Scrutiny', *Public Administration*, Vol. 62.
Weakliem, D. (1989) 'Class and Party in Britain, 1964–83', *Sociology*, Vol. 23.
Wedderburn, Lord (1989) 'Freedom of Association and Philosophies of Labour Law', *Industrial Law Journal*, Vol. 18, No.1.
Weekes, B. *et al.* (1975) *Industrial Relations and the Limits of the Law* (Oxford: Basil Blackwell).
Weir, S. and Hall, W. (1994) *Ego Trip: Extra-Governmental Organisations in their Accountability* (London: Democratic Audit and Charter 88).
Westergaard, J. and Resler, H. (1976) *Class in a Capitalist Society* (Harmondsworth: Penguin).
Wheeler, N. J. (1991) 'Perceptions of the Soviet Threat', in Croft, S (1991).
White, B. (1988) 'Britain and East-West Relations', in M. Smith, Smith and White (1988).
White, D. (1994) 'Scramble for Seats on a Mystery Ride', *Financial Times*, 10 January.
Whiteley, P. (1983) *The Labour Party in Crisis* (London: Methuen).
Whiteley, P. and Seyd, P. (1996) *The Dynamics of the British Party System: The Decline of Party Support* (Ann Arbor, Michigan: University of Michigan Press).
Whiteley, P., Seyd, P. and Richardson, J. (1994) *True Blues: the Politics of Conservative Party Membership*, Oxford: Clarendon Press.
Wilkes, S. (1993) 'Economic Policy', in Dunleavy, P., Gamble, A., Holliday, I. and Peele, G. (eds), *Developments in British Politics 4* (London: Macmillan).
Willetts, D. (1992) *Modern Conservatism* (Harmondsworth: Penguin).
Wilson, H. (1971) *The Labour Government 1964–70* (London: Weidenfeld & Nicolson).
Wilson, H. (1979) *Final Term* (London: Weidenfeld & Nicolson and Michael Joseph).
Wilson, J. (1994) 'Thatcher, Major and the Public Services', *Talking Politics*, Vol. 6, No. 3.
Wintour P. (1993), 'Winning the Battles but not the war', in McKie (1993).
Young, H. (1990) *One Of Us* (London: Pan).
Young, H. and Sloman, A. (1986) *The Thatcher Phenomenon* (London. BBC).
Young, J. W. (1993) *Britain and European Unity 1945–1992* (London: Macmillan).
Zifcak, S. (1994) *New Managerialism* (Milton Keynes: Open University Press).

Index

322 *Index*